THE STUDY
OF THE FUTURE

An Introduction
to the Art and Science
of Understanding and Shaping
Tomorrow's World

**By Edward Cornish
with members and staff of the
World Future Society**

WORLD FUTURE SOCIETY
Washington, D.C. 20014 U.S.A.

Published by
WORLD FUTURE SOCIETY
4916 St. Elmo Avenue
Washington, D.C. 20014 ● U.S.A.

Copyright © 1977 by
World Future Society

Second Printing, April 1978

Library of Congress Cataloging in Publication Data

Cornish, Edward
    The study of the future.

    Bibliography
    Includes index.
    1. Forecasting. I. World Future Society. II. Title
CB158.C67   001.4'33   77-75308

Library of Congress Catalog Number 77-75308
International Standard Book Number 0-930242-03-3

Design by Diane Smirnow
Typesetting by Unicorn Graphics

Price: $9.50
        $8.50 to members of the World Future Society
Please inquire for reduced multiple copy price for classroom use.

Contents

Preface

If anything is important, it is the future. The past is gone, and the present exists only as a fleeting moment. Everything that we think and do from this moment on can affect only the future. And it is in the future that we shall spend the rest of our lives.

Despite the importance of the future, scientists and scholars have traditionally paid little attention to it. They spend lifetimes trying to decipher ancient hieroglyphics or to determine authorship of a Renaissance play, but only rarely do they think seriously about what may happen to mankind in the years to come. Recently, however, some people have become seriously interested in the future, because the future is smashing into all of us so forcefully that it can no longer be ignored. A maelstrom of social change has engulfed the world—and things will never again be what they were.

The people who have become seriously interested in the future—people who now are generally styled *futurists*—emphasize that we can do relatively little to improve the present world, because basic changes require time, but we have great power over the more distant future. A seed of change planted today can become a mighty force in the years ahead. Recognizing that the crises of today have resulted from past failures to deal with emerging problems, we can hardly fail to see that what we do now will determine the sort of world that we will have 10, 15, or 20 years from now. The abolition of poverty, the establishment of world peace, the enjoyment of good health by people everywhere no longer need be viewed as idle dreams; these goals may actually be realized in the next few decades by intelligent human effort. Whether these goals are achieved will depend, in large measure, on our ability to understand the possibilities of the future before we are entangled in possible—but avoidable—catastrophes.

The study of the future may well be the most exciting intellectual enterprise of today. But it is more than an exciting adventure: it is an awesome responsibility. Though our future is darkened by the possibility of thermonuclear war, environmental destruction, and the potential collapse of the economic and social systems that sustain us, it is also brightened by the knowledge that we have it within our power to create a civilization incomparably superior to any in human history. In the following pages, we shall describe the new study of the future, and suggest how it can help people to build a better tomorrow.

Acknowledgements

This book is designed to meet the need for a brief, readable introduction to the study of the future. The need for such a book has long been felt by the staff of the World Future Society, but the means of meeting that need did not become available until 1975 when the Society received a grant from the National Science Foundation and the Congressional Research Service (Library of Congress).

The grant was for the preparation of a *Resources Directory for America's Third Century*, a work designed to serve as a contribution to the U.S. Bicentennial celebration. As described in the grant proposal, the directory would include an extensive introduction to the field, as well as a listing of organizations, individuals, and other information sources.

Work on the directory began soon after the grant was received and culminated in the submission of the report to the government agencies in March 1977. At the beginning of the project, the staff hoped that the report might serve as the book the staff had long dreamed of, but it proved impractical to serve that purpose satisfactorily and at the same time satisfy the governmental requirements. Accordingly, the staff decided that a new volume should be prepared, using many of the materials developed for the government project but designed specifically to meet the need for a general-purpose introduction to the futurists and their emerging field of study.

The present volume is the result of that effort. It is essentially a new work, but it owes its existence to the government project, and therefore a large debt is owed to all those who contributed to the report—a total of more than 500 people!

Though it seems quite impossible to accord proper recognition to everyone who has contributed in some way to the present volume, mention must be made of a few:

First of all, of course, a special debt is owed to the National Science Foundation and the Congressional Research Service, which provided funds for the antecedent project, and specifically to Lynn Carroll and Joseph F. Coates of NSF and Walter Hahn and Dennis Little of CRS. Without their vision and help, the Society could not have undertaken the project from which this book evolved.

Among those who have provided helpful editorial corrections, criticisms, ideas, and suggestions are: Roy C. Amara, Isaac Asimov, Philip H. Auerbach, Daniel Bell, Marvin Cetron, Arthur C. Clarke, Joseph F. Coates, Vary T. Coates, Sally Cornish, Howard F. Didsbury, Jr., Christopher T. Dede, Bertrand de Jouvenel, Hugues de Jouvenel, Gregg Edwards, H. Wentworth Eldredge, Victor Ferkiss, Jib Fowles, Willis W. Harman, Olaf Helmer, Frank Snowden Hopkins, Lane Jennings, Thomas O. Jones, Earl C. Joseph, Herman Kahn, Draper Kauffman, Kynoch Kendall, John McHale, Magda McHale, Michael Marien, Joseph Martino, Everard Munsey, Aurelio Peccei, Jerry Richardson, Donald C. Rosene, Glenn T. Seaborg, David P. Snyder, and Alvin Toffler.

Portions of the history chapter were reviewed by Roy C. Amara, Raymond Bauer, James Bright, Bernard Cazes, Henry David, Andre Clement Decoufle, Bertrand de Jouvenel, Hugues de Jouvenel, S. Colum Gilfillan, Walter Hahn, Theodore J. Gordon, Francois Hetman, Jerome Monod, and Charles W. Williams, Jr. A special debt is owed to Kathryn Humes for a manuscript that was especially useful for its description of future-related developments in the U.S. during the 1920s and 1930s.

The chapter on introducing the future into established organizations draws on a paper by James Webber of Lexington, Massachusetts, and Rebecca Ojala of the Cambridge Research Institute, as well as material supplied by Jay S. Mendell, Visiting Professor at Florida Atlantic University's College of Business and Public Administration. Other contributers to the chapter include Joseph F. Coates, now at the Office of Technology Assessment; Orville L. Freeman, President of Business International; the Ven. John J. Weaver, and Andrew E. Spekke.

The chapter on "Futurists and their Ideas" draws on papers prepared by Anne B. Cadman (Alvin Toffler), Jerome C. Glenn (Herman Kahn), Larry Schwartz (Herman Kahn), James Stirewalt (Willis Harman), and Guy Streatfeild (Robert Jungk and John McHale).

Proofreaders included Kristine Stroad, Jerry Richardson, Nancy McLane, Blake Cornish, Jefferson Cornish, Carol Ann MacArthur.

Staff assistance was supplied by Lucille Beard, Janet Carson, Jean Jacobson, Carolyn Kaufman, Virginia Kerney, Elaine Napoleone, and Rebecca Sinden.

Researchers and staff writers included Anne Cadman, Janet Carson, Roslyn Dauber, Richard Ferrara, Scott Finer, Theodore J. Maziarski, Cindi Ryland, James N. Stirewalt, and Andrew E. Spekke.

Special mention must be made of Peter Zuckerman, who coordinated the production; Philip Auerbach, the Research Director of the original government project, and Nancy B. McLane, who labored indefatigably in a variety of capacities.

The greatest debt of all is owed to the members of the World Future Society, without whose steady support since the Society's founding in 1966 this book could never have been realized.

1

An Age of Convulsive Change

The human race is now experiencing the most rapid change in its history. There is little agreement, however, on where this change is leading or what its ultimate outcome and meaning may be. We know for certain only that a hurricane of change is sweeping through all human institutions, upsetting, destroying, and creating more in a generation than was accomplished during centuries or even millennia in times past. No known force can stop this pervasive metamorphosis; generations may pass before the powerful social and technological processes now at work are controlled or dissipated.

The speed of the transformation is suggested by the enormous change that now occurs within the lifetime of a single individual. Since World War II the inventions and discoveries in almost every field have far surpassed the achievements of earlier ages; satellite television, oral contraceptives, electronic computers, photocopying machines, the Salk vaccine, and heart transplants figure in the massive explosion of new technology. Since 1945 man also has climbed the highest mountain (Everest defied all challengers until 1953), explored the depths of the ocean (the Marianas trench), lived for weeks in dwellings constructed hundreds of feet beneath the sea's surface, landed men on the moon, sent probes to the planets beyond earth, and set up radar telescopes to listen for signals from extraterrestrial civilizations. During the same period (1945-76), 82 new nations have appeared, bringing the current total to about 160, and the world population has swollen by 1,700,000,000, rushing past the four-billion mark in 1976. The gross world product (GWP) has increased even more rapidly. Just in the years between 1950 and 1970, the GWP climbed from $700 billion to $3.2 trillion (current prices).

The changes are part of a historical trend that now is surpassing all its previous records in speed and pervasiveness. The current transformation, says the humanistic scientist John Platt, "is as enormous as 10 Industrial Revolutions and Protestant Reformations, all rolled into one and occurring within a single generation."

Policy analyst Charles W. Williams, Jr., who was Staff Director for the White House's National Goals Research Staff, voiced a similar sentiment when he warned in 1972 that "the change during the next 30 years may be equal in scope to the change of the past two or three centuries!"

A peculiar feature of the current transformation is that people are aware that it is occurring. This was not true in the Old Stone Age or the Dark Ages, when life went on much as usual from day to day. Even the 18th-century English never knew they were experiencing the Industrial Revolution; they knew about such novelties as the spinning jenny, but few suspected the magnitude and significance of the overall change that was occurring. But people today know that they are living through a period of historic transition. No one knows what its ultimate meaning may be or what historians will call our age, but thoughtful people everywhere are well aware that human life now is changing drastically.

The current transition is not just a transformation; it is also a global crisis, perhaps the greatest that mankind has ever experienced. During the decades ahead, the human race will, in effect, make collective choices that may well determine its long-term future or even whether it is to have a long-term future. No one knows the precise nature of these choices or how they will be made, but scholars and scientists do generally agree on the portentous character of humanity's actions in the years ahead. As futurist sociologist John McHale states in his book *The Future of the Future*, "The next 50 years may be the most crucial of all man's history."

Complicating humanity's problem of making its awesome choices is the fact that so many problems now demand attention simultaneously. The crises are coming one on top of another. "Most administrations," says Platt, "are able to endure or even enjoy an occasional crisis, with everyone working late together and everyone getting a new sense of importance and unity. What they are not prepared to deal with are multiple crises, a crisis of crises all at one time." Furthermore, the governments and other human institutions that are trying to cope with these crises often operate at cross purposes—and even in open conflict with each other.

The Megacrisis: A World in Transformation

Though no one can know what future historians will call our period of history, we may provisionally term it the Megacrisis, because it is far more than a crisis by the standards of the past; it is a supercrisis. Optimistically, we can hope that it is a transformation to a far better life for everyone on the planet; pessimistically, we cannot rule out the possibility that it is the final convulsion of our civilization.

The Megacrisis might be defined as the rushing vortex of social and technological change that has engulfed civilization during the latter half of the 20th century. Though there is no standard way to measure social change, scientists and scholars generally agree that the pace of change has been speeding up steadily over the past few centuries. Through most of human history, conditions remained relatively static. Generals might go out on military adventures and seize vast empires; dictators might become kings, and tribes might wander from place to place, but to the peasant on a farm or the craftsman in a village, it meant little: the basic aspects of life went on unchanged. "There is nothing new under the sun," said Ecclesiastes, and in his time, it was a reasonably fair statement of the human condition.

As the Middle Ages receded, the pace of change gradually increased, and since the Industrial Revolution in 18th century England, the rate of change appears to have accelerated steadily. World War II unleashed a storm of political change that toppled the regimes of Japan and many European countries and hastened the freeing of the colonies in the postwar period. In view of what has happened since the end of World War II, it is curious to realize that people even then were worried about the pace of change. In 1946, social scientist Samuel Lilley declared that "the most prominent psychological feature of the world of 1946 is the very prevalent feeling of uncertainty about the future." In past generations, said Lilley, a man could never be sure if his country was going to be involved in a war, "but today he has the added uncertainty that he can hardly visualize what that war will be like—atomic, bacteriological, or what?" The average working-man has long lived with the uncertainty of not knowing if he would have a job next year, "but today he has also serious doubts as to whether the particular job for which he is skilled will exist at all in 10 years time."

In the years following World War II, the pace of change accelerated further. In 1959, Max Ways, an editor of *Fortune*, estimated that the pace of change had become "perhaps 50 times as great as the average pace of previous centuries." In 1961, theologian Alvin Pitcher of the University of Chicago asked, "How much flux can a man stand?" In an article in the *Harvard Business Review*, Pitcher argued that man needs a measure of order and stability and is being dehumanized by excessive change. Pitcher called for a slowdown in automation and other socially disruptive and "needless" changes. Later, Ways picked up the theme in a 1964 article on "The Era of Radical Change," in which he identified four categories of social change: gradual change, revolution and major disruption, rapid change, and radical change. Ways argued that the period from 1800 to 1950 was one of rapid change, but about 1950 an era of radical change had begun.

> The break between the period of rapid change and that of radical change is not sharp; 1950 is an arbitrary starting date. More aspects of life change faster until it is no longer appropriate to think of society as mainly fixed, or changing slowly, while a tide flows around it. So many patterns of life are being modified that it is no longer useful to organize discussion or debate mainly around the relation of the new to the old. So many old landmarks have been set in motion that they have become misleading as guides. Newness has become an even more treacherous beacon. In the late nineteenth century or early twentieth century, 'to be up to date' was a boast. In 1964 the very phrase sounds dated, for everyone knows that to be up to date means to be on the verge of becoming out of date.

About the same time Charles de Gaulle was saying, "It so happens that the world is undergoing a transformation to which no change that has yet occurred can be compared, either in scope or in rapidity." And the historian Marshall M. Fishwick was recalling the Angel Gabriel in *Green Pastures* as saying, "Everything nailed down is coming loose."

After the publication of Alvin Toffler's *Future Shock* in 1970, the phenomenon of radical change entered the consciousness of people all over the world. And yet that same year, some social scientists were forecasting that during the decade of the 1970s more change might occur than during the previous three or four decades; in other words, the pace of change was still increasing. If this theory is correct, a new category of change may be appropriate: we may now be in an era of *convulsive* change. What may have happened is that during the period of rapid change (1800-1950) technology changed rapidly but social arrangements were relatively unaffected. In recent years, however, the locus of rapid change may have shifted from technology to institutions. Already family solidarity appears on the verge of total collapse, as witnessed by the steep climb of the divorce rate in the 1970s. Religion is no longer the solid Rock of Ages; God is either "dead" or "just doesn't want to get involved." Government, business, science, and other institutions face a barrage of attacks from all sides—including each other.

During the current era of convulsive change, institutions are increasingly viewed as incompetent, irrelevant, and illegitimate, and are being attacked, circumvented, revamped, and replaced. But since institutions are highly interrelated, interlocking systems, changing them to meet new circumstances and requirements necessitates further change, which in its turn requires still further change in an endless sequence. Thus change propagates itself, racing faster and faster through our lives. Today change seems to be the only constant in our lives.

No one knows how long the period of convulsive change will last. Some scholars think the pace of change will start to slow soon. John Platt, for example, feels that the rapid growth in population, economic development, speed of transportation and communications, etc., now is approaching limits, which will cause the growth to slow. Platt likens the current rapidity of change to that in a colony of bacteria whose growth slows and stops as it uses up all available food. Economist Kenneth Boulding has suggested that humanity "may well be through the middle point of this transition and the age of very rapid change may well be over." But other scholars disagree, suggesting still more acceleration of change in the years ahead. For example, Willis Harman of Stanford Research Institute believes that the world is "headed for a climacteric that may well be one of the most fateful in the history of civilizations. This convulsion is now not far off and most people sense something of it—although interpretations vary widely, like the well-known interpretations of the elephant by blindfolded people who feel different parts of the animal."

Almost all the scholars seem to regard the extremely rapid change now occurring as a temporary rather than permanent aspect of human civilization, but "temporary" here means that the phenomenon may continue for decades (or possibly centuries) rather than millennia. Most scholars seem to assume that rapid change is abnormal, but man has no knowledge of civilizations more advanced than his own, so it is difficult to say what is a "normal" rate of change in a high-technology culture.

The Causes of Rapid Change

The rapid social change that we are experiencing is frequently attributed to advancing technology. As sociologist William F. Ogburn once wrote:

> There is no doubt that useful inventions and researches cause social changes. Steam and steel were major forces in developing our extensive urban life. Gunpowder influenced the decline of feudalism. The discovery of seed-planting destroyed the hunting cultures and brought a radically new form of social life. The auto is helping to create the metropolitan community.

But Ogburn added that social inventions, such as life insurance, the holding company, the League of Nations, etc., also play a major role in social change and can in fact cause changes in technology, instead of vice versa. "Indeed, the more one studies the relationship between mechanical and social inventions, the more interrelated they seem," Ogburn said.

Change, in short, is a process that feeds on itself. Each change leads to more changes. For example, the invention of movable type by Johannes Gutenberg led to the printing of more books. More books encouraged people to learn how to read and the existence of more readers (book buyers) made it possible to print more books. The resulting dissemination of information greatly stimulated scientific research and knowledge, which made possible further advances in technology.

Similarly, the Xerox machine decreased the demand for carbon paper and for batteries of typists to copy papers. It also made government security more difficult (as witness the Pentagon papers that were photocopied by Daniel Ellsberg), and led to numerous scandals. The Xerox machine made everyone a publisher, and threatened the livelihood of commercial publishers and authors, since it was now easy and cheap to make copies of printed matter. Educators began photocopying chapters of books rather than having their students buy them; as a result, the cost of textbooks began climbing, thereby intensifying the use of copying machines to avoid the higher price.

Technology often is thought of as consisting of such things as machinery and chemicals, but in a broad sense it includes all practical knowledge, including information about which plants are good to eat and which insects carry diseases, the words and grammatical structures with which we communicate, the models of reality that we carry around in our heads, and the social arrangements we have found effective. In the broadest sense, technology might be defined as the ability to do things. Such a definition might seem all inclusive, but it leaves out not only impractical knowledge, but questions concerning what it is we *want* to do, that is, our values.

In recent years, many authors such as French sociologist Jacques Ellul have blamed technology for causing many or most modern social problems. In the view of these authors, technology obeys its own dynamic, marching forward irrespective of the damage it does. Warren Wagar, for example, after listing five world calamities (total warfare, ecocide, etc.) in his book *Building the City of Man*, attributed them all to "the vastly accelerated material progress of Western civilization, which has made everything happen too fast and too soon. Like little boats caught in a maelstrom, we spin round and round, losing all sense of up and down and right and left."

Is technology or the material progress that technology has made possible really the cause of modern-day troubles or is it simply a scapegoat? Through the centuries people have searched for somebody or something to blame for their troubles. And it may be argued that people blame "Technology" today in the same unthinking way that they blamed "Wall Street" or "Communists" in times past. But there are reasons to believe that technology is not a totally innocent scapegoat. The application of new technology clearly is *causing* problems as well as solving them. Even though one may feel that on balance the rapid advance of technology is a blessing, there clearly are enormous costs. And if all the costs were properly weighed and a judicious decision made, society might reject much new technology that seems at first glance to offer only benefits.

Suppose the American people were asked to vote on whether to accept a new technology that would have the following costs:

- 50,000 people killed each year (adding up, through the years, to far more slain than in all the wars the U.S. has ever fought)
- 2,000,000 disabled each year, including perhaps 100,000 maimed for life
- $20 billion in property damage
- urban sprawl
- the decay of downtown areas
- a deterioration in public transportation
- sexual promiscuity and weakening of parental control
- pollution resulting in unknown thousands of deaths from lung cancer, emphysema, heart disease and other ailments
- U.S. subservience to the Middle Eastern nations
- the conversion of thousands of hectares of rich farm land and scenic countryside into asphalt
- billboards that obscure natural scenery
- the placing of a large burden of debt on individual citizens
- unsightly graveyards for rusting vehicles
and much, much more.

Neither the American people nor their representatives in Congress ever voted to accept the automobile, for which they pay such a terrible price. All things considered, the benefits of the automobile may outweigh the costs, but the automobile shows how technology exacts heavy costs even when it provides benefits. The fears and criticisms of technology may be exaggerated, but they are not without foundation.

Unintended Results of Our Activities

Advancing technology has greatly intensified an ancient problem: the unintended consequences of our actions. A primitive man might occasionally hurl a spear at a bear and hit his fellow hunter instead. But in the relatively isolated settings of the past, the unintended damage done by technology was generally minor. As technology has become increasingly powerful and the human race has united into a single interacting social system, however, the unintended consequences of technology have become more numerous and more important.

We can never do just one thing. Every action radiates forward in time and outward in space, affecting everything everywhere. The practitioners of the new art of technology assessment have convincingly demonstrated that the consequences of a new technology are often far different and far greater than the users of that technology may dream. Such technologies as the automobile, improved refrigeration, and television can illustrate this point.

The Hidden Effects of Technology: Three Examples

Automobile

First-order consequences: People have a means of traveling rapidly, easily, cheaply, privately door-to-door.

Second-order consequences: People patronize stores at greater distances from their homes. These are generally bigger stores that have large clienteles.

Third-order consequences: Residents of a community do not meet each other so often and therefore do not get to know each other so well.

Fourth-order consequences: Strangers to each other, community members find it difficult to unite to deal with common problems. Individuals find themselves increasingly isolated and alienated from their neighbors.

Fifth-order consequences: Isolated from their neighbors, members of a family depend more on each other for satisfaction of most of their psychological needs.

Sixth-order consequences: When spouses are unable to meet heavy psychological demands that each makes on the other, frustration occurs. This may lead to divorce.

Improved Refrigeration

First-order consequences: Food can be kept for longer periods in the home.

Second-order consequences: People stay home more because they do not need to go to stores.

Third-order consequences: As with the automobile, the residents of a community do not meet each other so often and do not get to know each other so well. In addition, there is more free time for the wife.

Fourth-order consequences: As with the automobile, people find themselves increasingly isolated from their neighbors. In addition, the added free time increases the demand for recreation and entertainment.

Fifth-order consequences: Same as for the automobile.

Sixth-order consequences: Same as for the automobile.

Television

First-order consequences: People have a new source of entertainment and enlightenment in their homes.

Second-order consequences: People stay home more, rather than going out to local clubs and bars where they would meet other people in their community.

Third-order consequences: As in the case of the automobile and improved refrigeration, television tends to keep residents of a community from meeting and getting to know each other. Television also makes people less dependent on each other for entertainment.

Fourth-order consequences: Same as for the automobile. In addition, television caters to the increased desire for entertainment to fill the time made available when people do not need to shop so often.

Fifth-order consequences: Same as for the automobile and improved refrigeration.

Sixth-order consequences: Same as for the automobile and improved refrigeration.

Tracing out the consequences of technologies shows that they can have important consequences not anticipated by the users of the technology. Few people who buy an automobile or a refrigerator recognize that their purchases may contribute to the deterioration of their community or their marriage. One reason that people do not perceive the relationship is that there generally is a time-lag between the use of a technology and its various effects on our lives. Automobiles, improved refrigeration, and television do not immediately destroy the personal relationships in a community; instead, the weakening occurs progressively as contacts between people decline. The gradualness of the change makes it hard to detect the culprit technologies.

But every major technology has many significant impacts on society. The automobile, for example, contributed to the growth of supermarkets and the decline of neighborhood stores; the development of motels; the weakening of parental control over children;

new courtship patterns; and a decline in a community's ability to control the behavior of its citizens. (For example, the automobile enabled people who lived in counties that banned the sale of alcoholic beverages to travel easily to places where alcohol could be bought.) And the initial consequences of the automobile were only the beginning: The development of motels contributed to the deterioration of downtown areas, thereby accelerating the flight to suburbia of people who could afford to leave—and the consequent growth of ghettos (whose inhabitants came to be people displaced by the introduction of improved agricultural technology in rural areas).

"Future Shock"

Despite the problems it poses, new technology is introduced with almost reckless abandon in many areas of our society. "We used to have one major advance every 25 years," a drug executive has said. "Now we have one every 24 hours." A manufacturer of electronic products has been quoted as saying, "If it works, it's obsolete." Such rapid change in technology poses a constant threat to businessmen. The basis of a whole industry can be undermined overnight. Blotters and carbon paper—in common use in 1950—have joined buggy whips and whale oil lamps in the parade of outmoded objects. And the rush of technological advance which unsettles the businessman can cost employees their jobs. Older workers of a company are laid off even while recruiters are hiring youngsters trained in the newer technologies.

The so-called "Paul Principle " focuses attention on the problem of employee obsolescence. This principle, developed by Paul Armer, director of Stanford University's Computation Center, holds that people become progressively less competent for jobs they once were well equipped to handle. "Perhaps an example will help explain what I have in mind," Armer says. "Let me take it from the computer field, since its technology is changing very rapidly. Suppose an individual has risen in a company to where he is responsible for all computer and data processing activities in the company. The demands of his management duties leave little time for actually working with the technology of computers and data processing. Over time, his proficiency in the technology becomes less and less current—he becomes technologically obsolete and less and less able to perform his job. Eventually, he may be demoted, pressured to resign, or even fired."

Armer and others have suggested that education must be provided on a continuing basis to keep people from becoming outdated. But Gordon Rattray Taylor in his book *Rethink* angrily replies that this is not an adequate answer.

To the objection that a man's skills may be obsolete when he is 40 the technomaniac replies: 'Then he must be retrained.' He does not see that this is putting production above the man. In all probability the man does not want to go back to square one, giving up his status as a skilled workman and becoming an apprentice again. Why should he? The satisfactions of stability in his life may be more important to him than increased material wealth. . . . For it is much more than a question of retraining a workman in an industrial skill. We are talking about changes which render whole life patterns pointless, which disturb value systems, create alienation, make life boring or frustrating or not worth living, raise crime and suicide and alcoholism rates, and much more. In anthropological terms we are talking about disacculturation. We are doing to ourselves what we have already done to many primitive peoples, plunging them into a technological world for which their institutions and values were unfitted. It is well known that this breaks a primitive culture up, leads to loss of motivation, to alcoholism and eventually total anomie. The invisible costs of change are enormous.

The advancing power of technology threatens not only man but nature. In ancient times, forests were cut down to obtain fuel and to plant crops, thereby changing the vegetation and climate over vast regions. Today the Mediterranean basin has barren wastelands that once produced grain and timber for the Roman Empire. In the 20th century, technological advances—and the population growth they have caused—have completely eclipsed the environmental destruction of earlier ages. Increasingly, technology has overwhelmed the self-restorative powers of the natural environment. The emissions of hundreds of thousands of automobiles pollute the air in many cities so thoroughly that citizens contract lung ailments, clothing quickly becomes filthy, plants wither, and at night the stars can no longer be seen.

Technological advance has had innumerable impacts on education, government, family life, the churches, and even intimate relationships and human values. Television, for example, has provided exciting visual entertainment that teachers and clergymen find difficult to equal, with the result that they face increasing restlessness in classroom and sanctuary. The generation gap widens as young people grow up in a world that is increasingly different from the one in which their parents were reared. Change turns the old morality into the new immorality. Motherhood, once held in reverence, now is often viewed as wicked, because it contributes to the population problem; patriotism becomes suspect in an increasingly interdependent world. Change has made institutions increasingly irrelevant to the needs of their clients, with the result that the institutions find their legitimacy attacked. And many people now appear to be alienated not just from specific institutions, but from the entire society, which comes to be seen as incomprehensible, fraudulent, hostile, and boring.

The psychological disorientation caused by all this rapid change is sometimes called "future shock," a term invented by Alvin Toffler and popularized in a best-selling book bearing that title. The term is graphic but a misnomer because the shock is not administered by the future but by rapid social change. A more accurate term would be *change shock*. But the disorientation that Toffler describes is real. People no longer feel certain of anything—job, spouse, church, moral principles, or whatever—because everything is changing. Hence, a pervasive uncertainty arising from change casts a pall of apprehensiveness over everyone in the modern world. The change may be "progress" but its price is very high.

Progress and Its Discontents

Progress may be defined as "desired change." Progress is the sort of change that we want to achieve—control of disease, adequate food and shelter for everyone, efficient communication and transportation systems, security from attack, good recreational facilities, etc. During the 18th and 19th centuries, mankind generally felt that the social and technological change of the day was really good; progress was real. In the 20th century, many people have come to feel that "progress" is illusory.

Progress has two ways of disappointing us:

1. It has unexpected costs. The price of riding in an automobile is not just the cost of the gasoline and oil. Many other costs—ranging from the risk of death in an accident to the costs of community disintegration—must be figured into the cost-benefit accounting.

2. New desires emerge when old desires are satisfied. Hence a change cannot provide permanent satisfaction.

Let us look first at the hidden costs.

Even if a change is very desirable, it will have some undesired aspects. In some instances, the undesirable aspects may even require urgent attention. Man's success in preserving human life has created the population crisis. His success in reducing back-breaking human toil has led to the energy crisis. Willis W. Harman has listed the following "problems of success":

"Successes"	*Resulting Problems*
Prolonging the life span	Regional overpopulation; problems of the aged
Highly developed science and technology	Hazard of mass destruction through nuclear and biological weapons
Machine replacement of manual and routine labor	Exacerbated unemployment, urbanization

"Successes"	Resulting Problems
Advances in communication and transportation	Increasing air, noise and land pollution; information overload; vulnerability of a complex society to breakdown
Efficient production systems	Dehumanization of ordinary work
Affluence	Increased per capita consumption of energy and goods, leading to pollution and depletion of the earth's resources
Satisfaction of basic needs	Worldwide revolutions of "rising expectations"; rebellion against non-meaningful work
Expanded power of human choice	Unanticipated consequences of technological applications
Expanded wealth of developed nations	Increasing gap between "have" and "have-not" nations; frustration of the "revolutions of rising expectations"

Similarly, Herman Kahn and Barry Bruce-Briggs, the authors of *Things To Come*, have identified these "mixed blessings of progress":

1. Defunctionalization—partial (but increasing) loss of meaning of many traditional activities through the development of shortcuts to gratification: erosion of "traditional societal levers"
2. Accumulation, augmentation, and proliferation of weapons of mass destruction
3. Loss of privacy and solitude
4. Increase of governmental and/or private power over individuals
5. Loss of human scale and perspective
6. Dehumanization of social life or even of the psycho-biological self
7. Growth of dangerously vulnerable, deceptive, or degradable centralization of administrative or technological systems
8. Creation of other new capabilities so inherently dangerous as to seriously risk disastrous abuse
9. Acceleration of changes that are too rapid or cataclysmic to permit successful adjustment
10. Posing of choices that are too large, complex, important, uncertain, or comprehensive to be safely left to fallible humans

There are few instances in which a person can do something that has no bad consequences for anyone. If man were granted the gift of unlimited longevity, there would surely be endless moaning; who would want to be a plumber's apprentice or a gas station attendant for 200 years? If war were eliminated, people would argue that we had lost one of mankind's great goals to progress. If poverty were eradicated, critics would complain that "everybody's just like everybody else" and "you can't get decent servants." If the weather in London became sunny and pleasant, there would be an outcry from people claiming that smog is a precious part of the city's heritage. If disease were finally eliminated, people would worry that there no longer was any acceptable way to get rid of old people.

In addition to the fact that good things have undesired aspects, much complaining about "progress" may arise from the all-too-human need to express bodily and psychic discomforts, whatever their origin. All forms of progress represent change, and a change attracts attention, thus becoming a convenient focus for our emotions. Any new development thus is likely to act as a lightning rod for people who need to discharge pent-up feelings. Thus, *desired change* often provokes far more complaints than *undesired continuity*.

One undesired aspect of progress that bears special mention is its ability to raise expectations, thus causing frustrations and disturbances when the expectations are not met. Progress toward attaining a goal makes people aware that progress is possible and they may become increasingly impatient with any delay in achieving their desires. This is sometimes known as the De Tocqueville Effect, because the 19th-century French writer pointed out that the French Revolution occurred during a period when the conditions of life had been *improving*, not deteriorating. Lyman Bryson in *The Next America* wrote:

> Men do not rebel when they have reached the limit of their patience, which seems, indeed, to have no limits. They rebel when there is evidence that cruelty has passed its limit and has begun to lessen, when their oppressors seem for the first time to acknowledge that they have any rights whatever, when there is a faint hope that betterment is not an utterly hopeless dream.

Once progress is made in reducing poverty (or racial discrimination or whatever), people become hopeful that the ancient evil can really be eliminated; then they become angry and rebellious because the task is not immediately accomplished.

Yet another undesired aspect of progress is that it almost always means the acquisition of new *power*—and power can be used for evil as well as good. Nuclear and thermonuclear energy epitomize the awesome power of technology. Thermonuclear power will hopefully have far more good effects than bad in the long run, but the possibility that it may be used for evil creates deep fear and anxiety.

The Elusiveness of Happiness

If people succeed in satisfying a desire, their satisfaction is momentary. Soon a new desire takes the place of the old and they again become frustrated when they cannot attain it. If they are successful in satisfying their basic animal needs, they become increasingly interested in the psychic needs that are peculiar to human beings. The late psychologist Abraham Maslow has identified five types of human needs, which are prioritized in the following order:

1. *Physiological needs.* To survive, man needs food, clothing, shelter, and rest in order to stay alive.
2. *Safety or security needs.* When the physiological needs are satisfied, man wants to keep and protect what he has. He starts trying to stabilize his environment for the future.
3. *Social needs.* As his environment becomes more stable, he seeks to be part of something larger than himself. He wants to belong, to share, and to give and receive friendship and love.
4. *Ego needs.* People want to feel good about themselves, to be self-confident, independent, and be recognized and respected by peers.
5. *Self-fulfillment needs.* Man has a need for growth, self-development, self-actualization. He wants to realize the full range of his individual potential as a human being.

At each level, needs determine the values and patterns of an individual's behavior. At the survival level, the individual prizes food, clothing and shelter most highly. Once these desires are satisfied, he moves on to try to satisfy the other needs. In the 20th century, man has been increasingly able to satisfy his physiological needs, hence the other needs have assumed increasing importance. Paradoxically, however, the abundance has often made it more difficult than before to meet the emerging needs. Thus, in addition to the Problems of Success, we must contend with the Scarcities of Abundance.

The Scarcities of Abundance

The ability of western society to produce abundant food, clothing, housing, and other material goods has led, paradoxically, to growing scarcities of certain non-material goods. These new scarcities may arise either because the supply tends to disappear under conditions of material abundance or because the demand for the goods tends to increase.

Among the new scarcities are:

● **Time.** Due to complicated life-styles (pleasure boats, tourism, dinners in restaurants, etc.), people find they lack time to do everything they want to do; hence, time becomes a major constraint on their activities. By contrast, people in earlier periods of history had more time because they lacked the money that allows one to have a complex life-style. Today many people feel frustrated because they don't have time to do all they want to or feel they should do. A person with two houses cannot live in both simultaneously nor keep up with two sets of friends in the way he might like to. Automobiles make it possible for us to travel wherever we want, but we have no time to go every place we feel called to. In times past, we had fewer amusements, but now we have television in our homes and this provides us with something else we have to find time for, and poses special problems of choice because we cannot watch two programs simultaneously.

- **Recognition.** The amount of recognition accorded the average (median) person in western society has declined as population has grown and the mass media have become all-pervasive. People now tend to focus their admiration on a few "stars" who appear in newspapers and magazines and on television. The stars may take pleasure in the great recognition they receive, but after a certain point the addition of millions more fans means little to them. By contrast, the average person goes unrecognized.

  Western society distributes recognition even less evenly than it distributes wealth. A famous television personality may now be known to 200 million persons whereas the average person may be known to only a few hundred. The maldistribution of admiration and attention may easily be 10 or 100 times greater than the maldistribution of wealth. What makes the average person's recognition-deprivation more agonizing is that the increasing dearth of recognition is occurring at a time when the desire for recognition is becoming increasingly important since food, shelter and other material needs are met. The frustration of the need for recognition may be the cause of the "ego-tripping"—attention-seeking behavior—encountered frequently in meetings and parties.

- **Wisdom.** Growing complexity and the glut of information, most of which is irrelevant, have made it extremely difficult to obtain the information required for wise decisions. The number of items for sale in a supermarket has grown rapidly in recent years, forcing the consumer to make many more choices, for most of which he has an inadequate information base. As life becomes more complex, individuals and organizations need more wisdom to survive and prosper. Unfortunately, wisdom does not seem to be increasing; on the contrary, it may be declining due to such factors as marital instability which makes it difficult for children to develop the emotional maturity needed for wise decisions.

- **Influence.** People want to feel they can have some influence on things, that they can effect changes, that they count for something. But the growing scale of organizations has made it increasingly difficult for individuals to have a recognizable impact on our various social systems, so the individual finds institutions "unresponsive." He tends to feel alienated, and to withdraw. You can't fight City Hall; you can't stop the bulldozers from sweeping away your home; you can't do anything to change the way things are done. Hence, many people retreat into the few areas where they can feel they have some influence—the pinball machine that a player can tilt, the garden where one can tend plants and see the results of one's care, the arts and crafts that allow people to express themselves.

- **Intimacy (Love, Friendship).** The attenuation of community ties, the substitution of mass media entertainment for conversation, high mobility, rapid changes in jobs, etc., have made it increasingly difficult for people to establish and maintain intimate relationships. As a result, there is now a movement toward "instant intimacy" through encounter groups and commercially arranged social affairs.

- **Stability (Permanence and Continuity).** Whole neighborhoods and towns change in character nowadays with remarkable swiftness. Even if the buildings themselves remain in place, the residents may change completely. Often a group of an entirely different culture takes over. In New York City, for example, blacks and Puerto Ricans have taken over neighborhoods formerly inhabited by Jews, Italians and other ethnic groups. To maintain some continuity with the past, many people have sought to affirm their past by learning more about their once-rejected ethnic culture. People whose ancestors have long been in the U.S. often become interested in antiques and old houses.

- **Security of Status.** A person's position in society is increasingly uncertain due to marital instability and rapidly changing technology. Overnight, he can lose his status as an employee with a regular income or as a husband, wife, or child in a two-parent home. Unemployment benefits, child-support payments, other family members, etc., may ease the extent of the deprivation, but they do not increase the basic security of status.

In addition to the increased risk of losing one's status entirely, there are relative losses, due to shifts in the value of that status. In fact, such feelings may be one of the biggest sources of the current malaise. In the United States, the admission of blacks into situations formerly reserved for whites meant that whites lost some of their status; in other words, their social position had worsened. The blacks, on the other hand, often felt highly insecure in their improved status. Thus the short-term effects often made both blacks and whites uncomfortable and unhappy, even though the long-term consequences of desegregation might be beneficial.

Conferring a higher status on increasing numbers of people has the effect of debasing the status. In recent years, millions of young people have been given college educations, which formerly were a ticket to prestige jobs. As the number of graduates climbed, the value of a college education on the job market declined.

"Since the war," says British economist E. J. Mishan, "the bachelor's degree has been virtually worthless. Today, even the Ph.D. has lost its power to evoke respect in the community, and can no longer be depended upon to launch the successful candidate toward the upper echelons in government or business. If present trends in mass education continue, there is every likelihood of millions of dissatisfied ex-students milling about American cities, their frail expertise unwanted (How many sociologists can the nation employ?), unwilling or unable to fit into the uninspiring niches provided by industry and government, and inevitably forming a sort of intellectual lumpenproletariat that will go far to aggravate the general unrest, dissent and desperation."

In Sweden there have been disturbances because the wage gap between white-collar and blue-collar workers has narrowed. White-collar workers have tended to resent their loss of status as the blue-collar workers rise toward equality with the white-collar workers.

The new scarcities are not yet well understood, but they help to account for the widespread feeling that the world is becoming "dehumanized" and that things are getting worse even when they look as if they should be getting better. Yet all these problems of change might be bearable if man could still retain his sense of purpose, for, as Viktor Frankl, a survivor of the Nazi concentration camps, once remarked, a person who has a *why* to live can bear with any *how*. Unfortunately, the *why* is also disappearing.

The Death of Hope

For thousands of years, people have believed in a happy world to come, a world offering eventual escape from the agonies and injustices of the present world. Down through the ages, the hope of eventually attaining such a Promised Land has given people comfort and purpose. During the past two centuries, belief in a heavenly kingdom has declined. But as the hope of heaven receded, a new hope rose to take its place—the hope of utopia. Heaven would be built on earth, and man could labor in the expectation that the earth itself would someday become Paradise. The ideologues of Capitalism and the ideologues of Marx shared a common hope for the secular heaven to come. However, the terrors of the 20th century have led to widespread fears that mankind may be moving instead toward *dys*topia—a totalitarian world in which thoughts are controlled by Big Brother or a world in which human beings are dehumanized and manipulated as in Aldous Huxley's *Brave New World.* The future, which once offered comfort and purpose in a world of pain and sorrow, has become itself a source of terror. Today man fears there may be no desirable future either on earth or in heaven. And lacking the image of a desirable future, he also lacks what such an image could provide: meaningful goals and a moral system that could develop from such goals. As consolation he has only material goods that provide momentary comforts, transient feelings of superiority over people with less, or, at best, some rudimentary self-transcendence when he shares his goods with those less fortunate than himself.

Lacking belief in heaven or utopia, modern man has placed his hopes on his "career." He has hoped for "success," that is, a social position offering prestige, power, and wealth. This success is earned by means of a steady progression in which one's merits are demonstrated by hard work and sacrifice. This vision of success offers a justification and consolation for the disappointments and sacrifices suffered in life. People who do not believe that a career will lead to success can still hope to reach the Promised Land by such alternative routes as gambling and crime. The possibility of a "big win" in the lottery provides substance for hope, and so does the possibility of a big heist. For a ghetto youth, the vision of a big heist may offer the same sustaining hope that enabled the early Christians to face the lions.

But success is a poor substitute for heaven and utopia, because most people eventually realize that it has eluded them. Very few people who go to work for a big company ever become Chairman of the Board; most employees eventually fall by the wayside on their way to success. And those who do reach the peak of the pyramid find that work and worry do not stop at the entrance to the executive suite. Success can be the religion of the middle class—while the middle class is small—but it loses its credibility as that class grows and the chances of attaining to a really superior position become vanishingly small. Thus the hope of success—like the hope of heaven and the hope of utopia—appears to be declining. In the view of increasing numbers of people, there now seems to be nothing in the future that is genuinely desirable and worth working for.

The collapse of hope for the future has led to a sharp rise in suicides among young people. During the 1970s, the suicide rate for 15 to 24-year-olds in the United States is *triple* the rate of the 1950s. Suicide now is the third major cause of death among the young (following accidents and homicides); among college students, only accidents still claim more lives than suicides.

Less obviously, the collapse of hope may be a major factor behind the widespread retreat from parenthood in rich countries like the United States and Germany. American women in 1976 did not have enough children to replace themselves, the replacement level of births being 2.1 children per woman. Young people are saying, in effect, "It's not fair to bring children into a world that faces such a bleak future."

The retreat from parenthood makes the future even bleaker. In the past, people could hope that even if they could not have a happy and successful life, they could help their children to reach it. The hope that people placed in their children provided another route to consolation and meaning amid the hardships of life. People could think, "My life has been painful and frustrating, but my children will benefit; they will enjoy the fruits of my labor, and my sacrifice will be justified."

Without children on whom to place one's hopes, the last barrier to despair is removed, and the only "hope" is world catastrophe, which will provide full justification for despair and apathy. Hence, the decline of belief in a Desirable Future World has been accompanied by mounting fears of world calamity. In the next chapter, we shall look at what the doomsday prophets are saying about the future, and explain why futurists—the people who are most seriously concerned with exploring the future—are surprisingly optimistic.

2

The Terrors of Tomorrow: Realities and Bugaboos

Anyone who is unhappy with the world as it is today can take cold comfort in the fact that many contemporary writers believe that things may be worse in the years ahead. Instead of a bang, the future may offer a whimper—a general deterioration and degradation from the way of life we have known. Discussing his computer projections of world trends, Professor Jay Forrester has commented, "We may now be living in a 'golden age' where, in spite of the worldwide feeling of malaise, the quality of life is, on the average, higher than ever before in history and higher now than the future offers."

The notion that the late 20th century may be a golden age might strike some people as ludicrous, but during the golden ages of Greece and Rome there doubtless were many people who would have laughed at any suggestion that theirs was one of the blessed eras of history. Yet, from many standpoints, our era does seem to be a golden age: people today live longer and have a far higher standard of living than the inhabitants of previous golden ages; science, education, and art are supported far better than in past eras (though not as well as their practitioners might wish). If our era does not seem golden, it may simply be that we are not looking back on it from some leaden era in the future.

Roberto Vacca, the Italian author who describes the future in a book entitled *The Coming Dark Age*, says that the inconveniences and discomforts of today's society are of negligible importance compared with what is to come. "Anyone who is preoccupied with them is—to use appropriate apocalyptic vividness—like a prisoner in a crowded, locked freight car who complains about the uncomfortable ride and gives no thought to the extermination camp that awaits him."

A similarly bleak viewpoint appears in Gordon Rattray Taylor's book *How to Avoid the Future*. Taylor asserts that the future will be "more violent than anything we can remember, more unstable socially, and more insecure. Life will be more inconvenient and frustrating, the material standard of living will fall, there will be financial disasters and whole classes will be wiped out. Food and resources will be in short supply, noise and pollution will be worse. There will be famines and no doubt wars, both civil and uncivil." To cap it all off, the world will be colder due to climatic changes.

Another catastrophist, Andrew Hacker, author of *The End of the American Era*, offers this grim glimpse of the future in a recent book review:

> In the books on the future there is one scenario that no one wants to write, chiefly because none of us cares to read it. It would show millions expiring of hunger, worldwide looting, the surviva: of only the pitiless. Rats and flies would share a terrain with radioactive ash and the rubbish of earlier generations. Even to a grim end, people would remain so convinced of their special quality that they would grab for themselves rather than accept standard allocations. From the jungle we came, and to a jungle we may return. There is no law of man or nature that says human civilization must continue indefinitely. Or even for another half century.

Ivory-tower intellectuals are not the only people making dire forecasts these days. In 1969, U Thant, then Secretary-General of the United Nations, had this to say:

> I do not wish to seem overdramatic, but I can only conclude from the information that is available to me as Secretary-General, that the Members of the United Nations have perhaps 10 years left in which to subordinate their ancient quarrels and launch a global partnership to curb the arms race, to improve the human environment, to defuse the population explosion, and to supply the required momentum to development efforts. If such a global partnership is not forged within the next decade, then I very much fear that the problems that I have mentioned will have reached such staggering proportions that they will be beyond our capacity to control.

The Extinction of *Homo Sapiens*

Warnings of impending doom now are so common that we can begin to collect and classify them. One category of possible catastrophe is the extinction of the human race. The modern catastrophists do not generally use the term extinction, but often speak as if that is what they have in mind. John Platt, for instance, said in the 1960s: "We may have even less than a 50-50 chance of living until 1980." However, few, if any, of these writers have presented a credible scenario suggesting exactly how extinction might actually come about. While there is no question that hundreds of millions of people might die in World War III, there is a considerable difference between the loss of millions and the extinction of more than four billion people. The world suffered stupendous losses during the

Black Death and World War II, but the extinction of *Homo sapiens* was hardly even a remote possibility in either case. The capability of modern technology has increased vastly in the 20th century, but it remains difficult to imagine how the human race might plausibly become extinct in the near future. Consider the following:

1. Despite all the crises of history, the human race is more numerous today than ever before. Though it is possible for a species with a large population to become extinct within a few years (e.g., the passenger pigeon), such an event is rare. In general, an animal is not added to the endangered species list until its numbers have dwindled to a few thousands or less (whooping cranes, orangutans, etc.).

2. The dispersion of the human population. People live all over the world, and not just in a single portion of the earth. There are people on almost all sizeable islands.

3. People have very varied habitats and lifestyles. Unlike other species of animals, man has an extremely wide range of habitats—and this wide range has been vastly enlarged in recent years. He now lives (at times) under the ocean and even in spacecraft far above the earth's surface. Within a few more years, he may have a colony on the moon.

4. Man has a vast amount of scientific knowledge, and techniques to combat any perceived threat.

5. The rapidly improving worldwide communications system can provide rapid warning of any situation that could threaten the very survival of the human race.

A "doomsday machine," a device that would destroy the entire world, was set off in the final scene of the motion picture *Dr. Strangelove*, but despite all the talk of such devices, there does not seem to be any realistic possibility that such a machine would be built, even if theoretically it could be. The destruction wreaked by a 100-megaton thermonuclear device is horrendous to contemplate, but it represents a mere pinprick in the skin of the earth.

If all the world's thermonuclear weapons were simultaneously launched at their targets, there is no question that huge numbers of people, perhaps hundreds of millions, would be killed. Cities would be wiped out, and fallout might cause agonizing deaths far away from the countries directly in the path of the attack. But there would probably be millions of survivors, many of them in good health. People in the jungles of Peru and Brazil and Africa and Borneo might survive, along with the inhabitants of the frozen wastes of Novaya Zemlya and the islands of the Indian Ocean. Humanity would have experienced a body blow—but it would recover.

Man's self-destruction seems to encounter limits similar to those faced by an insect exterminator. Pesticides can greatly reduce the insects in a given area, but never eliminate them completely and forever. Some insects always escape full exposure to the insecticide, and the species gradually develops immunity to it. All animals, including man, constantly adapt to changed conditions. Through history human beings have developed considerable immunity to diseases that once killed them, and they may well adapt to the many new hazards of existence.

Many environmentalists now talk as if the world might become totally uninhabitable. Warren Wagar, in *Building the City of Man*, discusses "ecocide" as a real possibility in the years ahead. Man, he says, "has the technical resources to make the earth actually uninhabitable for himself and most of his fellow species." But one may doubt that this is true—at least so far. Many hundreds of millions of people might die in a thermonuclear holocaust or a population collapse stemming from overpopulation and the exhaustion of resources, but such losses do not add up to extinction of the race. Even if man were bent on exterminating himself, it seems hard to imagine how he could effectively accomplish it. Millions or even billions of people might be killed, but survivors would probably still be left to breed. In the long run, people may prove as hard to exterminate as cockroaches.

The Collapse of Civilization

Though the persistence of *Homo sapiens* during the coming decades appears reasonably certain, the continuance of civilization may be far less so. Through history, innumerable kingdoms and empires have risen and fallen, and entire peoples have vanished with hardly a trace. Following the decline and fall of the Roman empire, civilization went into a period whose cultural activity was so limited (in comparison to the earlier period) that historians called it the Dark Ages.

A number of social thinkers are now worried that our civilization is so interconnected and dependent on the proper functioning of its various elements that a failure anywhere can cause problems everywhere. The disappearance of the Peruvian anchovy *(anchoveta)* caused a rapid rise in soybean prices in the United States and consternation in Japan when the U.S. limited its soybean exports. The price rise imposed by the petroleum-producing countries, and the power blackout in the Northeastern U.S. offer other examples of the interconnectedness of today's civilization. A strike of dock workers in France or postal workers in Canada can cause shipments to pile up on the docks and in warehouses in many other countries.

Experts also are worried because certain natural resources upon which civilization depends are now vanishing. Rising population and the exhaustion of easily obtained, cheap supplies of fossil fuels and minerals could lead to a declining standard of living, which might eventually reduce civilization to barbarism. The first things to go might be private automobiles and large houses, due to the sky-rocketing cost of fuel. As the level of affluence continued to decline, meat would become scarce; restaurants would offer simpler fare. Pleasure travel and resorts would decline. The horse and bicycle might return as standard transportation. People might grow their own food. Education might be cut back as a useless luxury, starting at the higher levels, but gradually working downward, leading to an increasing percentage of illiterates.

Television might be retained long after universities, libraries, modern-style hospitals, and legitimate theater had disappeared, but television itself might disappear as barbarism declined into a state of general social disintegration. The anthropologist Colin Turnbull has described the degradation of the Ik People of Uganda after they were ousted from their lands. In his book *The Mountain People* Turnbull tells how the Ik came to rejoice in the sufferings of others and lost all sense of group solidarity. Many Indian tribes in the United States disintegrated in a similar way after they lost their land.

If civilization actually does collapse, it might never revive. Various scholars have noted that the rise of our present civilization depended on the availability of easily accessible supplies of minerals, including coal and iron. Mankind now has used up the most readily available supplies, and they will no longer be available for future barbarians to use in another painful climb toward civilization. On the other hand, records and artifacts of today's culture might provide some alternate means for future barbarians to attain civilization.

A Population "Crash"

One of the key questions, many futurists feel, is whether man will succeed in controlling his population. The acceleration in the world population growth is generally viewed as unlikely to continue very long: something will bring it to a halt, but whether that something will be starvation and violence or effective birth control remains uncertain. The Scandinavian scientist Gota Ehrensvaerd has suggested the possibility that more than seven billion people might die off during a population crash that would occur during the three decades between 2020 and 2050. He suggests that population would fall back to the 1970 figure of three billion.

The crash could come much sooner. The world no longer has the large stocks of reserve grains that the United States maintained during the quarter century after World War II, and climatologists are voicing warnings about global droughts. Stephen H. Schneider, deputy head of the climate project at the National Center for Atmospheric Research in Boulder, Colorado, believes that a periodic series of droughts will lead to a worldwide food catastrophe. "I would say that the odds are at least 50% that we'll have massive famine in the next decade," Schneider said in a 1976 interview. He noted that people rarely die of starvation alone. In most cases, they die of a cold, a minor festering injury, or another ailment which their malnourished body cannot fight off.

Overpopulation may also exacerbate international tensions and intercultural relations, as suggested by the situation in Mexico where the population jumped from 20 million in 1940 to 60 million in 1975. It is forecast to reach 70 million in 1980, and if the present rate of increase persisted for 100 years, Mexico would have more than one billion citizens. Illegal immigration of Mexicans into the United States already is causing deep concern, but the current problem may be only a hint of what could happen in the decades ahead. In his book *Navigating the Future*, Bruce Murray, director of Caltech's Jet Propulsion Laboratory asks: "How will the United States react to massive human waves of the future as Mexico's race between births and deaths soars to its agonizing climax? Will the country symbolized by the Statue of Liberty be forced to form a lethal iron curtain to keep people out?"

War, Violence, and Totalitarianism

The number of nations possessing nuclear weapons or the capability of developing them has climbed steadily since 1945. In addition to the unimaginable horror of an all-out nuclear "exchange" between the U.S. and the U.S.S.R., the growing level of international terrorism suggests the strong possibility—if not the overwhelming probability—that atomic weapons will again be used before the bloodstained 20th century reaches its conclusion. Small nations, like Israel, would almost certainly consider using atomic weapons when survival becomes an issue. And underdeveloped nations might use nuclear weapons to extort wealth from the developed nations. As the editors of *The Ecologist* warned in their *Blueprint for Survival:*

> At times of great distress and social chaos, it is more than probable that governments will fall into the hands of reckless and unscrupulous elements who will not hesitate to threaten neighboring governments with attack, if they feel that they can wrest from them a larger share of the world's vanishing resources. Since a growing number of coun-

tries (an estimated 36 by 1980) will have nuclear power stations, and therefore sources of plutonium for nuclear warheads, the likelihood of a whole series of local (if not global) nuclear engagements is greatly increased.

The world is filled with ambitious dictators eager to strut across the headlines into history, and these political popinjays know that atomic bombs can give them the recognition they crave. And there may be more dictators—not fewer—in the future. During the 1960s and 1970s, the flame of democracy has flickered out in lands across the world. Some scholars in the democratic nations have begun to feel that democracy is incapable of coping with emerging world problems. Only "iron governments," Heilbroner has argued, are "capable of rallying obedience" to carry out the necessary tasks that people will not do voluntarily.

Planetary Impoverishment and Famine

Even if civilization is not gradually reduced to barbarism, there might be a severe fall-off in living standards. In effect, the citizens of the developed world might come to live like dispossessed aristocrats in genteel poverty, trying to keep the ancient color television set in repair and showing off photographs of the home, automobile , and boat they once owned. Alternatively, they might not accept their reduced circumstances quietly and use violence to try to regain what they had lost.

A number of thinkers fear that the world cannot stand to have many more people living at the consumption levels now enjoyed in the advanced countries. Jean Mayer, Professor of Nutrition at Harvard University, has made this point in striking fashion: "It might be bad in China with seven hundred million poor people, but seven hundred million very rich Chinese would wreck China in no time. It is the spread of wealth that threatens the environment." Economist Herbert W. Robinson, President of International Management Systems Corporation, has made a series of calculations suggesting the stupendous output that would be required in the year 2000 to give everyone the steadily rising standard of living that people everywhere dream of.

Even with dramatic technological advances, says Robinson, the question arises whether there is actual capacity of mineral deposits, forests, cultivatable land, airspace, water, etc., to support these levels of output.

Another question is whether the huge conurbations which would be created worldwide by the establishment of industrial capacity on this scale will create new economic and social problems, huge pockets of poverty and malnutrition, and political upheavals as yet undreamt of. Another question is whether this level of economic activity, and its associated outpouring of waste products, would not cause worldwide problems of clogging and pollution of the atmosphere, inland waterways and rivers, the ocean and even the land itself, which could only be solved at great additional expense. . . . We may be entering a period when nature's price for our materials and energy in the quantities in which we need them, and for an adequately unpolluted, orderly, and decent environment, is rising so steeply that real increases in productivity per head, and hence in output and income per head, will prove harder and harder to achieve with the investment funds available.

Through history, man has periodically exhausted the natural resources that he needed. When this happened, substitutions sometimes could be made, as in the substitution of coal for wood in England and other European countries. In recent centuries, the industrialized countries have pressed harder and harder on the world's natural resources; they developed the technology to dig deeper for fossil fuel, to refine lower grade minerals, and to exploit new sources overseas. But from now on, some scholars believe, the demand for raw materials—timber, fossil fuel, metal ores, etc.—will put increasing pressure on the available supply. Hence, prices of raw materials will rise rapidly, forcing down living standards. In the past, new technology has repeatedly come to the rescue—and it may again—but there is no guarantee of it. In principle, energy can be obtained from the sun, metals abound both in the oceans and in the crust of the earth, and there are numerous substitutes for lumber, but obtaining these substitutes with current technology requires a far higher price than is paid now.

New technology, reduced population growth and perhaps new values and life-styles offer hope that man can continue to improve his standard of living, but pessimists argue that living standards are more likely to fall in the years ahead due to the exhaustion of the cheapest sources of raw materials. Living standards may also be depressed by the growing need to protect the environment. In the past, industry used the air and waterways as convenient sewers for disposing of wastes. The situation could be tolerated in areas with few people, but population growth has forced industry to use more costly ways of disposing of wastes, and the costs will inevitably be passed on to the consumer. Whether the overall long-term cost of controlling pollution will depress the standard of living is somewhat debatable. Money spent in maintaining a clean environment may have a net economic benefit to the community as a whole (though less certainly to the polluter), as well as improving its quality of life.

Some thinkers now are calling for a reduction in living standards in the advanced countries on the grounds that the rich nations are, in effect, using the world's resources for themselves while poor countries continue in abject poverty. Warren Wagar in *Building the City of Man* writes:

> If the billions of people now mired in profound poverty are to experience even a modest increase in personal income, and if the human race is to strike a reasonable natural balance with its environment, the consumption patterns of the rich must change completely. We who find it 'difficult' to exist today on a per capita annual salary of several thousand dollars will have to learn to make do on considerably less than $1,000.

Whether the rich countries would agree to a voluntary reduction in their standard of living is, to say the least, open to question. Even countries with very high per capita incomes like Sweden, Switzerland, Kuwait, and the United States have many people who are poor —or at least consider themselves to be poor—and who would deeply resent the diversion of their wealth to other nations.

Thus, there appear to be reasonable arguments for believing that the world's living standards *might* decline in the future due to dwindling resources and to the growing cost of maintaining a livable environment as population and industrialization increase. The likelihood of such a decline in living standards is now the subject of much debate among futurists.

Miscellaneous Possible Horrors

Futurists foresee a number of other potential disasters:

- "Insane" Nations. The Israeli political scientist Yehezkel Dror warns that some national governments may exhibit highly irrational behavior in the years ahead. In his book *Crazy States*, Dror says that Nazi Germany offers a striking example of a crazy state and what it can imply for the international order. The scenarios that he develops might result in the following headlines in future newspapers:

**SOUTH AFRICA USES
NUCLEAR THREATS
TO SAVE WHITES**

**MEXICANS DEMAND
RETURN OF CALIFORNIA
AND TEXAS**

**CZECH STUDENTS ORGANIZE
SUICIDE SQUADRONS**

**STUDENT ANARCHISTS ADOPT
COUNTERPOPULATION TERROR**

- **Nuclear Crime.** The proliferation of atomic capability should make it increasingly easy for criminal groups to obtain enough capital to go into the nuclear bomb business. Nuclear theft and "fencing" of the stolen materials to terrorist groups could become a serious danger. Large corporations have paid thousands of dollars to ransom one of their executives; they might also pay handsomely to keep a "suitcase" atomic bomb from destroying one of their major facilities.

- **Economic Collapse.** Recent developments in the international financial community have heightened fears of hyperinflation, depression, and a general breakdown of the money system.

  Alvin Toffler in his book *The Eco-spasm Report* warns of a "general crisis of industrialism—a crisis that transcends the difference between capitalism and Soviet-style communism, a crisis that is simultaneously tearing up our energy base, our values system, our family structures, our institutions, our communicative modes, our sense of space and time, our epistemology as well as our economy."

  "What is happening, no more, no less, is the breakdown of industrialization on the planet and the first fragmentary appearance of a wholly new and dramatically different social order: a super-industrial civilization that will be technological, but no longer industrial." Toffler says that the economic breakdown "may be a symptom of a larger transformation and may be generated by forces that economists never think to study. Moreover, precisely because history does not repeat itself, because we are moving into a wholly new techno-culture, all the carefully constructed 'stabilizers' built into advanced economies to prevent a repetition of 1929 are largely irrelevant."

- **Death of the Oceans.** Brian Aldiss, a British science-fiction writer, has stated that there is now "very good reason for believing that pollution of our oceans, through dumping and distributions of poisons and chemicals and sewage, may already have reached irreversible proportions. The Great Lakes, the Baltic, the Mediterranean are rapidly dying, becoming unable to support their traditional life-forms, and there is no reason to suppose that this is anything but the beginning of a terminal process. With dead oceans, the rest of the world will die."

- **Climate Changes.** A number of studies have suggested that human activities on the earth are changing the earth's climate. The increase in atmospheric dust prevents the sun's rays from reaching the earth's surface, thus making the earth colder. This cooling trend, if it continues, would cause increasing areas of the northern regions to become unfit for agriculture, and thus adversely affect the world's food supply.

• **Destruction of the Earth's Ozone Layer.** Freon, the gas used as a propellant in aerosol cans used for paints, deodorants and other products, rises through the atmosphere and weakens the ozone layer that protects the earth from ultraviolet radiation. The increasing use of aerosols—and other human activities that weaken the ozone layer—have alarmed scientists because ultraviolet radiation causes cancer.

• **Racial and Cultural Strife.** A novel by Alan Seymour called *The Coming Self-Destruction of the United States of America* describes a nightmare world in which blacks and whites hunt each other with rifles. The book is assembled by an "editor" who, in about the year 2000, wanders through the abandoned houses and business offices of American cities and collects tape recordings, letters and diaries in order to reconstruct the events that led to America's destruction. Some of the tapes and letters describe the pleasure that both whites and blacks take in the torture of men, women, and children. In the late 20th century, cultural strife has arisen in many areas where it had long been quiescent. In addition to renewed battling between the Catholics and Protestants in Northern Ireland, some of the "subject peoples" of Europe—the Basques, Bretons, Scots, Welsh, etc.—have made new moves to free themselves from "alien" rule.

• **Family Breakdown.** In Sweden today, the majority of marriages now end in divorce or separation. The divorce rate has risen fairly steadily in the United States throughout the 20th century, and recently has reached the highest levels in history. The U.S. now has one million divorces every year. An American who gets married today faces a high likelihood that the marriage will eventually fail.

One result of marital instability is that increasing numbers of children are growing up in single-parent families. One out of seven American children under 18 now lives in a home without a male parent. The long-term consequences of increasing marital instability remain uncertain, but they may prove extremely serious. Sargent Shriver, first Director of the U.S. Peace Corps, commented during his campaign for the Presidency in 1976: "As society grows more complex, the family becomes more essential—as one place

where a sense of trust, a degree of discipline, a capacity to
love can all be nurtured, and often as the only place where
people are cherished because of who and what they are."

- **World Unemployment and Underemployment.** In the 1970s, India has needed 100,000 new jobs every seven days. An estimated three out of every four Indian college graduates are
unable to find work. Continued population growth may lead
to an almost unimaginable unemployment crisis. Factors contributing to the increasing glut of manpower are: the large
number of young people coming into the market from the
"baby boom" years following World War II; the entry of increasing numbers of women into the work force, and the constant pressure of business to minimize its use of manpower
because of the high cost of labor.

    Contributing to the problem is the training of large num-
bers of people for certain "prestige" job categories, with the
result that there come to be thousands of teachers, clergymen, and others who cannot find work in the professions
they have trained for. Many scholars believe that the thrust
for efficiency and productivity has resulted in a lasting condition of a potential labor force far greater than is needed to
conduct the necessary activities of society.

- **Loss of Religious Belief.** Most churches in the western world
have suffered declining membership in recent years, at least
in relation to the rate of population growth. Overall, the
peoples of North America and Europe appear to go to church
less frequently now than in times past, and to believe less in
religious doctrines. The decline in belief in God comes at a
time when such new "gods" as material success have also declined. "I am not sure," Warren Wagar warns, "that any kind
of civilization can long survive without religion, or without
the quest for transcendental meaning in life, which is the
same thing. One might as well ask a man to live without will
and desire, no matter how strong his rational powers or his
bodily health. But we fast approach a religionless social order in our century."

Surviving the Holocaust

A number of people who view the future pessimistically have
started talking about how to preserve civilization during the dread
period ahead. The Italian writer Roberto Vacca has elaborated his
plan in a book called *The Coming Dark Age.* Vacca holds that man's
great technological systems have become unstable and are now beginning to break down. The initial manifestations of the future Dark

Age will probably appear in the United States, Vacca says. Later the European countries will experience similar regressions to medievalism.

The Coming Dark Age describes how the breakdown will result in a sharp decline in population and the breakup of large systems into many small, independent and self-sufficient subsystems:

> A small number of people forced to rely on themselves will be unequal to the adequate maintenance of the buildings they are using, and they will give no attention at all to those they are not using. Empty buildings will be raided for fixtures or odd pieces having some structural value; and this, along with damage due to weather, will cause collapses. These will bring down other inhabited buildings. In the long run, therefore, houses will be much scarcer than they were before the KO [knockout of the world's systems] and new ruins will become a typical feature of the urban landscape. Ancient and noble ruins will be covered and obliterated by new ones in accordance with a process that was familiar in the former Dark Ages. Vandalism will add to collapse and destruction in cities, and inasmuch as it will not cause direct damage it will not be punished, but will be one of the few entertainments still available to the young.

To save the best elements of our civilization, Vacca proposes the establishment of monastic communities, located in high places "because in a dangerous age it is heights that are easiest to defend."

Vacca places his hopes in individuals and the small communities they may form in the future, because he has little faith in civilization as a whole. "Man's societies are going downhill," he says. "Powerful pressures make his existence increasingly unstable. There would be no sense in trying to reverse these tendencies simply by admonishing society and governments. It is the appeal to the individual that alone can have direct, albeit limited, results."

Warren Wagar, who also foresees a reversion toward barbarism, suggests the establishment of a renewal colony which could speed up the rebuilding of civilization when conditions again were favorable:

> Our colony must be located in a remote area, and extensive research would be necessary to sift out the various possibilities. Most of its facilities would be established deep below the earth's surface—possibly on an island in the southern hemisphere, in Antarctica, in the Andes Mountains, in southern New Zealand; or in some Arctic location, in or near Iceland, Greenland, or northern Norway. An important consideration would be the political security of the colony from outside interference during the years before Doomsday. It might seek extraterritorial rights from the country claiming jurisdiction over the land it uses; it would no doubt require protection from piracy; a mutually satisfactory arrangement with a country such as New Zealand or Iceland should be possible—for a price.

The colony would consist of perhaps 2,500 persons, including technicians in all fields, physicians, architects, geologists, journalists, psychologists, anthropologists, and specialists in management and public relations. It would have a particular need for men and women skilled in the arts of propaganda and persuasion, whose task it would be to link together the scattered fragments of postdiluvian humanity into a viable world order. . . .

A somewhat similar theme was developed earlier in Walter Miller's novel, *A Canticle for Leibowitz.* Already viewed as a classic of science fiction, *A Canticle for Leibowitz* begins tens of thousands of years after a large-scale nuclear war has wiped out modern industrial civilization. In the aftermath of that war, there occurred what was described as a "simplification," in which mobs roamed everywhere, lynching anyone who had any technological knowledge, on the assumption that it was technology that had brought the devastation. The mobs also destroyed all books and papers, so that people could go back to a simple pastoral life.

But tens of thousands of years later a strange thing happens. There are still Jesuit monasteries and the monks find a group of papers that had been carefully hidden by an electrical engineer named Leibowitz who lived in southern California in the 20th century. Leibowitz had hidden some circuit diagrams just before the mob reached him in the belief that the achievements of human intellect should be preserved.

The monks who discover the diagrams many centuries later do not understand what they mean. However, the diagrams are interesting and the monks set themselves the task of copying them and illuminating them. The monks also speculate about the diagrams and begin to notice there is a pattern. As centuries pass the monks begin to understand something of what St. Leibowitz had saved for them, and little by little bring back to the world the deadly knowledge. Once again, the path of technological development is followed, and as the book ends another nuclear war is again destroying civilization.

The Case for Optimism

Pessimism is now widespread among intellectuals, who complacently contemplate man's future destruction as the long overdue retribution for unpardonable folly and wickedness. Non-intellectuals seem to take less satisfaction from the coming collapse, but find it a useful excuse for apathy and self-gratification. Eating, drinking, and trying to make merry may be appropriate reactions to a future that has ceased to offer hope. Here and there, a few people have decided that the best course is to assume the worst and prepare for it. A number of American businesses now specialize in selling "survival" goods like dehydrated food that can be stored for long periods of time. People interested in survival are also heavy buyers of gold, which may perhaps still retain some value after a cataclysm, and weapons, which might be required amid the lawlessness following the collapse of the established order.

But is all this pessimism justified? It may seem curious that the people who think most seriously about the future—the people known as futurists—seem, on the whole, to be reasonably optimistic about the future. They are well aware of the dangers ahead and deeply concerned about them, but most seem to feel that mankind will manage to survive and perhaps even prosper in the years ahead. The optimism of futurists has been widely noted. For instance, educator Harold Shane, who interviewed a number of leading futurists on behalf of the U.S. Office of Education in 1971-72, reported that they have "a warmly optimistic view of what tomorrow holds in store for the United States." Similarly, George Boehm, a writer for *Think* magazine, described the typical futurist, as "conspicuous for his optimism in the face of nuclear proliferation, international tension, global pollution, the dull despair of the underfed, and other threats to civilization."

The optimism of futurists may be due, at least in part, to the self-selection of futurists: people who believe the future will be good are probably more likely to be interested in studying it than people who feel it will be bad. One should not expect members of a philately club to believe that postage stamps are ugly and uninteresting or the members of a gun club to argue that guns are immoral. A person who really believes that civilization will collapse into barbarism within 20 years will perhaps not be very interested in thinking seriously about anything except how to survive in the chaos.

But there are at least some suggestions that a few futurists became interested in the future because they were shocked by a vision of a horrifying future. For example, the advent of atomic weapons seems to have jarred a number of people into thinking about how catastrophe might be prevented and a desirable future created. Possibly people who have thought about the "unthinkable" become less afraid of it, or perhaps they see that the enormous power for evil is also an enormous power for good. Whatever the reasons, futurists in general do appear reasonably optimistic about the future. They are deeply concerned about the period ahead, but most seem to feel hopeful that man can learn to cope with the very dangerous new problems. Thus the consensus of futurist opinion might be described as "a deeply concerned optimism." The average futurist seems to have the mood of a sea captain whose ship is weathering heavy seas: he knows the dangers that the ship faces, but he hopes—and believes—that despite the perils, the ship will even-

tually sail safely into port, and that he will have a warm and joy-
ful reunion with his wife and children. Even if there were little or no
chance of such a happy ending, the futurist—like the sea captain—wants to struggle to the end and, if misfortune prevails, to go
down with the ship.

The optimism of futurists may derive more from their emotions
and basic personality structure than from any rational, scientific
analysis of the human situation in the late 20th century. But
futurists can and do make rational arguments for an optimistic point
of view. Most futurists are convinced that despite present-day
problems and the dangers ahead, human progress is real. However
troubled our era, it is better than any previous period. Most
futurists firmly reject the notion that progress is illusory. Though
there is no way to measure the level of human happiness through
the centuries, futurists point out that the average person today enjoys far greater comforts and protection from ills than did people in
past eras. In a modern nation, the ordinary person enjoys luxuries
such as television and airplane travel that even the wealthiest em-
peror could not have had in times gone by.

Famines occur today in Africa, on the Indian subcontinent and
elsewhere, but they are no longer the common lot of people everywhere. In the 18th century, death by starvation was an everyday occurrence throughout western Europe; in the 19th century, during
the potato famine, a million people starved to death in Ireland (and
another million escaped to America). Today the threat of mass
famine has been lifted from western Europe, North America, and
other parts of the world.

In past centuries, poverty was assumed to be the inescapable lot
of the mass of mankind. Only in the 20th century have certain countries succeeded in virtually eliminating poverty—at least the abject
poverty known in previous centuries. Many of the people who are
considered poor today would have been viewed as well-off in previous eras.

The 20th century is remarkable for the scale of its achievements—and its wars and genocides have been on a scale to match its
more positive achievements. But human life today is far safer than
in previous eras, as is shown by the great increase in longevity.
When Rome was at its height, the average person lived no more
than about 21 years; the triremes that plied the Mediterranean had
sweating slaves as their engines; death by crucifixion or mortal
combat was an everyday occurrence. From those harsh times, the
lot of the average man probably deteriorated as the Dark Ages de-
scended, but it began improving steadily and rapidly in the 18th
century.

With all the problems man faces today, life is probably far better now for the average person than at any time in the past. Many people still lead unhappy lives, but they can generally enjoy their misery in comfort and reasonably good health—and with television to take their minds off their troubles.

Happiness is a subjective and elusive phenomenon, and it could be that people in the 20th century are not really any happier than people in previous ages. But most futurists argue that the progress made so far in realizing human goals shows what human intelligence and effort can accomplish. This progress suggests what people can accomplish with effort—and time.

The Solubility of Human Problems

Man has myriads of problems, but he also has a growing inventory of solutions. Many seemingly impossible problems have been solved or are in the process of being solved. Where one approach fails, another may prove successful.

Often a new technology will offer a solution to a difficult social problem. If people will not accept abstinence from sexual intercourse as a means to control population, they may be willing to use contraception which permits the pleasure of sex without the problems of childbirth.

Technology has not provided a complete technological "fix" for the ancient problem of poverty, but enormous progress has been made. In the Marxist view, poverty was caused by the capitalist who deprived the worker of the fruit of his labor. But the capitalist's "profit" actually was only a small portion of the worker's earnings. What really kept workers in poverty was their low productivity. New technology permitted improvement in productivity, thus making it possible for increasing numbers of people to escape from poverty. In the future, such technological fixes may help solve a wide variety of social problems that now seem intractable—crime, poor education, inefficient government, etc.

Once we identify a problem clearly, we can often imagine dozens of ways to solve it or ease its impact. All that seems necessary in many cases is a willingness to make a serious effort to solve it. The air over Pittsburgh once was black with smoke and London's Thames River was an open sewer of human and industrial waste. Today the air over Pittsburgh is reasonably clear and the fish have returned to the Thames.

Every day the technological powers of the human race grow greater. Furthermore, the world is slowly uniting to form a single global civilization. Though the process will take many more years before it is completed, people all over the world now have joined in a wide variety of joint enterprises ranging from the International Telecommunications Satellite Consortium (Intelsat) to the International Postal Union. These international bodies work quietly and effectively while the wrangling continues in the United Nations General Assembly.

The work of science has hardly begun. It has been estimated that 85% of all the scientists who have ever lived are alive and working today. Little by little, they are solving the problems that can enable people to have a better life in the future, and many futurists feel that a cautious optimism about the future is amply justified. The Committee that planned the World Future Society's Second General Assembly, held in Washington, D.C. in June 1975, spent weeks trying to choose a theme for the meeting. The final choice, after seemingly endless hours of discussion, was "The Next 25 Years: Crisis and Opportunity." Those seven words reflect what appears to be a general feeling among futurists that the next few decades may be an extremely critical period of human history—a period during which mankind will make the decisions that can lead either to calamities that could dwarf any previous catastrophes in history or to a brilliant and happy future.

In general, futurists do not interpret the current megacrisis as the death struggle of civilization, but rather as the birth struggle of a new civilization that is emerging from the old. As Glenn T. Seaborg has put it:

> What we are seeing today in all our social upheavals, in all of our alarm and anguish over an environmental feedback, and, in general, the apparent piling of crisis upon crisis to an almost intolerable degree, is not a forecast of doom. It is the birthpangs of a new world. It is the period of struggle in which we are making the physical transition from man to mankind—a mankind that will be an organic as well as a spiritual whole on this earth. I see this transition as a natural evolutionary process, a continuation of the growth and growing complexity of life on this planet. I do not believe that this growth is malignant in nature. It will not destroy itself by devouring its host or poisoning itself in its own waste. Neither will it self-destruct after delivering its message. Rather it will self-adjust through listening to and responding to that message—one that for all the static surrounding it is coming through quite clear.

The consensus among futurists appears to be that the closing decades of the 20th century will witness even more rapid social change than the preceding decades. There may be megafamines and wars fought with nuclear weapons, but the human race will probably endure these terrible catastrophes just as it has withstood so many others in the past. The years ahead will not be easy, but the majority of futurists seem to believe that civilization will not self-destruct in the next few decades and the human condition may dramatically improve. Recognition that it is possible to avoid a worldwide cataclysm and to move decisively toward a peaceful, prosperous, and humane world suggests that this generation of humanity must bear a momentous responsibility for the future.

3

The Shape of Things to Come

Even the most optimistic futurists are willing to concede that the world will continue to experience violence, war, disease, starvation, totalitarianism, brutality, environmental havoc, and myriads of other ills during the years ahead. But these problems are hardly new. What *is* new is that there is reason to hope that the harsh lot of the average man may be vastly improved. Man's lack of the wisdom needed to manage the powerful technologies that now are at his disposal will make the years ahead extremely dangerous, but catastrophe is not inevitable. To the surprise of the doomsters, man may be able not only to avoid Armageddon but also to create a far better world than any known in the past. Whether the future turns out to be as bright as futurists hope or as dark as they sometimes fear depends on man's ability to manage the human enterprise with greater foresight than he has employed in the past. Such foresight depends, in turn, on his ability to understand the world of tomorrow, a realm that rapid social change has made even more mysterious and baffling than it was in the past.

One way to begin thinking seriously about the future is to look at current world trends. Tracing such trends from their historical origins to today's headlines is far easier now than in previous times, because of the growing wealth of information about human culture. Until the late 19th century so little was known about the origins of man that even learned scholars accepted the biblical myth of creation and thought that the world was created in the year 4004 B.C. But scholarly research during the past century has revealed a wealth of new information about the human past. Anthropologists like Louis S. B. Leakey have pushed back the advent of man by hundreds of thousands of years. Several million years ago, apparently in Africa or Asia, certain apes began to make and use primitive tools as a means of improving their ability to obtain food and protect themselves, and little by little through the millennia, these apes evolved into men.

A basic theme of human history through the eons is man's steadily growing power to accomplish his purposes whatever they may be. The increase in human capability has been accompanied by a number of dependent trends, including a longer life-span for human beings; increasingly rapid movement of people, goods, and information over vast distances; increasing literacy and education; increasing per capita wealth; increasing use of mechanical power in place of human muscle, etc.

Scholars generally agree on the existence of these trends, though they differ on just how to describe them and on how they interrelate. Some futurists believe that the trends really constitute aspects of a single major trend, which Herman Kahn and his colleagues at the Hudson Institute call the Long-Term Multifold Trend of Western Culture.

The Long-Term Multifold Trend of Western Culture

1. Increasingly sensate (empirical, this-worldly, secular, humanistic, pragmatic, manipulative, explicitly rational, utilitarian, contractual, epicurean, hedonistic, etc.).
2. Bourgeois, bureaucratic, and meritocratic elites.
3. Centralization and concentration of economic and political power.
4. Accumulation of scientific and technical knowledge.
5. Institutionalization of technological change, especially research, development, innovation, and diffusion.
6. Increasing military capability.
7. Westernization, modernization, and industrialization.
8. Increasing affluence and (recently) leisure.
9. Population growth.
10. Urbanization, recently suburbanization and "urban sprawl"—soon the growth of megalopolises.
11. Decreasing importance of primary and (recently) secondary and tertiary occupations; increasing importance of tertiary and (recently) quaternary occupations.

Another description of the trends in western culture appears in Burnham Beckwith's 1967 book, *The Next 500 Years*. Social scientist Beckwith lists 31 trends which he believes will shape the next few centuries, and notes that most of these trends are already in progress, and some are already more than 1,000 years old.

Among the trends that Beckwith lists are:
1. The growth of population
2. The growth of knowledge
3. The democratization of education
4. The decline of religion and superstition
5. The spread of birth control
6. The rise in real wage rates
7. The growth of leisure

8. Urbanization
9. Industrialization
10. Specialization
11. Professionalization
12. The increase in the scale of production
13. The rise of meritocracy
14. Cultural homogenization

A Shift in World Trends?

Will the trends that have characterized western civilization over the past few centuries continue or will they change in the years ahead? No one knows, and the question is now the subject of considerable debate. Some futurists feel that the basic trend toward increasing human capability is beginning to come up against limits imposed by the environment and soon there will be a radical change in the direction of the basic trends of our civilization. These futurists say that the earth's resources of fossil fuels and easily exploited minerals are disappearing, and the supply of arable land not already under cultivation has dwindled while the number of mouths to feed has climbed. Even more ominously, the natural environment no longer appears capable of withstanding the ever growing assaults of man's technology: the earth's air, water, and land increasingly are polluted. Eventually man himself may strangle in the pollution he has created.

In the years ahead there could be a sharp reduction of the human population, just as animal populations suddenly decline when they outgrow their food supply and starve to death. An alternative possibility would be a die-off due to environmental pollution; already, pollution is causing an increasing number of deaths from lung cancer, emphysema, etc., and, despite excellent progress in cleaning up the environment in certain areas, pollution continues to worsen on a worldwide basis. The underdeveloped countries, striving desperately to satisfy the material needs of their rising populations, generally feel they cannot afford stringent pollution controls, and since the air is shared by all the world's people, the quality of the environment everywhere will be affected.

This pessimistic view is countered by other futurists who believe that the world's population and per capita income can continue to increase during the coming decades. They argue that advances in technology have historically allowed man to exploit resources that earlier were unavailable to him. In the petroleum industry, for example, new technology has allowed oil men to drill deeper and deeper into the earth and even to drill beneath the ocean. The supply of metals is virtually inexhaustible because of the vast quantities in the oceans. At the moment, it is not economically feasible, in most cases, to extract them (magnesium is an exception), because there are cheaper ways to meet the current demand, but if demand rises and other supplies dwindle sufficiently, man will go to the oceans—and perhaps also to the moon and asteroids—for new supplies.

The "technological optimists" and "technological pessimists" now are engaged in a lively debate. Scholars and scientists of distinction may be found on both sides of the issue.

In general, the technological pessimists argue for drastic population control measures; the simplifying of life-styles (eating less meat, reducing automobile travel, etc.); decentralization of activities (to reduce the use of energy for transporting goods and people), and organic farming (to reduce the need for chemicals). The technological pessimists tend to be very critical of the petroleum, chemical and nuclear power industries on the grounds that they are highly polluting and dangerous. Solar, wind, and geothermal power should be used rather than nuclear power or petroleum; natural compost, crop rotation, and other techniques should substitute for chemicals in agriculture; chemicals should not be added to food. The technological pessimists point out numerous instances where nuclear energy and powerful chemicals have caused unanticipated and frightening consequences; the insecticide DDT, for example, has turned up in the bodies of animals all over the world, even in Antarctica; people who eat the flesh of hogs that have received antibiotics build up an immunity to the antibiotic which makes it useless to them when they are ill.

The technological optimists generally concede that technology has many unwanted side-effects, but argue that technology is essential to maintaining a high quality of life. Without modern technology, the technological optimists say, man would quickly return to barbarism. The opponents of modern technology, according to the technological optimists, are romantics who fantasize about the joys of simple rural living while forgetting the brutal realities of wresting a living from the soil without modern techniques. More technology is essential if mankind is to raise the living standards of the hundreds of millions of people who live in the most abject poverty and on the edge of starvation. Technology offers the only realistic means of improving their lot.

The technological pessimists often argue for a better distribution of the world's wealth (because the *amount* of wealth cannot safely be increased very much); they propose that the rich countries transfer much of their wealth to the poor nations. The technological optimists say that such a transfer would be impossible politically, because even the richest countries contain many people who are poor—or who *feel* poor. The solution to the poverty problem, say the technological optimists, is to invest more heavily in improving technology both in the rich and the poor countries. As the world's wealth increases, the poorer countries will, in effect, benefit more than the wealthy countries, because a doubling of the income of an Indian earning $50 a year will mean more to him than a doubling of the income of an American earning $50,000 a year. Technological optimists maintain that the poor countries can and will emerge from the worst poverty. In fact, the gap between the rich and poor countries is causing a lot of industries to transfer their operations to the poor nations where labor is cheap. Japanese workers have long produced electronic components for American firms, because labor was cheaper in Japan than in the United States; in recent years, Japanese wages have risen so high that firms are moving their production to Hong Kong, Taiwan, Korea, and other nations which still have cheap labor. As this process continues, the supply of cheap labor will eventually run out; at that point, there will no longer be any poor countries!

The optimists believe that things are going rather well for mankind—and will continue to do so. In their view, the desperate and seemingly eternal problems of human poverty will have been solved or greatly alleviated in the coming decades. Most misery will then derive from the anxieties and ambiguities of wealth and luxury rather than from physical suffering due to scarcities.

A similar debate between optimists and pessimists rages on the subject of the international order. The pessimists warn of increasing violence, including a growing possibility that nuclear weapons will be used; the optimists emphasize that despite widespread world conflicts and the wrangling in the United Nations General Assembly, the world is slowly but steadily uniting into a single planetary civilization.

Many of the conflicts of today's world have occurred when people became aware that they were in danger of losing their culture due to the impact of world unification. Many of today's problems result from the rapid integration of the world's separate nations into a single global community. The unification of North America, for instance, threatens the separate identity of French Canada; the unification of Europe threatens the traditional independence of many nations and cultures.

Signs of world unification include:

1. Standardization of measurements. The metric system has steadily gained converts and the United States (the last major hold-out) is finally accepting it.

2. Standardization of language. English has become widely accepted as the principal global language. Hence scientists and schol-

ars around the world now have a common means of communicating with each other.

3. International organizations. There are now thousands of international organizations, both governmental and non-governmental, that link up the world's nations.

4. International trade. Japan uses coal from West Virginia and iron ore from Australia to make steel for cars that it ships all over the world on ships powered by oil from the Persian Gulf and Indonesia. A typical American may shave in the morning with blades made in England, drink a cup of coffee from Brazil, and drive to work in an automobile made in Germany while listening to a tape-recorder made in Korea. The multi-national corporation has become a powerful instrument for combining the technical know-how, raw materials, and labor from a number of different countries in the production of goods. All decisions now are global in character, and there are no longer any problems that are purely local.

5. Wide recognition that the environment is shared by everyone in the world. Barbara Ward and Rene Dubos, in their book *Only One Earth*, have suggested that recognition of environmental interdependence could give the peoples of the world

> ... that sense of community, of belonging and living together, without which no human society can be built up, survive and prosper.
>
> Our links of blood and history, our sense of shared culture and achievement, our traditions, our faiths are all precious and enrich the world with the variety of scale and function required for every vital ecosystem. But we have lacked a wider rationale of unity. Our prophets have sought it. Our poets have dreamed of it. But it is only in our own day that astronomers, physicists, geologists, chemists, biologists, anthropologists, ethnologists, and archeologists have all combined in a single witness of advanced science to tell us that, in every alphabet of our being, we do indeed belong to a single system, powered by a single energy, manifesting a fundamental unity under all its variations, depending for its survival on the balance and health of the total system.
>
> If this vision of unity—which is not a vision only but a hard and inescapable scientific fact—can become part of the common insight of all the inhabitants of planet Earth, then we may find that, beyond all our inevitable pluralisms, we can achieve just enough unity of purpose to build a human world.

Space probes have at last enabled man to see the world from a point beyond the earth itself, and thus to recognize that the earth—the only home of all mankind—is a single unit, and all the members of the human race are passengers on the same "spaceship."

Some futurists warn that certain world trends may become less pronounced or even reverse direction in the years ahead. "We often assume (with considerable justification)," writes Willis Harman in *An Incomplete Guide to the Future*, "that the most probable future

is a direct continuation of past trends. Yet it is apparent today that
many long-standing trends cannot continue unaltered: world population cannot forever expand exponentially; world energy use cannot increase endlessly; patterns of world mineral consumption must
change. In fact, it has been apparent for several decades that
modern society has broken with the past in a number of important
respects. Peter Drucker has called our time 'the age of discon-
tinuity.'"

One trend which many futurists believe may abate in the years
ahead—at least in the developed countries—is the trend toward
ever more rapid economic growth. Economic growth has no discern-
ible limit from the standpoint of economics, physics, or technology,
economist E. F. Schumacher says, but it "must necessarily run into
decisive bottlenecks when viewed from the point of view of the
environmental sciences. An attitude to life which seeks fulfillment
in the single-minded pursuit of wealth—in short, materialism—does
not fit into this world, because it contains within itself no limiting
principle, while the environment in which it is placed is strictly
limited."

Has Western Culture Reached "Rock Bottom"?

Willis Harman believes that today's resource-devouring society
may be approaching a crisis similar to the "rock bottom" experience
of the alcoholic. The typical alcoholic, says Harman, refuses to admit
his powerlessness until his life becomes absolutely agonizing. At
that point he may find creative potentialities that make it possible
for him to rebuild his life.

"Something like these first two steps of Alcoholics Anonymous
may be needed for society," says Harman. "First, admission that we
face a set of dilemmas, of thwarted goals and intolerable trade-offs,
such that the future of society has become unmanageable. Second,
discovery of a nobler image of man and his potentialities than that
which has come to dominate the industrial age."

Harman anticipates a shift in the long-term world trend. He and
his colleagues at Stanford Research Institute believe that certain
recent developments may result in new trend components and
hence in an overall change in the trend. These developments include:

- "Spaceship earth" thinking. This includes awareness of the
  biosphere as a life-support system, and concern for the environment, ecological systems and resource control.
- "Alternative futures" thinking. Such thinking includes awareness of potential dangers of technological manipulation to
  shape the future, and of the new dimensions of human responsibility for the future of the planet and for life thereon.

- Shift from predominance of problems of inadequate capability to manipulate the natural environment to predominance of problems of technological success.
- Shift, throughout the industrialized world, from deficiency-need concerns to self-actualization concerns (to use psychologist Abraham Maslow's terms), occasioned by increasing levels of nutrition, education, and affluence. The shift of need-level concerns is characterized by changes in value emphases away from materialistic and status values and toward humanistic and spiritual values. Manifestations of such a shift can be found in survey results, new forms of worker discontent, new political and social emphasis on self-determination, new styles of management.
- Awareness throughout the lesser developed world and among poorer groups of major inequities in access to the earth's resources and of the power to change this. The awareness is brought about in part by modern communications and transportation.
- Beginning of a shortage of meaningful social roles, as a result of automation and cybernation. The employment statistics and survey data are equivocal with regard to the seriousness of unemployment and worker discontents. Nevertheless, the evidence strongly suggests that the thrust for efficiency and productivity, for replacement of men's muscles and brains by machines, had brought about by around 1930 a lasting condition of a potential labor force far greater than needed to conduct the necessary activities of the society. Furthermore, the division of labor has been carried to the point where many jobs are segmented to subhuman tedium. Meaningful work opportunity has come to be considered an increasingly scarce commodity, as witness the concern over unemployment and "exporting jobs," rising worker complaints over stultifying jobs, inflated job-entry requirements, forced early-retirement policies, featherbedding, makework practices, and generation of jobs through arms races and "pyramid building."
- "New Transcendentalism." There is new interest in meditation and other self-exploratory techniques.

The Next 25 Years

The world will change very rapidly during the next 25 years, most futurists agree. Whether the pace of change will continue to accelerate or begin to decelerate remains unclear, but there seems to be no question that the extremely rapid change that has characterized our era will continue for the next few decades. No known force appears remotely capable of bringing it to a halt, though ways may be found to slow it down.

Many very surprising developments are virtually sure to occur; in fact, the most surprising surprise would be an absence of surprises. In 1940 atomic power, space travel, and electronic brains belonged to the realm of science fiction; today they are everyday realities. Between now and the year 2000, there will probably be many such developments, though we can only speculate on what they may be. There are, however, a number of fairly well-defined trends that provide a basis for thinking about the world of the future. For example, the specific developments mentioned earlier— atomic power, space travel, and electronic brains—all are part of a steady increase in man's scientific and technological capabilities. This trend may be expected to continue during the next few decades, but it does not automatically guarantee a steady increase in human welfare and happiness. For one thing, the growth of human knowledge and ability is accompanied by other trends that have the effect of increasing the need for knowledge and ability. Greater knowledge and social organization are required to support a world population of six billion than a world population of two billion, especially if (as some scientists think) the genetic heritage of man is deteriorating because people suffering from hereditary illnesses or mental defects are increasingly able to reach maturity and have children. As the complexity of the world increases, so does the need for human brainpower.

Adding to the problems the world faces is the rapid depletion of the world's supply of fossil fuels and minerals. Unless offset by improved technology, the depletion of fossil fuels may pose one of the most urgent problems of the next few decades; the loss of these supplies can very likely be offset by new and improved technologies and changes in life-styles, but not without alteration of long-standing habits and industries—and such alteration will not be effected painlessly.

The integration of the world community may help to provide basic security for everyone, because improved communications will provide timely news of a developing famine and improved transportation will make it possible to ship food wherever it is needed. However, the integration of the world community eliminates the insulating space that helped to slow the pace of change. Henceforth, social, economic, and political developments will occur increasingly on a worldwide scale and with dramatic suddenness. (A song about World War III by comedian Tom Lehrer describes the conflict as lasting only an hour and a half!)

If recent trends continue (and the "if" must be stressed), the world of the year 2000 may differ from today's world by being:

- **More unified.** Improved communications and transportation will bind people increasingly into an integrated world community.
- **More standardized.** The metric system will be universally accepted. English will likely be the accepted lingua franca of mankind. People over most of the world will be using the same types of goods—often the identical brands. Styles in clothing, architecture, art, etc., will be global rather than national. A world currency may be in use; such a currency might develop gradually from the Special Drawing Rights established by the International Monetary Fund.
- **More affluent.** The average person in the western world will have a higher standard of living. However, many things may be relatively more expensive in the early decades of the 21st century. (For example, gasoline, fuel oil, water, food, servants, haircuts, electricity, etc., may become more expensive in relation to other goods and services while long distance telephone calls, computing services, videotape recorders, etc., become relatively less expensive.)
- **More leisured.** People will spend less time at their jobs.
- **Less integrated by family and kinship.** People will change mates more frequently. The family will have deteriorated still further and people may have increased emotional problems (unless steps are taken to offset the impacts of family disintegration on children).
- **Less oriented toward industry in the developed countries.** As a percentage of the working population, employment in manufacturing will have slackened in the developed countries. More people will work in services (health, education, etc.)
- **Longer lived.** Life expectancy will have reached new highs in the developing countries. However, in the western countries, life expectancy may not be much longer than it is today—unless scientific breakthroughs are made in understanding the aging process and how to retard or reverse it. Some scientists believe such breakthroughs could occur in the next few years.
- **More mobile.** People will move about with increased frequency—both for business and pleasure.
- **Less religious.** Belief in the spiritual realm will have declined. A greater proportion of people in the developed countries will be unchurched.
- **Better educated.** A larger percentage of the world's people will know how to read and write. The percentage of people with degrees from colleges and universities may also be higher.

Numerous other trends might be listed, but trends do not reveal what the future will really be like; they only provide us with a convenient point of departure for thinking about the future. Trends often conflict with each other; they accelerate or decelerate or reverse. (Who would have thought that the horse population of the United States, which had been declining since 1915, would start increasing again in the 1960s? Or that sales of Franklin stoves would boom in the 1970s?) The future has many cunning passages which can sidetrack the best-established trend and secret lairs that can produce one surprise after another.

Not content with simply projecting current trends into the future, today's futurists are actively seeking new and better ways to identify possible future developments. But to understand what they are doing, we need to see how man's attitude toward the future has changed in recent years and how the future has finally emerged as a subject for serious study.

4

The Discovery of the Future

The study of the future is sometimes confused with fortune-telling. Both are ways to anticipate the future; aside from that, however, they have little in common. Unlike fortune-tellers, futurists believe that the future world will be shaped by human decisions and actions rather than a divine fate. Furthermore, futurists use rational or scientific means to study future possibilities rather than tea leaves, tarot cards, and other mystical mumbo-jumbo. Another important difference is that fortune-tellers focus on the future of particular individuals; futurists on the future of civilization. Futurists do not try to answer questions like, "Will John Jones get married next year?" but rather "How may the institution of marriage change in the United States during the next 20 years?" To tell John Jones that he will get married next year is, for a futurist, not only impossible but insulting, for it denies Mr. Jones the freedom to determine his own future.

Futuristics (if it may be called that) is a distinctly modern phenomenon; fortune-telling was well known to the ancients. The ancients appreciated fortune-telling, but they probably would have had great difficulty understanding what futurists are talking about, because they had never experienced rapid cultural change. In ancient times, people lived essentially the same way, not only year in and year out, but century in and century out. Their culture seemed to them an eternal and changeless reality like the sun and the stars. Individuals were born, lived, and died. Battles were fought. Famines and plagues swept the land. But people's basic way of life changed so little that most people did not see that it was changing at all.

Tracing back the history of futuristics, we do not find that it originated as some necromancer's brainstorm. Instead, it was developed by scientists and scholars who wanted to apply knowledge to solving human problems. Futuristics takes historical fact and scientific knowledge and adds human values and imagination to create images of what may happen in the future. Futuristics is science standing on tiptoes; it is history seeking to look forward instead of back.

The Pre-History of Futurism

The origins of the study of the future may, therefore, be traced to the ancient inscriptions carved in wood, bone, stone, or pottery for the purpose of conveying some information or preserving a record. These scraps of writing were the beginning of history, of scholarship, and of science. Not the Delphic oracle but ancient Greece's *logographoi*, the first men who could be called historians, were the very distant ancestors of the modern futurists. The logographoi carried their inquiry beyond the written record and oral tradition to a study of the world around them. They became critics of tradition and the forerunners of Herodotus, the "father of history." Herodotus now would be viewed more as a travel writer than as a historian, but scholars still praise his work as a scholarly achievement that was remarkable for the period in which he wrote.

History reached a new high point with the Athenian general Thucydides, who lived in the fifth century B.C. Unlike the "chroniclers" of earlier times, who were more concerned with popularity than accuracy, Thucydides strove to make his reports completely accurate, and to verify all his facts. "As to the deeds done in the war," he writes, "I have not thought myself at liberty to record them on hearsay from the first informant or on arbitrary conjecture. My account rests either on personal knowledge or on the closest possible scrutiny of each statement made by others. The process of research was laborious, because conflicting accounts were given by those who had witnessed the several events, as partiality swayed or memory served them."

With Thucydides and other historians, men began to collect the data base needed to understand that (1) their way of life was not the only way, because there were people elsewhere who lived in very different ways, and (2) a way of life changes through time. The ancients did not grasp the second point very well, but the establishment of factual historical records made it possible for later people to understand the reality that we know as *cultural change*.

In addition to the ancient historians, the ancient philosophers contributed to the development of modern futurism. Plato's *Republic* started the utopian tradition that has played a major part in the development of future studies. In seeking to answer the question, "What is justice and how can it be achieved?," Plato developed a picture of an ideal society in which philosopher-kings rule. "We have agreed then, Glaucon," Plato writes, "that in the city whose constitution is to be perfect, wives and children and all education will be in common; so will war-like and peaceful occupations; and those who have shown themselves best in philosophy and war are to be their kings." The *Republic* makes clear that the systems which regulate human affairs differ in quality, that they can be analyzed and evaluated, and perhaps improved.

Plato's *Republic* marked the start of a long series of utopias and dystopias that have exercised human minds down through the centuries. "It is no extravagance to claim," said British writer I.F. Clarke recently, "that the entire body of utopian fiction is little more than a series of variations on Plato. As the first in the field he was able to present—once and for all—the basic dilemma that puts power and passion into the dullest utopia—the eternal conflict between individual desires and public necessities, between the happiness of the citizen and the security of the state. From Plato the literary tradition runs straight to Sir Thomas More and on to the many visionaries, ideologues and propagandists of the last hundred years."

Besides historical and utopian writing, the ancient world contributed a number of ideas that have gone into man's thinking about the future. Christianity, for example, developed three strikingly different approaches to the future, theologian Harvey Cox says, and all three still have adherents. The three views of the future are the *apocalyptic*, the *teleological*, and the *prophetic*.

Apocalyptic literature seethes with vivid symbolism, stemming mainly from Iranian religious influences with a complex angelology, weird demonology, and the stark dualism between this world and the next. Apocalyptic motifs produce a mood of world negation, fatalism, and a retreat from earthly chores. The ancients hoped for a miraculous deliverance after the cataclysm, but their secularized modern successors see only the cataclysm itself, Cox says. The motion picture *Dr. Strangelove* is a modern reincarnation of the apocalyptic mood, says Cox; the movie is "a deeply antipolitical exercise in chic nihilism, the modern nonbelievers' equivalent of apocalypticism."

The *teleological* perspective sees the future as the unwinding of a purpose inherent in the universe itself or in its primal stuff towards a fixed end. Modern secularized teleology is sometimes based in biology and points to a Great Intelligence moving toward still unthought-of forms of life.

The *prophetic* mood is the characteristically Hebrew notion of the future as the open field of human hope and responsibility. Prophecy has often been mistakenly confused with soothsaying and divination, says Cox, but nothing could be further from the truth. The Hebrew prophets envisioned the future in the prophetic utterances, but their only reason for talking about the future was to get people to change their present behavior. They did so because they believed the future was not predetermined, and that human beings shape it. A seer of the pagan tradition, says Cox, can foretell the future only because the gods have already determined each man's future. The seer speaks not to elicit repentance and a new course of action, as the prophets did, but to warn someone that striving to evade his fate is futile. By contrast, the Biblical prophets talk about the future in terms of what Jehovah will do unless his people change their ways. Jehovah is free to change his mind. The future is not determined.

"Prophecy," says Cox, "insists that the future will be shaped not by invisible malevolent forces or by irresistible inherent tendencies but by what men decide to do. . . . This unconditional openness to the future also allows prophecy to escape from the paralysis of past decisions and policies. The prophetic call always requires repentance, the candid recognition that one has made mistakes, but will now do something different. Policies need not be papered over with spurious claims that they are simply extensions of decisions made in the past. The prophetic perspective requires incessant innovation and the continuous reappraisal of past policies because tomorrow will not be just an unfolding of yesterday's tendencies but will include aspects of unprecedented novelty."

The Beginnings of Modern Futurism

The trends in the ancient world that might have developed into a conscious futurism collapsed with the decay of the Roman empire. During the Dark Ages and medieval period, man's interest in the future was directed toward heaven rather than earth. During this period of relatively slow cultural change, there appears to have been little recognition that civilization was changing, and little interest in forecasting such change.

But in Europe, during the 11th or 12th century, there began a movement that slowly gathered force through the 13th, 14th and 15th centuries. Europe's intellectual life quickened; the books of the ancient writers were revived and read; the New World was discovered, explored, and colonized; science developed more rapidly; technology advanced. In England, Sir Thomas More wrote *Utopia*, a satire on government and society that was inspired by Plato's *Republic*. *Utopia* relates More's supposed conversations with a fictitious mariner named Ralph Hythlodaye who had visited the island of Utopia, an ideal land characterized by community of goods, a national system of education, work for everyone, and a philosophy under which the desires of the individual are sacrificed to the common good. Modern readers find it curious that slavery and monarchy are accepted in Utopia, but More was writing in 1516 when both institutions were viewed as natural if not inevitable aspects of life.

As in Plato's *Republic*, the ideal state is a static community, or-
dained to continue unchanged for all time. *Utopia* gave its name to
the genre of literature that describes imaginary but desirable societies.

Scarcely more than a century later, another Briton developed a
utopia that proved even more significant, perhaps, in the development of futurist thinking. Sir Francis Bacon's *New Atlantis* described an ideal science-based community located on the imaginary
island of Bensalem, which has a research institute known as
Solomon's House standing at its center. All the island's citizens
have as their great purpose "the knowledge of causes and secret
motions of things, and the enlarging of the bounds of human empire,
to the effecting of all things possible." Bacon, unlike More, believed
the purpose of knowledge is to improve human life, and the logic and
attractiveness of his argument won him a wide audience, many
imitators, and enthusiastic followers. His *New Atlantis* powerfully
influenced the movement that produced the famed *Encyclopedie* in
France. Diderot and d'Alembert, who published the first volume of
the *Encyclopedie* in 1751, gave Bacon the major credit for the idea
of a universal dictionary of the arts, sciences, trades and manufac-
tures.

Bacon and the Encyclopedists ushered in an era of great confidence in the ability of man to improve his condition through science
and industry. Plato's dream of a perfect state was to be realized on
earth by means of Bacon's "profitable inventions." There was little
suspicion that science and technology could cause problems as well
as solve them. "For all his shrewdness and intelligence," writes I.F.
Clarke, "Bacon did not anticipate, for instance, that advances in
medical knowledge could lead to a rapid growth in population; and
the complacent account of the new weapons—'new mixtures and
compositions of gunpowder, wildfires burning in water and unquen-
chable'—is innocent of anxiety about the consequences that could
follow from improving on the means of warfare."

The idea that science had practical utility and could improve
man's lot on earth was the guiding star of Bacon's intellectual labor.
Bacon single-mindedly insisted that the true object of science is not,
as the Greek philosophers maintained, mere speculative satisfaction, but rather to increase human happiness. In the *Novum
Organum*, he saw clearly that three inventions unknown to the ancients—printing, gunpowder, and the compass—"have changed the
appearance and state of the whole world; first in literature, then in
warfare, and lastly in navigation; and innumerable changes have
been thence derived, so that no empire, sect, or star appears to have
exercised a greater power or influence on human affairs than these
mechanical discoveries." Never before had the impact of new

technology been so clearly recognized and proclaimed. Bacon saw that new discoveries were changing the culture in which he lived; by pointing out the cultural change, he opened the minds of men to the possibility of anticipating what changes might occur. Until people recognized that their culture was changing, they could have no serious interest in trying to forecast what changes might occur.

The Idea of Progress

Bacon was the first to formulate the Idea of Progress as it was to triumph in the 18th century. As described by J.B. Bury, this idea is the belief that "civilization has moved, is moving, and will continue to move in a desirable direction." Today, according to historian Warren Wagar, the idea of progress "is the religion of modern western man. Long after he lost touch with transcendence, he continued to believe that history recorded his own gradual approach to perfection."

The idea of progress was new and exciting in the 17th and 18th centuries, and marked a major turning-point in human thought. Charles Beard, the historian, has written:

> Among the ideas which have held sway in public and private affairs for the last 200 years, none is more significant or likely to exert more influence in the future than the concept of progress. With a few exceptions, ancient writers were imprisoned in a vicious circle; they thought that mankind revolved in a cycle through some series of stages. In the middle ages thought and practice were cramped by the belief that man was a sinful creature born to trouble as the sparks fly upward, that the world would come to a close sometime, and that life on earth was not an end in itself but a kind of prelude to heaven or hell. It was not until commerce, invention, and natural science emancipated humanity from thralldom to the cycle and to the Christian epic, that it became possible to think of an immense future for mortal mankind, of the conquest of the material world in the human interest, of providing the conditions for a good life on this planet without reference to any possible hereafter.

During the years that followed the publication of the *New Atlantis*, Europe's scholars crossed swords in a literary war over the comparative merits of ancient and modern writers. The quarrel of the Ancients and Moderns was part of the rebellion against the intellectual yoke of the Renaissance, which had revived the writings of the ancient Greeks and Romans. Classical enthusiasts argued that the ancient writers were superior to their modern counterparts, but scholars enthralled by contemporaries like Corneille, Racine, and Moliere refused to concede that the modern writers were inferior to the ancients. Underlying this seemingly petty quarrel was a deeper question: Were modern men the equals of the ancients, or intellectually inferior? Had humanity declined from a golden age? Was Louis XIV less great than Augustus? Entering the fray on the side of the Moderns was Bernard de Fontenelle, whose *Dialogues of the Dead* (1683) features an imaginary discussion between Socrates and Montaigne. Socrates says he expects that the age of Montaigne will show a vast improvement over his own, because men will have profited by the experience of many centuries. Montaigne says that it is not so and the vigorous types of antiquity, such as Pericles, Aristides, and Socrates himself, are no longer to be found. Socrates protests, arguing for the permanence of the forces of nature. Nature has not degenerated in her other works; why should she cease to produce excellent men? Socrates says that antiquity is enlarged and exalted by distance. "In our own day," he says, "we esteemed our ancestors more than they deserved, and now our posterity esteems us more than we deserve."

Five years later, in 1688, Fontenelle published a short pamphlet, *Digression on the Ancients and Moderns*, in which he formulated for the first time the idea of the progress of knowledge as a complete doctrine. At the same time, says Bury, "the import and far-reaching effects of the idea were not realized, either by himself or by others." Fontenelle's *Digression* displays his open-mindedness, and his readiness to follow where the argument leads. "No man of his time was more open-minded and free from prejudice than Fontenelle," says Bury. "This quality of mind helped him to turn his eyes to the future."

The prospect of the future was one of the two elements which were still needed to fashion the theory of the progress of knowledge, says Bury. The champions of the Moderns, reacting against the Renaissance and inspired by the startling discoveries of science, had prepared the way by establishing progress for the past and present. It remained for Fontenelle to extend progress into the future. Man will not degenerate and the intellectual achievements of successive generations will accumulate through the years ahead. Fontenelle also added to the theory of progress the belief that it is necessary and certain. Progress does not depend on particular individuals, because it is in the nature of things. "There is an order which regulates our progress," Fontenelle said in a later work. "Every science develops after a certain number of preceding sciences have developed, and only then; it has to await its turn to burst its shell."

By the mid-18th century, the doctrine of universal progress had become widely accepted among France's intellectuals, and had begun to develop a zealous following. On December 11, 1750, A.R.J. Turgot, later to become famous as an economist and statesman, read a paper on the "Successive Advances of the Human Mind" to a conference of clerics at the Sorbonne in Paris. He argued at length in favor of the new theory of progress and ended with a burst of enthusiasm for the advancement of mankind:

> Open your eyes and see! Century of Louis the Great, may your light beautify the precious reign of his successors! May it last forever, may it extend over the whole world! May men continually make steps along the road of truth! Rather still, may they continually become better and happier!

A belief in progress is a belief that one's culture will change for the better in the years ahead, but it does not in itself indicate just what alterations may occur in the human situation. The future would be better, yes, but just how would it be better? Who could describe the utopia that men would eventually be living in?

To answer this question a Frenchman named Sebastien Mercier published, in 1770, a book that described human civilization in A.D. 2440 and took as its motto Leibnitz's saying, "the present is pregnant with the future."

The Year 2440 was published anonymously in Amsterdam. Its circulation in France was rigorously forbidden, because it implied a criticism of the administration, but the book was reprinted in London and Neuchâtel and translated into English and German. The book tells about an 18th century man who wakes from an enchanted sleep to find himself in the 25th century when the world is made up of nations who live in a peace rarely disturbed by war. Slavery has been abolished. The long rivalry of France and England has been replaced by an indestructible alliance. The Pope still reigns but has renounced his errors and returned to the customs of the primitive church; France is still a monarchy but its population has increased by one half; Paris has been rebuilt on a scientific plan; private hospitality is so generous that inns have disappeared; dowries have been abolished and marriages are contracted only through mutual attraction; Latin and Greek are no longer taught in all the schools. Mercier offered, however, few prophecies of what science might accomplish and he did not foresee that scientific discoveries might transmute the human situation.

The Year 2440 is one of the earliest examples of prophetic fiction, but it is not quite the first, even if forerunner works like *The Book of Revelation* and the prophecies of Nostradamus are excluded. What might be viewed as the first work in the modern vein appeared seven years earlier, in 1763. This was *The Reign of George VI, 1900-1925*, whose anonymous author tried to describe life in the 20th century. The fact that a George VI did reign in the 20th century might make the work seem today to be a triumph of prophecy, but the author's originality in writing a book about the future was not matched by his abilities to forecast accurately what it would be like. The British critic I.F. Clarke comments as follows on *The Reign of George VI:*

> The author is so well satisfied with the state of society in his time that he cannot imagine anything different. He looks forward to the first quarter of the 20th century as a time when architecture, literature, politics, and government have been frozen into a splendid classical perfection. George III would have felt completely at home in this vision; for population has not increased, cities are still small, and the good news from America is that the colonists 'are in possession of perhaps the finest country in the world, and yet had never made the least attempt to shake off the authority of Great Britain.'
>
> The only changes that the author can foresee in his static world of the future are political and military moves within the European monarchical system, and here there is one perceptive anticipation. Although the Spanish empire in South America is still intact and the Turks continue to control the Balkans, Russia has advanced into Poland, Finland, and the Scandinavian countries. The great menace of the twentieth century is Russia, especially Russia in alliance with France; and the task for any sensible British monarch is to restore the balance of power in Europe by crushing the French.

The Reign of George VI was the first major forecast of its kind—the beginning of a form of fiction that in the last century became a prominent device for commenting on the state of society and for tracing the pattern of future developments. The anonymous author failed to anticipate how science and technology were to change civilization, although he did predict, correctly, some of the changes that would follow from the completion of the Worsley Canal in 1761. Within 20 years of the publication of *The Reign of George VI*, the Industrial Revolution was under way in England, and the failure of *The Reign of George VI* as a forecast became increasingly evident.

The Industrial Revolution, which brought with it the steam engine, the railway, the steamship, the electric telegraph and innumerable other inventions, became an incontrovertible demonstration that science was a social device for improving human life. Bacon's view now was buttressed by tangible evidence on every side.

Benjamin Franklin summed up the outlook of his time in a 1780 letter to the Unitarian theologian and natural scientist Joseph Priestley:

> The rapid progress true science now makes occasions my regretting sometimes that I was born so soon. It is impossible to imagine the height to which may be carried, in a thousand years, the power of man over matter. We may perhaps learn to deprive large masses of their gravity, and give them absolute levity, for the sake of easy transport. Agriculture may diminish its labor and double its produce; all diseases may by sure means be prevented or cured, not excepting even

that of old age, and our lives lengthened at pleasure even beyond the antediluvian standard. O that moral science were in a fair way of improvement, that men would cease to be wolves to one another, and that human beings would at length learn what they now improperly call humanity.

Franklin's letter was hardly more than a momentary excursion into forecasting, but a few years later there appeared one of the greatest classics in the study of the future, a book that correctly foretold many of the developments of the 19th and 20th centuries, and may still foretell the developments in the 21st. This great classic of futurism is the Marquis de Condorcet's *Sketch for a Historical Picture of the Progress of the Human Mind.*

Condorcet was a great admirer of Francis Bacon and even wrote a paper, *Fragment on Atlantis*, in which he carried Bacon's idea of a research institute, Solomon's House, to its logical conclusion—a world research center. Still more influential on Condorcet was his friend Turgot, who had delivered the paean to progress at the Sorbonne in 1750. Turgot wrote a book in which he viewed history as the story of man's progress from superstition and barbarism to an age of reason and enlightenment. Later Condorcet took Turgot's basic concepts, extended them to every department of human activity, and used them as instruments to deduce what the future would be like.

The victory of the Americans in their war for independence and the increasing volume of the movement against slavery heightened Condorcet's natural optimism and confirmed his faith in progress. He felt he was living through "one of the greatest revolutions of the human race," and he never lost his optimism even though the *Sketch* was composed in 1793 when he was a fugitive from Robespierre's terror.

Condorcet did not just affirm the certainty of progress in enlightenment and social welfare, he tried to forecast its direction and determine its goal. His forecasts have proved remarkably accurate. Probably no other prognosticator has survived the test of subsequent history so well for so long. Condorcet suggested that the colonies of the New World would become politically independent of Europe; today almost all are. He said they would make rapid progress because they could profit from the knowledge that Europe had acquired; they have, though some much more so than others. He predicted that slavery would eventually disappear; it has, almost everywhere. He predicted that science would make rapid progress; that farmers would produce more and better food on the same acreage; that people would have more leisure; and that birth control could become widespread. The world has unquestionably moved toward the kind of world that Condorcet foresaw, though many of his forecasts have not yet been fully realized.

Condorcet's *Sketch* has won praise for its accuracy from S. Colum Gilfillan, a 20th-century forecaster, who reported that nine students rated Condorcet's social forecasts right in three-quarters of the cases. Gilfillan credits Condorcet with formally originating and using the extrapolative method of prediction, and being one of the first to make conditional predictions, that is, forecasts of what is likely to happen *if* something else occurs.

The belief in progress, an exciting and even controversial idea in the 18th century, became part of the conventional wisdom of the 19th. By that time, progress was visible everywhere—in the steamboat and locomotive, in the expanding overseas empires of Britain and France, in the steady march of civilization across the Americas, in the fantastic new discoveries of physics and chemistry, in innumerable inventions like the cotton gin and the grain reaper, in the burgeoning factories pouring out an ever increasing quantity of goods, and in the development of programs for social welfare. The construction of utopia was underway!

The common people shared in the increasing prosperity. Nineteenth century life was harsh by today's standards, but living conditions advanced markedly over the 18th century. In 1750 two-thirds of the children born in London died before they reached the age of five, carried away by the privations and maladies that made life a constant battle for survival. With the coming of the Industrial Revolution, swift advances in agriculture, medicine, manufacturing and other areas rapidly reduced the rate of infant mortality, and as the age-old scourges of famine and plague retreated, Europe's population doubled—from 140 million in 1750 to some 266 million a century later.

Perhaps the most dramatic symbol of progress in the early 19th century was the railroad. The locomotive was something that even the ordinary individual recognized as a wonder of the age. Between 1830 and 1850 railway transport spread throughout Great Britain and was introduced on the Continent. Alfred Lord Tennyson traveled by the first train from Liverpool to Manchester in 1830 and was inspired to write *Locksley Hall*, a poem celebrating the idea of progress. The poem's narrator, disappointed in love, finds consolation in thinking about the future achievements of mankind:

Men my brothers, men the workers, ever reaping something new:
That which they have done but earnest of the things that they shall do:

For I dipt into the future, far as human eye could see,
Saw the Vision of the world, and all the wonder that would be.

Saw the heavens fill with commerce, argosies of magic sails.
Pilots of the purple twilight, dropping down with costly bales:

Heard the heavens fill with shouting, and there rain's a ghastly dew
From the nations' airy navies grappling in the central blue . . .

Till the war drum throbbed no longer and the battle flags were furled
In the Parliament of Man, the Federation of the World.

In 1850, a few years after *Locksley Hall* was published, the Prince
Consort, husband of Queen Victoria, spoke at a banquet at the Man-
sion House in London about the plans for the Great Exhibition, to be
held the following year. His remarks summed up the new dogma of
progress:

> Nobody who has paid any attention to the peculiar features of our
> present era will doubt for a moment that we are living at a time of
> most wonderful transition which tends rapidly to accomplish that
> great end to which indeed all history points—the realization of the
> unity of mankind. The distances which separated the different nations
> and parts of the globe are rapidly vanishing before the achievements
> of modern invention, and we can traverse them with incredible
> ease. . . . Gentlemen, the Exhibition of 1851 is to give us a true test
> and a living picture of the point of development at which the whole of
> mankind has arrived in this great task, and a new starting point from
> which all nations will be able to direct their further exertions.

When the Exhibition actually opened the following year, the leading article in *The Times* of London proclaimed that it was "the first
morning since the creation that all people have assembled from all
parts of the world and done a common act." *The Times* said the
Exhibition signified a new moral movement and foreshadowed universal peace. Tennyson's "Parliament of Man, Federation of the
World" seemed just around the corner.

Jules Verne and Science Fiction

Speculation on where progress might eventually lead became increasingly common in the 19th century. In Denmark, Hans Christian
Andersen in January 1852 entertained readers of *Foedrelandet*
with speculations on the tourists of the future. These would be
young Americans who would cross the Atlantic in steam-driven flying machines. With remarkable prescience, Andersen suggested
that their slogan would be "See Europe in Eight Days." But the
casual speculations of writers like Andersen were eclipsed by a
French author, Jules Verne, who achieved stupendous popularity
by using science as material for fiction. Verne became one of the few
writers whose works were read all over the world.

Verne did not set out to be a science-fiction writer. He studied
law, wrote for the theater, and was set up in business by his family
as a stockbroker. But his interest in science led him to write a sci-

entific treatise on controlling the altitude and navigation of a balloon. Publishers rejected his effort, but one suggested he turn it into an adventure story. Verne did, and the immediate popularity and financial success of *Five Weeks in a Balloon* (1863) determined his later career.

From then until his death in 1903, Verne turned out some 60 books. By the time *Twenty Thousand Leagues Under the Sea* was published in 1870, Verne was established as the great prophet of his time. He became so popular that when *Round the World in Eighty Days* appeared as a serial in *Le Temps* the Paris correspondents of foreign newspapers would cable it to their home offices.

Verne's fiction was solidly grounded on the latest findings of science. For example, in choosing a metal for the projectile that was to take men to the moon, Verne's characters consider one proposed metal after another, until someone makes the startling suggestion that aluminum might be used. In Verne's day, aluminum was known only as a rare metal, prohibitively expensive and unobtainable in useful form. But Verne had learned in his research that its production was practicable and that it had the qualities needed for the projectile. Almost unquestionably, his writing about aluminum encouraged interest in aluminum, and research eventually brought it into common use.

"Verne's writings have influenced the future he was writing about," says William T. Gay, an American writer specializing in utopian authors. "In fact, his success as a forecaster appears to be due in no small measure to the fact that many of his readers were inspired to realize the inventions and feats he dreamed about. Youthful aspirants to careers in science felt that they had a technical manual on how a flight to the moon could be accomplished. And the characters were so humanized that each young reader could imagine himself as one of the participating scientists or one of the world-hero astronauts."

The occurrence of the moon flights in 1969 and 1970 in a way similar to that described by Verne in such books as *From Earth to the Moon* (1865) was no accident, Gay says.

> It may reasonably be said that he did more than any other single man to make the flights a reality. Many scientists have in fact acknowledged the inspiration they received from him. Konstantin Tsiolkovsky, the Russian 'father of astronautics,' once said that the 'great fantastic author Jules Verne . . . directed my thought along certain channels.' Tsiolkovsky's American counterpart, rocket pioneer Robert Goddard, read Verne's novels while he was in high school. Astronomer George Ellery Hale, who led the successful effort to create the Palomar Observatory in California, used to recall that Jules Verne provided a huge telescope on a mountain in the West for keeping track of his space flights.

Though he based his mechanical contrivances on the best and latest work on scientific facts and principles of his day, Verne peopled his fiction with 19th-century characters living in a 19th-century world; he did not undertake the far more complex task of trying to imagine how society as a whole would change as a result of the mechanical wonders he imagined.

But other writers carried on the utopian tradition by describing whole societies. The British novelist Bulwer Lytton published, in 1871, a book called *The Coming Race* in which he describes an advanced group known as Vril-ya who have achieved a level of scientific knowledge and degree of control over nature far in advance of Victorian accomplishments. The Vril-ya have domestic robots, television, sleep teaching devices, flying machines, equality for all, and universal peace. But the Vril-ya are not happy, because their civilization has reached a saturation point and their energies, instincts, and ambitions have drastically declined.

Edward Bellamy's novel *Looking Backward 2000-1887* was perhaps the first predictive utopia to reach a world audience. Within 14 months of its publication in 1888, the book had sold a quarter of a million copies in the United States alone. The book was rapidly translated into most of the European languages, and in 1891 the historian Friedrich Kleinwachter reported that it was being read "in almost every village." Bellamy Clubs, bent on putting the author's ideas into practice, sprang up in many countries.

The narrator of *Looking Backward* awakens in Boston in the year 2000 after having fallen asleep in 1887. He finds that the civilization of 2000 has radio, electric lights, clean air, full employment, retirement at 45 on a good income, and community centers with enclosed sidewalks for protection against the weather.

H. Bruce Franklin, a professor of English who has specialized in what he calls "fictions of the future," says that Bellamy's *Looking Backward* was the most notable and influential of the 19th-century utopias.

> Bellamy's vision of the year 2000 saw in America a society of extreme interdependence and organization in which all needs were satisfied and selfless love, unity, and happiness were omnipresent. Needless to say, Bellamy's vision was much more extreme than Marx's, and among the hundreds of future-scene fictions written as responses to *Looking Backward* were many which viewed his view with alarm. The critics of the future-scene utopias no longer argued that it wouldn't happen or couldn't work; they were now terrified that it was certainly going to happen and would work too well.

Serious nonfiction attempts to forecast the future appear to have been uncommon during the 19th century, but a few examples can be noted. In 1871 a British parliamentary committee presented a

Report on Coal, which included an estimate of coal reserves still available for exploitation in the United Kingdom. A German author published, in 1892, a book entitled *A Look at the Great Discoveries of the 20th Century: The Future of Electrical Television.* The author, Max Plessner, discussed the possibility of using the power of a selenium cell to translate light into electric current, which could then be reproduced as sight or sound, after transmission through space by electric wire, or through time by a phonograph or a photographic recording.

One of the more interesting forecasts of the late 19th century was *In 100 Years* by Charles Richet, published in 1892. Richet presents a statistical projection of the growth of world population between 1892 and 1992 and concludes that as a consequence of the decline of European birthrates, the two most powerful nations in 1992 would be the United States and Russia. "Their combined population will probably be around 600 million, which will be much larger than that of all Europe," Richet wrote. This forecast today looks remarkably accurate, but Richet was less successful when he tried to forecast the future of colonial empires. Here Richet's chauvinism appears to have influenced his judgment: The French would remain in North Africa but Egypt would shake itself free of "British despotism." Turning to energy, Richet forecast that oil would replace the decreasing supplies of coal: he also suggested that it might be possible to exploit solar energy and the internal heat of the earth, but he was not hopeful.

The Theory of Evolution

Belief in progress drew new strength from the theory of evolution advanced by Darwin and Wallace in 1859. Though evolution sheared man of his glory as the being specially created by God to be master of the earth, the doctrine enabled him to take pride in having risen from the primeval slime to become a rational creature that could create a world civilization. Darwin himself gave an optimistic conclusion to *The Origin of Species* (1859):

> As all the living forms of life are the lineal descendants of those which lived long before the Silurian epoch, we may feel certain that the ordinary succession by generation has never once been broken, and that no cataclysm has desolated the whole world. Hence we may look with some confidence to a secure future of equally inappreciable length. And as natural selection works solely by and for the good of each being, all corporeal and mental environments will tend to progress towards perfection.

Just as higher animals evolve from lower, civilizations also evolve and humanity moves in a desirable direction through the centuries.

Among the educated people of the Western world, the optimistic faith in human progress largely replaced faith in the celestial rewards of the human soul. Progress also gave people an ethical principle—the importance of leaving a valuable heritage to future generations.

"Consideration for posterity," says Bury, "has throughout history operated as a motive of conduct, but feebly, occasionally, and in a very limited sense. With the doctrine of Progress, it assumes, logically, a preponderating importance; for the center of interest is transferred to the life of future generations who are to enjoy conditions of happiness denied to us, but which our labors and sufferings are to help to bring about."

The complete triumph of the idea of progress required that it overcome a psychological obstacle which Bury calls the "illusion of finality."

> It is quite easy to fancy a state of society, vastly different from ours, existing in some unknown place like heaven; it is much more difficult to realize as a fact that the order of things with which we are familiar has so little stability that our actual descendants may be born into a world as different from ours as ours is from that of our ancestors of the Pleistocene age.
>
> The illusion of finality is strong. The men of the Middle Ages would have found it hard to imagine that a time was not far off in which the Last Judgment would have ceased to arouse any emotional interest. . . . It is science, perhaps, more than anything else—the wonderful history of science in the last hundred years—that has helped us to transcend this illusion.

But fervor for Progress declined as people slowly realized that though the future world might be *good* it would also be drastically *different;* it would in fact be so different that it could not be understood. John Dewey voiced this view in 1897 in an essay entitled *My Pedagogic Creed:*

> The only possible adjustment which we can give to the child under existing conditions is that which arises through putting him in complete possession of all his powers. With the advent of democracy and modern industrial conditions, it is impossible to foretell definitely just what civilization will be 20 years from now. Hence it is impossible to prepare the child for any precise set of conditions.

But if the future is to be so different that people cannot understand it, how can they be enthusiastic about it? Indeed, how can they even know that it will be good? If the future world is good, it will be good by its own strange standards, not by the familiar values of today. Thus rapid progress, as it became less of a dream and more of an everyday reality, began to give man a feeling of uneasiness.

Utopia might indeed be realized, but he might not be at home in it. The perfect world might have no place for imperfect man.

5

How the Future Became Foreboding

The 20th century dawned auspiciously. Both Europe and America enjoyed unprecedented peace and prosperity. France basked in *la belle epoque*. England stood at the height of its power and prestige. Both British and French empires were prospering as never before, and the ancient rivals had become friends. American industry was booming. Ocean liners, railroads, telegraph and telephone were binding the world together.

And as science and technology forged ahead, European civilization spread enlightenment to the darkest corners of the earth. With such a bright future to contemplate, it is perhaps not surprising that a few writers began to speculate on the good things to come. Sir William White, long chief designer of the Queen's Navy, suggested how marine power plants might be improved in the next decades by means of the turbine, high pressure, oil fuel, nickel steel, and noncorroding alloys. R. H. Thurston, historian of the steam engine, made optimistic predictions for its future. *Harper's Weekly*, in 1900, published an article on "The Future of Long Distance Communications." And in 1901 George Sutherland published a book entitled *20th Century Inventions*.

Most of the writers of the early 20th century are now forgotten, but one, H. (for Herbert) G. (for George) Wells, helped to shape the course of history. H.G. Wells' first excursion into the future seems to have occurred in 1883 when he read a paper to his college debating society. The subject of his paper was no less than "The Past and Future of the Human Race." Later he explored the future in such fiction as *The Time Machine* (1895) and *When the Sleeper Wakes* (1899), but he also wrote about the future in nonfiction works like *Anticipations* (1901), a collection of essays in which he examined the new trends in society. In *Anticipations* Wells identified the factors making for change in transportation, communications, the size of cities, warfare, etc. He foresaw the decline of horse-drawn vehicles and the coming of motor trucks. He also suggested that all of Great Britain would become an urban region held together by a dense network of telephones and tubes for parcel delivery. More accurately, he foresaw the importance of aviation in warfare. "Once the command of the air is obtained by one of the contending armies," he said, "the war must become a conflict between a seeing host and one that is blind."

Wells explicitly called for a science of the future in a lecture given at the Royal Institution on January 24, 1902. Most people, he said, are wedded to the past but the future was being discovered, and increasingly, people were shifting their thinking toward it. "It is into the future we go; tomorrow is the eventful thing for us," Wells declared. "There lies all that remains to be felt by us and our children and all that are dear to us."

The failure to look forward, Wells suggested, was due to the fact that people believe the past is certain, defined, and knowable, and only a few people think that it is possible to know anything about the future.

"Many people believe," he said, "that there can be no sort of certainty about the future. You can know no more about the future, I was recently assured by a friend, than you can know which way a kitten will jump next. . . . It is our ignorance of the future and our persuasion that that ignorance is absolutely incurable that alone gives the past its enormous predominance in our thoughts. But through the ages, the long unbroken succession of fortune tellers— and they flourish still—witnesses to the perpetually smouldering feeling that after all there *may* be a better sort of knowledge—a more serviceable sort of knowledge than that we now possess."

Wells pointed out that science has enabled man to discover the past—through studies of rock strata and fossils—and suggested that science might also help him to discover the future.

> Is it really, after all, such an extravagant and hopeless thing to suggest that, by seeking operating causes instead of fossils and by criticizing them persistently and thoroughly as the geological record has been criticized, it may be possible to throw a searchlight of inference forward instead of backward and to attain to a knowledge of coming things as clear, as universally convincing and infinitely more important to mankind than the clear vision of the past that geology has opened to us during the nineteenth century?

Wells stressed that he was not suggesting that individuals could ever know their own personal futures in the same way that they know their past. "But the possibility of an inductive future to correspond with that great inductive past of geology and archeology is an altogether different thing."

If the specialist in each science is in fact doing his best now to prophesy within the limits of his field, Wells asked, "what is there to stand in the way of our building up this growing body of forecasts into an ordered picture of the future that will be just as certain, just as strictly science, and perhaps just as detailed as the picture that has been built up within the last hundred years to make the geological past?" In his own mind there was little doubt about the answer:

> I believe quite firmly that an inductive knowledge of a great number of things in the future is becoming a human possibility. I believe that the time is drawing near when it will be possible to suggest a systematic exploration of the future. And you must not judge the practicability of this enterprise by the failures of the past. So far nothing has been attempted, so far no first-class mind has ever focused itself upon these issues. But suppose the laws of social and political development, for example, were given as many brains, were given as much attention, criticism and discussion as we have given the laws of chemical combination during the last fifty years—what might we not expect?

Wells ended his discourse with a burst of enthusiasm for the great changes that would come in the 20th century. "If we care to look we can foresee growing knowledge, growing order, and presently a deliberate improvement of the blood and character of the race. . . . All this world is heavy with the promise of greater things."

In Wells, the study of the future had both an advocate and an exemplar. He moved beyond Jules Verne's interest in the immediate use of potential technology to a concern for its long-term consequences. Verne described submarines and spaceships furnished with Victorian elegance and operated by mid-19th century men in a mid-19th century world; Wells recognized clearly that the new technology would change the character of human life and showed how future changes in society might be anticipated by a combination of scientific knowledge and imagination.

World War I and the Collapse of Optimism

The study of the future leaped forward with Wells—but both soon came up against World War I, the worst cataclysm that Europe had experienced since the Black Death. Suddenly the future which had seemed to lie before mankind like a land of beautiful dreams became dark, sinister, and terrifying. The joy of Britain, the pride of Germany, the hope of France perished on the western front. Civilization suffered a body blow to its hopes—a blow from which it has never fully recovered. And that terrible blow was followed by others—the Russian Revolution, the disastrous inflation in Germany, the coming of Fascism in Italy, the Stock Market Crash of 1929, the worldwide depression, the rise of Hitler, World War II, atomic bombs, the Cold War—in a seemingly endless succession.

Pessimism did not, of course, originate in the modern age. In the

18th century William Blake complained about Britain's "dark satanic mills," and in the early 19th century the Italian poet Giacomo Leopardi wrote perhaps the most pessimistic verses ever composed. Throughout the 19th century certain thinkers harbored dark suspicions about the march of progress. The Danish philosopher Soren Kierkegaard wondered if life was not becoming too easy and someday we should need to make it more complicated. Henry David Thoreau questioned whether the telegraph was really an advance, and sought escape from the world around him by building a hut in the woods near Walden Pond. Thomas Malthus (1766-1834) warned that population growth tends to outstrip food production, thereby producing misery. Malthus explicitly opposed the notion of inevitable progress: His famed 1798 essay bore the title *An Essay on the Principle of Population, as it Affects the Future Improvement of Society, with Remarks on the Speculations of Mr. Godwin, M. Condorcet, and Other Writers.* Fyodor Dostoyevsky in his *Notes from Underground* (1864) suggested that the human will would always rise up to overturn a utopian paradise where things work perfectly.

But despite the misgivings of a few, most 19th-century people found solace in the continuous progress in the present world and the paradise they hoped to find in the next. During the 18th and 19th centuries, rising doubts about the heavenly paradise were amply compensated by the increasing faith in the secular paradise that was being built on earth. But with World War I, sophisticated western man, having lost faith in heaven, now lost faith in earth. Progress came to be widely viewed as a snare and delusion; the same science and technology that once seemed to provide only benefits now threatened to destroy humanity. Motor cars led to armored tanks. Airships carried bombs. The wonderful science of chemistry was applied to the manufacture of poison gas. People began to talk about a "moratorium" on science and inventions.

Wells, who had prophesied so ebulliently about the future before World War I, began speaking more soberly. "Human history," he wrote in *The Outline of History* (1920), "becomes more and more a race between education and catastrophe." Twenty-five years later, after the outbreak of World War II, he had become convinced that the race was over and catastrophe had won. In his last book, *Mind at the End of its Tether* (1945), he despondently declared: "The end of everything we call life is close at hand and cannot be evaded. . . . There is no way out or round or through the impasse. It is the end."

The onslaught of troubles that followed the outbreak of World War I brought with it a powerful new ideology, Communism, that claimed to provide an infallible guide to the future. A young American, John Reed, witnessed the Soviet Revolution and

enthusiastically declared that he had seen the future and it "works."
But other observers, both inside and outside Russia, were increasingly doubtful that the future would "work," especially under Communism.

The collapse of belief in a bright future resulted in the
development of a new literary genre, the anti-utopian novel, or
dystopia. The first great dystopia was Eugene Zamiatin's *We*,
written in Russia just three years after the Revolution. *We*
describes a future in which the world has one great nation, the
United State, populated by people whose names are numbers,
whose God is "We" and whose devil is "I." The United State offers
stability, perfection, and happiness, but the narrator, whose name
is D-503, gradually discovers opposing forces who incarnate chaos,
passion, energy, and rebellion. At the end of *We*, the Well-Doer who
heads the United State puts down the revolution by performing lo-
botomies on all the Numbers, including the narrator, whose last
words are "Reason must prevail."

We was not published in the Soviet Union and remained little
known in the west for many years, but it marked the start of a flood
of dystopian writings. Among the best known are Aldous Huxley's
Brave New World (1932), George Orwell's *1984* (1949), Kurt Vonnegut's *Player Piano* (1952), and Anthony Burgess' *A Clockwork Orange* (1962).

Pessimism could also be seen in the publication, between 1917 and
1922, of Oswald Spengler's *The Decline of the West*, which provided a ponderous intellectual justification for despair. Cultures
rose and fell through history, going through a series of stages,
Spengler argued, and the western world was now on a downward
slope. Events seemed to confirm him.

Though the world's hopes recovered a little during the middle and
late 1920s, they were again dashed by the stock market collapse of
1929, the Great Depression, and the rise of aggressive nations—
Italy, Germany, and Japan.

The Struggle to Tame Technology

Despite the bleakness of the future after the start of World War I,
efforts to forecast future developments continued. Charles
Steinmetz, the inventor, regaled readers of *The Ladies Home
Journal* in 1915 with a vision of all the wonders that electricity
would bring to the home: Electric heating would help the housewife
to escape the drudgery of making fires and the bother of the dirt
and ashes. Cooking would be done on electric ranges. Wireless telephones would bring concerts into the parlor. In 1920, A.C. Lescar-
boura published an article in the *Scientific American* on "The Future as Suggested by the Developments of the Past 72 Years." In

1922, *Popular Science Monthly* published the forecasts made by a symposium of inventors, including Thomas Edison and Nicola Tesla.

These early 20th-century forecasts appear to have been made rather casually by inventors or journalists who had no lasting interest in the art or science of forecasting. But one writer, sociologist S. Colum Gilfillan, became interested in determining the accuracy of earlier forecasters and in understanding the prediction process. Gilfillan may have been the first person to study methodologies seriously (starting in 1907) and he also may have been the first to coin a name for the "science of the future." In his master's thesis done for Columbia University in 1920, he proposed the term "mellontology," derived from the Greek word for "future."

In England during the 1920s a series of books by distinguished scientists discussed the future of various fields. In *Icarus: or The Future of Science* (1924), Bertrand Russell wrote what was now becoming the new conventional wisdom: "Science has not given men more self-control, more kindliness or more power of discounting their passions. . . . Men's collective passions are largely evil; far the strongest of them are hatred and rivalry directed toward other groups. Therefore at present all that gives men power to indulge their collective passions is bad. That is why science threatens to cause the destruction of our civilization." Once hailed as the motor of progress, science was now suspected of creating the dismal future that lay ahead.

In 1926, the great French generalissimo Ferdinand Foch described the next war, which he scheduled for 1946 (seven years later than actuality). Other forecasts published during the 1920s and 1930s included those by inventor Charles F. Kettering (1935), whose statement "My interest is in the future because I shall spend the rest of my life there" later became a slogan among futurists, and C.C. Furnas, a chemical engineer who published a book entitled *The Next Hundred Years: The Unfinished Business of Science* in 1935.

Meanwhile, the effort to anticipate future developments was moving forward in government. In February 1921 Lenin established a Commission for Elaborating a Plan for the Governmental Electrification of Russia, and soon the Soviet Union was operating under a series of Five-Year Plans. The idea that government should plan the economic development of a nation was a startling innovation in the 1920s and horrified many people in the west, especially businessmen who feared government interference and control.

But, despite their misgivings, the western nations moved toward increased planning. Until 1900, the U.S. Government had exercised little control over commerce. Theodore Roosevelt's intervention in the 1902 coal strike astounded his contemporaries. Frederick Lewis Allen in *The Big Change* says that Roosevelt himself was "profoundly aware that he had no power at all to intervene. What he was doing was quite outside the normal province of the United States Government." Since 1902 the U.S. Government has increasingly intervened in economic affairs, and when the Democrats came to power in 1933 with a mandate to "do something" about the disastrous economic depression, governmental activism came to be widely accepted as a necessity.

Underlying the increasing interest in and frequent insistence on government intervention and regulation was the development of an industrial society, in which workers had no farms to return to if a recession threw them out of their jobs. Boom-bust cycles with periodic financial collapse could be tolerated in a nation where most people grew their own food or had relatives who did, but not when a family's entire livelihood depended on jobs that could be lost during a business recession.

Herbert Hoover, though later accused of being a "do-nothing" president, was an early and vocal advocate of planning. Hoover played a dominant role in a Presidential Conference on Unemployment that met in the early twenties and eventually published two works, *Business Cycles and Unemployment* (1923) and *Regulation of Employment* (1925). These documents concluded that (1) it is a function of businessmen to "regularize" or stabilize employment, (2) means and methods to so regularize employment exist, (3) such activities by industry are consistent with business goals, and (4) management has been responsible for the employment irregularities of the past. Therefore, the Conference concluded that it was in the best interest of both the nation and business to construct and adopt five-to-ten-year plans.

After he became President in 1929, Hoover appointed a President's Research Committee on Social Trends, a group that eventually achieved what was almost unquestionably the most comprehensive assessment of the U.S. social system ever conducted. In 1932 the Committee published a mammoth work, *Recent Social Trends*, that is still revered by sociologists. The Committee's Director of Research was William F. Ogburn, a sociologist and one of the leading students of social change. "Ogburn was constantly envisioning the future from 1928 onwards," his long-time friend and associate Gilfillan recalled in 1967. "In 1935 he called for the establishment of a predictive science."

Ogburn's Committee made explicit the concepts of social impacts and costs and expressed Ogburn's deep interest in the social effects of technology. (Ogburn today is sometimes called the Father of Technology Assessment.) The Committee concluded that the ills of the nation were in large part due to the unequal rates of social changes in the twenties: growth in production exceeded growth in purchasing capacity, large corporations were growing faster than labor organizations. Such unequal rates of change were the dominant cause of the Depression and its persistence. The Committee therefore recommended widespread economic and social planning as the only solution.

After Franklin Roosevelt's 1932 election victory—widely viewed as a mandate for government intervention and national planning—Ogburn played a leading role on the National Resources Committee, which published, in 1937, a report on *Technological Trends and National Policy: Including the Social Implications of New Inventions.* The preamble states that the report was "the first major attempt to show the kinds of new inventions which may affect living and working conditions in America in the next 10 to 25 years. It indicates some of the problems. . . . It emphasizes the importance of national efforts to bring about the prompt adjustment to these changing situations." The report contains a chapter by Gilfillan, who argues that mechanical inventions can be forecast because an invention does not spring full blown from a single inventor's brain but rather is the result of a social process that can be studied and, to some extent, forecasted. "A great invention," said Gilfillan, "is an agglomeration of a vast number of detailed inventions, like the thousands that have been added to the automobile." The best seers, he decided, are "distinguished technical and scientific men, who choose to predict in their own general field." But he added that "they are liable to upsets from developments in outside lines, and from the tendency of the ordinary scientific or technical man to see little change ahead."

Technological Trends was also remarkable for calling attention to the social impacts that might come from the mechanization of the cotton industry in the South.

> Exhibitions and tests in 1936 of cotton pickers in Texas and Mississippi have led many people to believe that the key to complete mechanization of the cotton industry is closer to a reality today than ever before. It will require several years thoroughly to test the machines on different soils, topography and varieties of cotton. But if the confidence of the inventors is justified, the picker will inevitably create new social and economic problems . . .
>
> In exhibition tests one of these pickers is reported to have picked as much as 5,000 pounds of seed cotton a day, as contrasted to 125 to 150 pounds a day for the average picker . . .
>
> If we assume that cotton acreage will remain about the same, and that a successful machine will be produced in large quantities and sold to all who can afford to buy, tenant farming as it now exists in the South would undergo change. Some tenants and sharecroppers would still be needed as laborers in the cotton fields, but many would need to turn elsewhere for a livelihood.
>
> Would they pour into the North and seek employment in industry?

... Many of the people from the rural South have had almost no experience with industrial discipline and complicated machinery; could they be trained to useful and self-supporting employment? ...

The cotton picker would cut down sharply the greatest single source of employment for woman and child labor in America ... How else, it may be asked, are these people to make a living? ... Will northern industry move into the South and take up the slack in the labor supply?

Despite recognition of the problem of displaced agricultural workers, little was done about it, and in 1970, Orville Freeman, who served eight years as Secretary of Agriculture, commented:

The displacement of large numbers of rural people by mechanization is more responsible for the big city problems which resulted in the burning of cities in the United States in the 1960s than any other factor. . . .

I have visited cotton plantations in the American southland where in one year the labor supported by the plantations dropped from 100 families to five families. Some describe this phenomenon as efficiency and progress, proudly citing per capita output figures. Such an evaluation fails to consider the human and social cost of 95 black families with nowhere to go. They or their children made up the rioting mobs who cried "Burn, baby, burn" in Detroit, Washington, Cincinnati, Cleveland and Los Angeles.

World War II and the Death of "Tomorrow"

During the 1930s, science fiction developed as a recognized literary genre and attracted a very enthusiastic following, even though the genre was generally scorned by literary people and rarely carried in the "slick" magazines. In England, science-fiction fans formed the Science Fiction Association and began publishing a magazine called *Tomorrow: The Magazine of the Future.* The magazine offered a variety of short articles on science fiction and forecasts of coming developments in such fields as transportation. In the Spring of 1938 issue, Professor A.M. Low suggested that Britain should have a Minister for the Future.

I can conceive the day when there will be a Ministry of the Future, an institution which will be far more useful than many of the Ministries which have been created recently. It will be the duty of the Minister to collect data from all over the world, to tabulate, correlate, compare and calculate. He will be like a spider sitting in a web, drawing towards him all knowledge, and working out, on scientific lines, the effect that the latest developments and discoveries will probably have upon the human race.

H.G. Wells was the patron saint of *Tomorrow*, which had all the enthusiasm for the future that Wells had earlier in his career. But the timing was unfortunate: *Tomorrow* was barely launched before

World War II arrived, and its editors and writers went off to war.

World War II brought *Tomorrow* to an end, and it led to a more sinister development which also was inspired by Wells—the atomic bomb. Wells's 1913 novel *The World Set Free* forecast the discovery of artificial radioactivity, the liberation of atomic energy, the development of atomic bombs, and a world war fought by England, France and America against Germany in which all the major cities of the world are destroyed by bombs. In 1932 a physicist named Leo Szilard read the book while he was in Berlin. The following year Szilard was a refugee in England, and a speech by Lord Rutherford pooh-poohing the possibility of liberating atomic energy on an industrial scale made him think again of Wells's predictions. In 1934 Szilard worked out the theoretical equations which could govern a self-sustaining chain reaction, and assigned his work to the British Admiralty so that it could be kept secret. When Szilard later learned that other scientists had achieved the fission of uranium, he realized its possibilities and participated in the early explorations of chain reactions at Columbia University in 1939. Later he got Albert Einstein to inform President Roosevelt of the possibility of making the ultimate weapon to crush the Axis powers. Soon the Manhattan Project was on, and the nations of the world were racing to acquire new weapons of mass destruction.

6

A New Attitude Toward the Future

H.G. Wells dreamed of a "science of the future." He thought that social forces could be analyzed and the future deduced from them. Individual human beings—even the greatest leaders—do not make the future, Wells maintained; they are merely the pawns of progress. As he put it:

> There are those who will say that the whole world is different by reason of Napoleon. But there are also those who will say the whole world of today would be very much as it is now if Napoleon had never been born. There are those who believe entirely in the forces behind the individual man, and for my own part I must confess myself a rather extreme cast of the latter kind. I must confess I believe that, if by some juggling with space and time Julius Caesar, Napoleon, Edward IV, William the Conqueror, Lord Rosebery and Robert Burns had all been changed at birth it would not have produced any serious dislocation of the course of destiny. I believe that these great men of ours are no more than images and symbols and instruments taken, as it were, haphazard by the incessant and consistent forces behind them; they are the pen nibs Fate has used for her writing, the diamonds upon the drill that pierces through the rock.

But are individual human beings really nothing more than helpless instruments of destiny? A science of the future might be Wells's dream, but such a notion was abhorrent to many people at the end of World War II. They distrusted science not only for its new horrors, but for threatening the dignity of the individual human being. This mood appeared most clearly, perhaps, in France.

France's experience during World War II was different from that of the other great powers. She spent four years as a slave state, divided into two parts, one occupied by Nazi troops, the other controlled by a puppet regime run by Frenchmen who chose to collaborate with the German conquerors. Under these circumstances, each Frenchman constantly faced a terrible choice: to collaborate or to refuse to collaborate. Many Frenchmen deliberately chose to risk their lives by joining the Resistance, but even those who did not join the Resistance knew that they might be questioned on what they knew about Resistance activities, and tortured or killed if they refused to reveal what they knew. Thus Frenchmen found themselves asking basic questions about themselves and their values. Unable to fight actively they began to think about the philosophical and moral questions involved in fighting—about human freedom and choice, the importance of the individual, the dilemmas of human existence and the nature of man's future.

One French writer, Jean Paul Sartre, had the gift to express the new mood and give it a name—*existentialism*. Few Frenchmen read his abstruse philosophical works, but his novels and plays dominated the French intellectual scene in the middle and late 1940s. After the liberation of Paris in 1944, the Cafe de Flore which he frequented became a shrine and tourist attraction which ranked with the Eiffel Tower. Sartre's existentialism became popular because it fitted with the wartime experiences of the French, and because Sartre and certain other writers expressed the philosophy in plays and novels that many people could appreciate.

Sartre himself explained the wartime mood of the French in these words:

> Never have we been so free as under the German occupation. We had lost all our rights, first of all, the right to speak. We were insulted to our faces every day, and we had to remain silent. We were deported in large groups as workers, as Jews, as political prisoners . . . . Because of all that, we were free. Since the Nazi venom inserted itself even into our thoughts, each free thought was a victory. Since the all-powerful police tried to force us into silence, each word became precious as a declaration of principle. Since we were hounded, each of our movements was like a skirmish with the enemy.

Thoughtful Frenchmen, like Sartre, lacking the support of institutions, developed a strong individualized sense of responsibility for the future of France, and experienced a radical freedom to choose that future through their own acts. "If I can hold out," a Frenchman could think, "France will rise again." "Everyone of her citizens," as Sartre explained, "knew that he owed himself to everyone and that he could only count on himself; each of them realized, in the most total abandonment, his historic role and responsibility."

For Sartre and other existentialists, each human being creates his own future and should take full responsibility for his creation. He must not try to excuse his actions by saying that he is doing what his employer, his church, his parents, or some other outside force says he should do. That would be a deception, because he is always free to refuse to do what they want him to do. There is no one and nothing that can authoritatively prescribe what an individual must do. "You are free," said Sartre in a 1946 lecture.

"Choose, that is to say, invent. No general system of ethics can tell you what to do." (The phrase "inventing the future" became popular among futurists after it was used years later by physicist Dennis Gabor in an article, later a book, but the concept was clearly expressed by Sartre and other existentialists.)

The concept of the future as something to be invented or created rather than something that unfolds relentlessly regardless of human will appears to have been an important departure from the customary western view of the future. In most western thought, the future grows out of the past and is largely controlled by it. The existentialists suggested a fundamentally different character of the future—and of the past. For the existentialists, the future is free, virgin, unwritten, undetermined, and exciting; the past is finished, dead, permanently closed, and uninteresting. The critics of the existentialists have suggested that they think only of the present moment, but many existentialists appear to emphasize the present only because that is when the decisions are made that will determine the future.

The intellectual currents in France after World War II contributed to the philosophical frame of reference in which futurism developed among French intellectuals. Even more important, perhaps, may have been France's tradition of attempting to transform society by using science and technology directed toward achieving an ideal vision. The reconstruction and economic development of France after the war led to a series of national plans, which required assumptions about what would happen in the years ahead. A few French planners became seriously interested in exploring what assumptions about the future might be justified.

A key figure in French futurism during the 1950s was Gaston Berger, a philosopher, businessman, and educator. Born in Senegal in 1896, Berger worked as a businessman in Marseilles but his wide-ranging artistic and intellectual interests took him in many directions. He became an excellent photographer, studied musical composition and foreign languages, received a master's certificate in physiology at the Faculty of Sciences in Marseilles, and started studying to become a doctor. But he later abandoned both business and medicine to become an assistant professor of philosophy at the Faculty of Letters in Aix. Eventually he became director general of higher education in the French Ministry of National Education.

Berger's experience in high university administration, combined with his imagination and his earlier experience in business, led him to create in Paris in 1957 a Centre International de Prospective [International Prospective Center]. The following year the Center published the first issue of a journal, *Prospective*, which contained articles looking at many different aspects of the future. For example, Louis Armand, head of France's nationalized railroad system, contributed an article on the future of transportation.

Berger used the term Prospective to denote, first and foremost, a particular attitude of mind toward the problems of the future. Prospective was to be the "mirror-image" of *retrospective*. In the view of Berger and his circle, Prospective was not the same as forecasting, which they held to be an extension into the future of trends observed in the past. He explained his views of Prospective in the first issue of the new journal:

> In what does the Prospective attitude consist?
> Its principal characteristic consists obviously in the intensity with which it concentrates our attention on the future. We may be tempted to believe that this is something quite ordinary. But in fact nothing is rarer. As Paul Valery wrote, "We walk forward with our backs to the future." . . . On the contrary, we must look it in the face . . . grasp its intrinsic nature, and hence apply to it other methods than those which are valid for the present or the past.
> This turning of our faces, which seems quite easy and natural, actually requires sustained efforts because it runs counter to our most ingrained habits. Doubtless we often think about the future but we dream about it rather than construct it. Dreaming is at the opposite pole from planning. Instead of starting us off along the path of action, it turns us away from it; it allows us to enjoy in our imagination the fruit of a labor we have not accomplished.

In a later article, Berger tried to correct certain misinterpretations of Prospective.

> Prospective is neither a doctrine nor a system. It is a reflection on the future which seeks to describe its most general structure with the aim of bringing out the elements of a method applicable to our accelerating world.
> Now this description reveals that the future is quite different from our common perception of it. It is not a particular 'region' of temporal continuity. It is not simply the series of moments which have not yet arrived. Time, taken as a whole, is not a kind of continuous and fluid substance which proceeds in a regular flow and along which events are strung out. For man, past and future are heterogeneous. They are not moments in the same series. They have no concrete meaning, no human meaning, except when we relate them to our action: The Past is what has been done; the future is what is to be done. . . . To turn toward the future, instead of looking at the past, is not simply to make a change of scene, it is to pass from "seeing" to "doing". . . . To take a Prospective action is to prepare for action.

Like Sartre, Berger was a former professor of philosophy, and his thinking suggests the marriage of existentialism and planning. Prospective might be viewed as a socialization of existentialism. The reality of choice and creating one's own future was not limited to the individual but also concerned the nation and all humanity.

Berger and his Prospective group had a significant impact on French intellectual and governmental life. They appear to have stimulated and articulated the future orientation that France's planners had been groping for. Though Berger was killed in an automobile accident in 1960, the crystallization in French thinking that he had set in motion continued and even accelerated.

Among those active in the Prospective group was Pierre Masse, formerly Executive Director of the nationalized Electricite de France and then Commissaire General au Plan [High Commissioner for the Plan]. In preparing for the Fifth National Plan, Masse decided to enlarge the forecasting process taking place under his direction and created in 1963 a Committee of 1985, whose function would be to take a broader view of the future of France, its economic goals and social problems. This broader view would provide a horizon for the planners engaged in more immediate and limited forecasting. Masse's initiative created a link between the Prospective group and a number of young technocrats in the various branches of the French Government.

By this time, the Prospective group had developed a distinctive approach to studying the future. For one thing, the group's ad hoc study groups were highly interdisciplinary; people from different fields had to work together (just as they later did in working parties created for the French Government's National Plans). Another characteristic was the search for what Masse called *faits porteurs d'avenir* or "future-bearing facts." The study groups did not limit themselves to logical analysis but also used imagination and forecasts to make this image as comprehensive as possible and to take full account of what was desirable for man as well as what could be accomplished. This image of the distant future provided a background for the formulation of short-term plans and decision-making.

In 1960, the year that Berger died, another Frenchman, Bertrand de Jouvenel, set to work on a project that was to elevate French futurism to the attention of scholars around the world. De Jouvenel's project, for which he received funds from the Ford Foundation, was named *Futuribles* and consisted of a series of papers by leading scholars on what might happen in the future, especially in the political sphere. De Jouvenel and his colleagues became interested in the methods of thinking about the future and held several international conferences on methodology. In 1964 de Jouvenel published his now classic work *The Art of Conjecture*, which provides an epistemology for the study of the future, a general discussion of the possibility and utility of studying the future, and advocates the creation of forums at which the possibilities of the future could be systematically developed and debated. *The Art of Conjecture* is also noteworthy for its insistence that the study of the future cannot be a science, but rather is an art, a viewpoint that is emphasized in the book's title.

De Jouvenel has become not only a key figure in the movement but a bridge between several aspects of futurism. His writings provide a meeting ground for the science-oriented futurists (mainly American) eager to improve their methodology and the more philosophical and humanistic futurists (mainly European). De Jouvenel and his late wife Helene founded the Association Internationale Futuribles, which now is headed by their son Hugues. The Association publishes a journal *Futuribles* and sponsors meetings not only in Paris but elsewhere in France. (For details, see the biography of de Jouvenel elsewhere in this volume.) The French Regional Planning Agency *[Delegation a l'Amenagement du Territoire et a l'Action Regionale]*, headed by Jerome Monod, has also been active in orienting France toward the future. Elsewhere in the French Government, there are many future-oriented civil servants whose imagination has been shaped by the Saintsimonian tradition as perpetuated and refined in the *grandes ecoles*, where for decades France's top civil servants have trained. French futurist Francois Hetman, author of *The Language of Forecasting*, says, "Saint Simon's vision of a society guided by scientists, technicians, managers, and social planners has had an everlasting appeal to the successive generations of technocrats."

The French influence on the international futurist movement has been pervasive—and most of it has come through de Jouvenel and his Futuribles project. De Jouvenel provided the vital connections and essential intellectual foundation that enabled the study of the future to become an important intellectual activity not only in France but in Italy, the United States, and elsewhere. Thanks to de Jouvenel and his compatriots, the future is now generally recognized as not belonging to the scientists alone but also to the artist, the philosopher, and perhaps most of all, to the individual human being who in the privacy and mystery of his own soul is determining what he will do and, therefore, what the future will be.

Developing a Science of Forecasting

While French futurists explored the philosophy of futurism, scholars in the United States were approaching the future in a very different way. The main impetus behind the study of the future in the United States following World War II was the demand for national security. A Cold War in which the major contenders are armed with rockets that could carry for thousands of miles the most destructive power ever known to man was a new experience for the American people. No longer was the U.S. protected from its enemies by thousands of miles of ocean, and no longer could the nation hope to have advance warning of an attack. U.S. leaders charged with maintaining the nation's defenses received billions of dollars to protect the American people from whatever dangers might come. To carry out that assignment, they became perforce ardent students of the future.

One of the defense planners, H.H. ("Hap") Arnold, Commanding General of the Army Air Force, made two extremely important contributions to the futurist movement—though he probably had no idea that he was doing so: (1) He ordered what was perhaps the first major forecast of future technological capabilities, and (2) he created the first "think factory."

General Arnold made his first contribution to futurism in 1944 when he asked Theodor von Karman to prepare a forecast of future technological capabilities that might be of interest to the military. Von Karman's report, *Toward New Horizons* (1947), began a tradition of technological forecasts which resulted in the permanent Army Long-Range Technological Forecast. Von Karman's report made it clear that technological capabilities could be forecasted. Since the Cold War gave the military an abundance of funds, the defense establishment began expanding its technological forecasting capabilities. The need for forecasting became increasingly apparent. In his treatise, *On Thermonuclear War*, Herman Kahn pointed out that since 1945 there has been a complete technological revolution every five years. Any realistic attempt to make military plans extending more than five years into the future had to take account of revolutionary changes in technology. The magnitude of military forecasting is suggested by the Air Force's Project Forecast, a 1963 effort, which involved representatives from about 40 U.S. Government organizations, faculty members from 26 universities, representatives from 70 major corporations, and personnel from 10 nonprofit organizations. The end product was a 14-volume report which attempted to blueprint the technological characteristics of forces which could most effectively support the Department of Defense in the post-1970 time period.

Arnold's second and perhaps even more important contribution to future studies was his institutionalization of the process of analyzing policy alternatives. Arnold got the Douglas Aircraft Company to establish in 1946 a Project RAND (an acronym for Research And Development) to study the "broad subject of inter-continental warfare other than surface." In 1948 Project RAND split off from Douglas and became the RAND Corporation with the financial backing of the Ford Foundation; the new corporation's announced purpose was to "further and promote scientific, educational, and charitable purposes, all for the public welfare and security of the United

States." RAND thus shifted from merely studying alternative weaponry systems to exploring the policies of the nation.

As the first "think factory," RAND was a novelty quite unlike most organizations at the time. The notion of a relatively free, independent organization that is encouraged to speculate upon a host of "way out" ideas was an idea whose time had come. RAND indirectly gave birth to a number of other organizations, such as the System Development Corporation and the Hudson Institute. The new think factories were oriented toward scientific methodologies, but, unlike academic centers, the think factories were invariably multidisciplinary, possessed strategic links to the non-scientific and technological communities, had a large degree of freedom in attacking their assigned problems, and were concerned with broad areas.

Two developments at RAND were especially important to the study of the future, and Olaf Helmer, a mathematician, played a major role in both of them. In 1959 Helmer and fellow RAND researcher Nicholas Rescher published a paper on "The Epistemology of the Inexact Sciences," which provided a philosophical base for forecasting. The paper argued that in fields that have not yet developed to the point of having scientific laws, the testimony of experts is permissible. The problem is how to use this testimony and, specifically, how to combine the testimony of a number of experts into a single useful statement. Single experts sometimes suffer biases; group meetings suffer from "follow the leader" tendencies and reluctance to abandon previously stated opinions.

To overcome these problems, Helmer and another RAND staffer, Norman Dalkey, had earlier developed what they called the Delphi technique. This new procedure consists of a series of steps for using experts to make a group forecast which, hopefully, will be more accurate than an ordinary poll. In the Delphi method, each expert is questioned privately through the use of questionnaires in a series of rounds. The experts cannot know what others are saying except when the Delphi leaders inform them. In September 1964, Helmer and Theodore J. Gordon, a Douglas engineer, used the Delphi process in a major study of possible forthcoming developments (widespread use of teaching machines, moon colonies, and computer translations from one language to another). The results of this study, which employed a number of leading scientists and other experts, were widely reprinted.

The Delphi technique was important not only because of its own usefulness, but because it suggested that rational methods of exploring the future could be developed. During the 1960s, a large number of Delphi studies were made, and the method itself was studied and improved; the Delphi technique was also combined with computers in what came to be known as the Delphi Conference, and this opened the way toward more generalized use of computers as a means of continuous communication among a group of people for extended periods. (The term "Delphi conference" now seems to have yielded to "computer conference.")

The publication of a long-range forecasting study by Helmer and Gordon led to an invitation to develop a future-oriented game for Kaiser Aluminum Corporation. Twenty thousand copies of this game, called *Future*, were distributed to Kaiser Aluminum's corporate friends. This game made use of the "cross-impact" concept, which now is being developed, in the form of cross-impact analysis, into one of the more promising new techniques of futures analysis.

Besides leading the development of the Delphi technique, Helmer was a key figure in assembling a group of people interested in establishing an institute that would specialize in futures research on domestic, civil, non-security issues. The organizing committee issued a *Prospectus for an Institute for the Future* dated May 25, 1966. The prospectus was a committee product, written by such men as historian Henry David, who had served as a RAND consultant as early as 1947-48 and was then head of the Office of Science Resources Planning at the National Science Foundation, and psychologist Marvin Adelson, Chief Scientist and Assistant to the President at the System Development Corporation.

The prospectus proposed the creation of an Institute for the Future whose purposes would be:

1. to explore systematically the possible futures for our nation and for the international community;
2. to ascertain which among these possible futures seem to be desirable, and why; and
3. to seek means by which the probability of their occurrence can be enhanced through appropriate purposeful action.

The prospectus said that ability to deal effectively with the future "becomes increasingly important as the pace of change accelerates," and added:

Today, because resources available to governments are immeasurably greater than ever before, and the courses of action taken by governmental and private agencies are interacting in more intimate and complex ways, we are becoming more concerned over the need to understand what is implied by the alternative courses open to us. The cost and limitations inherent in piecemeal responses and short-term orientation have in recent years become sufficiently apparent for industry and government agencies to accept the idea that policies and programs designed to shape future courses of development must be planned and worked out more systematically than heretofore.

The prospectus also noted that the idea for the Institute arose from "a change in attitude toward the future."

The fatalistic view that it is unforeseeable and inevitable is being abandoned. It is being recognized that there are a multitude of possible futures and that appropriate intervention can make a difference in their probabilities. This raises the exploration of the future, and the search for ways to influence its direction, to activities of great social responsibility.

The Advisory Council for the new institute included 32 persons, mainly people associated with universities and think tanks, but a few with connections to the U.S. Government. In addition to Olaf Helmer, the founding group included Paul Baran, a communications expert at RAND; Arnold Kramish, a physicist from RAND; Theodore Gordon, an engineer-director of space stations from Douglas Aircraft; and Frank Davidson, who became the Institute's first President.

Henry David was instrumental in obtaining some initial funding for the Institute. Further support came from the Senior Executives Council of the National Industrial Conference Board (now the Conference Board), following recommendations by Bruce Palmer, the Board's President, and Charles M. Darling III, its director of projects. The Board "midwifed" the creation of the new institute, providing contacts and other support. Additional funding came from the Arthur Vining Davis Foundation, RAND itself, and the Ford Foundation. The Connecticut Research Commission provided an initial contract assignment and Edwin D. Etherington, President of Wesleyan University, invited the Institute to locate in Middletown, Connecticut, and work closely with Wesleyan University. The Conference Board also helped the Institute to obtain members for its Board of Directors.

By the time the Institute opened its doors in Middletown, Connecticut, in 1968, a total of more than $1 million in direct and indirect initial support had been secured. Since then, the Institute has made a large number of studies and has established a reputation for careful analyses of future possibilities. Now located in Menlo Park, California, the Institute has not developed into the RAND-scale enterprise that Helmer hoped for, but it has earned wide respect for its work. By 1977 the Institute had successfully completed scores of major studies, covering a wide range of topics—housing, plastics, telephones, etc. The Institute, said its president, Roy Amara, "has perhaps succeeded in institutionalizing research on the future more than any other organization elsewhere."

The Institute for the Future made Mother RAND a grandmother when staff member Theodore J. Gordon and two colleagues left in 1971 to set up the Futures Group, a profit-making research organization in Glastonbury, Connecticut. An investment firm, the Dreyfus Corporation, purchased 30% of the shares of the Futures Group, in 1972. By the end of 1975, the Futures Group had about 40 employees performing policy-oriented studies for corporations and government agencies, primarily in the United States. These studies for the most part involved inquiries into the need for or consequences of actions, in view of evolving trends and expectations about developments which would make the future different from the past.

The Hudson Institute may also be cited as part of the RAND legacy. Hudson was founded by former RAND analyst Herman Kahn, who brought with him the scenario technique and the habit of thinking about the future. Kahn and the Hudson Institute did major research on the future-oriented aspects of military strategy (reported in such books as *On Escalation: Metaphors and Scenarios* and *Thinking About the Unthinkable);* later he turned to the broader issues of the future, and with a Hudson colleague, Anthony J. Wiener, published *The Year 2000: A Framework for Speculation on the Next 33 Years.*

The Year 2000, published in 1967, was a new milestone in futurist literature. This 431-page volume, replete with charts, graphs, and tables of figures, presented a general picture of the direction in which the world appeared to be heading. *The Year 2000* did not go uncriticized (partly because many reviewers had never forgiven Kahn and Hudson for their links to the U.S. military and thermonuclear war), but it demonstrated that the world of the future *could* be studied in a serious, meaningful way, with tools of scientific and scholarly research.

The national security concerns which led to the founding of the think tanks also encouraged the study of the future in several other respects. For one thing, a small number of intellectuals began to think about the possibilities of determining—and eliminating—the causes of international conflict. A "peace research" movement became noticeable in the early 1960s, and scholars interested in peace wrote papers and books about the future. Donald N. Michael, a social psychologist then with the Peace Research Institute in Washington, D.C., wrote a book called *The Next Generation: The Prospects Ahead for the Youth of Today and Tomorrow* (1963); his colleague, historian Arthur Waskow, worked on *Notes from 1999,* and economist Kenneth Boulding, then head of a Center for the Study of Conflict Resolution at the University of Michigan, explored the future of man in a book called *The Meaning of the 20th Century* (1964).

The Korean War, which began on June 25, 1950, resulted in shortages of raw materials and consequent fears that the United States might lack an adequate supply of raw materials in the future. Accordingly, President Truman created a Materials Policy Commission to survey the nation's raw material supply. *The President's Report on Raw Materials*, which became known as the Paley Report, appeared in five volumes in 1952. The Ford Foundation later provided funds so that the nation's raw materials could be studied on a continuing basis. The mechanism is a nonprofit, Washington-based research corporation known as Resources for the Future, Inc.

Concern about national security took a new turn in 1957 when the Soviet Union launched the first satellite. Sputnik I incited U.S. leaders to mount a huge effort to recover the lead in space that the Russians had seized. Billions of dollars soon poured into the space program. The National Aeronautics and Space Administration mushroomed into a gigantic agency. Thousands of scientists, engineers, and technicians joined the effort, lured by high salaries and a chance to work on an exciting historic program.

The space race led to a new need for serious technological forecasting, because the space administrators had to know what could be done in space and what capabilities would be available in the years ahead. The money pouring into the space program also funded a wide variety of research and development projects. Colleges and universities also benefited because the government's space program provided a major source of direct and indirect funding of their programs.

Like the Manhattan Project, the space program was a powerful though unintended force in stimulating the study of the future. Neither of the massive projects was designed as an exercise in futuristics, but both demonstrated in an extremely convincing way that it is possible to forecast what can be achieved through technology, and then actually to do what one has decided upon. Furthermore, both demonstrated that man can shape the future. Though the realization of humanity's power over its own destiny is not always comfortable, it brings with it a new sense of responsibility. The power of the atom, demonstrated so frightfully but so convincingly, was power at the disposal of man, and this power, though it caused dread, also suggested hope, a hope that has since been realized (though somewhat uneasily) through the use of atomic power for peaceful purposes.

The landing of men on the moon was a similar achievement of accurate forecasting and, even more powerfully, stimulated people to recognize their own capabilities—and responsibilities—for their own future. "If we can land a man on the moon," people said, "why can't we conquer cancer, insure world peace, eliminate poverty?" The Manhattan Project and the moon landings unequivocally demonstrated that man could imagine a future development, evaluate its practicality and desirability, and then set out to realize it. Perhaps never before in history has man's ability to shape the future—at least in some measure—been so convincingly demonstrated.

Other social forces that encouraged the study of the future to develop during the period following World War II included the rapid increase of government funding for science. The U.S. Congress set up the National Science Foundation (NSF) in 1950; within a few years, the government was handing out hundreds of millions of dollars to fund scientific projects of the most diverse variety. During the 1950s, pure science enjoyed tremendous support because it was viewed as an "endless frontier" for exploration that would return enormous benefits for mankind. Funds were ample in relation to the number of scientists available to use them. But during the 1960s the supply of scientists caught up with the supply of funds, and hard questions began to be asked about which scientists should get how much money. The subject of science policy began to get serious attention, but intelligent science policy making requires a serious effort to know what society's needs may be in the future, because investments in science have perhaps the longest and most diverse—as well as greatest—payoffs of any investments that can be made. To decide what scientific research to support, government policymakers need to know what society will need in five, 10, 20 or 50 years. Hence many NSF staff members became seriously concerned with trying to understand the future.

The unintended side effects of increasingly powerful technology caused mounting concern during the 1950s and 1960s. People became increasingly aware of air and water pollution, solid waste problems, chemical additives, and a wide range of technological impacts. Among the many results of these new concerns were the creation of the U.S. Environmental Protection Agency, and the requirement that government agencies prepare environmental impact statements for major projects. These developments led to a new interest in trying to assess the future impacts of technology and even to philosophical concerns about a "high quality" life.

By the end of the 1960s, it was clear that two important changes were occurring in people's outlook on the future. First, they were becoming convinced that it is *possible* to study the future. H. G. Wells and others had, of course, advanced such a proposition long before World War II, but neither Wells nor his followers provided very convincing answers for an almost inevitable and highly embarrassing question: *How* does one study the future? The development of such methods as the Delphi technique, however crude they might be, provided futurists with a plausible answer.

The second important change was recognition that the future world is plastic: Human beings are not moving toward a predetermined future world, but instead are active participants in the creation of the future world. The study of the future is, therefore, not just an idle amusement of people interested in contemplating their destiny, but rather an essential enterprise for anyone who wishes to behave intelligently.

The two changes in people's view of the future added up not just to a rationale for the study of the future, but to a mandate. And the mandate was sensed not by scholars alone, but by government officials, businessmen, educators, and others. As people recognized that the future needs to be studied if man is to create a better world, they rushed to create the future-oriented institutions necessary for the task.

Futurist Groups Form

Before the 1960s there were few futurist organizations of any significance. But in the 1960s a great many sprang up, both in the United States and many other countries. In addition to research institutes, a number of associations or clubs developed. In Italy, Aurelio Peccei, an economist and businessman, formed the Club of Rome, an international group of scientists, humanists, planners, and educators interested in looking at the problems of the world from a global standpoint. Elsewhere in Europe, a group known as *Mankind 2000* took shape under the inspiration of Berlin-born author Robert Jungk. And in Washington, D.C., a group of private citizens formed the World Future Society, an association which grew rapidly from a few score members in 1966 to some 20,000 a decade later. Shortly after its founding, the Society began regular publication of a newsletter, *The Futurist*, which grew into a magazine by 1969. Elsewhere, other publications started up, including *Analyse & Prevision* (France), *Analysen und Prognosen* (Berlin), *Futuriblerne* (Denmark), *Futures* (London), *Futuribili* (Italy) and *Futurum* (Germany).

The people who have joined the new future-oriented organizations and subscribe to futurist publications tend to be well-educated people in a wide variety of occupations. University professors are well represented, especially sociologists and political scientists. In business concerns, interest in the future seems keenest among corporate planners, market researchers, systems analysts, and product developers. In government, strong interest appears among science policymakers, technology forecasters in the military establishment, demographers, and economists who have become increasingly aware that economics is being profoundly influenced by noneconomic forces.

The futurists tend to be rational, scientific, and pragmatic in their outlook. They are not idle dreamers; in fact, their interest in the future seems to arise out of a desire to be really effective. They want genuine, long-term solutions, not temporary palliatives. They are also sensitive to emerging problems and want timely action taken before a problem grows into a crisis.

7

Basic Principles of Futurism

Futurism implies certain assumptions about the universe and man's role in it. By identifying these underlying assumptions which futurists make, we can begin to understand why futurism offers a perspective which is fundamentally different from the traditional view of western culture, but which may be more in keeping with the tasks of humanity in the late 20th century.

We can start exploring the fundamentals of futurism by considering a simple question: Can the future be predicted? Scholars may respond yes, no, or maybe—depending on their mood or frame of reference—because the question is ambiguous. Some people use the word "predict" to indicate an absolutely precise, infallible knowledge about the future. Since people are fallible and make incorrect statements about the future (just as they make incorrect statements about the past), it is correct to say that no one can predict the future. But the word *predict* is also used in the sense of making a forecast of what will happen, that is, a statement about what one thinks will happen, even though one concedes that one may be wrong; in this latter sense, many future events can be predicted. A person crossing a street predicts that the passing automobiles will stop when the traffic light changes from green to red; in some instances, he may be wrong, but in most instances he is quite correct in his prediction. Thus it is also perfectly correct to say that the future *can* be predicted.

A second ambiguity is the failure of the question to state *whose* future is to be predicted. Astronomers can predict the precise time of an eclipse years ahead of the event. Meteorologists can forecast weather conditions with considerable (though hardly infallible) success.

On the other hand, predictions for many political, economic and social aspects of human life are woefully prone to error. Economists, political scientists, and sociologists have not yet fathomed the intricate workings of society, and therefore often make forecasts that turn out to be wrong. Yet, even their forecasts may be better than no forecasts at all. The social scientists give us *some* guidance about what to expect, even though they cannot offer the highly precise and accurate statements concerning specific events that we now expect from astronomers.

Some people argue it is possible to have knowledge of the past, but never of the future. The statement is a half truth that is generally used to support the view that there is no point in thinking about the future. The truth in the statement is that our knowledge of the world and ourselves is *derived* from our *experience*, that is, the perceptions and feelings that we have had in the past. But that does not prevent us from making accurate statements about what will happen in the future, and thus, in a sense, we "know" what will happen in the future just as we "know" what happened in the past. We may make mistakes in our forecasts just as we make mistakes in our recollections, but both forecasts and recollections are part of our "knowledge." I know that the sun will rise tomorrow even more certainly than I know the date of my birth. My forecast that the sun will rise tomorrow is based on my experience, but it is not just a memory from the past; it is an image of the future—that is, an idea of what will happen—that I have constructed on the basis of my experience.

Another point is worth noting: Though all our knowledge is derived from our experience, most of our knowledge about the past does not come from our own experience at all, but rather from the statements of others, which may or may not be accurate. The future is mysterious to us, but so is the past. Most of us could probably write a more accurate description of what the world will be like in 1995 than we could of what the world was like in 995; we would make our forecast for 1995 simply by describing the world in which we exist today—with perhaps a few modifications to allow for current trends and likely developments. Describing the world of 995 with equal accuracy would require a knowledge of history that most of us do not possess.

Forecasting the future is an action that is fundamental to human beings. Throughout our lives, we are constantly making forecasts, e.g., "If I don't get this job done, my boss will be angry," or "My husband will be on the 6 p.m. train from Philadelphia." Forecasting is not some new and strange activity; it is as natural and necessary as breathing. Futurists have not developed an arcane knowledge and practice; they are simply trying to make a very ordinary activity more rational and hence more successful. By studying the process by which forecasts are made, we can make better forecasts— and, even more important, we can develop better ideas about what can be done—and so improve the world in which we live.

Many people believe that knowledge consists of "facts" and there are no "facts" about the future. This is true—in a sense. The word *fact* derives from the Latin word meaning something that has been done, and clearly something that has been done is not something that has yet to be done. However, the word *fact* in its modern meaning refers to an accurate statement about reality. In this sense, the statement, "The sun will rise tomorrow," is just as much a "fact" as the statement, "The sun rose yesterday." We have many "facts" about the future that really are more accurate than the "facts" we have about the past. For instance, it is more certain that the Atlantic Ocean will still exist in 1992 than that Christopher Columbus discovered America five centuries earlier.

People who say, "You can't predict the future," often mean simply that they don't want to think about the future, or that unexpected events often occur. As weather forecasters know well, people relish catching a forecaster in error. The rain that spoiled the picnic after the weather forecaster spoke of sunny skies is long remembered; little notice is paid when a weather forecast proves accurate.

The Non-Existence of "the Future"

So far we have discussed "the future" as if it really existed. But in actual fact, it does not, and we must recognize the non-existence of the future if we are to clarify our thinking about it.

"The future" refers to a period of time that has not yet arrived, hence the future, by definition, does not exist. Furthermore, the future will not exist even in the future, because the future exists only when it becomes the present, at which point it automatically ceases to be the future. As one popular saying expresses it, "Today is the tomorrow you worried about yesterday."

The paradoxical character of the future arises from the fact that the future has no reality as an independent object. When we speak of "the future" we really mean the future of *something*, that is, some object or situation as it will be at a latter point in time. Ordinarily, "the future" is simply a shorthand way of referring to human civilization (or some portion of it) at a later point in time. Recognizing the non-existence of "the future" is, paradoxically, an essential preliminary to understanding why it is so important!

Since neither "the future" nor "the world of the future" exists, they cannot be studied. We can only study *ideas* about what the world may be like in the future. (We can also study the world as it exists in the present, because the world of the future will be created out of today's world.) Thus when we "study the future" what we are really doing is studying *ideas* about the world as it will be in the future, ideas developed largely from our perceptions of what the world was like in the past and how we believe it is changing.

The present is the constantly moving boundary between what has happened and what will happen. If the present were only this, we might conclude that it did not truly exist, any more than the future and past. But this paradox appears to arise from the limitations of language. For our purposes, the "present" is not just the present *moment*, but the brief period of time on both sides of the present moment in which we "live"; that is, the realm of our experiencing of ourselves and the world, a realm of time that includes both the immediate past and the immediate future.

The present, in this sense, is the period of time in which we experience and think, when the perceptions and memories of the past are reviewed, decisions are made, and muscles activated to carry them out. In this present, the immediate past and the immediate future are thoroughly intermingled. Perceptions of the immediate situation in which we find ourselves make connection with memories of past situations, with our own desires, and with our images of what we want; at the same time, perceptions of the actions we are taking are also reaching our brains and being evaluated. Thus, the present may be defined as the period of time during which decisions are made and actions are taken.

The Nature of the Future World

The future world does not exist, and yet it is the object of our actions. The purpose of almost everything we do is to improve the situation in which we will find ourselves in the future. Even when we think about the past, we are seeking to decide what we shall believe about it in the future. The future is the domain of goals and dreams, just as the past is the domain of memories. Since the world of the future does not yet exist, it may still be shaped according to our desires, unlike yesterday's world which is gone forever. We can, if we wish, do things today to change the world that we will experience tomorrow.

The plasticity of the future—the fact that we can shape the situations that we will experience at a later point in time—makes the future simultaneously more difficult to predict and more important to study. If the world of the future were totally predictable, it would have to be unchangeable, and the study of the future would serve no purpose except perhaps to satisfy our curiosity.

Some Postulates of Futurism

In the broadest sense, anyone who is seriously interested in the various possible developments that might occur in the future could be called a futurist. Generally, however, the term is limited to those who are interested in the longer-term future of human civilization and who use non-mystical means to identify and study possible future occurrences.

The modern futurist movement, which began developing rapidly during the 1960s, appears to be gradually forming a coherent philosophy or world-view. The crystallization of the philosophy is far from complete but it is now possible to speak—very tentatively—of certain basic principles that typify the thinking of today's futurists.

Among the emerging futurist principles are: (1) the unity or interconnectedness of reality, (2) the crucial importance of time, and (3) the importance of ideas, especially ideas about the future. Let us take a brief look at each of these principles because they appear basic to the futurist perspective:

The Unity of the Universe. Fundamental to almost all futurist thinking is the perception that the universe is all one piece, rather than an aggregation of independent, unconnected units. An insistence on the interconnectedness of everything in the world, including man, and on the impossibility of fully comprehending any single entity without considering its place within the whole, are fundamental precepts of today's futurism. This holistic thinking contrasts with the traditional view that man exists in the universe but is not really a part of it. In the holistic perspective of the futurist, man is as much a part of nature as anything else in the universe: Individual human beings owe their existence to the operations of the universe and cannot possibly be separated from it.

The unity of the universe is a unity of time as well as space, that is, the world of the future is being created out of the world of the present, and for this reason we can know much about the future world by looking carefully at what has been happening in the world during the recent past. The future is built largely with the materials of the present.

The Crucial Importance of Time. Most people are almost totally preoccupied with their immediate concerns. Thinking about what might happen five or 10 years from now seems to them merely idle speculation. But the fact is that the problems of today did not appear suddenly out of thin air; they have been building up, often for many years, and might have been dealt with fairly easily if they had been tackled earlier. The crisis that we face today is generally the minor problem that we neglected yesterday.

In addition to discounting the future, most people tend not to recognize *gradual* change. For example, a 2% increase per year in air pollution might attract little notice, yet it means that air pollution will double in 34 years! The doubling of the population of a city over the course of a generation means a drastic transformation of the life of that city for better or worse. Futurists generally want to identify such gradual changes, so that they can be monitored and timely action taken to avoid painful crises.

When a problem reaches the crisis stage—that is, when the pain of the situation has become unbearable—it generally gets attention. But at that point it can be solved only with fantastic expenditures of time and money, and in many cases it simply cannot be solved at all. The damage has been done, and people just have to live with it. On the other hand, a small change that is wisely introduced today can result in major improvements in the years ahead. Such a change may be likened to a seed that is planted in good soil and grows, almost by itself, into a great tree. Thus, time is a crucial element that can make things easy to accomplish—or impossible.

In thinking about the future, futurists tend to focus on the period from five to 50 years ahead. The reason for focusing on this period is that the immediate or near-term future (less than five years) constitutes what might be viewed as the domain of ordinary human concerns (although even five years from now would be regarded by many non-futurists as a very distant point in time!). In addition, one cannot do much to change the world that we will experience in the near-term future; there simply isn't enough time to decide upon and put into effect many basic changes. The period beyond 50 years also tends to be neglected because so much change will occur in the next half century that it is difficult to make any statements about it that might be useful for decision-making today. We cannot do much useful planning for the period 50 years from now because so many unpredictable events and unknown factors will exert their influence that anything we tried to do would likely be erased in the intervening years.

Just as the Eskimos have developed names for different types of snow and the Arabs for the parts of a camel, futurists are beginning to develop names for various parts of the future. Earl Joseph, Editor of *Future Trends*, published by the Minnesota Futurists, has identified five basic periods of the future: (1) Now: the immediate future (up to one year from now), (2) the near-term future (one to five years from now), (3) the middle-range future (five to 20 years from now), (4) the long-range future (20 to 50 years from now), (5) the far future (50 or more years hence).

Joseph makes two points that are important in futurist thinking:

1. *The world that we will experience in five to 20 years is being shaped by decisions made now.* Today's decisions will not change very much the world that we experience during the next five years, but they may dramatically change the world that we experience five to 20 years from now! This curious fact results from the time lag between the making of a decision and its final impact. People new to government have often been frustrated by their inability to get

their decisions implemented; U.S. President Harry S. Truman is said to have complained that he gave orders and absolutely nothing would happen! Yet the bureaucracy which responds so sluggishly to new commands may be changing pervasively in response to commands issued many months or years earlier but only now becoming fully implemented. In the U.S. Government, Republican decision-makers may preside somewhat helplessly over a bureaucracy steadily implementing policies and programs instituted by the previous Democratic administration! Later when the bureaucracy is finally implementing Republican policies, a Democratic administration may be again in power—and equally frustrated at its inability to get decisions implemented.

2. *Almost anything can be done in 20 years!* The statement is startling—until one recalls that, once the decisions were made, only four years were needed to unleash the awesome power of the atom and only eight years to put a man on the moon!

These two points underlie the futurists' insistence on making the more distant future an integral part of current decision-making. The whole point of studying future possibilities, futurists emphasize, is to improve the quality of decisions that are being made *right now.* Today's decisions are shaping tomorrow's world, yet only too often we make decisions with little concern about their impact on the longer-term future.

The Importance of Ideas. Since the future does not exist, it must be invented, that is to say, ideas about what may happen in the future must be generated and studied. Such ideas or *futuribles* are critically important because our thinking is shaped both by our concepts of what happened in the past and our images of what we may see in the future.

Ideas are the tools of thought. Without them, no thought is possible. Ideas may be divided into two classes: concepts and theories. A concept is a kind of mental map or picture of something; a theory (in this sense) is an interlinkage of two or more concepts to indicate how they relate to each other. For example, one may have a concept of a house, a dog, or an educational system, and a theory that mosquitoes (concept) lead to malaria (concept). A theory may be compressed into a concept by striking out the space that separates two concepts and creating a new concept that incorporates them both. For example, the concept of "boy" may be given the attribution of "bad," so that the new concept of "bad boy" emerges.

Concepts and theories are our mental models of how the world operates. They enable us to recall what happened in the past and to imagine what may happen in the future. Thinking consists of manipulating our concepts and theories in various ways. When we daydream, we let concepts emerge into consciousness without attempting to focus them on a particular problem. When we want to solve a problem, we seek to summon to consciousness only those concepts and theories that relate to the problem. In thinking, we play with our concepts, moving them about in various ways. We are pleased when we discover a concept or theory that seems to correspond well with reality. A theory that promises to "work" rewards us, because we enjoy the feeling of power that it gives us; it is like having a new power tool or a new house. Even before we have done anything with the fine new concept or theory, we feel a sense of competence.

As we go through life, we constantly try to develop our tool chest of ideas. As we acquire new and more powerful tools, that is, as we develop knowledge and wisdom, we feel enriched and become more secure within ourselves. We feel better able to meet the challenges of the future.

The power of ideas is not always clearly recognized, because they are invisible and hard to evaluate, but they represent an extremely valuable resource and, from an economic standpoint, are often more important than raw materials, industrial plants, and manpower when it comes to earning money.

Businessmen tend to emphasize material rather than intellectual capital because material wealth can be easily calculated, and readily exchanged. Yet intellectual capital is generally more important. After World War II, Germany's material capital was in ruins, but within a few years the German people were prospering as never before, because the war had not destroyed their intellectual capital, that is, the ideas in their heads, which were their greatest resource. On the other hand, if today's Germans were, by some miracle, replaced by an equal number of illiterate tribesmen, the German economy would immediately collapse. Within a few months, the steel mills and pharmaceutical firms would be infested with rats and weeds.

Ideas have made civilization possible and keep it advancing. For example, the division of labor is one simple idea that has proved extraordinarily powerful through history. If we want to do a job, this idea offers a success formula: Divide the job into separate tasks and assign these tasks to specific individuals. In this way, each person can become proficient in his part of the work and everybody benefits. Without the division of labor, or specialization, civilization would be almost inconceivable.

Another idea, Eli Whitney's notion of identical parts for a machine, provided the basis for the standardization of equipment and for assembly-line production methods. Other ideas, such as Copernicus' theory that the earth moves around the sun, rather than vice versa, displaced earlier concepts, which had proved unsatisfactory, and by so doing opened the way to new discoveries. Darwin's theory of evolution by means of natural selection was a similar powerhouse of an idea that could immediately be applied to solving all sorts of biological riddles. New ideas enable us to build more accurate and complete maps of reality. Useful ideas constitute an intellectual capital that we have available when needed. Education may be viewed as the mass reproduction and distribution of ideas that have proven their worth. The ideas are stored up in the brains of people so that they are available for later use.

If our ideas are powerful, we can dramatically change the world to make it a happier place. But if our ideas are weak, then we are extremely limited in what we can do. The power of ideas is itself a powerful idea. In recent years, government and business leaders in the advanced countries have come to realize that the major constraints on human achievement are not physical but conceptual, that is, the limitations are in our ideas rather than in the material resources at our disposal.

In social systems, more may depend on what people think will happen than on the "realities." A builder once explained how important it was for him to get people to think that a building was actually going to be built: If people believed that he was really going to build the building, then he would get the money from the bank and credit from suppliers and the building would indeed be built. The image of the future that people had in their heads played a crucial role in actually determining the future.

People often "cannot" do things because of a lack of ideas rather than a lack of muscle power, tools, or money. Armed with the right ideas about what to do, the "impossible" may quickly become possible. To get the right ideas, we can invest in the research required to develop them. In short, if we really want to do something that seems very difficult or "impossible," we invest time and effort in the development of ideas directed at achieving our goal. History is full of instances where an "impossibility" was simply a case where people did not see how something could be done. In recent years, governments have shown that the allocation of funds for research and development is an effective means of removing the obstacles to achieving their goals.

Firmly convinced that ideas can move mountains, futurists are extremely interested in the systematic development of ideas. Better ideas will make it possible to improve the human condition. With the right ideas in their heads, the people of the poorest underdeveloped nation in the world could probably become the richest in less than a single generation. With the right ideas, the people of the world might soon throw war, poverty, famine, and disease into the ashcan of history.

Ideas about the future world—sometimes referred to as "images of the future"—may be especially important. People think that their actions are based on past events and present realities, but their images of the future may play an even more critical role. Images of the future are the blueprints that we use in constructing our lives, and the blueprints may be more important than the materials we work with (our bodies, families, financial resources, etc.) in determining our success and happiness.

Just as a building can be built if people believe it will be, a desirable world might be created if it can be imaged properly, that is, if people can develop a consensus about what a desirable world would be like and how it might be achieved. To develop such a consensus, futurists believe, ideas about the future world should be systematically generated and studied, and that implies the development of the study of the future as a major human activity.

8

Methods for Studying the Future

Historians are fond of saying that the study of the past can help us to understand the future. Futurists agree, and point out that all our ideas about the future necessarily come from the past, not the future itself, for the very simple reason that the future, by definition, has never existed. What has happened in the past is our only source of guidance to what may happen in the future.

Futuristics might even be defined as "applied history." It picks up where history leaves off. Futurists are not content with just understanding what has happened in the past; they want to *use* their knowledge to develop an understanding of future possibilities. Futurists emphasize that the future, not the past, is the focus of human action, and that the value of the past is that it can be used to illuminate the future.

But how can the past be used to study the future? One way is to assume that conditions that have existed in the past will continue into the future. This is the Principle of Continuity. If we follow the Principle of Continuity, we anticipate that the future will be like the present: The situation that we observe today will remain the same or it will continue to change in the way it is now observed to be changing. The Principle of Continuity allows us to believe that the Indian Ocean will be in its customary place in the year 2025 and that the world's population in the year 2025 will be far higher than it is now.

The second principle, which may be called the Principle of Analogy, is based on our observation that certain patterns of events recur from time to time. If we observe an event that we believe is like a certain preceding event, we may forecast that the new event will be followed by certain other events similar to those that occurred after the similar, previously observed event. When the mercury in a barometer falls, we forecast that a storm may be coming. There are also "leading indicators" in the business cycle. The Principle of Analogy can also be applied in politics: for example, a new situation may be described as a "Munich," thereby suggesting that it may be followed by disastrous consequences similar to the appeasement of Hitler at the fateful meeting in 1938.

We all use continuity and analogy in our everyday forecasting. When we walk about a city we assume that we will see certain sights that we have seen in the past (continuity), and we also assume that if the traffic light turns red, the traffic will come to a halt, even though we may never have seen this particular traffic light or these particular vehicles approaching this particular intersection. In this instance, the analogy is so familiar to us that it almost seems like a type of continuity, and shows how analogy blends into continuity.

Knowledge of the past does not automatically become knowledge of the future. Knowledge of the future must be created by using data obtained in the past as raw material for fashioning ideas about the future. In fashioning such ideas, we use a number of mental tools as well as our experience with using those tools. The tools are concepts and theories that "work" for us. In our thought processes we also use our own desires, because a primary purpose of our thoughts is to decide what would really please us, so that we can take action to achieve it.

Our desires play a major role in shaping the ideas that we have about the future. We feel thirsty and we develop the idea of getting a glass of water. We feel restless and develop the idea of taking a walk. Thinking about ideas that please us is often downgraded as useless "daydreaming," but daydreams can help us discover what it is that we want and thus they may play an important role in helping us to make good decisions. By exploring pleasant (and unpleasant) thoughts we may develop a concept of the goals we want to achieve. A daydream can become an anchor that we can throw out into the future and use to pull our thoughts forward. In this way, our present *desires* give to our thinking a character that it would not have if we used in our thinking only the memories of what has happened in the past. Stored in the ten billion nerve cells of our brains is an unbelievable quantity of information about what happened in the past, but when we use this information to create ideas about the future we must be incredibly selective, because only a tiny portion can be used at any one moment in our conscious thinking. And one of the principal forces in selecting the memories to think about is our *present* motivation.

Our desires are not the only force affecting our choice of the memories that fill our thoughts. We also are exposed to an incredible barrage of sensory data from our present environment. These external stimuli have an immediacy and urgency that is generally lacking in the data stored in our brains. Sensory data also help shape the ideas that we have about the future. For example, if we happen to overhear someone say something interesting we may quickly decide to say something in response.

When we try to think seriously about what might happen in the future, we face a certain dilemma. Everything that we know is derived from the past. If we wish to think about what might please us in the future, we find that the only happy situations we can readily imagine are variations on those that we experienced in the past or that we have heard about someone else experiencing. It is very difficult to do much more than try various combinations of images stored in our memory; we cannot easily leap outside our memories and seize something truly new. There *is* one way, however, to develop ideas that are not based simply on memories and logical connections: We can exploit the chance connection of thoughts that ordinarily are kept separate. Two memories that normally reside in separate compartments in our minds can—through the operation of chance—come together and form a new idea.

The entry of chance into the process of human thinking may be likened to the effect of cosmic rays on human genes. As in the case of the cosmic rays, the results are generally poor, but occasionally they are extremely fruitful. Chance allows us to develop concepts that are beyond the power of memory, logic, and desire. The importance of chance events may seem strange, yet human beings owe their very existence to the operations of chance. We are the result of billions of years during which chance combinations of atoms and molecules and genes were seized upon and utilized.

Chance is an essential element in creativity. In trying to develop a new idea that might be used in writing a poem, developing a scientific theory, or imagining a new business, a person needs to do two things: (1) provide his mind with the needed structure, that is, familiarize himself with the problem and information that *might* be used in fashioning useful solutions and (2) introduce into his thinking an element of chance. Normally, this element of chance is provided by the events of everyday life. Unrelated events push the conscious mind in new directions so that a new connection is made and a new idea is born. The new idea is tested out mentally; if it seems to work well, the person becomes exalted: he has just had "a good idea."

Creativity allows us to generate ideas about what *might* be in the future—things that otherwise would be unimaginable. With creativity, we can fashion *possible* future worlds that have never existed, but that we might choose to build.

There are a number of simple techniques to enhance creativity through the element of chance. As we will see in a later chapter, Isaac Asimov, the prolific author, opens books at random when he is trying to get a new idea. An inventor in Canada has produced a device that he calls a *Think Tank*, consisting of a container filled with hundreds of words printed on small strips of plastic. A person seeking a new idea turns a knob which stirs the mixture and brings four or five words into a position where they can be read through a small window. A user of the Think Tank then tries to apply the randomly-presented words to his problem; hopefully, one of them will push his mind toward a creative solution.

Creativity cannot give us *knowledge* about the future, but it can help us to discover new concepts about things that *might* be possible. In effect, creativity helps us to use the past in new ways to discover the possibilities of the future.

Few people think of themselves as forecasters, yet all of us are constantly making forecasts. If we did not do so, our lives would be impossible. If we want to talk to someone, we dial a certain sequence of numbers, because we believe that if we do so we may soon be able to talk to him. In other words, we forecast that we have a reasonable chance of accomplishing our purpose by following a certain series of actions.

Much of our everyday forecasting is so routine that we do not even recognize that it involves a constant series of exercises in futuristics, that is, explorations of the future aimed at helping us to decide what to do. But when we move beyond our everyday situations into the more distant future, we become less sure of ourselves and more self-conscious about our "futurizing."

Forecasting may be viewed as the purest form of futuristics, but there are other activities that are closely related and often intertwined with forecasting. One such activity is goal-setting—deciding which possibilities we *want* to realize rather than those that are likely to occur. Another related activity is planning—setting forth the steps needed to reach our goals. Futuristics logically precedes goal-setting, that is, we identify *possible* goals before deciding which to try to realize. Planning logically follows goal-setting: After a goal is determined, we set forth a cost-effective series of steps to realize it. In actual practice, however, futuristics, goal-setting, and planning tend to become highly intermingled, and many of the same tools are used in all three. Among the tools are mechanical devices like computers as well as procedures like Delphi polls. Confusing the situation further is the fact that one class of forecasting techniques—the so-called "normative methods"—use goals as a basis for forecasts, thus reversing the "normal" sequence of moving from futuristics to goal-setting to planning.

Blunders of Forecasting

Down through the ages, the exploration of future possibilities and the making of the decisions that shape the future have been carried out in a casual, intuitive way. If there were a question of unusual importance, people might consult relatives, friends, and various authorities in the hope of understanding a little more about what might happen in the future or what action might best help them to achieve their goals. But thinking about the future has rarely moved much beyond this very primitive level. Furthermore, in the past even more perhaps than today, thinking about the future generally focused on the very near-term future and on immediate, practical considerations.

There have, however, been historical instances when a question or proposal of such magnitude occurred that the question was referred to that venerable instrument of policy-making known as a committee. For example, in 1486 a committee was organized at the command of King Ferdinand and Queen Isabella to study Columbus's plan to sail west to the Indies. After four years of work, the committee, headed by Fray Hernando de Talavera, reported that a voyage such as Columbus contemplated was impossible. Among the reasons offered by the committee: (1) The Western Ocean is infinite and perhaps unnavigable. (2) If he reached the Antipodes (the land on the other side of the globe from Europe) he could not get back. (3) There are no Antipodes because the greater part of the globe is covered with water, and because Saint Augustine says so.

Such blunders of forecasting make amusing reading today. For example, modern armies would still be fighting with bows and arrows if Colonel Sir John Smyth had had his way. In 1591 Smyth advised the British Privy Council: "The bow is a simple weapon, firearms are very complicated things which get out of order in many ways . . . a very heavy weapon and tires out soldiers on the march. Whereas also a bowman can let off six aimed shots a minute, a musketeer can discharge but one in two minutes."

In 1835 Thomas Tredgold, a British railroad designer, declared that "Any general system of conveying passengers—at a velocity exceeding 10 miles an hour, or thereabouts—is extremely improbable." Two years later, in 1837, the Surveyor of the British Navy, Sir William Symonds, declared the screw propeller was useless for driving steamboats. "Even if the propeller had the power of propelling a vessel," Sir William argued, "it would be found altogether useless in practice, because—the power being applied in the stern—it would be absolutely impossible to make the vessel steer."

A week before the Wright brothers' successful flight at Kitty Hawk, North Carolina, the *New York Times* ridiculed the notion that man might fly. Referring to a rival flying machine experimenter, the *Times* said: "We hope that Professor Langley will not put his substantial greatness as a scientist in further peril by continuing to waste his time and the money involved in further airship experiments. Life is short, and he is capable of services to humanity incomparably greater than can be expected to result from trying to fly. . . . For students and investigators of the Langley type there are more useful employments."

In 1945 Vannevar Bush, then President of the Carnegie Institution of Washington, offered his advice to President Truman on the atomic bomb. "The bomb will never go off," Bush declared, "and I speak as an expert on explosives."

Until the 20th century, little systematic effort appears to have been devoted to improving the methods whereby people think about the future. Exploring the future was almost always done with ordinary "common sense" plus consultation with experts; most exploration of the future is still done that way, but more sophisticated techniques are also appearing. Many of these new methods are often described as "forecasting methods," but most can also be used in goal-setting, decision-making, and planning. All these other activities normally appear in any serious exploration of the future, because we do not explore the future just as an idle pastime: we do so because we want to shape it.

Let us now look at a few of these methods.

Trend Extrapolation: A Method Everyone Uses

The simplest assumption about the future that we can make is that the future will be exactly like the past: things will remain as they are. The next simplest assumption is that things will change in the same ways they have changed in the past, that is, a change that has been observed in the past will continue into the future. If the population of a city is known to be increasing at the rate of 2% a year, we assume that it will continue to do so in the future, and we can use simple arithmetic to calculate what the population will be in five years. In other words, we can generate a forecast by observing a change through time in the character of something and projecting (extrapolating) that change into the future. In making a forecast, we naturally disregard short-term changes or *fluctuations*, such as the swelling of a city's population each morning as people come to work. What is important is the longer-term change, that is, the *trend*.

Trend extrapolation is one of the most commonly used ways to generate a forecast. City planners, economists, demographers, and many other specialists constantly extrapolate trends—consciously or unconsciously—when they think about the future. So, too, do ordinary people. Assuming that the future will be like the past or that past changes will continue in the same direction and rate is a perfectly sensible way to begin trying to understand the future. It should not, however, be the end of our endeavors, because trend extrapolation can be very misleading. For example, we might estimate that a child aged four has grown at the rate of five inches a year, and then calculate that this rate of growth means he will be more than 13 feet tall at the age of 34! We would not accept this forecast, because we know that human beings—of which the child is an example—never grow that tall. Long before he reaches the age of 34, we forecast, his rate of growth will slow and eventually halt at a height that will probably be somewhere between five feet and six and a half feet. In making this forecast, we have, of course, shifted from the Principle of Continuity to the Principle of Analogy.

This slowing down of growth is frequently encountered among living things: an organism or a colony of bacteria will grow rapidly for a time and then its growth will slow and eventually stop. If growth did not stop, the organism or bacteria would eventually become bigger than the world itself—and extrapolating still further, bigger than the solar system and universe. But growth does not continue indefinitely; eventually it slows because of limits either in the environment or in the organism itself.

Growth curves may be observed in social as well as biological phenomena. For example, during the 1950s and 1960s scientific research grew very rapidly in the United States. In fact, if the percentage of the U.S. population trained as scientists were to increase in the years ahead as fast as it did during the 1950s and 1960s, there would soon be more scientists than people! Of course, this theoretical limit to the production of scientists will never be reached. Long before then, the production of scientists will be curbed by such factors as the reluctance of taxpayers to pay the ever-increasing costs of scientific research and the exhaustion of the pool of people who might become scientists.

Similarly, a new technology may exhibit a growth curve strikingly similar to those found in biology. When railroads were first developed in the early 19th century, they found many customers eager for rapid, inexpensive transportation. Railroads developed rapidly during the 19th century, but in the 20th their growth slowed, because they began to saturate their market and because new competition appeared in the form of automobiles, trucks, and airplanes.

When growth is plotted on a graph, the resulting curve generally looks like an elongated S, which means that growth is slow at first, then becomes rapid, then slows again. Why? In the case of a biological system, growth normally begins with only a small base—a single fertilized egg or a plant spore. Even if the cell grows and divides quickly, the doubling in the number of cells only results in one additional cell. The second doubling adds only two more cells, and the third doubling only four. Since time is required for a cell to absorb nutrients from its environment and to divide, the total growth is small in absolute terms (though it may be very large percentage-wise). As the number of cells increases, so does the rate at which new cells are added, hence growth is very rapid. Eventually, however, the growth encounters limitations, such as the exhaustion of the nutrients in the environment. Animal populations often increase rapidly until the animals have eaten up most of the food in their environment; at that point, the animals starve and the population shrinks. Somewhat similarly, a new technology or business organization generally starts with a small base—little capital and few customers—but grows more rapidly as banks and customers become confident and provide more capital and business. Eventually, however, the market is saturated, competition develops, or problems occur, and growth ceases.

But sometimes growth does not follow the pattern we expect. Just when we expect growth to slow—or even when it has actually started to slow—it suddenly picks up again. Such situations have occurred in the history of technology, and when we consider the nature of technological development, we can understand why. In most technologies, many technical approaches are tried. Each approach encounters limitations, but just when the technology itself might seem to be encountering an insurmountable obstacle, a new technique arrives to keep the technology improving. For example, the top speed of aircraft has increased quite steadily during the 20th century despite the fact that the aircraft engineers kept encountering factors that seemed to make higher speed impossible. Almost as soon as a barrier was identified, a way around it was found, and airplanes got faster and faster. Fabric-and-wood airplanes gave way to all-metal craft; the open cockpit gave way to the enclosed cockpit, and the reciprocating engines gave way to jets. But forecasters of technology must be wary of assuming that the growth trend will always be saved by a new breakthrough; at some point, the curve will begin to bend over: Airplane speed will no longer increase so rapidly and may not increase at all. Interestingly—and typical of futuristics in general—the forces that will change the trend in technology will probably not come from technology itself, but from other fields—politics, say, or the natural environment—because technology is shaped by social forces which determine what technology is desirable or acceptable. These social forces influence the economic and managerial resources required to develop technology.

One of the raging debates among scholars today is over growth curves. Everybody agrees that the world population is increasing very rapidly and that it probably will reach about six billion by the year 2000. Projecting the population increase further into the future, one can anticipate world population rising to 12 billion or 24 billion or even 48 billion during the next century. But can the earth tolerate so many people, or will these vast numbers consume all the available food and die in huge numbers like a plague of lemmings? Perhaps even more critical is the economic growth which is raising humanity's standard of living but also is threatening to exhaust the world's natural resources and raise pollution to intolerable levels.

The problems posed by increasing population and economic development are graphically described in such books as *Awakening from the American Dream* by Rufus E. Miles, which (like many such books) calls for a drastic slowdown in economic as well as population growth to avert disaster. But other authors, like Herman Kahn in *The Next 200 Years*, are optimistic that economic and population growth can continue—indeed, *should* continue—and that the problems associated with growth can be effectively dealt with by improved technology.

But will technology really improve fast enough? No one knows for sure, since the factors that control the development of technology are not clearly understood. Optimists can point to the steady improvement of technology—and, with technology, the standard of living. Pessimists can stress the ominous parallel to the growth of biological systems. A practical policy-maker might take account of both positions by adopting measures aimed at (1) reducing the rate of population growth, (2) developing new technology that will be less harmful to the environment, (3) encouraging the development of life-styles that are not costly in environmental terms, and (4) encouraging technology that can raise the standard of living without also damaging the environment.

Scenarios: Making Up Stories About the Future

A scenario may sound exotic, but in its simplest form, it is very common. It is simply a series of events that we imagine happening in the future. Our everyday thinking is filled with little ventures into the mysterious world of tomorrow, or next week, or next year. And these ventures are scenarios, though rarely as well developed as the elaborate scenarios prepared by professional researchers working for government agencies, the military, and commercial enterprises.

A scenario begins when we ask, "What would happen if such-and-such occurred?" For example, "What would happen if we went to the theater on Saturday night?" Once this question is posed, we can begin to imagine the various consequences of the event. First, certain preparations would be necessary for this event to occur; for example, there would be the need for transportation to the theater. In addition, if the event *does* occur, there will be additional consequences, such as being absent from home at a time when we anticipate that a relative might come.

In our minds, we may develop a large number of scenarios in an effort to decide whether or not to go to the theater on Saturday night. We develop these scenarios intuitively and rarely bother to write them down. We may, however, discuss them with each other and with friends.

What does a scenario do for us?

First, it makes us aware of potential problems that might occur if we were to take the proposed action. We can then (1) abandon the proposed action or (2) prepare to take precautions that will minimize the problems that might result.

Second, the scenario gives us an opportunity to escape from a potentially disastrous action—or to realize a tremendous opportunity. Either eventuality may be tentatively identified by developing a number of scenarios. For example, as we develop a scenario we begin to think about how to get to the theater and how to get back. As we review in our minds the various alternative means of transportation, we recognize that the brakes on our automobile are defective. If we take the automobile to the repair shop today, it will be ready in time for our excursion to the theater. Otherwise, we might find ourselves using it on Saturday despite its unsafe condition, and possibly having a fatal accident.

Third, the scenario can mobilize others—get them involved in assessing a situation and planning action. People tend to become more involved in a situation when they are faced with a concrete choice. At that point, they must think about consequences and are led into the various aspects of the problem. Some writers have used the scenario as a useful technique to get people to focus on a certain problem. Novels like *Seven Days in May* by Fletcher Knebel and Charles W. Bailey II are, essentially, scenarios presented as fiction. In other words, they explore the question, "What might happen if—?"

The act of developing a scenario in a think-tank may differ very little in essence from the scenario-preparation that all of us do in our minds every day. However, a policy analyst generally prepares his scenario more carefully and writes it down so that other analysts can review and comment on it. Moreover, unlike the fiction writer, the policy analyst is generally not concerned with literary embellishments, but simply with identifying potential events that could have a major impact on the situation he is studying.

Arthur Waskow, a policy analyst at the Institute for Policy Studies in Washington, D.C., used a scenario to show how his proposed peace-keeping machinery might prevent wars in the future. Waskow proposed the creation of three different police forces to preserve peace in a demilitarized world, and then he created an imaginary Berlin crisis in 1999 to show how the peace-keeping forces

would act to prevent the crisis from mushrooming into a war. Waskow imagined a sequence of events, including worker and student
protests in East Germany that mushroom to the point of threatening the East German government, the Soviet Union accusing West
Germany of secret rearmament efforts, the western powers warning that Soviet intervention will bring an immediate response, etc.
In the end (according to Waskow's scenario), the new peace-keeping machinery worked, and the world settled back to normal.

Writing a scenario is not a difficult task. All that is required is
imagination and familiarity with the situation for which one wishes to write a scenario. A person wishing to probe the future of the
energy situation in the United States and its possible consequences
might begin by assuming that the U.S. Government's energy policies will remain essentially unchanged from what they were in 1977
when the Carter administration took office, and then proceed to
imagine what might happen on the basis of known trends. Here is
how the resulting scenario might look:

U.S. Energy Scenario Based on Known Trends 1977-1997

Consumption of petroleum and other fossil fuels continues
to rise.

U.S. reserves continue to decline, and imports to increase.

The petroleum-exporting nations steadily raise their prices,
hoping to conserve their dwindling reserves.

Wealthy nations like the U.S. suffer some decline in living
standards as the cost of energy rises, but find themselves unable to develop the political will required to halt the continuing rise in energy consumption.

Poorer nations are increasingly priced out of the market.
They no longer can pay for fuel and fertilizer needed in their
agriculture.

Millions in the poorer nations begin starving to death, but
U.S. food supplies are inadequate to prevent the calamity
without politically unacceptable consequences to U.S. living
standards.

Most people in rich countries ignore the plight of the starving in the poor nations, but a minority of sympathizers begin
turning to terrorism as a means of helping the poor countries.

Terrorists secure atomic bombs and threaten to destroy 10
major U.S. cities if the U.S. fails to send adequate food supplies to poor nations. To make their threat credible, the terrorists detonate a small atomic device in Palm Beach, home-
town for many millionaires . . .

(The scenario may be continued by listing subsequent
events that might occur as a result of the situation that has
developed.)

The foregoing scenario suggests how a government policy (or non-policy) can have disastrous consequences that may not be anticipated by the policymakers. The scenario may seem overdramatic and unlikely, but it is based on known facts: the decline in the world's petroleum stocks; rising petroleum prices; the dependence of poor nations on fossil fuel to grow food; the proliferation of atomic technology; and the rise of international terrorism. Putting all the facts together gives us a rather terrifying scenario that suggests one possible series of consequences of decisions being made today. By identifying the possible consequences now, we can take action to make them less likely.

When we develop a scenario, we free ourselves from strict bondage to the past. No longer are we assuming that the future will be like the past except more so (as in trend extrapolation). Instead, we have begun to see the future as offering a wide variety of possibilities (including some that seem fantastic). Furthermore, the realization of these possibilities may hinge on decisions that we ourselves make. The future now is a realm of infinite possibilities, many of which may never have occurred in the past. The scenario is not just a means of exploring possible interactions of various events, but a way that we can shape the future. The typical scenario indicates, in fact, a number of points where human decisions will be made, and how these decisions will affect later events.

Scenario-writing introduces imagination and creativity into the tool-box of futuristics, and the creativity-enlarging techniques, discussed earlier, may legitimately be used in developing scenarios. If we are seriously interested in exploring the future we must make a special effort to look at "far-out" possibilities, because one of the few things that we can be sure about is that the future will be filled with them.

Ways to Map the Future

The scenario technique allows us to think freely about the future, but thinking about the future is not always easy, because we lack a structure on which to hang our thoughts. Fortunately, there are simple ways to provide structure for our thinking and stimulate our imagination. These devices have fancy names—morphological analysis, relevance trees, mission flow diagrams, etc.—but despite the jargon, the techniques are basically quite simple, and an ordinary person can easily use them to deal with his everyday problems. These intellectual tools generally require nothing more than pencil and paper, and in their simplest form they consist of nothing more than lists of events, goals, characteristics, or whatever is being scrutinized.

Let us take a simple exercise in futuristics: Deciding what to do next Saturday night. First, we will imagine a series of alternatives that we put into categories: whether to go with friends or by ourselves, where to eat, what sort of play or movie we want to see, and where to have a nightcap. Then we will structure the alternatives as follows:

Group	*Entertainment*
Ourselves and Couple A	Movie A
Ourselves alone	Movie B
Where to eat	Movie C
Restaurant A	Play A
Restaurant B	Play B
Restaurant C	*Nightcap*
Restaurant D	Bar A
Home	Bar B
	Home

Though this is a very simple situation, we find that it represents four areas of choice, and when we multiply the alternatives in each category—2 x 5 x 5 x 3—we find that we have, in effect, written a capsule description of 150 different scenarios! Furthermore, the scenarios are stated very concisely in a way that may help us to think clearly about what is involved.

For some purposes, we may wish to diagram these alternatives in this way:

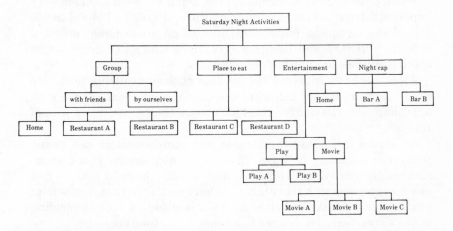

The diagram can be extended further, of course, by bringing in such choices as menus at the restaurant and the various friends one could choose to go with.

The foregoing type of diagram, known as a *relevance tree*, does not really provide any more information than a simple listing of the alternatives, but it provides a visual scheme that indicates the pattern of choices. An alternative means of presentation is the *mission flow diagram:*

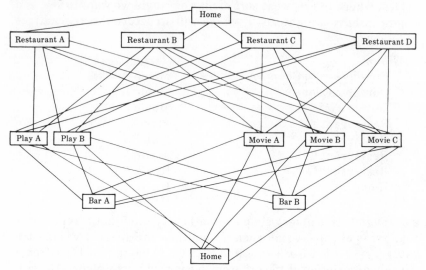

It should be clear that relevance trees and mission flow diagrams do not tell us what the future *will* be, but do clarify what the future *could* be. They can help us when we try to decide what sort of future we want to try to realize. Ordinarily, we do not want to bother with analyzing our choices so carefully, but when we want to make very important decisions concerning our future, it may be helpful to use one of the foregoing techniques, just as do government officials, military planners, and business executives who make decisions involving millions or even billions of dollars.

After we have analyzed the various choices available to us, we must select from our "menu" of choices those alternatives we wish to realize. The alternatives that we choose then constitute a plan of action.

As shown in the above example, the same situation can be described in a variety of ways. The "best" way depends on circumstances. Generally, a mission flow diagram may be most useful when one is concerned with scheduling a sequence of events such as a trip; a relevance tree may be better for a static situation such as deciding on the characteristics desired in a house one intends to build.

Another technique for structuring our thinking about the future is what is called a *cross-impact matrix*. This technique, which sounds quite mysterious, is also quite simple, or at least *can* be very simple. It helps us to identify the interrelationships between two sets of events, trends, or other data. For example, we may want to use the cross-impact matrix to help us understand more clearly the decisions we are making for Saturday night.

Let's suppose that we decide we want to have dinner at a restaurant and then to go see a play or movie. We also decide that the earliest we can start dinner is 7 p.m. and that we want to have dinner at one of four restaurants and go to one of five theaters that are offering two plays and three movies that sound interesting. The restaurants and theaters are all in the same general area and we estimate that 10 minutes will be enough time to walk from any of the restaurants to any of the theaters.

As we think about what to do, it occurs to us that the restaurants do not offer the same speed of service. Restaurant A is a fast-food establishment while Restaurant D has a very leisurely atmosphere and it is almost impossible to dine there in less than an hour and a half. Restaurants B and C lie between the two extremes. We also note the plays and movies begin at times varying from 7:30 to 8:30 p.m.

As we think about our situation, we decide on certain goals:

1. We do not want to miss the beginning of the play or movie that we choose.

2. We do not want to have to wolf down our food or skip dinner.

3. We would like a small amount of leeway in our schedule in case we are delayed at any point. We decide that the ideal amount of leeway is 20 minutes—enough for a little windowshopping if we are not delayed, but not so much that we will find ourselves not knowing what to do with the extra time.

To clarify our decision, we lay out our options in the form of a cross-impact matrix as follows:

	Restaurant A 30 minutes to dine	Restaurant B 40 minutes to dine	Restaurant C 1 hour to dine	Restaurant D 1½ hrs. to dine
Play A 7:30 PM	Impossible	Impossible	Impossible	Impossible
Play B 7:30 PM	Impossible	Impossible	Impossible	Impossible
Movie A 7:30 PM	Impossible	Impossible	Impossible	Impossible
Movie B 8:00 PM	Possible (20 minutes leeway)	Possible (10 minutes leeway)	Impossible	Impossible
Movie C 8:30 PM	Possible (50 minutes leeway)	Possible (40 minutes leeway)	Possible (20 minutes leeway)	Impossible

This matrix shows that we cannot eat at any of the restaurants and see either of the plays or Movie A. We can, however, eat at restaurant A or B and see either Movie B or C. We also can eat at restaurant C and see Movie C. Since we decided earlier that the ideal leeway time is 20 minutes, we are left with only two combinations that meet all our criteria:

Restaurant A and Movie B

Restaurant C and Movie C

At this point, we may decide that on the whole we prefer the first combination. This is a relatively simple decision to make once we have eliminated all the other combinations through our cross-impact matrix.

The cross-impact matrix can become infinitely complex as we add various factors into the decision-making process. With our human limitations, we might soon reach a point where we give up and rely on our intuition to make the right decisions. However, computers now are being used to identify the best choice in certain highly complex situations beyond the power of human beings to deal with in any reasonable period of time.

Making Better Use of Experts

In times gone by, a king who needed to make an important decision would call in his wise men and ask their opinion. He would listen to their views and then make his decision. Curiously, a modern executive—including the chief executives of today's nations and multi-national business concerns—follows almost exactly the same procedure. After all, what else can he do? He recognizes that his own judgment may be faulty, and that he lacks certain specialized knowledge, so to prevent a critical mistake he gets the judgments of others. Often the stakes are very high as when President Kennedy, during the 1962 Cuban missile crisis, convened his cabinet and went around the room getting the opinions of his most trusted advisors on what should be done. Despite the gravity of the situation, he never got the opinions of *all* his advisers during one of the most crucial meetings. Some were not asked for their views, those who were had to be very brief because of the shortage of time; all were busy men with little time to study the situation in great detail. The crisis came to a peaceful conclusion when the Soviet missiles were withdrawn, but the incident demonstrated a shocking mismatch between the technology used in presidential decision-making and the technology of modern warfare.

One approach to helping leaders get better forecasts and advice from their advisors is the Delphi technique, invented by Olaf Helmer and Norman Dalkey at the RAND Corporation in the late 1950s. The Delphi method recognizes human judgments as legitimate and useful inputs in generating forecasts, and also that the judgment of a number of informed people is likely to be better than the judgment of a single individual, who may be misinformed or highly biased. In popular parlance: "Two heads are better than one." However, if a group of people are brought together, a great many socio-psychological interactions occur that detract from the development of a good forecast or a good decision. The Delphi technique is a way of allowing only those interactions to occur that are likely to improve the quality of the forecast or decision.

Here's how a typical Delphi poll might work:

First, the person coordinating the poll identifies experts willing to participate and instructs them on the procedure, which may consist of a series of questionnaires sent by mail. Typically, a Delphi expert does not know who the other experts are or at least does not know who makes the statements reported to him during the course of the poll. All he knows is what the Delphi coordinator tells him about the results of the poll.

Second, the same questions may be presented to the experts several times. After the first time, however, the experts are informed about the results of the previous poll. The Delphi coordinator makes known what the "average" forecast was and perhaps what the range of opinions was. He may ask those persons who offered "extreme" opinions to state the reasons for their views. These reasons are reported to the group as a whole.

Third, the experts can freely revise their views on the basis of reasons offered by their colleagues, but are also free to adhere to their original judgments. No one except the Delphi coordinator will know which expert has switched his opinion.

The result of a Delphi poll is a consensus forecast or judgment. And this result is uncontaminated by "follow the leader" tendencies and other social phenomena that occur in normal group interaction. The opinions of people who tend to keep silent at meetings due to shyness or modesty have equal weight during a Delphi poll with those who normally dominate a meeting through aggressive verbosity.

The Delphi technique has been used in many situations since the early 1960s, and is generally recognized as offering a refinement of the traditional way of getting a consensus opinion. Furthermore, it can be computerized; each expert can be interviewed by means of a computer terminal located almost anywhere, even on another continent, and the results tallied by a single central computer connected by telephone lines to the various terminals.

The Delphi technique has been widely used to generate forecasts in technology, education, and other fields. Studies of consensus views arrived at through the Delphi technique suggest that the

Delphi poll can indeed improve the quality of forecasts. However, the technique has certain drawbacks. For one thing, many people *want* the recognition that comes from giving their views in a group and may also want to be identified with certain opinions and information (some of which may even be of a proprietary character); deprived of this recognition and credit, some experts may not wish to give their views at all. In addition, there is a potential problem in that the results of a Delphi could be used as a substitute for the careful formulation of alternative policies through research and analysis—or even substitute for the decision-maker. A chief executive, who is given responsibility for the welfare of an organization, should not be allowed to shift responsibility for mistakes onto a Delphi panel.

The use of experts allows us to escape from the assumption that current trends will continue. For instance, a 1964 Delphi study forecast that the rate of acceleration in world population growth would taper off in the next few decades. The experts could not base their forecast on the population growth rate itself, which was continuing to accelerate; instead, they recognized trends in other areas—such as improving birth control techniques and growing affluence—that would slow population growth.

Models, Games, and Simulations

Everyone is familiar with models, in the form of miniature replicas of airplanes, ships, and rockets. There are also models of human beings, or dolls, and model towns that children can build with blocks. Generally, a model is something that is smaller and easier to handle than the thing it represents. But since it has many characteristics of the original object, we can learn a lot about the original by studying the model.

Children learn the characteristics of automobiles and ships by looking at models of them. By moving the models around, children can simulate the movements of real automobiles and ships, and learn how they function in real situations. The children can also play games that involve interactions with several children in a simulation of human activities involving cars. For example, one child may crash his car into another's; the other child may angrily protest, whereupon the first child may bring a model tow truck to the rescue. Thus children, by playing games, learn about the situations they may encounter in the future.

Models, simulations, and games now are becoming increasingly important as tools not only of educators but of business and government policymakers. The principle of all three is that we can learn about something by studying something similar but easier to deal with. The distinction between the three terms is fairly simple in principle: a model is static or something that is being thought about in a static phase; a simulation involves changes through time; a game adds human motivations to a simulation. A miniature automobile is a *model*, but when a child plays with it he creates a *simulation* of the movements of a real automobile. If he has a companion, the two children can play a *game* in which each plays the role of a motorist and their cars crash into each other. A game includes the human elements of private interests, competition, jealousy, etc. The distinction between the terms is often blurred in practice, because a *game* is a *simulation*, and a *dynamic model* is one that is used in *simulations*.

Some medical schools use model "patients" to train students without endangering anyone's life. One such "patient" was developed by the University of Southern California's School of Medicine and Aerojet General engineers. The robot patient, actually a computer-controlled manikin, is sufficiently lifelike to look like a human patient on an operating table. Skin-colored, skin-textured plastic covers the frame of the model. The manikin's jaw opens and closes in normal human fashion. Inside the mouth are tongue, teeth, epiglottis, vocal cords, trachea, etc. The robot also has a heartbeat, carotid and temporal pulse beats, blood pressure, diaphragm movements, etc. The model is programmed to respond appropriately to the injection of four different drugs, administered in varying dosages, as well as to the administration of both nitrous oxide and oxygen.

The simulated patient is not, of course, *precisely* like a real patient. But it does permit medical students to find out what might happen to real patients under their care.

The U.S. Navy tests model ships and submarines at the Naval Ship Research and Development Center at Carderock, Maryland. The Center has a model basin that looks like a large indoor swimming pool, but few of the admirals and scientists that use it ever plunge in. Instead, they watch the performance of their model ships and submarines in the model ocean.

While the admirals are playing with their model ships, the generals are engaged in *war games*. In a typical military exercise a Red army will contend with a Blue army, with actual soldiers playing the role of the contenders. Such war games provide military commanders with an opportunity to test alternative strategies; at the same time, both the commanders and the troops gain experience under combat-like conditions.

War games need not involve actual soldiers. The games can also be played on a grander but more abstract level by military experts using only pencil and paper. These games are, in effect, sophisticated versions of "Battleship," the popular child's game in which the players secretly mark certain squares on a piece of graph paper as the location of their warships, and then each player takes turns calling out certain squares in the hope of hitting his opponent's warships. War games in the U.S. military may be exceedingly elaborate. A game may involve a number of teams located at various think tanks, military installations, and government agencies, and use a nationwide network of teletypes and computers.

Games played by RAND Corporation analysts are credited with having had a major influence on the development of U.S. military policy. For example, a series of games begun during the 1950s examined the possible role of the Air Force in a war in the Middle East, while another series of games initiated during that period dealt with the role of the military in limited wars. Together these games cast doubt on the then prevalent doctrine of "massive retaliation," and suggested that the nation must also be prepared for limited warfare as well.

Games are also used to simulate international political affairs, because the military planners must be alert to circumstances in which political leaders, such as the President of the United States, may require military support. In some games, players assume the roles of individual leaders (e.g., the President of France or the Secretary General of the United Nations) or of entities such as "East Germany" or the "Soviet Union."

War games contribute to an endless series of assessments of the strength of nations and what might happen in a test of strength within a specific set of circumstances. These games enable decision-makers to see more clearly what might happen if they took certain actions. Such bloodless battles can prevent the shedding of real blood in actual encounters: If Napoleon and Hitler had known from war games that they would lose their campaigns against Russia, the battles of Borodino and Stalingrad would presumably never have occurred. War games have probably played a major role in preventing World War III by showing both sides what they would lose if the forces symbolized in the game were employed in actual combat. In a sense, World War III may already have occurred—in fact, a series of World Wars—as military strategists repeatedly took certain actions (often on the orders of politicians) but kept playing games that enabled them to see accurately the terrible losses that would occur in real conflict. Napoleon and Hitler thought they could conquer Russia easily; today's military planners know that Russia, even in defeat, could inflict terrible punishment on her conquerors. War games may seem macabre, but most people would rather have the fighting done with paper and computers than with bullets and bombs.

Games can also be used to understand the operations of a city. One player may be designated as the mayor; another plays the role of a slum lord; a third is the head of a labor union, etc. The game master can then describe the situation in which the players are to interact. As the game proceeds, the slum lord may make demands on the mayor, the mayor may appeal to the labor leader for support, etc. Each player tries to respond as he thinks his real-life counterpart might. Such a game can help players to grasp the highly complex interactions in a city and understand the various interests involved.

A complex system, like the economy of a city, can also be simulated by means of a mathematical model, that is, a series of equations showing how different variables affect each other. The equations can be fed into a computer, and then the computer can be given data representing the situation as it is. At that point, researchers can change one or more of the variables to see what happens. What would happen, for example, if the real estate tax were raised 10% or the sales tax abolished?

Computer models of the U.S. economy are now standard apparatus in the making of U.S. economic policies. The number of equations is often staggering: Data Resources, Inc., one of the leading economic forecasting firms, uses a model that has 900 equations (trimmed from 1,200!). One of these equations may represent automobile sales, written as a function of real national income less transfer payments; the relative price of cars; the existing stock of cars; consumer debt; operating cost; family wealth, etc.

Computer models are also used outside of economics. For instance, Professor Jay Forrester of the Massachusetts Institute of Technology has developed models for the way a city grows and stagnates. Such a model can help a city policy-maker understand the possible impacts of various proposals such as a new sales tax or a rise in real-estate assessments. Forrester has also pioneered in the construction of models of the entire world, and his research group at M.I.T. did the now-famous "limits-to-growth" study under the auspices of the Club of Rome.

One interesting aspect of a complex system such as a city or a nation's economy is that it does not work the way human beings expect it to work. In Forrester's terminology, a system is *counterintuitive*, because it does not passively accept a change introduced into it, but actively responds—often in ways that directly contradict the wishes of the people who introduced the change. The counter-intuitive character of social systems means that people who want to improve a social system—for example, by reducing poverty or pollution—need to watch out that their supposed remedies are not useless or even worse than the condition they are trying to correct.

Let us look at a few highly-simplified examples of social problems and what may happen when policy-makers ignore the refractory, almost mischievous way in which a social system can frustrate well-meaning attempts to make it behave better:

Problem 1: A road is constantly jammed with traffic.
"Solution": Enlarge the road.
Result: More drivers are attracted to the improved road and it is even more crowded than the old one.

Problem 2: Poverty in cities.
"Solution": Build government-subsidized housing projects and make them available at low rent to poor people.
Result: Poor people become concentrated in the housing projects and adjacent areas, where there are few business enterprises or wealthy people who can provide jobs. The poor people find they cannot afford either to travel long distances to work or to move closer to jobs.

Problem 3: Pollution.
"Solution": A campaign to get people to turn in old newspapers for recycling.
Result: Waste paper floods the market, causing the price of scrap newsprint to drop. Junk dealers and their suppliers find it is no longer economically feasible to buy and sell waste paper, and stop doing so. The waste-paper campaign slows as volunteers become bored and stop working. The air becomes more polluted than ever from burning waste paper.

In each case, the people who propose the "solutions" mean to be helpful, and the solutions they propose sound reasonable to other people. Elections often are won by politicians proposing such "solutions" precisely because they *do* seem reasonable, even though they are, in fact, unworkable. Thus democratic societies face the problem of helping their electorates to become more sophisticated in evaluating social remedies and in judging the proposals offered by politicians. Otherwise, the nations will remain a prey to quacks peddling social nostrums—programs that are largely or totally ineffective in meeting urgent social needs and may even do major harm to the body politic.

Identifying real as opposed to false cures for poverty, pollution, family breakdown, mental illness, and other social maladies may increasingly be a task for computerized simulations. So far, scientists have succeeded in building only a few prototype model social systems, but the work done thus far is encouraging. Researchers may eventually discover *real* solutions to intractable problems like poverty and overpopulation.

The building of a good model of a highly complex system like a factory or an economy is, of course, extremely difficult. Work must begin with careful study of the system to be modeled so that all the essential variables can be identified and their interrelationships determined. This work is sometimes called "premodeling." At the Institute for the Future in Menlo Park, California, where a lot of research on futuristic methodology is done, researchers use cross-impact matrices, relevance trees, and graphs in their premodeling. Often the model-builders discover major gaps in knowledge that must be filled—gaps that other researchers have overlooked because they did not need to state precisely how a process actually works. "Often, in compiling the assumptions for constructing a model," notes systems analyst David Snyder, "systems designers become the first people to 'see' how common everyday phenomena actually occur, since our specialized world seldom gives any one individual or organization an opportunity for such a broad overview."

Eventually, the researchers may reach a point where they can express most of the significant interrelationships in mathematical formulas. When this task is completed, they are ready to put the model into a computer and begin feeding in data to fit into the formulas. Once in the computer, the model allows anyone—even people who know nothing about mathematics and computers—to ask all sorts of "What if—?" questions. Just as the medical student can see what might happen if he gives a certain medicine to his patient, a mayor can see what might happen if the city increases the real-estate tax and a business executive can see what might happen if he raises his prices by 20%. A good model—one that can accurately simulate the behavior of a real situation and can be easily used—allows anyone to explore the various possibilities of the future, and hopefully arrive at better decisions.

In addition to the five procedures discussed in this chapter, several others warrant a brief mention: operations research, cost-benefit analysis, systems analysis, and technology assessment. Each of these terms is applied to a variety of research activities, and the meaning of the term tends to change a bit with each user, but despite the ambiguity, the methods (or their lineal descendants) are increasingly important in government and business forecasting, goal-setting, and planning. Some of these procedures, it should be added, are not always recognized as belonging to futuristics, yet they are so closely tied in with exploration of the future that they may be included under the rubric of futuristics.

Operations research is the oldest of these procedures. Military planners during World War II used techniques and information from many different sciences to solve such problems as how to move troops, equipment, and supplies most expeditiously from

one point to another. Operations research demonstrated that knowledge developed by scientists could be applied to military problems.
When this application succeeded, government and business planners decided that the technique might also be useful in non-military
areas. Since World War II, operations research has been used in
many industries, from metallurgy to textiles; in hospital planning;
and in government operations. Among the analytical tools used in
operations research are mathematical statistics, linear program-
ming, queuing theory, Monte Carlo simulation methods, stock and
production control models, decision and game theory, operational
gaming, cybernetics, and information theory.

Cost-benefit analysis was used initially in the 1930s to evaluate
U.S. water resource programs. In the 1950s it came to be used by
military planners who referred to it as "cost-effectiveness" analysis. Since then, cost-benefit analysis has merged into systems engineering. The idea in a cost-benefit analysis is to identify the criteria to be used in making an evaluation, describe all the alternatives, specify mission performance and cost for each of the selected
alternatives, etc., so that decision-makers can choose more sensibly
between alternative programs and policies.

Systems analysis focuses attention on the fact that planners are
almost always concerned with *systems,* and systems have characteristic features. A system may be defined as a group of resources
with a definite objective (for example, a steel mill, a city, or a government agency). Or it may be defined as almost any group of interacting entities, such as the human body or a clique of schoolgirls.
A systems analyst tries to help the decision-maker to select among
alternatives by comparing the alternatives according to their cost,
effectiveness, and risk. Robert McNamara introduced systems
analysis into widespread use in the U.S. Government in 1965 when
he was Secretary of Defense.

Technology assessment is a systematic forecasting and planning
process that describes the costs and benefits of various technologies, with explicit emphasis on environmental and social considerations external to the program or product that is being studied.
The technology assessment movement began in the U.S. Congress
in the 1960s amid rising fears about the introduction of powerful
new technologies that could have important harmful impacts on
society and the natural environment.

Many other methods are used by futurists and new techniques
(or refinements of old ones) appear frequently. It is not possible to
discuss them here. Our purpose has been simply to show that the
idea of exploring the future through rational and scientific methods is a perfectly practical undertaking.

9

Futurists and Their Ideas

There is no such thing as an "average" futurist. Futurists live in different nations, speak different languages, practice different religions, and work in different fields. Sociologists and planners are well represented in futurist circles, but there are also mathematicians, governmental officials, salesmen, and people in many other occupations. The young have an especially big stake in the future, but many of the most enthusiastic futurists are elderly. The future is often viewed in terms of highly sophisticated technology, but many committed futurists are more interested in preserving the natural environment. Unusual innovations attract many futurists, but others place greater emphasis on maintaining the values of their heritage.

Each futurist has had a unique series of experiences that have led him to develop the special orientation that characterizes a futurist. To understand that orientation, it may be helpful to take a brief look at a few noted futurists, who can suggest, through their lives and thinking, what it means to be a futurist.

All the individuals described in the following pages may be called futurists, in that they have demonstrated an intense interest in the future, have participated actively in meetings dealing with the future, and have written considerably about future possibilities. Though they all are well-known, they are not *the* leading futurists. Dozens of other persons could be named who would have an equal or better claim to be among the top futurists. The choice of futurists to be described here was heavily influenced by such extraneous factors as the ready availability of suitable information. Thus the individuals that will be discussed here constitute a totally unscientific sampling of what might be called prominent futurists, but readers who like to play psychological detective can look in these biographies for clues to the causes of a future-orientation.

The following biographical sketches are presented in order of their birthdates, starting with Margaret Mead, born in 1901 and concluding with Alvin Toffler, born in 1928. Each individual is described as a futurist, not as a total personality; for example, de Jouvenel's books on politics and Asimov's historical writings receive only passing mention. Each biographical sketch seeks to suggest some of the concepts and techniques that characterize the subject's approach to the future. The chapter concludes with a set of hypotheses concerning the commonalities of these futurists' thinking.

Margaret Mead: Children as Guides to the Future

Margaret Mead brings to futurism the perspective of an anthropologist concerned with human beings living in a rapidly changing culture. As the human life span lengthens and social change accelerates, Mead points out, old familiar things fade rapidly from people's lives, and strange new things spring up faster and faster. The world that people experience now is changing swiftly everywhere. From now on, Mead says, "no one will live in the world into which he was born, and no one will die in the world in which he worked in his maturity."

One of the urgent problems the world faces, Mead feels, is the need to understand the nature of change in the modern world, including its speed and dimensions. "The primary evidence that our present situation is unique, without any parallel in the past, is that the generation gap is world-wide," she writes in her book *Culture and Commitment*. "The particular events taking place in any country—China, England, Pakistan, Japan, the United States, New Guinea, or elsewhere—are not enough to explain the unrest that is stirring modern youth everywhere."

The new conditions that have created world-wide youthful dissidence include the emergence of a world community, Mead says. "For the first time human beings throughout the world, in their information about one another and responses to one another, have become a community that is united by shared knowledge and danger."

Today all over the world people who are bearers of vastly different cultural traditions are entering the present at the same point in time. "It is as if, all around the world, men were converging on identical immigration posts, each with its identifying sign: 'You are now about to enter the post-World War II world at Gate 1 (or Gate 23 or Gate 2003, etc.).' Whoever they are and wherever their particular point of entry may be, all men are equally immigrants into the new era—some come as refugees and some as castaways." Everyone born and bred before World War II is now an "immigrant in time," just as his forebears were immigrants in space.

One of the striking changes in today's society, Mead suggests, is that human society has shifted from a "postfigurative" culture—

one in which the young learn from the old—to one that is "cofigurative," that is, one in which both adults and children learn chiefly from their peers. She believes that the next stage, already emerging, will be the development of a "prefigurative" culture, in which the old learn from the young. In a prefigurative culture, she suggests, the future dominates the present, just as in a postfigurative culture, the past (tradition) dominated the present.

Mead's terminology may be clarified by considering how the human condition has changed in the 20th century. In the past, there was relatively little change in the way people lived, and such change as there was tended to be recurring—wars, ceremonies, the death of leaders, etc. The elders had experienced more of these recurring events and thus could describe what the future would be like. For example, an elder could advise his fellow tribesmen on the supply problems of a forthcoming war and suggest practical steps to take. But when the culture of a group of people is changing, new events are not like those in the past, hence the elders' ideas about the future are less useful. Under these circumstances, people tend to rely on their contemporaries for guidance because they are not locked into past conceptions that are clearly inappropriate. As the pace of cultural change accelerates, people recognize that the younger members of society have absorbed the latest aspects of the culture and therefore are in closer touch with the future.

In today's fast-changing culture, people who want to understand what the future will be like can turn to the young, who will populate the future and may already suggest through their attitudes and behavior the shape of things to come. Already, older people frequently imitate young people in their dress, language, and manners. In the United States, casual dress styles, long hair and beards, and sexual freedom seem to have been adopted first by the young, who later influenced many of their elders to accept them. The influence of young people on their elders is attested by the success of popular musicians and singers in introducing new words into the language. The young people who listen to the popular stars quickly pick up new terms and pass them on to their parents.

In the postfigurative (traditional) cultures of the past, there were elders who could instruct the children in what they needed to know to live their lives effectively. Today there are no such elders. "It is not only that parents are no longer guides, but that there are no guides, whether one seeks them in one's own country or abroad," Mead says. "There are no elders who know what those who have been reared within the last 20 years know about the world into which they were born." Thus the current cofigurative culture, in which both young and old learn from their contemporaries, may soon give way to a prefigurative culture in which the child—not the parent or grandparent—represents the future.

"Instead of the erect, white-haired elder who, in postfigurative cultures, stood for the past and the future in all their grandeur and continuity, the unborn child, already conceived but still in the womb, must become the symbol of what life will be like."

If the old must learn from the young, who will teach the young and how? Mead suggests that people must seek "prefigurative ways of teaching and learning that will keep the future open."

"We must create new models for adults who can teach their children not what to learn, but how to learn and not what they should be committed to, but the value of commitment. Postfigurative cultures, which focused on the elders—those who had learned the most and were able to do the most with what they had learned—were essentially closed systems that continually replicated the past. We must now move toward the creation of open systems that focus on the future—and so on children, those whose capacities are least known and whose choices must be left open."

Mead believes that the development of prefigurative cultures will depend on the existence of a continuing dialogue in which the young, free to act on their own initiative, can lead their elders in the direction of the unknown. "It is only with the direct participation of the young," she says, "that we can build a viable future."

Though better known as an anthropologist and social critic than as a futurist, Mead has long exhibited a general future-orientation in both her writings and lectures. In the 1950s she suggested that every university should have a Chair of the Future, like a Chair of the Middle Ages or of Classical Greece. She wanted people who would be as responsible concerning the next decade or the next 50 years as a Medievalist might be about the Middle Ages, someone who would fit together a carefully thought-out picture of the future. She also stressed the need for "a reasoned belief in the future of human living," because the world now is haunted by the destructive powers released during the 20th century.

Mead has been continuously involved in studying and reflecting on man's cultural evolution since 1925 when she began her pioneering field work with tribal cultures in Samoa. She has made repeated trips back to the tribes she studied in the Twenties so that she could do follow-up studies. Studying a new culture would be more fun, she says, but she feels that her most valuable contribution is to continue to use her lifetime experience in the South Seas. "It is far more useful, because now I have the great-grandchildren of the people I studied."

Mead was born in Philadelphia on December 16, 1901, the daughter of a sociologist mother and an economist father. She was educated at Barnard College and Columbia University. At the age of 23, after completing her graduate work in anthropology, she spent nine months living with and studying the isolated inhabitants of American Samoa. The result of this first field work was *Coming of Age in Samoa*, which became a classic following its appearance in 1928. Even before its publication, Mead had become a member of the staff of the American Museum of Natural History and had begun her career as a specialist in Pacific cultures.

In Samoa, Mead focused her attention on adolescents, but when she went to New Guinea to study the Manus tribe, she shifted to young children. (*Growing Up in New Guinea* appeared in 1930.) Still later she investigated the male and female roles in several New Guinea tribes and also did work on infant development. She published these findings in *Sex and Temperament in Three Primitive Societies* (1936) and *Male and Female* (1949).

At various times, Mead married and divorced three men. She once commented: "We have got to face the fact that marriage is a terminable institution." By her third husband, anthropologist Gregory Bateson, she had a daughter, Margaret Catherine, who is also an anthropologist. Mead worked with Bateson in Bali (Indonesia) from 1936 to 1939. Following her return to New York City and the birth of her daughter in 1939, she concentrated on applying anthropological insights to wartime problems (at the Office of War Information in London) and modern societies. In 1953 she began her long series of trips back to the locations of her prewar expeditions so that she could study the adults who had been children or infants during her initial visits. *New Lives for Old* (1955) was the first fruit of this effort. In 1967 she made a motion picture entitled *Margaret Mead's New Guinea Journal.*

Mead has received such world-wide recognition that she may well be the most famous living social scientist. She has served as President of the American Anthropological Association, the World Federation of Health, the World Society for Ekistics, and the American Association for the Advancement of Science. Since 1969 she has been Curator Emeritus of Ethnology at the American Museum of Natural History. She also continues to teach as an adjunct Professor of Anthropology at Columbia and in the Department of Psychiatry at the University of Cincinnati's Medical School. She writes a monthly column for *Redbook* magazine and serves as chairman of the Fordham Liberal Arts College at Lincoln Center.

Mead sees the world in a period of stupendous transformation. "We know that we are in a transformation period, and we know that this is as important as the Copernican Revolution, the Industrial Revolution, or the period when man stopped being nomadic and became sedentary." But despite the tremendous dangers that the world now faces, Mead sees an opportunity for the human race in the fact that pollution now is a world-wide phenomenon.

"The whole world has never shared the same dangers before, and it may not continue to share them," she says.

> It's quite conceivable that in 25 years we may discover ways of boxing off parts of the world. Our interdependence at present depends on trade, on certain kinds of technology, on communication, and on a few beliefs, such as the belief in the brotherhood of man and we might get over that. (We haven't believed in the brotherhood of man very long and we could stop quite rapidly.)
>
> But at present we have a climate of opinion that recognizes that we're all one species, that the world is highly interdependent, and that the air is endangered. That endangered air gives us something to share . . . . So this is an ideal moment in history—a moment that we can possibly seize to build interdependent social institutions that we haven't had before.

As an anthropologist, Mead says that Western civilization has located the future ahead of us, beyond our knowledge, out of reach. The future is always "about to" but never is. But in some other cultures, she says, the future has always been, that is, it is behind rather than ahead, but only revealed bit by bit. An individual in such a culture views the future as always just "catching up" to his position. In order to make use of the past rather than be its prisoner, Mead suggests moving "the future" to the present. The often-heard phrase "The future is now," is, for Mead, a tool with which we might restructure our thinking.

One way in which the future exists in the present is in the form of children. Mead still takes special interest in children, especially her own grand-daughter Sevanne, whose pictures she proudly shows off. "The one way that you cannot avoid thinking about the future is if you have a two-year-old child in front of you who is growing. When you think about 10 years from now, that child will be 12; when you think of 20, that child will be 22 and you begin to wonder: What will that child's children be like? This biological guarantee of foresightedness has carried human beings forward as they forgot the troubles of their past and present in concern for the future."

Bertrand de Jouvenel: The Inventor of Futuribles

France's best-known futurist, Bertrand de Jouvenel, was only 16 when the peace treaty that ended World War I was signed at Versailles, but he saw the treaty as "loaded with the seeds of another great war." On the day the treaty was signed, de Jouvenel decided that "responsible statesmen are unable to recognize that an ending is a beginning."

As the son of a diplomat, de Jouvenel had enjoyed a box seat on the momentous negotiations that concluded what had been the most terrible war in history up to that time. The war had lasted over four years; almost every European family had its dead or maimed; whole regions were devastated, and the political regimes of Russia, Germany, Austria-Hungary, and the Ottoman Empire were overthrown. At the end of it all, thę statesmen gathered in Paris to recast the map of Europe.

De Jouvenel was a fascinated—but deeply concerned—spectator. He later gave this description of his feelings:

> To the youthful minds entranced by the course of events the Conference of Paris was proof positive that the world could be remade deliberately, and this well or badly. Keynes became our hero for denouncing the inherent absurdity both of interallied debts and reparations and the extension of national debts. A further absurdity, of which I happened to be an indignant witness, was the humiliating manner in which the Treaty of Versailles was presented to liberal representatives of a new German Republic, who were bidden to sign on the dotted line. This was unprecedented; nothing so degrading had ever occurred in the history of civilized Europe. The treaty also included the famous Article 231 that charged Germany with exclusive responsibility for the war—an injustice of which Hitler was to make much. Any schoolboy could see that such inequities would have to be redressed, and that the Polish corridor was a dangerous device. But subsequent events only demonstrated the resistance of politicians and public opinion to a rectification of these obvious errors.

Four years later, after the signing of the treaty, de Jouvenel was in Geneva for the 1923 meeting of the League of Nations.

> It was a bliss at 20 to witness its September assembly, and an even greater joy to watch small clusters of delegates from different countries locked in friendly discussion. The scene at Geneva stretched on both sides of the Leman from the distant Secretariat to the Hall of the Reformation, embracing the hotels housing the various delegations; to and fro went Jean Monnet, a creative go-between, inciting coalitions to advance the good work, inventing formulas. Here indeed was the building of the new world by men of good will! But had they power?

De Jouvenel's diplomat father, Henry de Jouvenel, and Britain's Lord Robert Cecil strove mightily to insure a lasting peace. Their efforts culminated in the 1924 signing of the Protocol for the Pacific Settlement of International Disputes. The so-called "General Protocol" bound signatories to abstain from war, to submit their disputes to arbitration, to proceed gradually to disarmament, and in the case of aggression, to apply sanctions to the aggressor and to cooperate in resistance to such aggression. "It was a great triumph," says de Jouvenel, "but one devoid of any practical sequel. Power diplomacy went its own way, ignoring the display at Geneva."

Other events confirmed de Jouvenel's perception that politicians do not take proper account of the long-range consequences of their actions. "Statesmen would do such crazy things" de Jouvenel says. "In France's case, treaties of alliance were signed with Czechoslovakia and Poland, but the French forces were organized solely for defense. We promised to intervene if either country were attacked, but such intervention could take no other form than an offensive into Germany, a role for which our army was not prepared." Years ahead of time, de Jouvenel and others foresaw what eventually happened in 1939 when Germany invaded Poland: "The French army sat uselessly in its defensive positions, having been designed for nothing else." De Jouvenel notes that a French military officer made an explicit forecast in 1929 of the eventual fate of the French army in a book titled *Feu l'Armee Francaise* [The Late French Army].

De Jouvenel emphatically rejects the notion that he has any special prescience in politics or any other field. "I have to my credit no feat of prediction based otherwise than on the simplest common sense," he said in a letter written in 1975. But he can give many examples where a forecast based on common sense might have prevented disaster, if it had been acted on. For example: "In the winter of 1951-52 I sent to our leading politicians a brutal short report on Algeria, announcing that it was going to spring into fire. The revolt actually started in October 1954. The forecast was quite easy: it only took a visit to Algeria. Anybody could foresee what was going to happen. Of course, there can be no foresight of the future if one refuses to look at the present." In none of these forecasts, de Jouvenel says, did he use any method "other than not closing one's eyes."

The man who has devoted a lifetime to not closing his eyes was born in Paris in 1903. His father, Henry de Jouvenel des Ursins, was an aristocrat as well as a diplomat, and in due course, Bertrand de Jouvenel inherited the title of baron, though he prefers to be known simply as Monsieur de Jouvenel. Educated in law, biology, and economics, the younger de Jouvenel became known in the 1930s as a journalist and writer concerned with European political and economic developments.

He wrote his first book, *L'economie dirigee* (The Directed Economy) when he was 25. In this discussion of *dirigisme*, or economic planning and control by the state, de Jouvenel discussed "things I thought to be evident and were evident—so there was really no need to say them." But they were not so evident to others, and *dirigisme*, which de Jouvenel coined, became an English as well as a French word. (It is listed in the *Webster's New International Dictionary, Third Edition, Unabridged,* 1971.)

Since World War II, de Jouvenel has published a number of books that reflect not only his deep knowledge of European history and diplomacy, but his understanding of systems theory, simulations, and other modern innovations in the fields of economics and politics. His style mingles Latin terms and references to ancient history with comments on the latest economic intelligence from Washington and London. Among his postwar works are *On Power* (Viking Press; French original edition published in Geneva in 1945); *On Sovereignty* (Chicago University Press, from original published in 1955); *The Pure Theory of Politics* (Cambridge and Yale University Press). His latest published work is *La Civilisation de Puissance* (The Power Civilization, Fayard, Paris, 1976).

For futurists, de Jouvenel's outstanding work is his classic treatise on forecasting and the future, *The Art of Conjecture*. Even before its translation, *L'art de la conjecture* was read by future-oriented people in the English-speaking world and helped inspire a number of the organizers of the World Future Society.

The Art of Conjecture, which exhibits its author's ability "not to close his eyes," has been an eye opener for many readers. In a sense, de Jouvenel may be viewed as saying—in a rather erudite way—a number of things that are obvious, except that most people had somehow failed to see them. Like *Future Shock*, by Alvin Toffler, *The Art of Conjecture* focuses on a subject that everyone is familiar with, yet rarely thinks about. Like Toffler, de Jouvenel uses a wide variety of examples to explain aspects of everyday life that are important yet generally ignored.

In his preface to *The Art of Conjecture*, de Jouvenel says that the subject of his book "forced itself on me," because he had constantly sought to forecast events and therefore was led to analyze what he was doing. He reasoned that if people can find out what they are doing when they make forecasts (which they do routinely everyday), they can begin to compare forecasts and decide which are most likely to be accurate.

In trying to understand how people make forecasts, de Jouvenel looks at the nature of the future and finds it fundamentally different from the past:

> With regard to the past, man can exert his will only in vain; his liberty is void, his power nonexistent. I could say: 'I want to be a former student of the Ecole Polytechnique'—but this is utterly absurd. The fact is that I did not go to the Ecole Polytechnique, and nothing can change this fact. Imagine that I am a tyrant and that my authority is sufficient to have the school records changed so that they show me as a member of the class of 1922. This would merely record a falsehood, not a fact. The fact that I did not go to the Ecole Polytechnique cannot be changed. The fundamental impossibility of changing the past accounts for those very important moral sentiments—regret and remorse.

The past is the domain of facts over which one has no power, de Jouvenel says. But it is also the domain of knowable facts. "It is not always so easy to determine whether alleged facts are true or false, but we always consider that they are in principle verifiable." The future, by contrast, is the realm of uncertainty. Future events cannot be attested to and verified in the same way as an accomplished fact. (De Jouvenel uses the Latin terms *facta* and *futura*, to contrast past events with possible future events.)

De Jouvenel explains further:

> When I say: "I saw Peter on my way here," I am testifying; but when I say, "I shall see Peter on my way back," I am making a supposition. If we are faced with two conflicting opinions regarding a past event, we try to determine which one is true; if we are faced with two conflicting opinions regarding a future event, we try to determine which one is more plausible.

Strictly speaking, de Jouvenel maintains, we can have positive knowledge only of the past, but the only useful knowledge relates to the future.

> A man wishing to display his practical turn of mind readily says, "I am only interested in facts," although quite the opposite is the case. If his aim is to get to New York, the time at which a plane left yesterday is of small concern to him; what interests him is the take-off time this evening (a *futurum*). Similarly if he wants to see somebody in New York, the fact that this person was in his office yesterday hardly matters to him; what interests him is whether this person will be in his office tomorrow. Our man lives in a world of *futura* rather than a world of *facta*.
>
> The real fact-collector is at the opposite pole from the man of action. One erudite scholar might spend years establishing the facts about the assassination of Louis, duc d'Orleans, in 1407, while another might devote his time to tracing Napoleon's itinerary day-by-day. Here are *facta* that could have no effect on our judgments concerning the future and on our present decisions.

A practical man is interested in facts only so that he can use them in dealing with the future. If he is worried about whether his plane will leave on time, he can be reassured by the knowledge that the flight has left at the appointed time each day for the past month. The only real use of facts, says de Jouvenel, is as raw material out of which the mind can make estimates of the future. The purpose of studying the forecasting process is simply to try to improve a natural activity of the mind.

Man's ability to forecast might be thought to increase with human progress, but the opposite is actually the case, de Jouvenel points out. The future state of a society would be known only in a perfectly static society, whose culture is changeless. In a rapidly changing society, knowledge of the future is inversely proportional to the rate of progress. When social change is accelerating, an increasing number of problems confronts government leaders and other public policy makers. Urgent questions demanding decisions become increasingly frequent and begin to overwhelm the people who are responsible for dealing with them. "It seems natural and even reasonable," says de Jouvenel, "to take the questions in order of urgency, but the results indicate that this is a vicious practice. No problem is put on the agenda until it is a 'burning' issue, when things are at such a pass that our hand is forced. No longer is any choice possible between different actions aimed at shaping a still-flexible situation. There is only one possible response, only one way out of the problem hemming us in."

Faced with a crisis, public leaders bow to necessity and later excuse themselves by saying that they had no choice. "What is actually true is that they *no longer* had a choice, which is something quite different: for if they cannot be blamed for a decision that was in fact inevitable, they can hardly escape censure for letting the situation go until they had no freedom to choose." To keep from becoming a victim of necessity, de Jouvenel stresses, public leaders must identify emerging situations while they are still manageable, before they have developed into crises. "Without forecasting," he warns, "there is no real freedom of decision."

In *The Art of Conjecture,* de Jouvenel develops his concept of *futuribles,* a term he coined for "possible futures." Futuribles are events or situations that might logically develop from the present. In other words, a futurible is a plausible future development based on what one knows about a situation.

To develop and evaluate futuribles, de Jouvenel has proposed the establishment of what he calls a "Surmising Forum" (*un forum previsionnel*) which would provide a means to develop ideas about what may happen in the future. "Since the passage of time brings new situations and new beginnings," de Jouvenel adds, "the forum clearly should be in continuous operation. The future cannot be envisaged once and for all, but rather must be discussed continuously. The Surmising Forum should be conceived as a true institution where very different types of experts will submit specialized forecasts which will be combined into more generalized forecasts."

The Surmising Forum would be a kind of "market place" of ideas to which various speculations about the future could be brought, discussed, and criticized in order to create images of attainable and desirable futures. As a political scientist, de Jouvenel is particularly anxious to revitalize what he calls "government by discussion." In all the countries he is familiar with, the legislature is not the supreme power, with the executive branch merely enforcing the

laws. Instead, long-term policies are worked out in the executive
branch, and the legislative body is called upon to make whatever
rules are needed from time to time to implement the executive's
long-term policies.

De Jouvenel would like to change this situation through his Surmising Forum. Here would be displayed the surmises, or forecasts,
that seem to call for long-term programs. The legislators—and the
general public—would debate the options, and political choices
would be made early enough so that technical details could be
worked out.

Even before *The Art of Conjecture* appeared, de Jouvenel had an
opportunity to create a first approximation of a Surmising Forum.
At a 1958 symposium on the Greek island of Rhodes, de Jouvenel
spoke on the trend toward authoritarian governments among the
world's new nations in Africa and Asia as well as elsewhere. His
remarks caught the attention of a young man who represented the
Ford Foundation, Waldemar Nielsen. Later, without de Jouvenel's
knowledge, Nielsen successfully campaigned within the Ford Foundation to obtain financial support for de Jouvenel.

With Ford money, de Jouvenel launched, in 1960, a project known
as Futuribles. This international venture was governed by a Board
made up of seven scholars. In addition, there was one person officially listed as a collaborator—Daniel Bell, then a professor of sociology at Columbia University. Under de Jouvenel's leadership,
the Futuribles group got experts from a great variety of fields to
speculate about likely social and political changes in the future.
The papers were published from 1961 to 1965 in the *Bulletin* of
the Paris-based Societe d'etudes et documentation economiques,
industrielles et sociales (S.E.D.E.I.S), which de Jouvenel edited.
Some 130 papers were produced before Ford support ended in 1966.

In a 1964 lecture, de Jouvenel explained what he wanted to accomplish through the Futuribles project: "The purpose is to generate a habit, the habit of forward-looking. We feel that as this grows
into a habit, we, or our successors, shall develop in this exercise
greater skill, thanks to self criticism and mutual criticism. At the
outset we encountered in the authors we solicited a great reluctance
to embark upon such speculation. They said it was unscholarly,
which of course it is, but it happens to be necessary. It is unscholarly perforce because there are no *facts* on the future: Cicero quite
rightly contrasted past occurrences and occurrences to come with
the contrasted expressions *facta et futura: facta* what is accomplished and can be taken as solid; *futura* what shall come into being,
and is as yet 'undone,' or fluid. This contrast leads me to assert vigorously: 'there can be no science of the future.' The future is not the
realm of the 'true or false' but the realm of 'possibles.' "

At the outset of the Futuribles project, de Jouvenel did not ask the scholars to use any special method for speculating about the future, partly because it was difficult enough to get scholars to think about the future at all. But as the project progressed, de Jouvenel and others became curious about the methods the scholars were using.

To find out how the scholars were developing their forecasts, de Jouvenel and his colleagues organized a methodological conference in Geneva in June 1962. This was followed by a second conference in Paris in July 1963 and a third at Yale University in December 1964. The conferences led a number of American and European scholars to think about methods of exploring the future. Daniel Bell, for example, produced a memorable essay, "Twelve Modes of Prediction—A Preliminary Sorting of Approaches to the Social Sciences" (*Daedalus*, Summer 1964). Some scholars also launched future-oriented projects of their own. Bell became chairman of the Commission on the Year 2000, sponsored by the American Academy of Arts and Sciences in Boston; Herman Kahn wrote (with his colleague Anthony J. Wiener) *The Year 2000*, and Olaf Helmer, a mathematician, left the Rand Corporation to help set up the Institute for the Future at its first site in Middletown, Connecticut.

A later meeting, held in Paris in April 1965, was not focused on methodology, but brought together about 120 scholars—perhaps the largest assemblage of future-oriented scholars up to that time.

When Ford support for the Futuribles project came to an end, de Jouvenel's wife, Helene, took up the challenge and founded, in 1966, a monthly journal *Analyse & Prevision*, which she edited. The following year, she founded the International Futuribles Association to take the place of the project's Board, which disappeared with the ending of Ford support. "People think that she helped me," de Jouvenel said, many years later. "This is utter nonsense. She did it all by herself, and I was no great help to her. Rather, on some important decisions, my recommendations were erroneous."

Both the journal and the Association went into a brief eclipse when Helene died, but revived in the mid 1970s, thanks to the energetic efforts of the de Jouvenels' son Hugues. Born in Lausanne, Switzerland, on July 2, 1946, Hugues Alain de Jouvenel had trained in law at the University of Paris and worked at the United Nations Institute for Training and Research in New York. He now is serving as executive director and secretary general of the Association, while working on his doctoral dissertation in sociology and philosophy.

In 1975 the younger de Jouvenel started a new journal, *Futuribles: Analyse, Prevision, Prospective*, as a successor to *Analyse & Prevision*. The new journal, a quarterly edited by Hugues himself, emphasizes practical as opposed to theoretical issues and is written in a more popular style than its very scholarly predecessor. The first issue contained articles on a wide variety of subjects—waste, Quebec, Europe, Morocco, and hyper-tankers (super super-tankers)—but the format remains somewhat scholarly and reminiscent of *Analyse & Prevision*.

Based in Paris, the International Futuribles Association now has a specialized library of 2,500 volumes in the futures field, a reference service consisting of some 40,000 index cards relating to various documents, and an international exchange network consisting of more than 300 researchers and institutes throughout the world. The Association organizes "round-table" discussions in Paris on a variety of future-oriented topics, and has branches in Lille and Toulouse.

Bertrand de Jouvenel, who inherited from his father the desire to create a more peaceful and prosperous world, is proud of his son's efforts, which he considers brave "given the condition in which he found Futuribles." But the proud father now tries not to meddle in the Association, saying: "I think a doting father is a very poor advisor."

Retired and living outside Paris at his home in the Oise Department, Bertrand de Jouvenel now writes for his son's journal. In the first issue of the new *Futuribles*, de Jouvenel discusses La Fontaine's fable of the 80-year-old man who was planting a tree. When some young people pointed out that the old man could not possibly live to enjoy the fruit of the full-grown tree, the old man said, "My great nephews will be grateful for the shade." If modern economists were advising the octogenarian, says de Jouvenel, they would suggest that the old man plant a poplar rather than oak, because the poplar could be cut down in 25 years and the lumber sold for profit. Through successive reinvestments his children could become wealthy. But de Jouvenel imagines the old man asking them: "What shade would there be then for those who live here a hundred or more years after we are dead?"

Concern for the welfare of future inhabitants, whoever they may be, is far different from concern about accumulating capital, says de Jouvenel. An oak tree that offers little profit in the short run but will shade people a century hence "bears witness of the efforts and spirit of past generations and is a message of friendship from ancestors who wanted to increase the human heritage. We owe to people who disappeared long ago the lasting beauties that are the source of our present pleasures. I hope that we will do as much for the people who come after us."

Glenn T. Seaborg: Using Science to Create a Better World

"The League of Frightened Men" was the name given to the atomic scientists who developed the bombs dropped on Hiroshima and Nagasaki and then were awestruck at the force they had unleashed.

One of these scientists was Glenn T. Seaborg, a lean, six-foot two-inch chemist, who had participated in the discovery of a new element, plutonium. Seaborg and his colleagues had enjoyed the rare exhilaration that comes from making an epochal scientific discovery, but a mere five years later the element they had discovered was being used to make the most terrifying weapons ever devised.

In the years following World War II, Seaborg remained in the laboratory and, with his fellow workers, discovered one new element after another. In 1952, he won the Nobel Prize, science's top award, for his work.

Despite the terrible way in which atomic power was first demonstrated to the world, Seaborg remained convinced that ultimately it would benefit mankind. Through the years, nothing has shaken that conviction and the energy "crises" of the 1970s—which he had long forecast—have further convinced him that nuclear power may have arrived in the nick of time to help prevent intense world-wide suffering due to lack of energy.

In his book *Man and Atom* (written in collaboration with William R. Corliss), Seaborg says:

> Human civilization is rapidly approaching a series of crises that can be managed only through some radical departures in man's dealings with the relationship between energy and matter. Nuclear energy holds one key—a crucial one—to the successful resolution of these crises. Without it there is no doubt that civilization, as we know it, would slowly grind to a halt. With it not only will we be able to raise a great part of the world's people to a decent standard of living, but we will be able to move all mankind ahead into a new era of human advancement—human advancement which takes place in harmony with the natural environment that must support it.

Seaborg is convinced that atomic energy, along with coal, is an essential component of the solution to the energy problem in the years ahead. Therefore, he says, "we must learn to live with the atom wisely. This means we must recognize, anticipate, and deal with all the environmental aspects and prospects of nuclear energy. I believe we are doing this and doing it well. This type of technological development is something that has never before been attempted in the history of man. No technology has been born and developed with the regard for human safety and well-being that is inherent in the development of nuclear energy."

Seaborg has stated that "the tremendous amount of knowledge we have accumulated over some 20-odd years has made us almost overly conservative in the development of nuclear power."

> I have often thought that if the potential health and safety implications of so many aspects of our lives—our chemical products, our foods, our transportation systems, our athletic, even our sleeping habits to name a few—were so well-known and documented, that we would have a very apprehensive public, one literally afraid to eat or drink or go anywhere or do anything.

Seaborg has vigorously defended the development of atomic energy against those environmentalists who fear that nuclear energy endangers either the natural environment or human health. He strongly supports and devotes much effort to the safeguarding of the natural environment as a member or leader in numerous organizations, including the San Francisco Bay Area's "Citizens for Urban Wilderness Areas," for which he serves as chairman. However, he believes government also has "a responsibility to help our people with power to run a technologically sustained society." In 1969 he delivered a strong warning to Congress.

> In the years ahead, today's outcries about the environment will be nothing compared with cries of angry citizens who find that power failures due to lack of sufficient generating capacity to meet peak loads have plunged them into prolonged blackouts—not mere minutes of inconvenience, but hours perhaps days, when their health and well-being and that of their families may be seriously endangered. The environment of a city whose life's energy has been cut, whose transportation and communications are dead, in which medical and police help cannot be had, and where food spoils and people stifle and shiver while imprisoned in stalls, subways or darkened skyscrapers— all this also represents a dangerous environment that we must anticipate and work to avoid.

Nuclear energy and other peaceful uses of the atom, Seaborg feels, will give man the ability to transform his life—the ability to create a peaceful and prosperous world. Seaborg has traveled in 60 countries of the world to spread that message.

The man behind the energy message was born on April 19, 1912, in the small mining town of Ishpeming, Michigan. His mother was a Swedish woman who had come to the United States in her teens. His father was born in the United States, the son of Swedish parents who emigrated to the United States in the 1860s. (Seaborg still speaks Swedish.) When Glenn Seaborg was 10 years old, the family moved to California and settled in a suburb of Los Angeles. Young

Seaborg mowed lawns and had his own paper route. He had no particular interest in science until Dwight Logan Reid, his science teacher in high school, inspired him with an intense interest in chemistry and physics. Seaborg matriculated at the University of California at Los Angeles in 1929 and at first paid his way with his earnings as a stevedore, apricot picker, assistant in an industrial laboratory, and apprentice linotype machinist. From 1931 to 1934 he worked as an assistant in the chemistry laboratory at UCLA and, encouraged by his professors, decided during his senior year to pursue a career in nuclear chemistry. After getting his bachelor's degree in 1934, he moved to the University of California at Berkeley and held a teaching assistantship while earning his doctorate, in 1937, for a dissertation on the interaction of fast neutrons with lead. By 1939 Seaborg was an instructor in Berkeley's College of Chemistry, continuing his research, mainly on new isotopes of common elements.

In recounting how he came to discover plutonium, Seaborg explains that while he was still a graduate student he began reading the exciting papers coming from scientists in Europe—Enrico Fermi, Emilio Segre, and their co-workers in Rome, and equally fascinating papers by Otto Hahn, Lise Meitner, and Fritz Strassmann in Berlin. "They were studying the interesting radioactivities that were produced when uranium was bombarded with neutrons and which they attributed to isotopes of transuranium elements," Seaborg says. "I remember how I devoured those early papers and how I considered myself something of a minor expert on the 'transuranium elements'." He read and reread every available article on the subject. "I was puzzled by the situation, both intrigued by the concept of the transuranium interpretation of the experimental results and disturbed by the apparent inconsistencies in this interpretation."

During a seminar in 1939, Seaborg and his colleagues got the exciting news that Hahn and Strassmann had performed a "beautiful" experiment demonstrating that atoms can be split. "At first . . . the fission interpretation was greeted with some skepticism by a number of those present," Seaborg recalls, "but, as a chemist with a particular appreciation for Hahn and Strassmann's experiments, I felt that this interpretation just had to be accepted. I remember walking the streets of Berkeley for hours after the seminar in a combined state of exhilaration in appreciation of the beauty of the work and of disgust at my inability to arrive at this interpretation despite my years of contemplation of the subject."

Seaborg's colleague, Edwin McMillan, thought he had detected a new chemical element, element 93, after bombarding uranium with neutrons. Another scientist, Philip Abelson, joined McMillan in the

spring of 1940 and together they were able to chemically separate
and identify element 93. Seaborg lived only a few rooms from Mc-
Millan at the Faculty Club and much of their conversation—whether
in the laboratory, at meals, in the hallway, or even going in and out
of the shower—had something to do with element 93 and the search
for element 94. McMillan left Berkeley to go to MIT to conduct war
research, but Seaborg stayed behind and experimented with the
bombardment of uranium with deuterons (nuclei of an isotope of hydrogen). Eventually he and his colleagues created and identified a
new element with the atomic number 94.

During the complex, time-consuming, arduous, and painstaking
search for element 94, Seaborg and his colleagues maintained a
self-imposed secrecy in view of the potential implications of their
discovery for national security. When they feared they might be
overheard, the group used the code name "Silver" for element 93
and "Copper" for element 94. "This worked just fine," Seaborg later recalled, "until for some reason I cannot recall now, it became
necessary to use real copper in our work. Since we continued to
call element 94 'copper,' on occasion we had to refer to the real thing
as 'honest-to-God-copper'."

On the stormy night of February 23, 1941, in an experiment that
ran well into the next morning, one of Seaborg's associates performed the oxidation that gave the group proof that what they had
made was chemically different from all other known elements. The
experiment took place in room 307 of Gilman Hall, a room that today
is a National Historic Landmark.

The group debated what name the new element should eventually
receive. Since McMillan had named the element 93 neptunium, because Neptune is the next planet after Uranus, which had served as
a basis for the naming of uranium 150 years earlier, the group decided to name element 94 for Pluto, the next planet beyond Neptune.
For a time they debated whether to call the element "plutium" or
"plutonium." They liked the sound of the latter much better and
finally adopted that name and the provocative symbol "Pu."

After the Japanese attack on Pearl Harbor in 1941, Seaborg
moved to the University of Chicago to carry on his plutonium research at the Metallurgical Laboratory, where Manhattan Project
scientists were concentrating on the creation of the atomic bomb.
Seaborg had the task of devising a chemical process for separating
plutonium from uranium and intensely radioactive fission products.
Seaborg planned and put into operation a program of ultra micro-
chemical research, using quantities of plutonium a thousand times
smaller than had previously been considered necessary. He made
these hitherto undreamed-of experiments possible by using the
cyclotron to manufacture plutonium, and in 1942 the first extremely

small fraction of a gram of pure plutonium compound was isolated and weighed. The total scientific effort of Seaborg and his scientific colleagues culminated in the dropping of the atomic bomb on Nagasaki in August 1945. He tried, however, to prevent this use of the atomic weapon as one of seven signers in June 1945 of the Franck Report, which recommended a demonstration test as a deterrent that should make its actual use unnecessary.

While at Chicago in 1944 and 1945, Seaborg helped establish the existence of two new elements—americium (no. 95) and curium (no. 96). He returned to Berkeley in May 1946 to resume his teaching and to direct nuclear chemical research at the Lawrence Radiation Laboratory. Continuing his investigations, he and his colleagues synthesized and identified berkelium (no. 97), californium (no. 98), einsteinium (no. 99), and fermium (no. 100). In 1955 the laboratory announced the discovery of mendelevium (no. 101). By 1975, the Lawrence group was up to element 105. Seaborg however, curtailed his research in 1958 when he was appointed Chancellor of the University of California at Berkeley. During the following three years he presided over what has been described as "possibly the best faculty in the United States." But in 1961 he accepted President Kennedy's call to be the first scientist to head the Atomic Energy Commission. Seaborg served as Chairman of the AEC throughout Lyndon Johnson's presidency and during the first years of Richard Nixon's presidency. He resigned in 1971 to return to the Lawrence Laboratory. He now is University Professor of Chemistry and teaches various courses, including elementary chemistry, at the University of California. He is married to the former Helen Griggs. They have six children.

Seaborg's writings suggest that he has a well-integrated philosophy of life, which might be approximated in two sentences:

1. Man is basically good and will become better (and happier) in the future.

2. Man can improve his lot both through science and technology (including specifically nuclear power) and through international, intercultural cooperation based on mutual love and respect.

Any discussion of Seaborg's philosophy must recognize his tremendous enthusiasm for science. For Seaborg, science is not just an occupation, but a sacred vocation. Science is a mind-expanding force in human society. It enables man to free himself from ignorance and explore the fascinating beauties of the universe. At the same time science enables man to improve his material situation.

> Throughout the ages men, from peasants to kings, have believed and acted on the belief that their material world was like the proverbial pie of a certain size, that it contained just so much and that the more it was divided the less each person received. From this it fol-

lowed that life was a constant struggle to see who could get more at the expense of the others who consequently would get less. If some, through their intelligence, daring, or sheer power, managed to gain a great deal, the share of the others diminished greatly and many suffered.

Today we are still thinking and acting strongly on the basis of this belief, but through modern science and technology I believe we can prove that the belief is no longer totally valid. In a sense the pie can be made continually larger and more satisfying if we who share it would only devote the time and energy we spend disputing over each portion as intelligently, and perhaps fanatically, to the solving of some basic human problems.

To put it a bit more scientifically, although our world is not unlimited in its resources, we have potentially more than enough energy, materials, and space to sustain a population far greater than the number of people on earth today at a living standard at least as high as that enjoyed in most of the developed areas.

Science leads to technology and from technology come diversified sources of energy. Unlike some scholars Seaborg sees energy as basically good, because he believes in man's ability and willingness to use power for good. His special concern, of course, has been nuclear and thermonuclear power. During his chairmanship of the Atomic Energy Commission, especially, Seaborg worked to convince people and governments of the desirability of building more nuclear installations. He believes that nuclear power is essential to supplement and eventually replace disappearing fossil fuels and can be made safe both for people and the natural environment. Uranium and thorium ores can last for decades as fuels and, when thermonuclear power is properly brought under control, man will have enough energy for almost any conceivable use.

Like other atomic scientists, Seaborg dreams of nuplexes (nuclear powered agro-industrial plants). In each nuplex, a nuclear plant would generate electricity and desalt millions of gallons of sea water. The plant would irrigate and fertilize thousands of acres of crop land. Through nuplexes, the peoples of the world could enter a new era of plenty. However, he realizes that, in view of their high capital cost, the present economic situation precludes the early building of such installations. Unlike most scientists, who prefer their laboratories to crowds, Seaborg enthusiastically mingles in groups and participates actively in group activities. He is a member of many associations and boards of directors and deals easily and effectively with people. Part of his success in dealing with people arises from his natural human warmth, but he appears also to want to do everything possible to educate the public in the work that scientists are doing. More than the Nobel Prize, Seaborg takes pride in the Pacific Science Foundation Arches of Science award that he received for his contributions to the public understanding of science. If people understand what science is doing, he feels, they will be able to use science for human betterment.

In his dealings with people, Seaborg constantly promotes consensus and cooperation. This belief in harmonious human relations extends to all mankind. Seaborg believes that man is now experiencing a world-wide trend toward a unified civilization.

The next 30 years, Seaborg believes, will see the world engaged in "what may be the most crucial struggle of mankind's existence—the struggle to prove that one 'mankind' as a physical entity and not just as a glorious idea can be created and can survive."

> I am talking about mankind as a global civilization—men and nations not only co-existing with each other and with nature but essentially living and acting as an organic whole. This is more than a utopian dream. It is the new imperative, the whole toward which we must all move. Though each may phrase it somewhat differently, this seems to be the consensus of most of the thoughtful philosophers, scientists, and educators speaking, writing and thinking today. There seem to be few if any viable alternatives to moving in this direction.

In recent years Seaborg has shown great interest in the possibilities of the future and in developing more effective ways for mankind to improve it. "We have a greater interest in the future today because we realize how much we can do toward directing it—toward building the kind of world we believe we would like to live in or at least turn over to our children," Seaborg has said. "The importance of all the 'future studies' being made today is not in the 'gee whiz' speculation they provide. What I believe we are interested in is the recognition of possible alternative futures so that we can carry out meaningful and rational activities and not merely be swept along in the tide of change. It is particularly important in a democratic society to present alternative futures to the public and to have an enlightened public that can see the importance of supporting certain programs and opposing others."

Seaborg feels that the time has come for "more consensus and commitment toward common goals and common dreams." It is not desirable to have a single master plan for humanity, but we need to establish goals worthy of a massive degree of effort. "If we are to arrive at the year 2000 and view about us a world worth living in and worth turning over to future generations, we must conceive most of that world today and build it with every succeeding tomorrow."

Robert Jungk: The Future-Creating Workshop

While Robert Jungk was in Hiroshima in 1960 making a film about atomic weapons, a bomb victim slowly dying of leukemia told him,

"Now you protest against the bomb, but it's too late. You always begin too late."

Jungk suddenly realized that he had spent his life protesting against things that had already happened. As a journalist he had fought the Nazis for years—after they were already in power. He thought to himself: "We must do something to prevent the crises of tomorrow so that we can avoid disasters. We must mobilize people ahead of time."

Jungk was not certain how to mobilize people ahead of time. But in 1963 he had an idea: It came to him when he was approached by a young Canadian Quaker, Garry Hunnius. Jungk suggested that a Quaker organization might sponsor an exposition portraying a peaceful future world, because a positive vision of the future would help mankind to achieve peace. Peace by itself is simply the absence of war, and does not generally inspire people to make a major effort.

Hunnius took Jungk's suggestion seriously and preparations soon were underway on a project which came to be known as Mankind 2000. The Quakers and others sponsoring the Mankind 2000 project organized a conference that brought together a stellar assemblage of international thinkers to look at the future and the problem of developing a favorable vision of a peaceful world. The conference was jointly sponsored by the Peace Research Institute in Oslo and the Institute for the Future which Jungk had founded in Vienna. Held in Oslo in 1967, the conference was the first of a series of international meetings that brought a wide variety of scholars together to think about the future. The conference also helped put Jungk in the forefront of the world's futurists.

Jungk's journey to futurism started with the circumstances of his birth on May 11, 1913. His parents were an actor and actress, who happened to be Jewish, and Jungk was born in Berlin, then the center of Germany's fledgling film industry. Like many liberal Jews, the Jungks had almost forgotten their Jewishness when Adolf Hitler was named Chancellor of Germany. Suddenly, Jungk's father, Max, could not sell the screen plays he was writing and was being forced out of the theater. By that time, Jungk was studying psychology and philosophy at the University of Berlin in preparation for becoming a psychologist. His studies came to a sudden halt in March 1933 when the police arrested him as suspect in the Reichstag fire. The arrest occurred on a day when Jungk had gone to classes as usual, and found the University buzzing with talk of the Reichstag fire the previous night. Nazi students had posted their party paper's article blaming the Communists for the fire on all the campus bulletin boards, not just their own. Outraged at this breach of the University rules, Jungk ripped down all the sheets and pinned them on the Nazis' bulletin board. A little while later he was under arrest and being questioned at the police station. When his pockets were emptied police found a box of matches. Jungk did not smoke, but had bought the matches from a street beggar as an act of charity. The Berlin police felt the matches were grounds enough for holding him long hours before eventually releasing him to his parents. Jungk feels he was most fortunate that the police kept him instead of turning him over to the SS, who might have killed him. The family decided that Jungk had better leave the country until things calmed down, so he joined a ski party to the Austrian Tyrol and made it safely across the frontier. During the next few months it became clear that Hitler was growing stronger, so Jungk moved to Paris to continue his studies. While in Paris he tried to help his parents financially by writing short stories and also spent time helping refugee directors. In 1935 Jungk returned illegally to Berlin where he lived with his parents for more than a year until some of the articles he was writing under an assumed name for the German resistance attracted the Gestapo's attention. Jungk fled on skis across the Czech border. In Prague he founded a commercial feature service called Mondial Press and wrote anti-Nazi articles for newspapers in central Europe. He brought his mother to live with him in Prague but his father remained in Germany, dying there in 1938. As the Germans advanced across Europe, Jungk relocated his operations first in Paris and later in Zurich. In 1943 the Nazis discovered who was behind all the pseudonyms and pressured the Swiss government to clamp down on Jungk. Charged with endangering Swiss neutrality, Jungk was given the choice of an indefinite jail term or leaving the country. He chose imprisonment. During his eight-month stay in jail, Jungk wrote his doctoral thesis. He had assembled all the material for his thesis but had never had the time to write it until he landed in jail. The subject of the thesis was, under the circumstances, ironic: the evolution of freedom of the press in Switzerland from 1823 to 1830.

When the war turned against the Third Reich, the Swiss released Jungk and for the first time he could use his real name. He traveled all over Europe covering such stories as the first United Nations conference in London and the Nuremburg trials. In 1946 he went to the United States as Washington correspondent for 10 Swiss and Austrian newspapers. In New York he met Ruth Suschnitcky and soon married her. She did not like Washington's climate and convinced Jungk to change his beat to Los Angeles. From Hollywood, Jungk wrote less about screen stars than about the growth of the aerospace industry and armament centers, the atomic cities in New Mexico, and the uranium hunters in Colorado. At Ruth's urging he wrote an outline of a screen play and sold it for $9,000.

Jungk's experiences in America led to a book entitled *The Fu-*

ture Has Already Begun: America's Omnipotence and Impotence.
Published in Germany in 1952, the book became a best seller and
made Jungk a celebrity. The book offered a critical look at technological progress which seemed to be hurtling forward blindly, dehu-
manizing everyone and everything. (The book was published later
in English as *Tomorrow Is Already Here: Scenes From a Man-Made
World.)*

Jungk's next book dealt with atomic energy. *Brighter than a
Thousand Suns* reported on the discoveries in nuclear energy that
led to the atomic bomb. Jungk later traveled across the Pacific to
Hiroshima and spent months interviewing survivors of the atomic
blasts and their neighbors, friends and children. The result, *Children of the Ashes: The Story of a Rebirth*, appeared in 1960. The
book was a big success, and was translated into 22 languages. All
the Communist nations published it.

When Jungk returned to Hiroshima in 1960 to make a television
documentary on the bomb's long-term victims, he met the bomb victim whose words did so much to turn him toward futurism. "I clearly remember the old man," says Jungk. "He probably wasn't over 50
but he looked 80." In a very quiet voice, the old man said: "How
could all those intelligent people have dropped this bomb without
thinking of the consequences?"

The old man's words haunted Jungk. He began to think about how
one could prevent crises. Returning to Europe he established an Institute for the Future (Institut fur Zukunftsfragen) in Vienna and
soon was involved in creating a plan for a European "look-out" institution under the auspices of the Council of Europe at Strasbourg. In
his first draft of the proposal, completed in April 1967, he declared:

> The need for the proposed institution was brought about by the un-
> precedented acceleration of change, which has become one of the main
> characteristics of our age, and even more by the sudden jump of incis-
> ive, even shattering power inherent in modern technology, which
> makes it imperative for human society to gauge and control the new
> forces.
> Fortunately, the ability to forecast and to anticipate future devel-
> opments has been dramatically improved in recent years. The ever-
> increasing stream of fresh data informing man not only about the
> present state of the world, but also about the impact of his actions is
> one of the least acknowledged and most hopeful post-war develop-
> ments.

Jungk suggested that a serious "forecasting gap" might be a
deeper reason for the much-discussed "technologic gap" separating
the United States and Europe. "It is therefore high time that not
only European industrial concerns but also the national and interna-

tional concerns of Europe devote more attention to the forecasting of long-range possibilities, dangers, and opportunities."

Jungk left Austria in 1968 to return to his native Berlin as a professor at the Technical University of Berlin. There he lectured on technological forecasting and the comparative methodology of futures research. He also held seminars, at the Free University of Berlin, on social imagination and the impact of politics on technology. Though teaching in Berlin, Jungk set up a permanent headquarters in Salzburg where he and his wife still maintain an apartment crammed with papers and books. Besides his trips to teach in Berlin, Jungk spends much time roaming the globe. In a letter to a friend in 1967, he wrote that he was "a bit torn between my curiosity, which makes me run from conference to conference, and my desire to sit down and think and write."

His 1968 book, *The Big Machine*, described the European synchrotron at the CERN laboratory located on the Swiss border just outside Geneva. CERN, which stands for Conseil Europeen pour la Recherche Nucleaire, is a consortium of 13 European nations which share the cost of the laboratory. The motive for establishing the CERN laboratory was the feeling that if European scientists were to maintain their front rank position in the rapidly expanding new research field of high energy particle physics they would have to construct the "big machine." Jungk was impressed by the unique atmosphere of the international laboratory. He had expected to find this newest example of "big science" infested with national rivalries and bureaucratic regulations. Instead he found freedom of access, open discussion, and a casual atmosphere.

In 1973 Jungk published a German-language book called *Der Jahrtausend Mensch* [Millennial Man] in which he argues that scientific and technical research has created a crisis which will become deeper between now and the year 2000. Only a changed human being can prevent this development from ending in catastrophe.

Jungk hopes to get the general public to participate in the exploration of the future. Unless this is done, he fears, militarists and big businessmen may create a tomorrow that will be as unpleasant as what befell the inhabitants of Hiroshima. At present, military establishments and large business firms dominate research on the future because of its high cost. "This is creating a dangerous monopoly. Those of us working on a smaller scale do not realize how handicapped we are in trying to debate with these powerful groups." Jungk believes that the study of the future could be democratized by establishing independent look-out groups sponsored by organizations such as trade unions, which can afford to do it, or by independent services within universities or by departments within parliaments. "These services could then be consulted by every group in society, either free or for a relatively modest fee. They might not be sufficiently objective at the start but they could be one step in the direction of a more equitable distribution of power."

Jungk fears that experts in the future may join forces with governments or industries both in the East and West to divide up the power. In Jungk's words: "I fear a sort of alliance, a combination of experts in futurology with governments or managers of governments and industry both in the East and West—a sort of plot involving both the experts in the future and those in power. Dividing up this power—and they have the technical means to do so—they will seize possession of the future and perhaps close it to others. In the three conferences that I have organized to found small groups of informed citizens, I have said: 'If you leave the future to the big "think factories" they are the ones who will make the future and not you.' "

Jungk says that the Western world is now experiencing what he calls a "participation crisis."

"The division between those who eat and those who are hungry has always existed," he said. "But a new division is emerging: a division between those who do interesting work which is non-routine and others who are not informed and who can never make decisions, influence the course of things, or create. These people form a new class of poor people. They are condemned to be toys, or copiers. This causes a deep malaise, which has nothing to do with economic demands. A human being is basically a creative being, yet most people are increasingly dependent and manipulated. Therefore they justly demand that those who have intellectual power or information address the problems that they experience. If not, the 'new poor' is in danger of abdicating or expressing itself only through violence."

In addition to his deep conviction that ordinary citizens must be involved in planning the future, Jungk is also very interested in using their imagination to develop new "social inventions." To do this he has organized a number of "future-creating workshops." In these workshops the participants generally sit around informally and try developing new ideas about a better world in the future. Jungk is eager to encourage people to think about the desirable future and not just the probable or possible future. To develop people capable of using their imagination to create visions of a better world, Jungk suggests introducing into meetings of social planners more of the people who have traditionally been creative—artists, poets, and writers. "They might help to supply the imaginative quality that is now lacking in almost all social planning," he says. Jungk believes that the future-creating workshops constitute a new method of revolting against the establishment. The old way of making revolutions—with brickbats, bombs, and barricades—is likely to destroy more than it creates. "Our industrial civilization has become too vulnerable and puts us all in the same boat. We must invent new forms of revolution."

Though he worries about the problems of the future, Jungk exudes optimism as well as energy and friendliness.

"I believe that there is no problem in the world that is hopeless. If you combine anticipation with imagination and if you don't attack the thing frontally but ecologically, you should be able to devise a possible solution. We must rehabilitate public understanding and appreciation of the visionary. We ought to give him back the prestige and importance he had in classical and ancient times."

Arthur C. Clarke: The Father of the Communications Satellite

In 1945 a young Royal Air Force radar officer had a flash of inspiration: He suddenly saw how it would be possible to relay radio and TV waves around the world.

Broadcasters had long been frustrated because radio waves travel in a straight line and therefore do not reach distant points on the curved earth. The young Briton, Arthur C. (for Charles) Clarke, realized that three satellites could be placed in orbit 22,300 miles above the earth's equator so that broadcast signals could be beamed from them to receivers almost anywhere on the globe. Clarke detailed his idea in the British journal *Wireless World*. Three decades later the communications satellite that he imagined had become a major link among the nations of the world.

Today Clarke is best known as a science-fiction writer, whose 50 books have sold more than 20 million copies in 30 languages, but he still views the communications satellite as "the most important idea of my life."

"Had I realized how quickly it would materialize I might have patented it," he says with dry humor. "Of course, I had the idea before I saw commercial TV!"

Clarke still speaks with the accent of England's "West Country" where he was born in 1917 in the coastal town of Minehead, Somerset. Clarke spent his childhood on his parents' farm, but his mind was soon climbing the skies. At 13, he made his first telescope from an old lens and cardboard tube. "Before long, I knew the lunar landscape much better than my native Somerset," he says.

"Throughout my teens, while my widowed mother was struggling to make a living from our small farm, I spent my time building scientific gadgets. The most ambitious was a photophone transmitter made from a bicycle lamp, which could send speech for several yards along a light-beam. I also attempted the audio-modulation of sun-

light by purely mechanical means and a device based on this principle has now been developed for space communications.

When he was 14 he saw his first copies of *Amazing Stories* and
Astounding Stories, two science-fiction magazines. "At once my life
was transformed, and for years I collected every science-fiction
magazine I could lay my hands upon."

At 19 Clarke passed the Civil Service Executive examination and
moved to London, where he began working for His Majesty's Ex-
chequer and Audit Department. In his off hours, he pursued his
interest in space and joined 12 other enthusiasts in the British Interplanetary Society, a group which met in London pubs in the
years before World War II. The Society was one of the few groups
then advocating research aimed at space flight; members were
viewed as harmless cranks.

In 1941 Clarke joined the Royal Air Force as a radar instructor,
later becoming a flight lieutenant. While in the RAF he published
several articles on electronics and sold his first science-fiction stories. After the war, he attended Kings College at the University of
London on an ex-serviceman's grant and earned a bachelor of science degree in two years with honors in physics and mathematics.
After he had completed only one term of graduate studies in astron-
omy and mathematics, he became Assistant Editor of the journal
Science Abstracts. Clarke held the position for two years, and found
it fascinating. Science journals in many languages from around the
world arrived on his desk. "It was a job which suited me perfectly,"
he says, "but in two years my books and articles had started to sell.
My part-time income was higher than my full-time. I resigned and
that was it."

Clarke published his first book, *Interplanetary Flight*, a non-fiction discussion of astronautics, in 1950. The following year his second volume, *The Exploration of Space*, became a Book-of-the-Month
Club selection. His first science-fiction novel, *Prelude to Space*,
appeared in 1952, and the following year he had critics raving with
a new novel called *Childhood's End*.

"In *Childhood's End*," said a reviewer in *The New York Times*,
"Arthur Clarke joins Olaf Stapledon, C.S. Lewis, and probably one
should add H.G. Wells, in the very small group of writers who have
used science fiction as the vehicle of philosophic ideas. Having said
that, one must hastily add that it is as readable a book, from the
point of view of pure narrative, as you are likely to find among today's straight novels."

Childhood's End, still regarded as one of Clarke's best science-
fiction novels, describes a time when a group of "overlords" have
taken control of the earth and created a sort of utopia where there
are no wars and everybody has enough to eat. Eventually, it is re-

vealed that the Overlords themselves are under the command of a mysterious Overmind whose purposes are obscure.

Throughout the 1950s and early 1960s, Clarke continued to write prolifically both fiction and non-fiction. For futurists, his best-known book is the non-fiction volume, *Profiles of the Future: An Inquiry into the Limits of the Possible.*

Clarke set out in *Profiles of the Future* to try to define the boundaries within which possible futures must lie. "If we regard the ages which stretch ahead of us as an unmapped and unexplored country, what I am attempting to do is survey its frontiers and to get some idea of its extent," he says. "The detailed geography of the interior must remain unknown—until we reach it." If the book seems completely reasonable and the extrapolations convincing, Clarke adds, "I will not have succeeded in looking very far ahead; for the one fact about the future of which we can be certain is that it will be utterly fantastic."

Scientists, Clarke stresses, make rather poor prophets, even in their own specialties.

> Time and again, distinguished astronomers and physicists have made fools of themselves by declaring publicly that such-and-such a project was impossible . . . and have been proved utterly wrong, sometimes while the ink was scarcely dry from their pens. On careful analysis, it appears that these debacles fall into two classes, which I will call 'failures of nerve' and 'failures of imagination.'
>
> The failure of nerve seems to be the more common: It occurs when even *given all the relevant facts* the would-be prophet cannot see that they point to an inescapable conclusion . . . 'they said it couldn't be done' is a phrase that occurs throughout the history of invention . . . .
>
> It is now impossible for us to recall the mental climate which existed when the first locomotives were being built, and critics gravely asserted that suffocation lay in wait for anyone who reached the awful speed of 30 miles an hour. It is equally difficult to believe that, only 80 years ago, the idea of the domestic electric light was pooh-poohed by all the 'experts'—with the exception of a 31-year-old American inventor named Thomas Alva Edison.

The most distinguished turn-of-the-century scientists argued that aviation was an impossibility, Clarke continues gleefully. Astronomer Simon Newcomb even "proved" it—just a few months before the Wright brothers flew at Kitty Hawk. Lord Rutherford, the distinguished atomic scientist, "frequently made fun of those sensation mongers who predicted that we would one day be able to harness the energy locked up in matter." Britain's Astronomer Royal, Richard van Der Riet Wooley, declared that "space travel is utter bilge" in 1956, one year before the first sputnik.

The best forecaster, Clarke suggests, is not the man who knows the most about a subject, but the person who combines "sound scientific knowledge—or at least the *feel* for science—with a really flexible imagination." Flexing his own imagination, Clarke foresees all kinds of possibilities, such as communicating with distant civilizations, but he also indicates what appear to him to be impossibilities, such as traveling to the center of the earth. Just what the future will bring remains unknown, but Clarke is certain the future will be fantastic.

In the mid 1950s, Clarke was "badly bitten by the skin-diving virus," and now is almost as fascinated by the sea as by space. In 1956 he moved to Colombo, Ceylon (now Sri Lanka), which he found to be "a lovely country, good skin diving, no television or other distractions." He now lives in a large house in Cinnamon Gardens, a fashionable section of Colombo.

From 1964 to 1967 he collaborated with film producer Stanley Kubrick on the script for the science-fiction film *2001: A Space Odyssey.* To insure scientific and technical accuracy for the film (which had its germ in a Clarke story called "The Sentinel"), Clarke and Kubrick consulted more than 40 top industrial and scientific firms and NASA experts. Before filming began, 36 technical designers from 12 countries worked for months on sets and props.

Since the release of the film, Clarke has continued to write and to lecture. Recent publications have included *The Lost Worlds of 2001* (1972), *The Wind from the Sun* (1972), *Rendezvous with Rama* (1973), and *Imperial Earth* (1975).

Clarke's personal life has included a marriage and a terrifying experience with paralysis. In 1953 he married Marilyn Mayfield of Jacksonville, Florida, but the marriage ended in divorce in 1964 and Clarke says: "No, I won't marry again. That's very definite." In 1962 he hit his head on a doorway at the height of a polio epidemic and became paralyzed, though physicians still are not sure why. "Over the next two or three years, I slowly recovered from an initial state of complete paralysis and am no longer seriously handicapped. I recommend the experience to anyone who has come to take his body for granted."

Friends describe Clarke as very friendly and generous but somewhat dreamy. "His head," says old friend A.V. Cleaver, "is in the clouds, or should I say it's really in outer space or even probably under water." Clarke himself says that he used to suffer from vanity before World War II and his nickname was "Ego." But he adds, "now that I've got over my self-conceit, I'm one of the nicest guys I know."

In 1975 Clarke proudly showed friends photographs of his latest acquisition: a receiving station that the Indian Government had given him so that he could tune in to NASA's new communications satellite, ATS 6. He believes that the eventual impact of the communications satellite upon the whole human race will be "at least as great as that of the telephone upon the so-called developed societies," and will lead to a United States of Earth.

"We are now about to witness an interesting situation in which many countries, particularly in Asia and Africa, are going to leapfrog a whole era of communications technology and go straight into the space age," Clarke declared at a 1971 ceremony of the International Telecommunications Satellite Corporation (INTELSAT) in Washington. "They will never know the vast networks of cables and microwave links that this continent has built at such enormous cost both in money and in natural resources. The satellites can do far more and at far less expense to the environment."

In a village of the underdeveloped world, an antenna to capture broadcasts can be erected simply and cheaply. Only one antenna per village is needed to start a social and economic revolution, Clarke says, and the cost would be only about $1 per person per year. "The engineering problems of bringing education, literacy, improved hygiene, and agricultural techniques to every human being on this planet have now been solved."

Willis W. Harman: The Coming Transformation

As a young officer in the U.S. Navy, Willis W. Harman came ashore on a Pacific Island and found the beach incredibly beautiful. He cabled his new bride to come join him as soon as possible, and hang the expense. She did, and for three months they lived an idyllic existence, in a large house with two other young naval couples. And then the idyll came to a sudden end, because Harman and his wife were living in the Manoa Valley near Pearl Harbor, and the date was December 7, 1941.

"The morning of December 7, I was ashore, home in bed," Harman recalls. "We heard the planes come over and some explosions, and turned on the radio. As soon as we grasped the news we rushed out to Pearl. We couldn't see the *Maryland* (Harman's ship) because of all the smoke, and when we got there the *Oklahoma* was already capsized alongside, the *West Virginia* was sunk astern, and the *California* was immobilized just ahead of us. We were still afloat, but couldn't move. It was two days before we could get out and move across the harbor to the Navy Yard for preliminary patching up. We had only a couple of bomb hits, having been well protected by the other sunken ships around us."

Harman's dramatic experience at Pearl Harbor may have conditioned him to think about the sudden developments that can change a person's life overnight. In any event, he has become one of the futurists who believes most strongly that the future cannot be forecast simply by projecting past trends. His rude awakening at Pearl

Harbor may be likened to the drastic changes that he believes western culture faces in the years ahead.

Harman was born in Seattle, Washington, on August 16, 1918. His father was an electrical engineer who worked most of his life at a hydroelectric plant on the Cedar River in Washington's Cascade Range. His mother was a piano and organ teacher who ran a musical kindergarten before she married. He got his early education in a two-room schoolhouse, which had a total of 30 students; Harman's own grade had six to eight children and was the largest in the school's history. He went on to a secondary school which had 96 students, then to Western Washington College of Education and later the University of Washington, where he received a degree in electrical engineering in 1939. After college he worked for the General Electric Company before going on active duty as an Electrical Officer in the U.S. Navy. In January 1941, he received orders to join the U.S.S. *Maryland* on the West Coast. "I telephoned Charlene Reamer, an Indiana girl living in Connecticut, whom I had been dating, and proposed marriage. Two days later we were married in her sister's home in Schenectady and headed west in my model A Ford. We caught up with the ship in Long Beach and shortly after that the ship sailed for Pearl Harbor. Charlene went north to North Bend, Washington, to stay with my folks."

After the war, Harman taught electrical engineering at Stanford University and then at the University of Florida. He returned to Stanford in 1952 and has been a professor there ever since, although he has become increasingly involved in his work at the Stanford Research Institute rather than the University. He might have remained an "ordinary" professor of engineering if it hadn't been for an experience in 1954: "I was beguiled into attending a two-week summer seminar on some of the profound questions of life. I didn't know it at the time, but I now recognize that this seminar was a forerunner of what later on was called sensitivity training or encounter groups or growth groups. Anyway, it had a hell of an impact. I had been quite remote from my feelings for many years, and this intense experience opened up vast areas I didn't even know were there. It completely changed my concept of what is important in education, and in time led to various activities in the field of humanistic psychology.

"We are quite tolerant, in our culture, of persons going through the metamorphosis called adolescence. Bizarre behavior, confusion, erratic floundering around, are all tolerated. There is no such tolerance for persons who are undergoing a sort of 'second adolescence' in mid-life—at least there wasn't in the mid-Fifties. I was fortunate in that my department head and Dean were unusually tolerant as I spent great amounts of time, after returning from the seminar, reading and exploring in areas like gestalt psychology, group therapy, Jungian psychology, psychotherapy, religious philosophy, and mysticism. I started a seminar, for graduate students across the University, called 'The Human Potentiality'—a fresh phrase at the time, but somewhat overused recently. This centered around the questions: What is the highest potentiality of man? What does the question mean? What can be found out about it and how? How can the potentialities be actualized?"

In 1956 Harman encountered a group of scientists and others— the best known of whom were Aldous Huxley, John Smythies, and Gerald Heard—who were engaged in an audacious plan: They were convinced that man now has the tools, including biofeedback and psychedelic chemicals particularly, to carry out a systematic exploration of human subjective experience, diverse states of consciousness, and hence to learn more about the deepest value commitments which have guided the lasting human cultures. "This knowledge," says Harman, "is particularly important to our modern industrial society which, in its overfascination with 'controlling' nature and replacing the natural order with a technical order, lost touch with the root experiences on which the basic Judeo-Christian values had been based. Thus the plan of this group was not only to explore and order the knowledge gained but to offer to world leaders the opportunity to conduct such explorations themselves and use the knowledge so gained in this intellectual and political work. Various members of the United Nations and national governments did indeed participate and the activities had some influence. However, in 1961 Timothy Leary came along with a different idea—distribute psychedelic chemicals widely throughout the younger population and change the world faster. By the mid-Sixties our more conservative approach had pretty much disappeared from the scene and the action had shifted, very conspicuously, to the campuses."

Harman's close association with the Stanford Research Institute began with the idea that systems analysis techniques developed from defense work could be applied to social problems, but it became apparent very soon that this idea was very simplistic and wasn't going to work at all. On the other hand, the holistic alternative futures approach looked more and more promising.

Harman and his associate, William Linvill, learned that the U.S. Office of Education was planning to fund educational policy research with a strong emphasis on alternative futures. They received a contract in 1967, and Harman plunged whole-heartedly into research aimed at identifying the possible future directions of U.S. society. As Harman saw it, society's big task in the 1954-65 period was to restore the balance between the exploitation of outer, objective, technology-oriented knowledge and the neglect of inner, subjective knowledge. But after he got into futures research in 1966, "the picture of our acute transformational crisis began to build up, and the central task seemed more to be sounding the alarm about the fundamental nature of societal problems."

During the late 1960s when Harman and his colleagues were working for the Office of Education, the main projects were (1) a major effort to develop a systematic approach for generating alternative future histories which would highlight the nonquantifiables of particular relevance to educational policy, and (2) various auxiliary analyses to add some flesh to this skeleton. After 1970, however, Harman and his associates largely abandoned that approach, partly because of personnel changes at the Office of Education. Instead of the broad exploration of the future of the United States, Harman's group turned to producing largely statistically-based analyses of specific policy issues, usually relating directly to pending legislation.

"Since the Office of Education was no longer interested in the broader futures work, we expanded the field of policy issues and sought new clients and new funding. Our plans were ambitious. Charles W. Williams, Jr. (formerly Staff Director of the White House's National Goals Research Staff) joined us and we set up a Washington group in the Stanford Research office in Rosslyn, Virginia. We expected to have a core activity doing the broad futures work, and, surrounding this, supporting it and being served by it, a number of different applied policy analysis activities in different areas (e.g., welfare and employment, energy, resources and environment, corporate planning). We tried to do too much, overextended ourselves, and in a very painful process had to shrink back to our present very modest level of activity."

Despite funding problems, Harman has steadily developed his own distinctive perspective on the future. One salient characteristic of his thinking is his belief that western society will undergo a pervasive transformation in the years ahead, because the industrial era "paradigm"—the underlying orientation of our culture—is leading to critical problems that cannot be solved within the framework of the paradigm itself. For example, certain "failures" have resulted from the successes of industrialism: e.g., prolonging the human life span has led to overpopulation; efficient production systems have "dehumanized" work, etc.

In developing a variety of "future histories" for American society, Harman found very few which manage to avoid a time of serious troubles between now and 2050. "The small number of desirable paths to the future—desirable in the sense of leading toward the national goals implicit in the nation's founding documents—appear to require a drastic and prompt shift in the operative values of the society and a corresponding change in its institutions."

The dilemmas of industrial civilization constitute what Harman and his colleagues have come to term the "world macroproblem." This macroproblem results from the *micro*decisions of individuals, corporations, government agencies, and others, which add up to form unwanted macrodecisions. For example, the decision of millions of individuals to use aerosols may result in a weakening of the ozone layer in the atmosphere which protects human beings from cosmic rays, and thus greatly harms the health of human beings everywhere. As a result of the growing number of problems that frustrate human desires, the basic goals and institutions of the industrial system are now being challenged. Harman believes that there now are signs of a very profound transformation of western society —"a conceptual revolution as thoroughgoing in its effects as the Copernican revolution and an institutional revolution as profound as the Industrial Revolution."

Harman suggests that post-transformation society might resemble the orientation described by Aldous Huxley in *The Perennial Philosophy* (1945). Huxley defined the perennial philosophy as: "the metaphysic that recognizes a divine Reality substantial to the world of things and lives and minds; the psychology that finds in the soul something similar to, or even identical with, divine Reality; the ethic that places man's final end in the knowledge of the immanent and transcendent Ground of all being."

The post-transformation society may espouse a pair of complementary ethics which, Harman feels, are most congenial to the transformation necessary to resolve the contemporary societal dilemmas. One is an "ecological ethic" which recognizes the limited nature of available resources and sees man as an integral part of the natural world. The other is a "self-realization ethic," which asserts that the proper end of all individual experience is the further evolutionary development of the emergent self and of the human species, and that the appropriate function of all social institutions is to create an environment which will foster that process. "The two ethics, one emphasizing the total community of man-in-nature and the oneness of the human race, and the other placing the highest value on the development of selfhood, are complementary, not contradictory. Together they encourage both cooperation and wholesome competition, both love and individuality. Each is a corrective against the excesses and misapplications of the other."

Harman believes that the main strength of his approach lies in its whole-system emphasis, which "results in the raising of questions that are less likely to come to the fore with some of the other futures methodologies." His approach is also unusual in its emphasis

on unconscious processes. "We have recently, since Freud, learned
to deal with the powerful influence that unconscious processes have
in the life of an individual. I think that the next really great advance
in thinking about how the societal organism chooses among its alternative futures will involve appreciation of the powerful role played
by unconscious processes and understanding of both how these contribute to thwarting rational planning and how their creative side
can be employed to lead us toward a fully humane society."

Daniel Bell: The Post-Industrial Society

During the past 100 years, the United States has changed from an
agricultural society to an industrial society. Today, the nation is
moving beyond industrialism and becoming what sociologist Daniel
Bell calls a "post-industrial society." Famed as an explorer of the
transformation of U.S. society, Bell has outlined his views in a 507-
page tome entitled *The Coming of Post-Industrial Society.*

The dramatic social change that Bell outlines can be seen in a few
simple statistics: In 1790, 90% of the U.S. workforce was employed
in agriculture; today agriculture comprises only 4% of the workforce. During the 19th century, the percentage of workers employed
in manufacturing rose quite steadily, but in recent years the percentage of workers in manufacturing has dropped as factories have
automated their production. Between 1947 and 1968, for example,
the percentage dropped from 30% to 25%, and the Bureau of Labor
Statistics has projected that by 1980 the percentage will decline to
about 22.4%.

Where has the work force been going? Into services—education,
medicine, insurance, banking, hotels and restaurants, etc. Every
society has a component of services: In pre-industrial society, it is
household help; in industrial society, it is utilities, transport, and finance; in post-industrial society, it is human services and professional services. Today the U.S. employs more than 65% of its labor
force in services. And during the next 20 to 30 years the changes
that have occurred in the U.S. economy may be replicated in many
Western European nations.

Bell is not ready to call the U.S. a service society, nor to use such
terms as "knowledge society," "information society," or "professional society." The terms are somewhat apt, in describing salient
aspects of what is emerging, but Bell feels it is safer to say simply
that the U.S. now has entered a post-industrial period. But he suggests that whereas the landowner and the soldier were dominant
figures in pre-industrial civilization, and the businessman in industrial society, the post-industrial society is dominated by scientists and researchers. In the move from an industrial to a post-in-

dustrial society, the locus of power shifts from the business firm to the university and research institute.

Bell was born on Manhattan's Lower East Side on May 10, 1919. His parents were Polish Jewish garment workers and until the age of six he spoke only Yiddish. By the time he was 13, however, he had little difficulty with English, and was reading Karl Marx and John Stuart Mill and expounding on their views for Norman Thomas, then leader of the Socialist Party and perennial candidate for President of the United States. At 16 Bell graduated from high school and at 19 from the City College of New York where he specialized in ancient history and sociology. The year of Bell's graduation was 1938, when the U.S. was near the depths of the Great Depression, and Bell gravitated toward the anti-communist left. Vitally interested in socialist ideals, he joined the Young People's Socialist League, but even then was critical of the ideological dogma that he found.

By 1940, Bell had completed most of his graduate course work in sociology at Columbia University and was writing regularly for the liberal weekly *The New Leader.* After four years of editorial experience, including a brief stint as editor of the journal *Common Sense,* he decided to return to an academic environment. In 1945 he went to the University of Chicago to teach social science for three intellectually productive years. In 1948 he so impressed the editors of *Fortune* with a memorandum on labor-management relations that he became the magazine's labor editor. For the next decade, he wrote a monthly column for *Fortune* and edited social science articles, but he maintained his association with the academic community as a part-time lecturer in sociology at Columbia from 1952 to 1956. In 1956 *Fortune* gave Bell a 15-month leave of absence to go to Paris as the Director of the Congress for Cultural Freedom, a project supported by the Ford Foundation. A year after returning to America, he resigned from *Fortune* to spend a year as a fellow at Stanford University's Center for Advanced Studies in the Behavioral Sciences. In 1959 he returned to Columbia as an associate professor of sociology.

Bell's reputation as an original social thinker began with the publication in 1960 of *The End of Ideology,* a collection of 16 essays he had written over the preceding decade. Now considered a classic in modern thought, *The End of Ideology* argues that Western society has passed through its ideological phase, and has outgrown the need for simple rubrics to describe and justify public conduct. Ideologies, Bell suggests, offer attractive but often unworkable solutions for human problems.

The End of Ideology won high praise from reviewers like political scientist Andrew Hacker, who said Bell "clearly ranks among the outstanding essayists of our generation. As a journalist-turned-professor his style and intelligence combine the best of both worlds." On the substance of Bell's thesis, Hacker added: "There is a sense of relief in being able to discuss Medicare or civil rights or the anti-trust laws without having to cope with the specter of Socialism, Wall Street, or Mongrelization. Not only have intellectuals and politicians thrown aside the prisms that once clouded their eyes, but the general public too is increasingly suspicious of catchalls and catchphrases."

Bell joined in founding a new quarterly journal that would provide insightful analysis of public issues. *The Public Interest*, which began appearing in 1965, sought to discuss domestic social issues in nonideological ways and was dedicated not to politicians but to the administrators who are concerned with housing, welfare, science, etc. Bell served 10 years as editor of *The Public Interest* and now is chairman of its publication committee.

In addition to insightful analysis, the creation of a better world required the anticipation of future developments. Bell's interest in forecasting found expression at least as early as 1964 when he published an essay entitled "Twelve Modes of Prediction." Here he systematically defined the modes in which forecasters can operate. Among the 12 modes he suggested are trends and extrapolation, structural certainties, prime movers, alternative futures or scenarios, etc.

Bell's essay appeared in *Daedalus*, a journal published by the American Academy of Arts and Sciences in Boston. A year later, in 1965, the Academy named Bell to be Chairman of a Commission on the Year 2000. Bell accepted the task in part because "I was appalled by the fact that the Kennedy and Johnson Administrations had 'discovered' the problems of poverty, education, urban renewal, and pollution as if they were completely new. The real need in American society, as I saw it, was for some systematic efforts to anticipate social problems, to design new institutions, and to propose alternative programs for choice."

Bell hoped that the commission would begin the design of alternative solutions "so that our society has more options and can make a moral choice rather than be constrained, as is so often the case when problems descend upon us unnoticed and demand an immediate response."

The commission, whose members ranged from physicist Herman Kahn to urbanist Daniel P. Moynihan, held plenary sessions in 1965 and 1966 before breaking up into smaller groups to look at specific aspects of the future. The plenary sessions resulted in a volume, edited by Bell, of reports and papers. The volume was published as the Summer 1967 issue of *Daedalus* under the title *Toward the Year 2000*.

The commission's final report, originally scheduled for 1972, has been long delayed because the very busy members have found it difficult to find time to write their papers. But one working group, headed by urban planner Harvey S. Perloff of the University of California at Los Angeles, produced a thick report on *The Future of the U.S. Government.* In an introduction to the volume (edited by Perloff), Chairman Bell said that the United States is experiencing three structural changes of overarching importance. These three changes—going back 30 years and forward another 30—include not only the creation of the post-industrial society but also the creation of a national society and a communal society. Though the U.S. has long been a "nation" in that it had a national identity and a national symbolism, the country has only in the past 30 years become a national society in the sense that changes taking place in one section of the society have an immediate effect in all others. The development of a national society stems from the revolution in communications and transportation—the rise of national newsweeklies, jet transport across the country in five hours, etc.

The emergence of a national society has led to three broad problems:

1. Social problems are now national in scope. As Bell puts it, "Just as the New Deal, in the 1930s, had to grapple with the problem of a national economy—and create institutions for the regulation and management of the economy—so the Great Society has had to deal with a national society in welfare, education, health, housing, and environment. The institutions we set up now will shape our lives for the next 30 years, just as the regulatory mechanisms of the last 30—the Securities and Exchange Commission for finance, the National Labor Relations Board for collective bargaining, and the Council of Economic Advisors for employment policy— shaped our present economic structure."

2. The inadequacy of the present administrative structure. "In a national society," asks Bell, "what is the rationale for a structure with 50 quasi-sovereign states, each with tax powers resting on varied and often inadequate tax bases? What is the rationale for the present crazy-quilt pattern of townships, municipalities, counties, and cities, plus the multifarious health, park, sewage, and water districts? The functioning of any society necessarily depends on the efficiency of its administrative structure. In the U.S., that structure is largely out of step with the needs of the times."

3. The rise of plebiscitary politics. The ease with which tens and even hundreds of thousands of people can pour into Washington, D.C., within a 48-hour period "makes the national capital a cockpit for mobilization pressures in a way this society has never before ex-

perienced." The mobilization tactics underline the problems of violence.

The emergence of a communal society, says Bell, is caused partly
by the growth of nonmarket public decision-making, that is, problems increasingly are decided by public authorities rather than
through the market. The Government rather than private parties
plays an even larger role in determining the planning of cities, the
organization of health care, the financing of education, the cleaning
up of the environment, and so on. "The items that need to be purchased are public goods, not divisible among individual consumers.
No one can buy his share of clean air or clean water in the marketplace; everyone must use communal mechanisms to deal with pollution."

While serving on the Commission on the Year 2000, Bell has continued his academic activities, both at Columbia University and
elsewhere. In 1966, he served as visiting Professor of Sociology at
the University of Chicago, and the following year was Phi Beta Kappa visiting scholar speaking at 20 campuses. In the spring of 1968,
Bell gave a graduate workshop for his Columbia students on "Problems of Long-range Forecasting." He divided his students into
teams which studied various aspects of the future (population, resources, labor force, intellectual manpower, etc.) and eventually
prepared reports. But the study of the future was interrupted by
the violence of the moment: "We had heard about five reports when
the disruptions at Columbia during the spring broke up the work of
the Seminar. Some students could not finish papers because they
had been involved in the sit-ins; several of the sessions, at the initiative of the students, were devoted to a discussion of the events at
Columbia."

In 1969 Bell turned his full attention toward thinking about
America's future, and spent a year's sabbatical at the Russell Sage
Foundation located in mid-Manhattan. In his 1973 book, *The Coming
of Post-Industrial Society*, he offered this description of his activities:

"During the past decade I have pursued several overlapping and
divergent intellectual interests: the work on the post-industrial
society, the development of social indicators, the interest in long-
range social forecasting and the year 2000, an assessment of
theories of social change and the idea of axial structures as a way of
organizing the field of macro-sociology, and a large concern with
what I have called the disjunction of culture and social structure."

The Coming of Post-Industrial Society is only the first of a
number of books that Bell plans to publish in the next few years. A
second, *The Cultural Contradictions of Capitalism*, published in
1976, points out that capitalism as an economic system requires ra-

tionality and efficiency but capitalist culture places ever greater emphasis on such values as "feeling" and personal gratification.

On the personal side, Bell is round-faced and heavy-set. He now has a gray moustache. He is a fluent and erudite talker who mixes a little wit into his conversation. For example: "Cooking is the perfect moral act," he says. "You have complete free will. You can put in as many herbs as you like. But in order to know what you've got, you must taste the consequences." Bell has been married three times. His daughter by his first marriage has taken her doctorate at Columbia in northern Renaissance history, a subject her father knows little about. He has a son in high school. His third wife, the former Pearl Kazin, edited the entire manuscript of *The Coming of Post-Industrial Society*. Bell describes her as his "most severe yet loving critic."

Less loving critics on the left complain that Bell belongs to the political and intellectual establishment, and that he is overly conservative in his approach toward reforming society. Bell might respond that he is simply being realistic, and that it is dangerous to merge reality with utopia. He says:

> In the wisdom of the ancients, Utopia was a fruitful impossibility, a conception of the desirable which men should always strive to attain but which, in the nature of things, could not be achieved. And yet, by its very idea, Utopia would serve as a standard of judgement on men, an ideal by which to measure the real. The modern *hubris* has sought to cross that gap and embody the ideal in the real; and in the effort the perspective of the ideal has become diminished and the idea of Utopia has become tarnished. Perhaps it would be wiser to return to the classic conception.
>
> Men in their imagination will always seek to make society a work of art; that remains an ideal. Given the tasks that have to be solved, it is enough to engage in the sober construction of social reality.

Isaac Asimov: Where Science Is Taking Humanity

"Predicting the future," Isaac Asimov once said, "is a hopeless, thankless task, with ridicule to begin with and, all too often, scorn to end with. Still, since I have been writing science fiction for over a quarter of a century, such prediction is expected of me and it would be cowardly to try to evade it."

Asimov now is frequently called on to predict the future (and often complies despite the risks), because he got his start as a science-fiction writer in the late 1930s and is still thought of as a science-fiction writer though he writes on many other subjects. "After the dropping of the atomic bomb, a new hindsight respectability fell upon science fiction," Asimov recalls. "Many who had thought stories about atomic warfare (printed in reasonably accurate detail as early as 1940) ridiculous—or even pathological—revised their thoughts hurriedly."

When space travel arrived, the public's opinion of science fiction rose still further, and it came to be viewed as prophetic rather than escapist in character. Like other science-fiction writers, Asimov takes some satisfaction from the change: "It is an odd form of escape literature that worried its readers with atom bombs, overpopulation, bacterial warfare, trips to the moon, and other such phenomena decades before the rest of the world had to take up the problem. If science fiction escapes, it is an escape into reality."

Asimov's own journey into reality began with his birth on January 2, 1920, in Petrovichi, 50 miles south of Smolensk, in the Soviet Union. His father was an accountant in a mill owned by his grandfather. In 1923, the Asimov family left Russia and settled in Brooklyn where Isaac's father opened a candy store.

The older Asimov forbade Isaac to read any of the pulp fiction sold in the store—except for science fiction, so Isaac read science fiction avidly. But his first venture into fiction was a novel in the Hardy Boys tradition that he wrote in pencil in a nickel notebook. Asimov now is a compulsive writer who works regularly eight hours a day, seven days a week. "Most writers," he explains, "like getting ideas and like having their books published, but they don't like what comes in between." But Asimov does: He is thoroughly absorbed by the actual act of writing, and types 90 words a minute.

Graduating from high school at the age of 15, Asimov enrolled at Columbia University as a chemistry major. But though he kept up with his studies, his real interest lay in writing, especially science fiction. In June 1938 he completed his first short science-fiction story and personally took it to John W. Campbell, then editor of *Astounding Science Fiction*. "He had never met me before but he took me in; talked to me for two hours; read the story that night; mailed the rejection the following day along with a kind two-page letter telling me where I had gone wrong. Over the next four years, I saw him just about every month, always with a new story. He always talked to me, always fed me ideas, always discussed my stories to tell me what was right and what was wrong with them."

Asimov credits Campbell with revolutionizing science fiction. "He demolished the stock characters who had filled it; eradicated the penny dreadful plots; extirpated the Sunday Supplement science. In a phrase, he blotted out the purple of pulp. Instead, he demanded that science-fiction writers understand science and understand people, a hard requirement that many of the established writers of the 1930s could not meet . . . . Campbell went to work to fill the gap left by the forced retirement of some of the best-known names in the field. He began to develop new talent in a new generation of writers—and succeeded. Those who flourished under Campbell's tutelage and learned to write in his uncompromising school lifted the field from minor pulp to high-art." Campbell later recalled that aspiring author Asimov did not know how to write and his first story was "completely hopeless." But, said Campbell "he could tell a story. You can teach a guy how to write, but not how to tell a story." Campbell became Asimov's greatest source of encouragement. After a total of 12 rejections, Asimov sold his first story, "Marooned off Vesta," to *Amazing Stories* in October 1938. During the next two decades, his stories appeared in virtually every science-fiction magazine.

But writing did not deter Asimov from his educational goals, because he felt that he could not support himself by writing alone. After serving in World War II as a chemist for the Naval Air Experimental Station, and briefly in the U.S. Army in 1945-46, he returned to chemistry studies at Columbia University and obtained his Ph.D. in 1948. His doctoral thesis was *The Kinetics of the Reaction Inactivation of Tyrosinase During Its Catalysis of the Aerobic Oxidation of Catechol.* Asimov did postdoctoral research on nucleic acids at Columbia before accepting, in 1949, an invitation to teach biochemistry at the Boston University Medical School. He joined the medical school faculty as an instructor and became an associate professor six years later. (He still has the title of Associate Professor of Biochemistry although he no longer teaches.) During his teaching career, he continued to write science fiction, and also joined two university colleagues in writing a textbook *Biochemistry and Human Metabolism.* "That introduced me to the delights of nonfiction," he says. "I went on to the even greater ecstasies of writing science for the general public."

Books like *The Chemicals of Life, The World of Carbon, The Bloodstream: River of Life,* and *The Intelligent Man's Guide to Science* poured from his typewriter. And he moved from science into history (*The Roman Empire, The Near East: 10,000 Years of History*) and other fields.

By May 1977 his production amounted to an awesome total of 184 published books.

Asimov's *Foundation* trilogy, which deals with empire-building in the universe of the future, is widely viewed as his best work of science fiction. *Foundation* relates the first 400 years of a millennial effort to deflect the largely inexorable current of history along a more socially beneficent course. The epic struggle is undertaken by a foundation of dedicated social scientists armed with a formidable tool known as "psycho-history"—a science which makes possible the prediction, with reasonable accuracy, of the reactions of vast human conglomerates to certain socio-economic stimuli.

Asimov was influenced in the *Foundation* series by Arnold Toyn-
bee's *A Study of History* (1934) and Edward Gibbon's *Decline and
Fall of the Roman Empire* (1776-88), which provided both historical
analogies and the concept of cyclical civilization (growth, maturity,
decline), challenge and response to external pressures, and the basic long-term multi-fold macro-historical trend. However, the actual genesis of the *Foundation* series was somewhat whimsical.
It all began, Asimov says, when he was riding a subway train to
meet with his editor, John Campbell.

> On this subway ride I had no story idea to present him with so I tried
> a trick I still sometimes recommend. I opened a book at random, read a
> sentence, and concentrated on it until I had an idea. The book was a col-
> lection of Gilbert and Sullivan plays which I just happened to have with
> me. I opened it to *Iolanthe* and my eye fell on the picture of the fairy
> queen kneeling before Private Willis of the Grenadier Guards. I let my
> mind wander from the Grenadiers, to soldiers in general, to a military
> society, to feudalism, to the breakup of the Roman Empire. By the time
> I reached Campbell I told him that I was planning to write a story about
> the breakup of the Galactic Empire.

Foundation embodies the theme that if utopia ever comes it will
not be through an altered environment, but through the altered
minds and attitudes of men. The *Foundation* trilogy places discussions of power, free will, and the ultimate destiny of man into a sort
of galactic perspective. Hence, it has become popular among college
professors as a means of encouraging undergraduates to think more
deeply.

For many years, Asimov lived in a ranch-style house in the sub-
urbs of Boston with his first wife Gertrude, whom he married in
1942, and two children David and Robyn Joan. He now lives in New
York City with his second wife Janet, a psychiatrist. Stocky, five-
feet nine-inches tall, Asimov has blue eyes and graying brown hair.
He talks volubly about everything, regaling his listeners with hilar-
ious anecdotes and sallies that portray himself as conceited and
lecherous. He will allude to his being "the world's greatest science-
fiction writer" and say that his university lectures were the best the
students ever got at Boston University. Holding court at a science-
fiction convention, he may embrace two female admirers while playfully flirting with a third. But he is deadly serious about one subject: air pollution. He will refuse to be interviewed by people who
are smoking and sometimes wears a button saying, "Thank you for
not smoking."

Asimov is most serious about his writing, pursuing it with a rare
single-mindedness, producing between 2,000 and 4,000 manuscript
words a day. "I write as a result of some inner compulsion," he says.
He does little traveling because, "I hate to leave my typewriters."

His restless intelligence leads him into many subject areas—all of which he writes about—but his devotion to science fiction remains steadfast. Science fiction, he says, is based on the fact of social change. "In a sense, it tries on various changes for size; it tries to penetrate the consequences of this change or that; and, in the form of a story, it presents the results to the view of the public, a public that needs more and more to have the possibilities of change pointed out to it before it is disastrously overwhelmed by it." The writers of science fiction, Asimov feels, are the eyes of humanity turned toward "the exciting and dangerous future, not of this individual or that, but of the human race as a whole."

John McHale: Planetary Planner

Many people claim to be citizens of the world, but John McHale is more than just a citizen of the world, he is actively planning the future of the globe. "There are no local problems anymore," McHale says. "We have reached the point in human affairs at which the basic ecological requirements for sustaining the world community must take precedence."

The development of a single world-wide culture stems from the diffusion of cultural styles and technological achievements throughout the world, improved communications between peoples, and the development of shared attitudes and experiences. As a planetary planner, McHale wants the peoples of the world to purge their minds of the ideas and inhibitions of the past which keep them from thinking clearly. He would like for people to look at the modern world of science and technology with fresh eyes, and to address themselves imaginatively to the problems of planning the common future of mankind.

Though he now makes his home in the United States, McHale was born in Glasgow, Scotland on August 19, 1922. He began his working life before World War II as a laboratory assistant at Glasgow University's Department of Pathology and Bacteriology. The war interrupted that career and replaced it with five years of active service with the Royal Navy in the Mediterranean. Back in Britain following the war, McHale moved from science to art. He worked as an artist and designer from 1951 to 1962. During that period he spent a year in the United States on a fellowship at Yale University School of Design.

Pop Art caught the imagination of the artistic world during the early 1950s. England was a major center of this movement, which marked the reunion of art with mass culture. The theoretical underpinnings of the pop art movement became the focus of a small group of artists and architects called "The Independent Group," of which McHale was the co-convener. Their discussions of "the sociology of the pop arts" led to an exhibition in London in 1956 entitled *This Is Tomorrow* in which some members of the Independent Group, notably John McHale and his wife Magda, focused on the elements and styles of mass culture as providing the socio-cultural indicators of the future.

During the late 1950s, McHale also wrote the first biography of and several papers on the work of Buckminster Fuller. McHale later worked with Fuller as Executive Director of the World Resources Inventory at Southern Illinois University in Carbondale, Illinois. The Inventory program was extraordinary for its time, for it predated the recent concern for the environment and resource depletion. Of all the studies of the future during the 1960s, the Inventory was one of the most persistently global. Fuller stated the theme in 1961 when he invited the International Union of Architects to invest 10 years in a continuing study of the problem of making the total chemico-energy resources of the world adequate to the service of humanity at higher standards of living and total enjoyment than have ever been previously experienced. The Inventory collected data documenting world trends. In effect it asked: What are the ripples today that will be the waves, high-tides, and even the floods of tomorrow? What do we have to work with in the way of comprehensive design and planning technology?

McHale threw himself enthusiastically into the project, which eventually resulted in a six-volume set called *World Design Science Decade 1965-1975*. The first volume, *Inventory of Resources, Human Trends and Needs*, was a collection of data—much of it reduced to graphic form—which often jolted the reader by its startling juxtapositions of various trends. The second, third and fifth volumes were devoted mainly to Fuller's concepts and designs, but McHale was the prime author of the fourth and sixth volumes. In the fourth volume McHale outlined plans for the Inventory and brought together trends and speculations about alternative futures and design strategies. A reviewer reported enthusiastically that the volume was "superbly and excitingly illustrated," and a tribute to McHale's artistry. The sixth and last volume *The Ecological Context: Energy and Materials*, treated the topic of world energy and materials within the overall context of global ecology. The volume was updated and republished in 1970 as *The Ecological Context*. The book vividly demonstrates McHale's ability to synthesize data of the most varied kind into a meaningful total picture. For example, in tracing the movement of the element carbon through the earth's biosphere McHale's mind races about, noting the 73,000 tons per year of star dust which brings carbon into the earth's atmosphere as well as the volcanoes that bring carbon up from the interior of the earth.

He also notes the carbon released from plant and animal respiration, industrial combustion, and microbial activity.

McHale's scholarly style suggests the French Pointillistes: He uses innumerable dots of data to paint a picture of the highly complex interreacting reality that is the world. His mind seems to move effortlessly from the ocean—the ultimate depository of everything eroded from the continents—to the infinite reaches of space. McHale insists that no large-scale human problem may now be solved outside of the planetary context. "The resources of the planet can no more belong, by geographical chance, to any individual, corporation, country or national group than the air we breathe. National ownership of a key watershed, mineral deposit, or scientific discovery is as farcical and dangerous a proposition as our supposed national sovereignty of an 'air space'."

In 1968 McHale moved to Binghamton, New York, where he became Director of the Center for Integrative Studies in the School of Advanced Technology at the State University of New York at Binghamton. John and Magda McHale set up shop in the basement of the women's gym. The newly formed center began using converted squash courts for displays of charts and graphs that monitored energy problems, population growth, etc. In 1976 the McHales moved the Center to the University of Houston at Clear Lake City, Texas. The official business of the Center is to study the long-range and cultural implications of scientific and technological developments. The Center's full-time staff is small, never more than five or six. But the number is frequently supplemented by graduate and undergraduate students from the University as well as outside consultants. Magda McHale works actively with her husband at the Center. Hungarian by birth, Magda is a naturalized British subject. Like John McHale she is an artist and has had her work widely exhibited. Most of McHale's projects lead to a collage of apparently unrelated information which is typically drawn together in factual and conceptual charts. The style is perhaps most readily apparent in his book *World Facts and Trends*. The book consists primarily of tables, charts and graphs with only a small amount of interconnecting text.

McHale's charts provide dramatic evidence of the world transformation. The first charts, for example, show the increase in travel speed (from about four miles per hour in the case of the small 15th-century sailing vessel to thousands of miles per hour in the case of manned satellites in the 20th century); the rapid rise in life expectancy during the 19th and 20th centuries; and the increase in the speed of change: It took photography 112 years to progress from initial discovery to widespread application, but the transistor required only three years to make a similar transition.

The McHales now are engaged in a study aimed at assessing the basic needs of the world's poorest people and considering how these might be given priority in accelerated development within the context of sound environmental management.

McHale's views on the future are presented most fully in his book *The Future of the Future*. The book gets its title from a somewhat cryptic motto which McHale devised some years earlier:

The future of the past is in the future.
The future of the present is in the past.
The future of the future is in the present.

McHale opens the book by noting that the future is an integral aspect of the human condition: "Man survives uniquely by his capacity to act in the present on the basis of past experience considered in terms of future consequences. By assuming a future, man makes his present endurable and his past meaningful. Past, present and their alternative futures interweave in the anticipation and prediction of his future actions."

McHale says that the centrality of the future in human affairs is attested by the great variety of social roles and institutions devoted to the prediction and possible control of future events. But the idea of the future in the sense that the concept is now employed is relatively new in human experience. In the past, people had very different concepts of the past, present, and future. For some people, the future was largely a continuation of the past. Some societies, particularly in the East, operated with the cyclical model—recurring cycles of individual birth, death, and rebirth, which occurred in a predestined sequence leading to the unknowable.

The Western view of the future, which is relatively unique, "embodies within it the idea of progress—both material, in terms of the improvement of human welfare in the present or near future, and metaphysical in the terms of perfectability of human institutions and, to a degree, of the perfectability of man and his society." McHale says that the Western view of the future arises out of a complex series of value developments and assertions, and carries with it many normative assumptions about ideals and possibilities. In recent years the assumptions have crystallized around the idea that the future of individual and human society are within human control.

McHale argues that man's present state of knowledge—social as well as scientific and technological—gives him an enormously enhanced capacity to choose his future, both collectively and individually. There is no future other than as we will it to be. If we conceive of a future state as desirable, we tend to orient ourselves toward it and to initiate the course of action necessary to its attainment. Of course, willing connotes more than wishful thinking; it involves an action-oriented commitment to the future in ways that transcend past constraints and present obstacles. The latter are often more apparent than real in our current affairs, where lip-service to change is the norm that conceals even the strongest investments in the status quo.

McHale says that the collective aspect of choice concerning the future is reflected in the growing concern about long-range social programs. "We begin to agree, for example, that investments in prenatal care, child welfare, and pre-school education, which may not pay off for 20 or 30 years, are realistic social strategies. We attempt to control and legislate the future pollution of the waters and the air, the future state of our cities, and the allocation of other living spaces on the same basis."

Though fascinated by scientific and economic data, McHale believes the main determiners of the future lie in the area of values, conceptions, and social arrangements. The future will be what people determine it to be. It will be shaped by the ways in which people conceive of its possibilities, potentials, and implications. "Our mental blueprints are its basic action programs."

The Future of the Future reflects McHale's openness to new ideas and his belief in a diversity of values. McHale finds significance in hippie communes and youth fads as well as technological data. In thinking about the future of the city, he suggests that the cities of tomorrow might specialize. Some cities might concentrate on recreation, as Las Vegas already does; others might specialize in museums, as Florence and Athens now do. There could be ceremonial cities, scientific cities, festival cities, and experimental cities.

McHale argues strongly for acceptance of the full range of human idiosyncratic requirements. "The 'aseptic and well-lighted' place characteristic of many current city and planning practices is not accommodative of many human desires and proclivities. Planning for those that fall out of the normal range is relegated to means of *controlling* the deviance and seaminess of the bohemias and the bar strips. Yet a considerable measure of aberrance may be expected in any human group. To plan only for the *control* and *surveillance* of those areas of human behavior that do not accord with present norms is not future but past-oriented."

McHale's formula for creating a better future world includes the following: (1) an active exploration and thorough understanding of the world as it is in all its complexity and interactions, (2) the development of a wide variety of alternative future developments, (3) a reconceptualization of human thought concerning the human situation and human values, and (4) the design of new social arrangements that will operate more effectively toward creating the better world that man aspires to. "Our prime need is to devise new agencies, new organizations, and models of social action that will enable us to escape our largely artificial dilemmas," he says. "The key to many of our difficulties lies in the identification of those social organizations that in the past had great survival value, but which may now endanger our survival in the present, or cripple our approach to the future."

Herman Kahn: The Unthinkable Optimist

"Is there really a Herman Kahn?" asked an outraged reviewer when Kahn's ominous treatise *On Thermonuclear War* appeared in 1961. "This is a moral tract on mass murder: how to plan it, how to commit it, how to get away with it, how to justify it," fumed James R. Newman, and added darkly that the "evil and tenebrous book . . . is permeated with a bloodthirsty irrationality such as I have not seen in all my years of reading."

On Thermonuclear War established Kahn—in some eyes—as the prototype of a new species of moral monster—the defense intellectual. The new ogre, immortalized in the title character of the film *Dr. Strangelove*, cold-bloodedly calculates the number of megadeaths needed to bring an enemy nation to its knees and speculates calmly about a "doomsday machine" that can destroy the world in a single flash. Kahn's colleagues at the Rand Corporation saw *On Thermonuclear War* differently. As one put it: "He [Kahn] did what nobody else had the guts to do—he took the secret stamp off all of those estimates of nuclear destruction because he believed it was time for the rest of the nation to get in on our debates."

Today Kahn's treatise on thermonuclear war is largely forgotten except as a reference and text in university courses. But a new group of critics is asking, "Is there really a Herman Kahn?" Much of their rage focuses on what they view as his over-optimism about the future. In a period when many people feel that the world is only a few years from a nuclear or environmental Armageddon, Kahn talks exuberantly about an era of peace and prosperity. In an interview with *U.S. News*, he said:

> I think there are good prospects for what the Europeans would call *la belle epoque* or, if you will, a good era similar to that experienced between the turn of the century and World War I—a worldwide period of growth, trade, peace, and prosperity on the whole, and a time, generally speaking, of optimism about the future.

Kahn thinks that the idea that he is an optimist is "basically wrong"; he claims that he is simply a realist. "I'm looking for solutions and if you can find solutions, you're optimistic," he says. "Are we running out of energy? The answer is absolutely no. No way. Are we running out of resources? Absolutely not. No way. Are we running out of the ability to feed people from a technological and economic point of view? Absolutely not. No way. Can we retain clean air and clear water and a reasonably esthetic landscape? Absolutely."

Kahn concedes, however, that there will be tragedy, and the most likely kind is widespread starvation. "The big problem is stockpiles," he explains. "It doesn't pay any country to have enough stockpiles so that the poor won't suffer when you have a bad harvest year or bad weather. It's up to the food exporting nations to rise to the occasion and assume responsibility for such stockpiles."

Kahn believes that the widespread gloom among intellectuals concerning the future comes from many things, one of the most important being that they usually belong to the upper-middle class. A person raised in this class, he says, does not get a "kick" out of increasing his income, because he always had an income due to his parents. Good things came to him on a platter; as a result, he does not have the joy of winning them in later life. Furthermore, the upper-middle class in the U.S. does not enjoy the status it has in poorer countries.

Kahn himself was born in modest circumstances on February 15, 1922, in Bayonne, New Jersey, one of the three sons of Abraham and Yetta Kahn. The family lived in New York City for some years before moving to California, where Kahn graduated from Fairfax High School in Los Angeles in 1940. He enrolled at the University of Southern California but later transferred to the University of California at Los Angeles. While in college Kahn worked as a ship steward, checker in a supermarket, and machinist in a camera shop to help pay his expenses. His studies were interrupted by World War II and two years' service in the Army, but Kahn eventually won his bachelor's degree from U.C.L.A. and began work with the Douglas Aircraft Company as a mathematician. While working for Douglas, he became a teaching assistant at U.C.L.A. and attended classes at the California Institute of Technology.

While at Douglas, Kahn worked as a laboratory analyst for Project RAND, a unique experimental institution that Douglas had set up in 1945 in collaboration with the U.S. Army Air Force. In 1948 Kahn became Senior Staff Physicist for RAND, his primary task being a study of the relations between weapons and tactics. Kahn soon became an expert in military strategy and weapons design, and he was conducting lectures and seminars for selected U.S. military and civilian leaders.

A series of lectures Kahn delivered at the Princeton University Center of International Studies in 1959 became the foundation for *On Thermonuclear War*. The "evil and tenebrous" book argues that there exists a strong possibility, even probability, of nuclear war *sometime* in the future, because disarmament talks and deterrence strategy probably cannot succeed for all time. On the other hand, the "realistic" possibility of nuclear war does not necessarily mean the end of human civilization, because such wars can have a number of "degrees of awfulness," partly depending upon degrees of preparation and tactics used. Kahn criticized as irresponsible those who argue against a "realistic civil defense program," which would greatly diminish the number of victims so that "normal and hopeful lives would not be precluded for the survivors."

Though it provoked much outrage, the book helped decision-makers on the Soviet as well as the U.S. side to think more flexibly about responses to nuclear threats and perhaps even consider moves toward detente.

In 1961, with $15,000 lent by the founders and a $25,000 loan from Harvey Picker, president of the Picker X-Ray Corporation, Kahn and attorney Max Singer established the Hudson Institute. The initial location was White Plains, New York; the Institute later moved to nearby Croton-on-Hudson. In a jocular vein, Kahn says that when he and Singer started Hudson they thought they would put down on paper during the first year everything that a good Secretary of Defense would want to know, the second year a good Secretary of State, the third year a good President, the fourth year a good Secretary General of the United Nations, and the fifth year a good God. The Institute would then close up shop.

"Unfortunately," chuckles Kahn, "in 1966 Singer pointed out that we were six years behind in the five-year program."

Small in size compared to "Mother RAND," Hudson now has about 50 permanent fellows and 100 consultants. The Institute's original motto was "National Security—International Order," but Hudson has decreased its dependence on military funding, and the present mix of about half military and half civilian work is reflected in its new motto: "Policy Research in the Public Interest."

Kahn has so much influence at the Institute that it has come to be called "Herman-on-Hudson." Critics of the Institute sometimes suggest that it is simply an extension of Kahn, while Kahn's detractors suggest that he just parrots ideas he gets from the Institute. Both theories may be plausible when considered separately, says one Hudson associate, but they do not live well together. Most observers agree that Kahn and Hudson enjoy a remarkable symbiosis. As one staff member put it, "There are two institutions here: Herman and the Institute. They go together like a great opera and a great star."

The Institute, now housed in a former institution for alcoholics, displays a remarkable degree of informality: Dress is casual and most staffers determine their own working hours. The style of Hudson reports has been to make bold, outspoken, and very general statements about the current status, objectives, and directions of policy for each issue discussed.

From a futurist's standpoint, Kahn's principal books are:

• *The Year 2000: A Framework for Speculation on the Next Thirty-three Years* (co-authored with Anthony J. Wiener, 1967). This 431-page volume, packed with tables and charts, was perhaps the first major statement of Kahn's views on the broad issues of the future. (Earlier works were more limited in scope.) Widely hailed as one of the most impressive futurist works to appear, *The Year 2000* presented Kahn's ideas about the Basic Long-Term Multifold Trend of Western society and his "surprise-free" scenarios for the future.

• *Things to Come: Thinking about the 70s and 80s* (co-authored with B. Bruce-Briggs, 1972). Kahn restated his case for the need to speculate on the problems and possibilities of nuclear disasters. He continued to refine and discuss the Basic Long-term Multifold Trend, described in the earlier work.

• *The Next 200 Years: A Scenario for America and the World* (co-authored with William Brown and Leon Martel, 1976). Perhaps the most readable of his books to date, Kahn here states his optimistic view of the coming decades. (The title was chosen because of the U.S. Bicentennial celebration, but the focus remains primarily on the next 50 years.) This book offers a strong rebuttal to the "limits-to-growth" school, and argues that Americans will become increasingly prosperous in the years ahead. Improved technology will, Kahn believes, compensate for both the problems of pollution and the depletion of natural resources.

Kahn has become a sharp critic of the intellectual and educational establishment, which he blames for a condition he calls "educated incapacity." Education has, in his view, decreased many people's ability to deal with certain problems. For example, he says, for a long time the educated elite viewed public demands for law-and-order as appeals to racism, whereas such demands reflect simply the average person's desire not to be robbed or assaulted—a desire shared by black and white alike. He believes the U.S. educational system now is failing to teach discipline and good work habits. "It's unbelievable how badly the schools are doing," he says. He also worries that young people are being led to believe that their parents' generation has immorally destroyed the basis of human life. "And that's just not true."

"We [Americans] get excited about problems when they are actually on the road to solution," he says. "Take the environment. Our air and water are cleaner today than 10 years ago. We're worrying about our population, but the fertility rate is down to 1.8—well below the replacement rate now."

Over the past 10 years, Kahn's interest has shifted from military affairs to the more general questions of the future. He has become a prophet exploring the major world trends of the next quarter century. Hudson has moved beyond such studies as "Post-Attack Social Organization" and "An Analytic Summary of U.S. National Security Policy Issues" to analyze youthful rebellion and alienation (a study underwritten by Coca Cola) and Office of Economic Opportunity poverty programs (funded by the OEO). Hudson recently completed "The Future of the Corporation," a major project sponsored by 100 U.S. and foreign corporations.

In 1969, Hudson received $100,000 from a large Portuguese manufacturing company to look at Angola, then a Portuguese colony. The project gave Hudson an opportunity to try a new analytical technique called the "Flying Think Tank." Four light twin-engine airplanes flew multidisciplinary teams of experts around Angola for a ten-day period; the teams met each evening to discuss what they had seen and to plan the next day's flights. The system was supposedly designed to expose the team to a maximum amount of information in a minimum amount of time. The resulting two-volume study on the development of Angola contains a variety of scenarios and predictions based on the impressions of people who only flew over the country in airplanes and an essay by Kahn, who didn't even go. The product was clearly pro-colonial in its findings. In his book *Think Tanks*, Paul Dickson complained that "Hudson's antipathy to self-determination in Angola and its suggestions for perpetuating dictatorial rule display the mentality of Kahn's think tank at work. The Institute clearly feels free to roam the world hunting for projects without having to worry about the political or moral repercussions of what it says or does." Dickson argues that the "flying think tank" is *a priori* a superficial means of probing for information, and "ideally suited for keeping aloof from issues on the ground."

Whatever critics may say, most people find Kahn a warm, hospitable, humorous, and thoroughly engaging character. White-bearded and obese, the one-man megamind often seems to contain the heart of a flower child. Closing one of his long pontification sessions, he will smile playfully, slap the table, and say, "Gentlemen, this meeting is over, and I love you all."

Alvin Toffler: From Future Shock to Anticipatory Democracy

Alvin Toffler's 1970 best-seller *Future Shock* probably contributed more to the popular notions of the future than any other single work. This provocative best-seller, which sold six million copies in

20 languages, warned of the "dizzying disorientation" of too-rapid social change as technologically-advanced societies whirl into a new age. Toffler wrote:

> We are creating a new society. Not a changed society. Not an extended, larger-than-life version of our present society. But a new society. Unless we understand this, we shall destroy ourselves in trying to cope with tomorrow. What is occurring now is not a crisis of capitalism, but of industrial society itself, regardless of its political form.
>
> We are simultaneously experiencing a youth revolution, a sexual revolution, a racial revolution, a colonial revolution, an economic revolution, and the most rapid and deep-going technological revolution in history. In a word, we are in the midst of the super-industrial revolution.

The new age creates serious stress caused by many demands for assimilating and controlling change. Toffler termed this stress "future shock," a phrase that has now entered the language.

The author who electrified the public with *Future Shock* was born in New York City on October 4, 1928, to parents who were both Polish Jewish immigrants. He became interested in writing when he was only seven years old. In high school he worked on the school paper, and later, as an English major at New York University, he founded an inter-collegiate literary magazine.

After earning his B.A. degree in 1949, Toffler worked for several years as an auto assembly worker, truck driver, punch press operator, and foundry millwright. During the Korean war, he served briefly, in 1953, as a private in the United States Army. His "hard-hat" experiences led him to become a staff writer for a daily newspaper published by the International Typographical Union. The newspaper was devoted to economics, politics, and labor relations. In 1957, he became a Washington correspondent for a Pennsylvania daily, *The York Gazette*, and free-lanced for publications like *The Christian Science Monitor* and *The New Republic*. He later commented that his Washington experience cleared away "the cardboard stereotypes we get at college" so that "political figures emerged as human beings."

In 1960 and 1961, Toffler worked as associate editor and labor columnist for *Fortune* magazine and wrote an article on the rising mass interest in the arts and the falling financial status of the artist. He later expanded the article into the book *The Culture Consumers*.

Toffler first described his "future shock" concept in a 1965 magazine article—five years before his book on the topic made the best-seller lists. Toffler defined future shock as "the shattering stress and disorientation that we induce in individuals by subjecting them to too much change in too short a time." He spent the next five years visiting scores of universities, research centers, laboratories, and government agencies, reading countless articles and scientific papers, and interviewing hundreds of experts on different aspects of change, coping behavior, and the future.

Toffler's research led him to the disturbing conclusion that more and more people are suffering from future shock. Furthermore, "in the most rapidly changing environment to which man has ever been exposed, we remain pitifully ignorant of how the human animal copes."

In *Future Shock* Toffler explains that technology now presents man with a bewildering variety of decisions, a condition that can be called "over-choice." For instance, a computer has calculated that today's car has so many variations of style, color, and accessories that a buyer faces 25 million potential choices.

Toffler analyzes three aspects of today's rapidly changing world: transience, novelty, and diversity. Transience is seen in throw-away products—and throw-away human relationships. Novelty appears in new gadgets, in "happenings," and in unprecedented scientific and political problems. Diversity bombards people with new products and new life-styles. Other areas of future shock include: the data deluge (made possible by computers, new analytical tools, and new communications technology), genetic innovation (artificial wombs, embryo transplants), and "adhocracy" (the task-force operations that replace bureaucracy).

To find ways to cope with the future, Toffler explored education and edited two books: *The Schoolhouse in the City*, a collection of papers presented at Stanford University's Education Facilities Laboratories in June 1967, and *Learning for Tomorrow*, which contains 18 papers by educators and other experts on the theme that "all education springs from images of the future and all education creates images of the future."

Toffler has also sought to develop a political approach to the future. In 1975 he played a leading role in forming a Committee on Anticipatory Democracy. "Under conditions of high-speed change," he explained, "a democracy without the ability to anticipate condemns itself to death. But an anticipatory government without effective citizen participation and, indeed, control may be no less lethal. The future must neither be ignored nor captured by an elite. Only anticipatory democracy can provide a way out of the contradiction in which we find ourselves."

The Committee on Anticipatory Democracy organized a conference for members and staff of Congress on September 11, 1975. Senator John Culver of Iowa and Representative Charlie Rose of North Carolina were among the 30 congressional sponsors of the Capitol Hill meeting. Toffler and other speakers urged the legislators to make use of future-oriented research in order to "re-invent

democracy." Warning that Congress as it now functions is an outmoded institution, he said: "People are asking, 'How come the energy squeeze? How come we built more schools than we needed?
Why weren't we forecasting these things?' " Toffler urged the legislators to be future-oriented but also to be skeptical of glib forecasts;
to avoid straight-line extrapolation; to use computerized data but
avoid reliance on technologists alone; and, above all, to do "imaginative thinking about parliamentary democracy." Many congressmen
and staff members expressed interest in his points but some noted
that congressmen must face re-elections every two years and cannot focus too much on the future if their constituents are interested
only in the present.

Six feet two inches, 172 pounds, with green eyes and brown hair,
Toffler goes to the movies and writes poetry for recreation. A li-
censed pilot, he flew a plane across much of Australia after completing a lecture tour down under in 1974. He is married to the former
Adelaide Elizabeth Farrell, whose nickname is "Heidi." The Tof-
flers have a daughter, Karen, and maintain a home in Washington,
Connecticut. Mrs. Toffler does research and editing for her husband's books and is a member of the Committee on Anticipatory
Democracy.

Toffler's latest thinking is summed up in a brief book *The Eco-
Spasm Report*, which began to take shape when the editors of *Es-
quire* magazine asked him to undertake a lengthy examination of
"the next depression." Toffler agreed to do an article, but felt that
the depression of the future would not be a depression at all, but
"something novel, strange, and far more difficult to overcome."

After months of research, he decided that his initial hesitancy to
use the term depression was justified, and he eventually wrote a
lengthy article entitled "Beyond Depression." For lack of a better
word, he called the phenomenon he sensed coming "an eco-spasm."
The article was expanded into a short book entitled *The Eco-Spasm
Report*, in which he explains:

> What we are seeing today is not simply an economic upheaval,
> but something far deeper, something that cannot be understood with-
> in the framework of conventional economics. This is why increasingly
> mystified economists complain that 'the old rules don't work any
> longer.' What we are seeing is the general crisis of industrialism—a
> crisis that transcends the differences between capitalism and Soviet-
> style communism, a crisis that is simultaneously tearing up our en-
> ergy base, our value systems, our family structures, our institutions,
> our communicative modes, our sense of space and time, our episte-
> mology as well as our economy. What is happening, no more, no less,
> is the breakdown of industrial civilization on the planet and the first
> fragmentary appearance of a wholly new and dramatically different
> social order: a super-industrial civilization that will be technological,
> but no longer industrial.

Toffler continues to place his hopes in anticipatory democracy as a means of futurizing democratic institutions and democratizing futurism. Despite his somewhat alarming references to the collapse of industrial civilization and eco-spasms, Toffler remains fundamentally optimistic. He concludes *The Eco-Spasm Report* with these words:

> The years immediately ahead will no doubt be painful. But if the notion of automatic "progress" is naive, so is the notion of inevitable "retrogression." If we can look beyond the immediate, we glimpse breakthroughs to something not merely new, but in many ways better and more just. To quote Raymond Fletcher (a member of Britain's Parliament) again: "All these alarming symptoms that so frighten us—they may be birth symptoms instead of death symptoms."

The Futurist Perspective

The future-oriented writers described on the foregoing pages represent only a tiny sampling of the thousands of people who might be termed futurists. Still, it is tempting to use them as a basis for speculation on what it is that gives a person a future-oriented outlook and what other characteristics seem to go with that outlook. Here are a few hypotheses:

Openness to Experience. Futurists appear to be remarkably open to all types of ideas; in fact they seem to be constantly searching for new information about the world, and are never so happy as when they have found a genuinely exciting idea. They are constantly playing with ideas: Jungk claims "brainstorming" as his favorite method of exploring the future. Mead is so ready with provocative ideas that she has been described as "the fastest opinion in the West." And no new idea seems to faze a futurist: Herman Kahn writes calmly about millions of people dying in a thermonuclear war; Arthur C. Clarke looks seriously at the question of travel backwards through time.

Global Outlook. With few exceptions, futurists have traveled a great deal and lived for extended periods outside their native lands. They all seem to think in global rather than national terms; indeed, in several instances (Arthur C. Clarke and Isaac Asimov, for example), the perspective seems to have become extraterrestrial if not universal.

Long-term Time-perspective. By definition, futurists are oriented toward the future, and therefore have a time perspective that extends some distance into the future. But it also appears that the time-perspective of the futurists runs backward in time. Bertrand de Jouvenel has a rich knowledge of the ancient Greek and Roman worlds as well as French history. Isaac Asimov has written whole books on historical topics (e.g., *The Roman Empire; The Near East: 10,000 Years of History).* In general, the futurists seem to have a lively sense of *human evolution through time,* and constantly scrutinize the past for clues to the future.

Ecological Orientation. Closely related to the breadth and length of the futurists' perspective is a sense of the infinitely complex interrelationships of the human and natural environments. The futurists are not environmental fanatics, but they seem to share a deep concern about preserving the natural environment, which can so easily be damaged inadvertently by powerful technologies. De Jouvenel worries about oil spills and Asimov about air pollution; Seaborg hopes that thermonuclear power will make it possible to restore the natural environment.

Broad Concern for Humanity. Because of their global and long-term time perspective, the concern that futurists feel for mankind is not limited to any particular time or place. Apparently, as they began to think about distant places and distant times, they have developed empathy for the inhabitants of those distant times and places. Futurists seem to exhibit a genuine concern for all living humanity—plus the generations yet to come. A concern for posterity is perhaps clearest among the older futurists, but it seems to be a common characteristic. Futurists are concerned about their children's children, and even the unknown people who will inhabit the world a century or millennium hence. De Jouvenel cites the story of the old man who plants a tree whose fruit he cannot live to enjoy and Mead speaks, almost reverently, of the little children who will run tomorrow's world.

Rationality. Though open to experience, futurists quickly reject notions that lack an adequate scientific or rational basis. They seem to have little time to waste on mystical forecasting (palmistry, tea leaves, astrology, etc.). By contrast, they have great respect for science and historical facts. The futurists rely heavily on facts to construct and test their concepts. They could even be described as "fact freaks" though it is ideas that seem to excite them the most.

Pragmatism. As a group, the futurists seem to be primarily interested in what will "work," that is, what will be really effective in improving the human condition over the long term. The test of effectiveness is not any ideology of left or right (Daniel Bell's book *The End of Ideology* makes this point explicit), but rather good data and methods, genuine concern about people, realistic assessments, and well-planned programs. Futurists also appear unusually hospitable to experiments and innovations in the effort to improve human life.

Reality of Choice. The futurists seem to be deeply conscious of the freedom of individuals to make decisions that will have tremendous consequences for good or ill. The futurists seem to have an existentialist's concern about the act of decision-making, which occurs in the present but creates the future. Most would probably agree with existentialist philosopher Jean-Paul Sartre's statement that everyone is, in a sense, a lawmaker, determining through his acts what mankind shall be. Though they want to improve the future and stress its importance, they see the present as crucially important because it is the time one makes the decisions that bind the future.

Interest in Values. Because of their concern about the future and their belief that they are, through their actions, building the future, the futurists exhibit a deep interest in values, the criteria by which one decides what to choose. The value that most futurists seem to agree on is a desire for the happiness of all human beings in all times and places.

Optimism. The futurists generally seem to believe that mankind will survive and perhaps prosper in the years ahead. Kahn and Seaborg are perhaps the most explicitly optimistic, but the thinking of all the futurists seems to assume that the world will not self-destruct during the next few decades. They even seem reasonably confident that if people will only use their heads, life will be much better in the years ahead.

Sense of Purpose. The futurists seem to be very hard-working people with a sense of mission. They seem to feel that what they are doing is important and will help to create a better world.

In addition to the foregoing hypotheses, it might be interesting to speculate on whether there are certain critical events in a person's life which may give him a future-orientation. De Jouvenel appears to have been profoundly affected by his perception that "seeds of war" were planted at Versailles in 1919. Jungk appears to have had a soul-moving experience when a survivor of Hiroshima wondered why the people who were responsible for the bombing had not foreseen the consequences. Seaborg and Kahn also had intimate experiences with atomic weapons and may have been driven to seek alternatives to the horror that circumstances had forced them to face. In a sense, it may seem ironic that Seaborg, the atomic scientist who discovered the material used in the Nagasaki bomb, and Kahn, the philosopher of thermonuclear horrors, appear to be the most optimistic futurists, but this may come from a deep feeling that the fantastic power of modern technology can, and hopefully will, be used to build a better world.

10

Futuristics in Practice
(With Case Histories)

A modern organization must cope with a rapidly changing technological, economic, and social environment. The demand for the
goods and services that it produces may skyrocket—or disappear—almost overnight. At the same time, the availability and costs
of obtaining the financing, people, and supplies needed for its operations may shift dramatically due to changing conditions.

Top leaders of business, government, and other organizations
generally acknowledge the need to plan for world changes in the
years ahead, but most have developed relatively little capacity to do
so. The most apparent reason is simply that the organizations are
so preoccupied by the crises of today that they feel they have no
time to prevent the crises of tomorrow. An organization obviously
must survive the present or it will never reach the future, but if it
concerns itself only with the present, it may find itself unable to
cope with future circumstances. In retrospect, it is often clear that
the problems an organization is facing today could have been
averted if they had been anticipated yesterday and appropriate action taken. We were too busy with yesterday's crisis to forestall another crisis today. Now, of course, with a crisis on our hands we feel
too busy to head off a crisis tomorrow.

The time perspective of organizational leaders often is startlingly
short, generally no more than a year and often less. One futurist
who was trying to convince a businessman of the need to think in
long-range terms thought he was making progress until the businessman said, "Yes, I think you are right. We should take time occasionally to think beyond the next quarter." For many businessmen,
especially smaller businessmen, any thinking beyond the next pay-
roll may be viewed as "long-range planning."

Lack of foresight among organizations has contributed heavily to
their failure to deliver the goods and services that their clients expect from them—and often to the collapse of the organizations themselves. The United States currently has about 300,000 business
bankruptcies every year, and bankruptcies (or government bailouts

from bankruptcy) occur not only among smaller businesses but a-mong corporate giants like Lockheed, the Penn Central Railroad, and W.T. Grant & Co. Though precise figures cannot be given, it seems reasonable to believe that a large number of these failures stem from inadequate reckoning with the future. In fairness to business, of course, it may be pointed out that many of its problems resulted from the lack of foresight among government regulators and contract officers.

Business organizations often show remarkable insensitivity to trends in their environment and make mistakes that cost hundreds of millions of dollars. The DuPont Corporation successfully developed Corfam, an artificial substitute for leather, but the market failed to respond, so DuPont sold Corfam to another company. Later, leather became increasingly costly and demand for Corfam became brisk. DuPont lost twice—first by introducing Corfam when the market was not ready for it and second by selling it shortly before demand boomed. Similarly, the Ford Motor Company developed the Edsel, a market failure so disastrous and famous that it contributed a new word to the English language: Any product that a company labors to produce but people do not want to buy is now known as "an Edsel."

The failure of business corporations to see the possibilities in new technology is legendary, as a few instances will illustrate:

• In 1876 the inventor of the telephone, Alexander Graham Bell, offered exclusive rights to the new invention to Western Union, then the largest communications network in the United States. WU President William Orton was unimpressed. "What use could this company make of an electrical toy?" Orton asked. Later, Western Union officials watched helplessly as the "electrical toy" gobbled up most of its market.

• In 1878 gas company securities dropped because an American inventor named Thomas A. Edison had announced he was working on an incandescent lamp that would use electricity. The British Parliament named a committee to look into the matter, and to the relief of the gas companies witnesses testified that Edison's ideas were "good enough for our transatlantic friends . . . but unworthy of the attention of practical or scientific men."

• Chester Carlson, who invented the Xerox machine, tried for years to get U.S. companies to invest in his invention. The IBM Corporation looked over the contraption twice and turned it down both times. Finally the Haloid Corporation, an ailing firm desperate enough for a wild flyer, gambled on the machine's development. Sales of Carlson's machine boomed and the Haloid Company metamorphosed into the Xerox Corporation.

One instance of how visions of the future can affect business corporations occurs in the histories of two great merchandising concerns, Sears Roebuck and Montgomery Ward. At the end of World War II, the leaders of the two companies acted on very different assumptions about the future. Montgomery Ward's President Sewell Avery believed there would be a depression and carefully conserved the company's cash; when the depression came, the company would expand, partly by buying up its ruined competitors. Sears Roebuck, by contrast, foresaw a boom in demand and expanded to meet it, thus enlarging its share of the market.

Many educational institutions have been hurt badly in recent years when they failed to foresee swift changes in the environments in which they operate. Somewhat ironically, the unfortunate results appear to have been due in some measure to long-range planning that failed to scan the horizon for forthcoming changes that would necessitate alterations in the long-range plans. Based on past enrollment trends, some universities made major capital investments in buildings on the assumption that there would be plenty of students to use them—and pay for them. When the rising tide of students abated in the 1970s, some universities were caught with excess capacity and insufficient income. About the same time, the scientific establishment found itself oversupplied with researchers and undersupplied with funds; yet the signs of the new situation that pained universities in the 1970s could have been perceived when the universities were still in the halcyon sixties.

Religious and other institutions may also experience similar changes that could be foreseen, at least in broad outline, and prepared for. The shortage of clergy during the 1950s became an oversupply in the 1970s, but this could have been anticipated on the basis of demographic factors such as the low birthrate during the 1930s.

Since World War II, organizations have begun making a much greater effort to deal with the future in a conscious way. In addition to seeking outside consultants to advise them on possible future developments, many organizations have developed in-house capabilities so that they have staff members who are familiar both with the organization and with current forecasts and ideas about the environment in which the organization will operate in the years ahead.

The biggest in-house forecasting capacities are found in the defense establishment. Though generals are accused of always fighting the last war, military agencies may be the most forward looking of all organizational groups. The U.S. Department of Defense has the most sophisticated and best-funded forecasting and planning capabilities of any organization in the nation, if not the world. The work is largely secret, but knowledgeable people appear agreed that the magnitude of the military's exploration of the future dwarfs that of virtually any other organization. Similar efforts are believed to exist in the military establishments of the Soviet Union and other major nations.

The strong future-orientation of the military appears to stem from several factors, including:

First, international competition. New weapons—from the long-bows to atomic bombs—have given their owners a tremendous advantage over rivals. Hence, military men are constantly seeking to identify potential future threats and to develop new military capabilities.

Second, contingency preparation. The military is expected to be prepared for all types of situations.

Third, availability of funds. The military in the U.S. and in many other countries benefits from deep public concern about national security. This concern means that funds are generally available for military purposes even when civilian needs are scanted.

Fourth, worldwide involvement of U.S. Government. The U.S. now is heavily involved in nations around the world. As a result, the military thinks in worldwide terms about security and other problems that may arise almost anywhere on the face of the earth.

Business organizations appear to have intensified their forecasting efforts in recent years, but, as with the military, much of their work is kept secret because the organizations hope to gain competitive advantage from it. Much business interest centers on what new technologies can be developed and how successful they will be. Interest in technological forecasting reached new heights during the space program of the 1960s when billions of dollars were spent to achieve something which many people doubted was even possible—putting a man on the moon. Companies involved in space had to make forecasts of what technology might become available and when, and some firms went so far as to hire full-time forecasters. For example, General Electric employed scientist-futurist Dandridge Cole to study space and the technologies that would be needed to explore it. Cole developed a wide variety of concepts including the idea of hollowing out asteroids as livable habitats for man. *Fortune* magazine took note of business's interest in forecasting in a 1964 article entitled "The Wild Birds Find a Corporate Roost."

TRW, Inc., made an elaborate "probe" of the technological future in the late 1960s in order to determine what the company should be doing. The results of the first probe, basically a poll of experts using the Delphi technique, were made public, but subsequent studies were kept secret. TRW's Vice President, Harper Q. North, and his assistant, Donald L. Pyke, explained the rationale for the company's forecast as follows:

The faster a racing car travels over a cross-country course to its
destination, the farther ahead the driver must look if he is to avoid
collisions and manage the obstacles in front of him. This image applies
very accurately to the technologically oriented company of today: the
company itself corresponds to the racing car, the pace of industrial advance to the race forward; the company's corporate goals to the destination at the end of the race; technical difficulties, market variabili-
ties, and competition to the obstacles in the course; and technological
and market forecasting to the driver's distance vision. Unlike the racing car, however, the company may not even have a fixed destination—its goals are likely to shift as the world changes.

For many years, especially in the mature industries, companies
have shown themselves myopic on the subject of long-range planning.
But the technological pace in most industries today demands that
companies try to achieve a longer view of the future—even if it must
be a slightly blurred view—if they want to stay in the business race.

The research and development departments of large companies
are naturally among the sections most likely to be interested in the
future, and to make some attempts to study it. Similar efforts are
likely to be made in the corporate planning and marketing sections.
Marketing has had to become future-oriented in part because of
rapidly changing social needs. In the United States, the Government's decision to invest heavily in space following the Soviet sputnik was soon translated into a demand for all kinds of goods and services that could be useful to the space program. When the space program was later scaled down, companies had to switch to other products for which there would be a market.

Corporate planning, research, and development and even marketing might seem obvious departments to be interested in the future.
But in the General Electric Company, concern about the future developed in the industrial relations department. Ian H. Wilson, a full-
time GE consultant, led a group which developed a major report entitled *Our Future Business Environment*. Published in 1968, the report attracted wide interest throughout the company and in business enterprise elsewhere, for it necessarily looked at many aspects
of the modern business environment in which all departments of
all businesses must operate. Wilson and his associates found evidence of major shifts in human values, and these shifts would
greatly affect the company's operations. Since 1971 GE has developed alternative scenarios as a framework for the company's strategic planning. The analysis and prioritization of societal pressures on
corporations goes to the Board of Directors' Public Issues Committee. Wilson's analyses of trends led the company to develop a
"pro-active" approach to equal opportunities for minorities and
women.

To understand how organizations are trying to deal with the future, it is useful to look at specific examples.

A Power Company Has a Change of Heart

Back in the 1960s, the Northern States Power Company found itself in the unenviable position of being viewed as Public Enemy Number One by many of the people it served. The Minneapolis-based company was embroiled in costly, head-on battles with environmentalists, who were outraged at the company for polluting the air and water, cutting down trees, and otherwise wreaking havoc on the natural environment. The environmentalists repeatedly succeeded in blocking company plans for new power stations and transmission lines, thereby causing huge losses to the company.

NSP's top management sensed that the company's problem was not just the environmentalists, but rather its own crisis-oriented, reactive decision-making process. Once the company succeeded in coming to terms with the environmentalists, it would find itself facing another crisis—unless it could develop a better way of anticipating future developments. In 1969 Earl Ewald, then Chairman of the Board of NSP, and D.F. McElroy, then Vice President (later President), created an Environmental Affairs Department. To head it, they tapped Roland Comstock, a lawyer who had undergone a consciousness-raising experience during the environmental conflicts. Comstock created an open planning system for the selection of sites for power plants and invited citizen groups and government officials to participate. He also established an educational program to raise employees' awareness of the outside forces impinging on the company. To head the program, Comstock brought in Donald O. Imsland, a future-oriented professional educator.

Imsland and his colleagues decided that their first task was to learn about the future, and arranged for teams of NSP employees to interview more than 20 leading futurists, including Glenn T. Seaborg, then Chairman of the Atomic Energy Commission; author Isaac Asimov; and Orville L. Freeman, President of Business International Corporation. The teams gathered nearly 25 hours of taped materials and 1,500 photographs which provided material for an audiovisual program entitled "Profiles of the Future." The program was first presented to NSP's Board of Directors at a meeting in the fall of 1971, and later shown many times to other groups, both inside and outside the company.

A next step was a training program for company employees. Known as the Future Trends Program, this pilot effort provided intensive education in the future for 35 selected company employees. The experimental program consisted of 30 sessions of two hours each, conducted during prime work times. Participants were assigned 15 books, 40 reprints, and 20 tapes. In addition, they saw films, heard guest lecturers (many of national stature), and partici-

pated in field trips. The faculty for the nine-month course included
Professor Arthur Harkins and two colleagues from the University
of Minnesota.

"The Future Trends Program was well received," Imsland says,
but "we were reaching only 35 employees and at that rate it would
take several years to make a significant impact. Furthermore, the
course was much too long and required too much of the employees'
time." So Imsland and his colleagues redesigned the program to
overcome its limitations. They capsulized the information in a fast-
moving, highly visual series of multi-media presentations. Each
segment of the series, called "Futures Report," includes a descrip-
tive brochure, a 20 to 30-minute show, and a learning packet. Imsland reports that reaction to the series has been enthusiastic.

Other features of NSP's futures program include:

• A series of week-long retreats dealing with the "New Industrial
Man," defined as a person "who has the substantial knowledge of
business and technology but, in addition, is aware of changing environmental problems and needs." Both employees and non-em-
ployees (community representatives, government officials, and representatives of other companies) attend these seminars.

• An Environmental Resource Center. Company employees can
find in the Center all references utilized in the seminars and Future
Trends Programs.

"Our efforts thus far must be viewed as experimental," says Imsland. "We are trying to avoid institutionalizing the educational programs too quickly. The overriding purpose is to make our company
more anticipatory in its outlook."

Tentative lessons to be drawn from NSP's experience include:

1. A company should try to learn about the future before attempting to plan for it. The company only now is beginning to introduce
its futures information into its planning and resource allocation process.

2. The encouragement and support of top management is crucial.

3. The openness of the educational process, both in terms of having information coming from the outside and having outside participants in the learning process, has helped to create awareness of
issues and broaden the outlook of company management. Unlike
many companies, NSP has shared widely the information and insights it has gathered about the future.

An Oil Company Turns to Scenarios

Until 1973 the Shell Oil Company each year developed an energy
forecast for planning purposes. The forecast was a 10-year analysis
of energy supply and demand using the best economic, demographic
and political premises available.

The single forecast approach worked well during most of the 1960s but came under question as predictability decayed in the early 1970s. Accordingly, Shell added scenarios in addition to the energy forecast for the 1972 planning cycle. The following year—the year that the OPEC nations quadrupled oil prices—the company abandoned the old energy forecast entirely and instead provided three scenarios.

Shell settled on three scenarios after considering six and trying four. The reason, according to Rene Zentner, head of the company's futures group, was that when planners were given too many scenarios, some were just ignored. But two scenarios would be too much of an either/or situation. At the same time, Shell did not choose a most probable future, so that the planners would give equal emphasis to the alternative scenarios. A theme provides a focus for the factors included in each scenario. A theme for a 1975-90 extrapolative scenario is: "The Future evolves through a series of ad hoc compromises between conflicting public demand for protection of the environment, fuel, energy, and economic growth." The Shell futurists avoid giving the planners a great deal of detail. By eliminating the references employed and assumptions used, a scenario can be compressed to 25 pages. All scenarios have the same length and degree of detail.

The data used in the scenarios comes primarily from study efforts throughout the year. The studies cover issues and alternatives in the social, economic, political, and technological environments. In addition, outside consultants are used for certain specialized inputs. The group that prepares the scenarios is small but contains a mix of skills and personalities. Disciplines include economics, engineering, law, and sociology.

The multiple scenarios are a component of the formal planning process. As part of the scenario development process, planners within the company review and comment on the drafts prior to presentation to senior management. Following approval or revision, the scenarios are distributed and presented to the planners, who then incorporate them in their planning effort. Each scenario requires a different corporate strategy to deal with it. The planners develop a variety of plans to cope with the several scenarios.

"The future," says Zentner, "is likely to be filled with unexpected and unlikely events and trends, arranged in unfamiliar ways and racing at us with terrifying speed." But some managers behave as though they expect the future to be a replay of the past and find scenarios hard to accept. Shell's answer has been to move toward early involvement of planners in the scenario development process to clarify obscure elements and to modify those that are "unbelievable."

A Trade Association Monitors Social Trends

One industry-wide effort to apply futures in a systematic way is the Institute of Life Insurance's Trend Analysis Program. The brief summaries of trends in areas relevant to the life insurance industry, accompanied by a bibliography of sources for further information about these issues, appear in a publication called *Trend Report*. Each issue of *Trend Report* is organized around a theme or topic which is likely to have some impact on the life insurance industry. The publication is circulated to members of the Institute who, together, represent 92% of all life insurance assets in the U.S.

The Institute of Life Insurance was originally oriented toward public relations efforts but, after World War II, the ILI became increasingly interested in keeping insurance executives attuned to forces in society which impact on the insurance industry. ILI sponsored a conference on "The Changing American Population" in 1961 and later made a broad, systematic forecast of the business environment in the form of a Future Outlook Study. In 1968 the idea emerged of organizing a formal, continuing program to gather and analyze information about relevant future developments.

Socioeconomic conditions and values strongly affect the life insurance industry and a lack of sensitivity to changes in these areas could be disastrous for the industry. Insurance executives now realize that the past assumptions about U.S. family structure and social values cannot be used as unquestionable truths in future planning. Open marriage, the decline of the nuclear family, and other phenomena may profoundly alter the demand for life insurance. To track such evolving phenomena, individuals from member companies of the ILI are assigned publications to monitor for articles describing such trends. The monitors are instructed to submit abstracts about articles which might have long-range implications for the life insurance business and which would ultimately be relevant to management's operating decisions. The final product, *Trend Report*, is organized around such topics as "Aging and the Aged" and "Frontier Technologies."

Trend Report helps keep insurance executives aware of imminent changes and their implications for the insurance industry. The publication is itself part of a trend—one which the National Association of Associations encouraged in a report in the early 1970s—the increased interest of industry associations in scanning the environment of the industries which they serve.

The ILI recently conducted a survey to determine how the *Trend Report* is being used. The results indicated that the report is read widely, is considered very interesting and informative, and frequently provides material for speeches and house publications.

However, the report so far has had only limited practical application, partly because insurance companies find the information difficult to use on a day-to-day basis and, more importantly, because the lack of commitment of top management means that the data do not get serious consideration in the planning process. The interest of top life insurance management may perk up if they encounter many disasters similar to that of the automobile insurers (like the Government Employees Insurance Company of Washington, D.C., which faced bankruptcy in 1976).

Congress and the Future

"What America needs is an early warning system to protect man against his own inventions," former Presidential science advisor Jerome B. Wiesner told a subcommittee of the U.S. House of Representatives in 1965. Wiesner's testimony struck a responsive chord, and in its report for 1966, the subcommittee made the first mention in a public document of the term *technology assessment*, a concept that suggested a major new responsibility for Congress.

The Chairman of the subcommittee, Representative Emilio Q. Daddario, introduced a bill in the House in March 1967 to create an Office of Technology Assessment. The bill failed to pass the first time it was introduced, but steadily gained support and was eventually signed into law in October 1972.

OTA became operational in January 1974 with Daddario as its first director. Unlike most Federal agencies, it is located within the legislative rather than executive branch of government, and is overseen by a 12-member Congressional Board, composed of six senators and six representatives. The first Chairman was Senator Edward M. Kennedy, who was succeeded by Representative Olin Teague of Texas.

OTA's Board selected six major areas for immediate investigation: food, energy, the oceans, materials resources, health, and transportation. Among the early contracts let by OTA were studies on new technologies for urban mass transportation, automobile safety considerations, and the rehabilitation of America's railroads. The OTA assessments of mass transit technologies and auto safety led to initiatives within Congress to improve upon proposals coming from the executive branch of government.

OTA has recently let contracts for research on systems to provide better information about the supplies (and potential shortages) of materials vital to the U.S. and world economy. Scientists and scholars, working with OTA money, are also evaluating the potential risks and benefits of oil and gas development in the waters off the New Jersey-Delaware coast, since there is high interest in Congress in petroleum exploration on the federally-owned outer continental shelflands.

OTA now is issuing a steady stream of reports designed to assist Congress in judging the impact of new technology. Each document attempts to help the Congressional decision-makers by impartially outlining the pros and cons of different actions the government might take. For example, one 401-page document, *Automated Guideway Transit: An Assessment of PRT and Other New Systems*, describes various personal rapid transit (PRT) systems, and their potential role in the future, the problems connected with them, and the various ways the systems might be developed. Another report, *The Financial Viability of Conrail*, evaluates a plan for reorganizing rail service in the 17-state region covered by the Regional Rail Reorganization Act.

The usefulness of OTA is now generally recognized. Certainly, almost no one questions the need to determine whether new forms of technology are really in the public interest. As physicist Murray Gell-Mann put it, "It used to be true that most things that were technologically possible were done. . . . Certainly, in the future, this cannot and must not be so. As our ability to do all kinds of things and the scale of them increases—for the scale is planetary for so many things now—we must try to realize a smaller and smaller fraction of all things that we can do. Therefore, an essential element of engineering from now on must be the element of choice."

OTA is not the only future-oriented innovation in Congress. The development of a second began in 1973 when the House of Representatives established a Select Committee on Committees, under the chairmanship of Representative Richard Bolling, a Missouri Democrat who had written two books on improving the functioning of the House, *House Out of Order* (1965) and *Power in the House* (1968). The Bolling Committee was charged with recommending changes in the House committee system, which provides the specialization needed for effective law-making, but also fragments the process—and goes out of date as time passes. The committees had last previously been overhauled in 1946, and the big concerns then were not the big concerns of 1973. The urgency of revamping the committees was summed up by committee member John C. Culver of Iowa (now a Senator) who said, "The past 25 years have seen a revolution in areas of public policy and concern and have added dimensions to Congressional responsibilities which were not—and, in many instances, could not—be foreseen in 1946."

The Bolling Committee conducted a thorough and comprehensive examination of congressional operations. At one of its hearings, three noted futurists (Victor Ferkiss, Willis W. Harman, and Charles W. Williams) testified concerning the problems that the

United States faces and emphasized that a solution to one problem often has unforeseen effects on other problems. Culver described the futurists' testimony as "the most provocative and challenging presentations that this committee has received to date."

The Bolling Committee eventually adopted a reorganization plan which the House passed in October 1974. In doing so, the House gave approval to what has since become known as "the foresight provision."

> The foresight provision, contained in Rule X, section 2(b)(1) of the House rules, states that each committee, except Budget and Appropriations, . . . shall review and study any conditions or circumstances which may indicate the necessity or desirability of enacting new or additional legislation within the jurisdiction of that committee (whether or not any bill or resolution has been introduced with respect thereto), and shall on a continuing basis undertake futures research and forecasting on matters within the jurisdiction of that committee.

To support the committees in meeting this requirement, the Congressional Research Service, a division of the Library of Congress, established a Futures Research Group in 1975. The Group, which has five full-time scholars, responds to requests from individual Members, committees, and their staffs for future-oriented information, including research, analysis, trends, forecasts, etc. The Group is also developing an information system for future-oriented information to serve the Congress.

In addition to OTA and the Futures Research Group, Congress now has a Congressional Clearinghouse on the Future, formed with the support of Congressman Charlie Rose, a North Carolina Democrat. The Clearinghouse has the following goals:

1. To assist Members as they become aware of the ways in which the future is affected by today's decisions.

2. To help committee members implement the foresight provision by identifying witnesses, suggesting questions, and developing model hearings on foresight.

3. To assist Members in gathering information regarding the long-term impacts of legislation on state and local government.

4. To identify new methods of citizen involvement which Members might use with constituents, and identify those citizen groups which are committed to work in the planning processes of government.

The Clearinghouse publishes a monthly newsletter called *What's Next?* which alerts the Congressional community to future-oriented publications, meetings, and other activities. In addition the Clearinghouse organizes seminars for Congress and maintains a Talent Bank of citizens willing to answer inquiries from a future-oriented viewpoint on specific subjects.

Congress has not yet finished orienting itself toward the future. The Senate currently is considering several proposals that would give it the equivalent of a "foresight provision." And other approaches to the future are being proposed: For example, Senator Hubert Humphrey has sought to establish a Congressional Office of Policy and Planning, which would provide the information and analysis that Congress needs to set national goals and priorities. And Congress also has ideas about the Executive Branch: Senator Edward Kennedy has proposed the creation of an "Experimental Futures Agency to serve as a national showcase for promising new technologies." Kennedy said that the proposed independent federal agency "could design experimental communities which could show us what would eventually be possible for all Americans in all communities: Clean air and water; reliable personal rapid transit; computerized health services and educational systems; safe streets and homes; environmentally sound energy sources—all on a community scale attuned to human needs."

Citizens Plan the Future of Their States

Thousands of U.S. citizens currently are participating in groups that seek to develop goals and plans for the future of their states. Going by such names as *Vermont Tomorrow* and *Iowa 2000*, the statewide groups provide extensive citizen participation in the middle- and long-range planning processes of their states.

The organizations have several common characteristics: First, they operate outside the regular state government structure. Second, they involve private citizens. Third, they are concerned with all aspects of the future of the entire state.

One of the most effective efforts, in the opinion of many observers, began in the State of Washington in late 1972. The *Alternatives for Washington* program was developed initially by a task force organized by the Seattle-based Evergreen Chapter of the World Future Society. According to Tom Sine, the Evergreen Chapter's project director, Alternatives for Washington owes much of its dynamism to the personal energy and commitment of its chairman, Edward Lindaman, President of Whitworth College in Spokane, Washington.

The initial year-long program included classroom sessions, interchanges, workshops, and "futures creating sessions" for the members of a 150-member task force, chosen by Governor Daniel Evans from a list of 4,000 nominees from all walks of life. An additional 1,500 citizens participated in regional conferences which reviewed the findings of the task force.

"The greatest benefit of the program," Lindaman says, "was in the transformation of the typical citizen, exposed to the future invention process, into a regular addict for futures planning. After 200 hours of work over the course of a year, seven out of 10 members of the task force were totally committed to the futures planning process."

At first, Lindaman reports, the average citizen had extreme difficulty in thinking more than one year into the future. A farmer's wife was so confused by the second day of task force meetings that she asked Lindaman's permission to leave. He convinced her to stay. Later in the session, she came up to him and said, "I want to thank you, Dr. Lindaman, for urging me to stay. The future involves our farm, our children's education, and our own well-being just as much as it concerns government. We have the right and the obligation to make our preferences known."

Towards the end of the program, the citizens were able to describe 11 alternative futures for their state and eight integrated areas of general policy recommendations for state action. The alternatives and problems were submitted to the public through a series of television programs, phone-in radio talk shows, and a press campaign. In late October, newspapers published a 40-item ballot so that citizens could vote on questions relating to the state economy, industry, population growth, land use, transportation, housing, education, human development, and governmental processes. They also were asked to identify which of 11 general alternative futures they most preferred and least preferred for the State. Over 40,000 citizens submitted ballots.

In the balloting, Washingtonians expressed their desire for the following:

• A "human environment" offering meaningful work opportunities and/or decent incomes for all citizens, including opportunities for education and social contribution.

• A diversified, moderately growing economy built on the state's huge natural resource base and including light manufacturing and other high-technology industries to supply employment for the state's young people.

• A more even distribution of population and economic activity to counter past trends toward urban concentration in eastern and western parts of the state.

• New communications technologies such as regional satellites to provide access to resources now available only in large urban centers.

• Vigorous environmental protection including conservation, recycling, and the use of renewable rather than nonrenewable resources on a "sustained yield" basis.

• Responsive, flexible government.

"The Alternatives program has been an effort on the part of state government to reinvolve the people in a public decision-making process," says Nicholas Lewis, who directed the Alternatives for Washington program for the State Planning Division. "The participants determined what government *ought* to do. The technicians in the planning office were then charged with a more appropriate role of figuring out how to translate citizens' goals into program recommendations."

The people's recommendations currently are being reviewed through another series of meetings and surveys. The basic goals need to be refined, and the citizens must examine the trade-offs between goals, agree on specific policies, and resolve the question of how to implement the resulting programs.

God and Futurism in California

"What in the world is the Bishop trying to do, delving into the future?" some California Episcopalians have wondered. The shocked reaction, reported by the Venerable John J. Weaver, Archdeacon of the Diocese of California, may be only natural because the Episcopal Church is better known today as a repository of tradition than a seedbed of futurism. Nonetheless, the Diocese has made a major effort during the last decade to futurize itself. To do so, it must endure criticisms from Church traditionalists who feel "God will provide" in the future and from non-Church people who want to know what right the Church has to "meddle with the future."

The Church began meddling with the future after a former Navy chaplain, C. Kilmer Myers, succeeded the famed James A. Pike as Bishop of California in 1966. Under Myers' leadership, says Weaver, the Diocese sought to create "an instrumentality that might guide it in its determination of the stance of the Church as it moved with mankind into the mysteries of the 21st century." The instrumentality became a Think Tank and Futures Planning Council.

"In their quest for the guidance they sought," says Weaver, "the Bishop and his associates were moved by a historical awareness that religion has been the 'glue' which has held society, from its most primitive beginnings, together—the core refuge to which men could repair in their time of trouble or despair. But they realized that the glue no longer seemed to be holding and the core of refuge, as it had been during the Reformation and the fall of Rome, was losing its magnetism of solace and comfort. It must be restored to its power of spiritual cohesion if the Church were to accompany, let alone lead, man into the uncharted paths of the coming ages."

When Myers took over, the Diocese had the traditional three branches of government—an Executive Branch (the Bishop), a Legislative Branch (the Diocesan Convention and Diocesan Council), and a Judicial Branch (a division little known even to Episcopalians). What was needed, the Bishop decided, was a Planning Branch, and from that concept blossomed, in 1968, the Futures Planning Council and its Think Tank, a smaller group within the Council.

The Council has 120 members, all volunteers drawn from many disciplines, ethnic groups, and denominational persuasions. "Their one common concern," says Weaver, "is the future of mankind and his habitat. Their one charge, the stance of the Church in relation to that future as mankind and the Church move into the coming century."

During the first six months, the Futures Planning Council and the Think Tank identified some 250 problems they felt should be studied. Then they went to work to seek alternative and affirmative courses they could recommend to the Bishop. "They met, they discussed, they debated, they studied, and they acted," Weaver reports. "In the course of months and years their work brought some 60 papers, scientifically documented, suggesting possible courses of action to meet the exigencies of the situations they foresaw in the coming ages of man's role on earth. They then reflected upon their own work, their own conclusions, and, with their documented reasons, sent them on to the Bishop."

Weaver says the papers already have had an appreciable impact upon the Church. The papers cover a wide range of subjects—work and leisure, guaranteed income, amniocentesis, the energy crisis, and drug abuse. The Planning Council now has 26 separate task forces studying topics ranging from "Alternative Educational Systems" to "Alternatives for the Aged." Once a year the entire Council and the Think Tank gather at a retreat center in Menlo Park, California, for a three-day session dealing with a specific topic.

After eight years of experience with the Futures Planning Council, Weaver says the biggest difficulty has been to keep together the "hard" and the "soft" scientists.

"For example, if our yearly conference is devoted to, say, Higher States of Consciousness, the noetic members, the philosophers, the teachers, the psychiatrists, the religious-minded, will be the first to sign up to attend, while the agronomists, the geneticists, the economists, and the engineers show up reluctantly, if at all. On the other hand, should the subject be economics, all the hard scientists quickly respond, but personal appeals are necessary to get the anthropologists, the philosophers, the social scientists, and the rest of the soft roster to take part."

But despite the problems, the futures group continues the task of futurizing a venerable institution. "The work has been good,"

Weaver says. "It has been God's work, in the sense that He works through the minds and will of men. The Council and the Think Tank have provided guidance and decisions; the ultimate impact of their work can only be measured as the long tick of time unfolds the future we ponder today."

Staff Futurists and Thirty-Year Projections

Other organizations are using a wide variety of approaches to the future. A few examples:

• The First National Bank of Minneapolis conducts a Social-Environmental Audit of the Twin Cities metropolitan area. The Audit attempts to measure the existing quality of life using ten indicators. The results of the Audit are used in setting priorities for the Bank and in specifying actions which the Bank ought to pursue.

• Bethlehem Steel has a panel of top managers selected from each department to receive reports from departmental task forces on issues which are likely to affect the steel industry in the next 10 to 20 years.

• Mobil Oil's Long-Range Analysis Group develops regional and worldwide scenarios concerning the supply and demand of energy in general and hydrocarbons in particular, using an unlimited time frame. The studies are used in the company's strategic decision-making, and they provide a long-range thinking framework for the division and corporate planners who prepare five and 10-year plans.

• Uniroyal initiated a Technological Audit in 1964. The Audit identifies hundreds of scientific advances for possible use by the company's Research and Development staff. The Audit was later expanded to include technological and social advances that might affect Uniroyal's commercial developments and their potential impact on the marketplace in general. More recently, an Advanced Conceptual Plan was formulated by various operating divisions and staff departments. The plan is a set of scenarios outlining how Uniroyal's businesses and staff functions might be operating in 15 or 20 years.

• Business International, a research firm, with its world headquarters in New York City, holds forecasting round tables in virtually every country in the world. BI's President Orville L. Freeman reports that the firm has recently done "a very ambitious sectoral forecast on what the automotive industry will look like in the year 1990." Another study under consideration would project what the global food and agricultural situation will look like in 1990.

• The Electronic Industries Association sponsored a conference which examined trends and events which would affect the electronics industry in the next 10 years. Industry executives, economists, and market planners used this perspective to make projections about the world and the electronics industry, and consequently to identify future business opportunities in electronics.

• The Prudential Insurance Company has a futurist whose job is to identify relevant trends, challenges and opportunities likely to appear in the next 30 years. Based in the Public Affairs Department, the futurist discusses his findings with management and also presents them in special reports and seminars, as well as regular training programs.

• Volvo assigns the task of exploring the future to its divisions, except when there is an issue of general interest to the company, in which case the central staff handles it. The divisions consider the business, political, social, and economic environments, as well as technological developments, in developing a 25-year projection of the state of the world.

• Western Electric's Corporate Environmental Scanning Program takes a broad look at future trends which may be relevant to the company, and its findings are presented at an Annual Planning Conference.

• Weyerhaeuser's New Business Planners are specifically interested in identifying potential for new business. To do so, they construct scenarios demonstrating ways in which the company might take advantage of that potential.

• Gillette's futurist, Joseph L. Shapiro, holds the title of Director of Commercial Research. Using a composite projection of the total environment in the year 2000, Shapiro has been able to locate potential opportunities as well as pitfalls for Gillette, and his general observations have been used successfully in Gillette planning. The futurist's role goes beyond research to include advising company executives on the future potential of any proposal, such as the possible acquisition of another company.

• Coca-Cola uses an analysis of resources, both physical and human, and the total business environment as a preliminary step in the planning process. Strategies and goals are worked out principally on the division level, due to the decentralized nature of the firm.

• General Mills' Director of Governmental Relations tracks the evolution of issues which may someday affect General Mills. The Director, Graham Molitor, incorporates into his job the task of alerting the company about environmental trends, using an annual report to the senior vice president as his medium in addition to serving as an advisor and investigator to anyone in management who requests information about an issue.

How to Introduce the Future Successfully

Introducing a futures perspective into an organization requires considerable tact, suggests Jay S. Mendell, a consultant on corporate strategy who now is a professor at Florida Atlantic University's College of Business and Public Administration. The gist of his advice is: "Seek top management approval and avoid triggering fears."

"I have talked to a hundred or more futurists (and would-be futurists) in business and government," says Mendell. "There is almost unanimous agreement that without strong support from the top of the organization, a futures group cannot survive at all."

Unfortunately, says Mendell, it is often difficult to enlist top management support for futurism since "tunnel vision and short-sightedness (the antitheses of futurist thinking), carefully managed and nurtured, have in the past been positive, not negative, in propelling executives to the top." But Mendell, who once headed a two-man futures group in an aviation company and is now introducing futurism into the strategic process of a financial institution, can report some success stories: "One successful futurist in the chemicals industry discovered futurism with his boss' boss, and with understanding and support from the top gradually emerged over a period of years as a manager of futures studies. Another futurist, in communications, works for a very large company which aborted several early attempts at futurism. He studied their mistakes; conceived a sound and practical attempt; implemented it, and judiciously convinced top management that it had been *their* baby all along, that he was carrying out *their* program."

Mendell says that to be effective a futurist must get out into the organization to teach and influence, but as he asks people to invest themselves in learning he will almost certainly make them anxious or fearful at times. If he wants to survive, he must take care not to increase their anxiety too much. "Futurism forces people to learn to play a new game. To futurize, one must learn to think creatively and speculatively, to tolerate ambiguity, and to separate speculative from analytical thinking. Most people cannot do this, and they certainly do not enjoy learning these skills on the job and in front of their colleagues."

People's ideologies frequently get in the way of futurism, Mendell says. If an individual is opposed to the decline of the traditional family structure, he may not wish even to discuss it, even though such a trend in the business environment may have a very important impact on the organization. People also may not want to think about important changes that may occur in the organization itself. "Often individuals do not want to discuss the future because they know that the environment will force a change in the mission and fundamental character of their organization. They are 'railroad men,' for instance, and they want their organization to define itself in railroad terms, not transportation terms. This goes beyond worrying about their *personal* future status. They *believe* in the current mission and don't want it changed."

Some people rapidly become excited about exploring the future, but others do not. "When the future environment comes into focus as fast-changing, complicated, and danger-fraught," says Mendell, "they see 'no future in the future,' that is, they see no way that they, or their organization, can survive environmental changes without making changes too drastic to contemplate. These persons move back to apathy—with a vengeance. And they remember who frightened them—the futurist."

James B. Webber and Rebecca A. Ojala of the Cambridge Research Institute in Cambridge, Massachusetts, agree with Mendell on the need for top management interest and support for futurism to succeed. They also point to such other obstacles as the fact that managers do not understand how to use information about future possibilities. "A future study, almost by definition," say Webber and Ojala, "is rarely timely for a particular decision. Its main contribution to decision-making is to build an appreciation in the executive's mind that allows him to broaden his future-oriented considerations when making a decision."

Webber and Ojala offer the following tips on how to succeed in introducing the future into an organization:

• *Understand the decision setting of your organization.* A company whose environment is simple and stable does not need complex studies.
• *Seek the seekers.* Find allies within the company.
• *Plan to learn first* (as the Northern States Power Company did), then plug the techniques into a planning system.
• *Decrease the resistance to change by minimizing the appearance of futures as a "big new deal."* Trumpeting the exotic, complex newness and originality of future studies is not the best way to win friends. Make the new approach sound as if it has a significant relevant advantage over the old way but is, in fact, only a small change because it is compatible, simple, divisible, and reversible. You can try little bits of the new approach and back off if you are not satisfied.

In the past, most organizations paid little attention to the long-range future but the rapidity of social and technological change today is causing business, governmental, and other groups now to search for ways to anticipate possible future developments. Though most organizations still do little or no strategic futures planning, more and more executives are beginning to take a broad look at the future in its various social, political, and other aspects. The dangers of ignoring future developments in a fast-changing world are generally recognized, and organizations are expected to become increasingly serious and systematic in thinking about the problems and opportunities that they will encounter in the years ahead. In business, government, and other fields, we can expect to see increasing efforts to develop an anticipatory mode of operating.

11

The Coming Revolution in Education

Down through history, most scholars have shown a remarkable capacity for ignoring the present as well as the future. Antiquarian by temperament, they have steadfastly looked backward, extolling the wisdom of bygone ages rather than opening their eyes to what was around and ahead of them. Thus the scholars insisted on the correctness of Aristotle even when Galileo offered visible proof that Aristotle was mistaken. The antiquarian bias of the scholar passed into teaching, and the teacher's function became that of filling the empty heads of students with the culture of the past. Even now, in school rooms across the world, there are school children desperately struggling to memorize Latin declensions, decipher novels that are of little interest today, and master mathematical problems that they will never use once they are out of school. Meanwhile, the same young people desperately need the knowledge required to cope with a rapidly changing, highly complex world.

But a revolution is brewing, due to the increasing exasperation of students, teachers, parents, and the public at large with the general irrelevance of so much of today's education. And the secret weapon in that revolution is futurism.

The future provides a touchstone for testing the worth of what is taught in schools. Young people have urgent learning needs if they are to be well equipped for the future, and courses that do not provide essential learning should be completely revamped or dropped from the curriculum. We should recognize that today's curriculum is the residue of traditions dating back thousands of years, and generally reflects what teachers want to teach more than what young people need to learn. Teachers have invented many ingenious arguments for their subjects, because they want to protect their livelihoods, but we should not let ourselves be deceived. And teachers should not be overly alarmed by the coming revolution; they can learn new subjects, and they can also revise their approach to current subjects to make them more relevant to the students' learning needs.

A Future-Oriented Curriculum

Just what *should* be taught in a future-oriented curriculum? Draper Kauffman in *Teaching the Future* offers the following list of six basic skills, with some of their components.

> *Access to Information:* Reading; listening and seeing; direct experiment; libraries and reference books; computerized data-retrieval; data from newspapers, businesses, government agencies, etc.; asking experts; judging reliability; managing information overload.
>
> *Thinking Clearly:* Semantics, propaganda and common fallacies; values clarification; deductive logic; mathematics; analytical problem-solving; scientific method; probability and statistics; computer programming; general systems; creative problem-solving; forecasting and prediction.
>
> *Communicating Effectively:* Speaking informally; public speaking; voice and body language; cultural barriers to communication; formal and informal writing; grammar, syntax, and style; drawing, sketching, still photography, film making, etc.; graphic design and layout; outlines, flow-charts, charts, tables, and graphs; organization and editing; handwriting, typing, dictating.
>
> *Understanding Man's Environment:* Astronomy, physics, and chemistry; geology and physical geography; biology, ecology, and ethology; genetics, evolution, and population dynamics; fundamentals of modern technology; applied mechanics, optics, and electronics.
>
> *Understanding Man and Society:* Human evolution; human physiology; linguistics; cultural anthropology (including history and the humanities); psychology and social psychology; racism, ethnicity, and xenophobia; government and law; economics and economic philosophy; changing occupational patterns; education and employment; issues in human survival; prospects for mankind.
>
> *Personal Competence:* Physical grace and coordination; survival training and self-defense; safety, hygiene, nutrition, and sex education; consumer education and personal finance; creative and performing arts; basic interpersonal skills; small group dynamics; management and administration; effective citizen participation; knowledge of best personal learning styles and strategies; mnemonics and other learning aids; biofeedback, meditation, mood control; self-knowledge and self-motivation.

Kauffman emphasizes that these are *objectives* for the total curriculum and not a list of courses. No program of study, he adds, can provide the necessary breadth and depth unless each component is designed to serve multiple learning goals. In the period ahead, there may be growing demand for those who can teach, for example, "small group dynamics" and "effective writing" in the process of teaching "biology" or "contemporary world issues."

It is worth noting that despite the immense variety of topics on Kauffman's list they all are part of a deliberate attempt to equip a student for his future roles in society. As this list demonstrates, the futurist perspective can convert the jumble of subjects offered in most schools into a meaningful program. Futurism offers the missing link between education and life.

Selecting the subjects that are likely to help a young person manage his future life is only one aspect of futurizing a curriculum. A second is orienting a given course toward the future instead of the past. A social studies teacher can ask students "What do you think will happen in the future?" as well as "What happened in the past?" The question is almost certain to stimulate student interest, and it also frees the students, at least to some extent, from the fear of getting the "wrong" answer. Since the future is the realm of possibilities rather than actualities, students can imagine many different things, and the teacher cannot mark them wrong. Orienting a course toward what might happen in the future turns students from antiquarians into planners, that is, from passive research into the past to active participation in shaping the future.

No matter how future-oriented a curriculum may be, it cannot anticipate completely a student's future learning needs. For this reason, education must be revamped to allow people to move easily in and out of education. At present, education is traditionally bunched at the beginning of a person's life. This custom must stop, most futurist educators believe. In general, they suggest that young people might interrupt their formal schooling for brief periods during their late teens in order to work, travel, or engage in other learning experiences. Later, they should resume their formal education.

Professor Harold Shane of Indiana University has proposed a "paracurriculum," which would be a supervised work program that would give youngsters an opportunity to do productive labor, starting when they are 13 to 15 years of age. The school would supervise the young person's move from the world of the school to the "real world," and monitor the student's on-the-job performance. After a period of work, he would return to school to continue his education. The paracurriculum concept would eliminate "drop-outs" and "push-outs": young people bored with school could easily leave and do something else for a time until they were ready to continue their formal education.

And, by spreading work throughout a person's career instead of bunching it in the middle, preceded by education and followed by retirement, futurists hope to provide a better opportunity for people to refurbish their skills in mid-career. Many futurists believe that people will be changing careers—not just jobs—with increasing frequency in the years ahead, partly because their previous careers will have disappeared and partly because they will have developed new interests.

As the paracurriculum concept suggests, futurists are well aware that most learning does not occur in the classroom, but in the home, neighborhood, and elsewhere. Furthermore, *everyone is a teacher as well as a learner.* In the future, steps may be taken to help non-professional teachers to teach more effectively.

At the same time, major efforts need to be made to improve the ease whereby adults can acquire new understanding and skills through formal education. At present, young people are still led to believe that once they graduate from high school or college—or are simply old enough to escape the compulsory education laws—they are finished with education. Many people remember their time in school as a period of excruciating boredom, painful humiliation, and psychological degradation. They have little inclination to start learning again in later life. Yet they have important learning needs if they are to function effectively in modern society. Since there is little likelihood that the pace of social change will slow down, people who stop learning at any point in their lives will find themselves increasingly unable to understand the world around them. They may find it difficult to earn a living or cope with the requirements of everyday life. Hence legislatures may eventually lay down legal requirements for adult education: The notion that people aged 50 or 60 may someday be trying to hide from truant officers is not completely fanciful! More desirable, of course, would be the making of education into a normal and desirable aspect of life for everyone.

Courses in Futuristics

Besides trying to orient the general curriculum or their own courses toward the future, many teachers now are giving courses in the future itself. No one knows who taught the first course in futuristics, but as far back as 1943 a political science professor, Ossip Flechtheim, wrote an essay urging that the future be taught as a subject. Author Alvin Toffler taught one of the first courses on the future in 1966 at the New School for Social Research in New York City. The number of such courses began growing rapidly in the late 1960s and mushroomed in the 1970s. H. Wentworth Eldredge, Professor of Sociology at Dartmouth College, identified at least 475 such courses during a series of surveys from 1969 to 1974. Based on inquiries received by the World Future Society during the mid 1970s, instruction in futuristics now is so widespread that some future-oriented activity appears to be occurring at a majority of the major college and university campuses in North America; in addition, courses in futuristics appear increasingly at the high school level and also, though less frequently, at the elementary level.

Educators have found many intriguing ways to introduce futuristics into the curriculum. At Canisius College in upstate New York, historian James Duran's students examine the attitudes toward the future held by various heads of state; for example, how did Lenin's view of the future affect Soviet policy? At Pennsylvania State University, Ronald Abler, a professor of geography, has taught a course on "The Geography of the Future." Other courses deal with such topics as "The Sociology of the Future," "Technology Assessment," etc.

The University of Massachusetts at Amherst pioneered in 1970 with its Future Studies program in the School of Education. Courses include futuristic methodologies, alternative futures of education, and future-oriented curriculum design and teaching methods. The University of Houston at Clear Lake City initiated a full-scale graduate futuristics program in 1974. Candidates studying for an M.S. degree in studies of the future may construct their programs from 25 future-oriented courses and from courses offered by other university programs. The courses include forecasting techniques, educational futuristics, and apocalyptic images. In addition, a specialized master's degree in educational futures is available.

Elementary and secondary educators are demonstrating a wide variety of ways to teach the future to younger students. The Fort Myer Elementary School in Arlington, Virginia, has a program known as *Projecting for the Future* which acquaints students with possible developments in the future and also some of the career choices they have. Priscilla Griffith of Florida's Melbourne High School, near Cape Canaveral, taught one of the first known high school courses on the future in 1966. She says that high school students need a "gyroscope"—a center of stability—to help them adapt to the severe stress coming from a rapidly changing society and their rapidly changing minds and bodies. During adolescence, students often have a great personal need to understand change and adapt to stress. It is particularly important, she says, for them to understand that there are positive alternatives to the problems of the present and the frightful scenarios of future disaster need not come about.

Courses in futuristics provide a way for students to put together a coherent picture of the future and how they might fit into it. The holistic imperative of futuristics helps young people to make the connections between what they are learning in school and their future careers as workers, parents, and citizens. By demonstrating the relationships of individual courses to their future lives, futuristics can help motivate students to put forth greater efforts in their studies. A student can come to see his education as a meaningful preparation for great tasks ahead rather than a senseless activity dictated by an unfeeling and indifferent society.

Courses in futuristics differ greatly in character, but a few gen-

eralizations may be made. Futuristics teachers tend to favor "learn-
ing-by-doing" and other innovative teaching techniques rather than
traditional lectures. Class projects and learning games are popular.
Many teachers use classic scenarios like George Orwell's *1984* or
Aldous Huxley's *Brave New World* to stimulate versions of trend
projections, cross-impact analyses, simulations, and other futuristic techniques.

The introduction of futuristics into the educational system appears to have come mainly from initiatives taken by individual
teachers rather than the institutions for which they work. Most educational innovations, such as open classrooms and programmed
instruction, have originated in the results of educational and psychological research and have filtered through extensive debate in
professional circles into the upper echelons of school administration
and teacher education and finally into the classroom. By contrast,
futuristics courses, so far, have generally appeared on the initiative of a single enthusiast, who has pioneered without an order or
suggestion from his superiors. Thus futuristics is essentially a
grass-roots movement in education.

The Student's Image of the Future

We are used to thinking that the causes of the present lie in the
past. But in a very real sense the causes of the present may lie in
the future. That is to say, the image of the future that people have
in their heads can have a dramatic effect on what they do right now.
For example, research by sociologist Arthur Stinchcombe indicates
that the image that high school students have of their future plays
a major role in determining whether they will rebel by dropping out
or flunking their courses. Young people who expect to become manual workers see no clear connection between what they are doing
in school and their future occupational status. Thus their current
performance loses its meaning. After all, if what you are learning
is probably going to be a waste of time, there is not much point in
exerting yourself. You might just as well hang around on street corners or in pool halls.

Similarly, researchers looking into the factors that affected children's performance in an Operation Head Start type program in
Ypsilanti, Michigan, found that parents' image of a child's future
was among "the best predictor variables for cognitive growth in
pre-school among a disadvantaged population." Sociologist Benjamin Singer says there is good evidence indicating that the pre-
dominant American middle-class orientation is toward the future,
and that parents brought up in the Protestant Ethic typically pass
on to their children "a time perspective that discounts the present
and looks toward the future. This concern with the future, when

transformed into personal terms, carries with it the ingredients for success in a culture geared to the future rather than the past." Such a future-oriented time perspective is lacking in many lower-class homes.

For youngsters to function well in school, they should feel that they are moving into a world in which they have desirable and meaningful roles. Unfortunately, many schools do not give their students such an image of their future roles in the world. Even if they try, the schools may not be able to undo the negative image inculcated by parents and others who shape the child's view of his future.

In times past, young people had a fairly good idea of their future roles. A boy would follow in his father's footsteps as a farmer, a smith, or a miller; a girl would become a wife and mother. Today few young people see their future roles in anything like those simple terms. Most do not know what occupation they will follow or whether they will ever marry and have children. Hence, when they think about the future, they see it as uncertain and threatening. This vision of an uncertain and threatening future can easily lead to despair and to a fixation on momentary pleasures.

Educators cannot make society give to each student the career that might appeal to him—movie star, famous scientist, President of the U.S., etc.—but they can help him to understand the incredible diversity of a job market that offers tens of thousands of distinctively different jobs, each offering challenges and satisfactions for the right person. Teachers can also help young people to appreciate the dignity and value of *all* work, paid and unpaid, for self and for others. Most important, teachers can encourage young people to develop a positive image of themselves as capable and worthy people, who can learn the new skills needed to succeed in a fast-changing job market and can serve mankind in myriads of significant ways.

In addition to uncertainty about their roles in the future world, many young people now despair of the future of the world itself. Though the younger (elementary school) students tend to have optimistic images of the future, the older students (secondary and college) tend to be very pessimistic. This pessimism stems in large measure from their growing uncertainty about their own roles in the future, but pessimism also comes from overemphasis on the problems of the world. Many teachers feel they have a duty to warn young people about world problems; but too much dwelling on problems can result in so much pessimism that the young people feel that the effort is useless. Gloom is not the best mood for effective action.

"There are two perilous attitudes toward the future," says Professor Howard F. Didsbury, Jr., Executive Director of Kean College of New Jersey's Program for the Study of the Future. "One is belief in a 'technological fix'—the notion that science and technology will snatch us back from the abyss just in time; this attitude tends to encourage complacency. At the other extreme—and equally dangerous—is the great temptation to exaggerate or overemphasize the complexities and difficulties that lie before us. Such an overemphasis tends to make the problems seem so great that students grow apathetic or feel completely ineffectual."

Didsbury says that teachers need to determine the attitudes of their students so as to judge the proper approach. At the beginning of each course, he asks his students to prepare papers answering these questions: "Would you consider yourself an optimist or a pessimist with respect to the future? How malleable to human will do you believe the future to be? Justify your position." If the students appear unduly optimistic, Didsbury will emphasize the problems the world faces; if on the other hand, they already are gloomy, he will take special pains not to "scare the wits out of them" any further.

Students' attitudes toward the future can improve dramatically as a result of a futuristics course. "Before I participated in futuristics," reported Steve Mathews, a Minnesota high school student, "I suffered from a type of doomsday syndrome. I saw myself as being insignificant in the making of the future, like it was some kind of immovable tidal wave, so I never really gave it much thought." After completing a full year of futuristics, Steve changed his mind. "Futuristics means a lot to me, because it has opened my eyes to many roads that we can take, instead of the narrow path I thought was inevitable."

One of Steve's teachers, Penny Damlo of Burnsville (Minnesota) Senior High, says that his evaluation is fairly typical. Many people are scared of the future when they first try to think seriously about it, but after studying it for a while they begin to feel that they can do something about it. Sister June Wilkerson, a teacher at Regina High School in Minneapolis, says that tests given before and after a course in "The Future and Social Change" showed that the course significantly improved students' images of the future. The course, taught by Sister Wilkerson and Joe Epping, focuses on three topics: a diagnosis of what's wrong with the present, a prescription of what could be done in the future, and an analysis of how to get from where we are to where we want to be, with emphasis on what students can do to work for change.

Despite the newness of futuristics as a school or university subject, the evidence clearly indicates that educators can play an important role in helping students to develop constructive attitudes toward the future and can get young people moving toward the creation of a better world.

12

The Uses of the Future

Almost everyone in today's rapidly changing society faces hundreds of clamoring problems, each of which demands more from him than he can possibly give. Pressed by the urgent problems of the present, he may have little patience with anyone who suggests that he should think about the future. His natural reply is likely to be, "How can you ask me to think about the future when I'm trying to deal with a crisis right now?"

Yet today's crisis is one of the best reasons for thinking about the future. Almost always, the crisis has resulted from a failure to deal with problems before they reached the crisis stage. In retrospect, it is generally easy to see how a modest amount of thought and effort—if invested earlier—could easily have forestalled the crisis, thus effecting huge savings in money and grief. Recognition of this simple truth is expressed in folk sayings like "An ounce of prevention is worth a pound of cure" and "A stitch in time saves nine," yet this simple folk wisdom is often forgotten in the hurly-burly of what seems to be an endless series of crises.

Due to the acceleration of social change, government officials, businessmen, and private citizens all have found themselves increasingly in the position of responding to crises rather than preventing them. U.S. Senator John C. Culver has offered the following description of "government-by-crisis" and its impact on the public:

> Recent energy and environmental problems demonstrate that as a nation we are reacting to problems rather than anticipating them before they grow into national emergencies. For instance, environmental degradation offers a classic case of government by crisis. We had no idea several years ago that our form of industrialization and urbanization would have such an adverse environmental impact. Now we are frantically trying to recover from what we failed to foresee.
>
> As a consequence of these major crises that have come upon our society from the blind side, I believe there is a growing sense among the public that its institutions are rudderless.

The disasters caused by failure to deal promptly with emerging problems are clear, but escaping from the treadmill of successive crises often seems difficult or impossible, because the current emergencies pre-empt all the available blood, sweat, and tears, leaving no resources to think about avoiding emergencies yet to come.

To escape from the crisis mode of operation, we need to recognize two facts:

1. Massive efforts to solve crises often result in little progress because time is required. Trying to solve overnight a crisis that has developed over a number of years may result in a horrendous waste of resources.

2. Crises often solve themselves, with little or almost no intervention. In many cases, the best policy may be one of deliberate inaction or only token action, because major expenditures of effort would be wasteful and possibly even harmful.

In general, a crisis grabs our attention, but it should not receive *all* of our attention. A certain expenditure of time and money may be wise, but after a certain point, further expenditure produces only marginal results. At that point, the resources should be diverted elsewhere, even though the crisis has not been "solved," and clients, constituents, or associates are still demanding an immediate and perfect solution. Politically, it may be desirable to continue an official posture of full commitment to resolving the crisis, but quietly shift resources as much as possible to areas where they can be more productive.

Identifying the potential crises of the future so that they can be averted is one important function of futuristics. In effect, the systematic exploration of future possibilities can serve as a distant early warning system so that timely action can be taken to deal with problems before they become disasters. In addition to spotting the potential crises of tomorrow, futuristics can identify potential "anti-crises"—situations offering unusual opportunities for significant gains. An "anti-crisis" may result from a scientific breakthrough, which suddenly opens an exciting new approach to tackling certain problems or a change in public opinion which allows politicians to take needed actions that previously would have provoked popular outrage or violence. Every real crisis is accompanied by an anti-crisis, that is, a bonanza of opportunity. Scholars have noted that the Chinese ideograph for "crisis" is an amalgam of the symbols for "danger" and "opportunity," and neatly expresses the insight that a great danger or an agonizing problem often makes it possible to accomplish things that otherwise would be impossible. The Japanese attack on Pearl Harbor, for example, provoked a national crisis in the United States, but it also created an anti-crisis, because public opinion was instantaneously prepared for actions that earlier would have been unacceptable. The anti-crisis aspect is so important that William James long ago sought a "moral equivalent of war"—something that would galvanize people's energies in the way that war does.

Crises and anti-crises are, of course, only the most dramatic types of future developments that may be identified through the systematic study of futuribles (ideas about what may happen in the future). Many other potential developments may also be identified, so that decision-makers can take effective action.

In thinking about the uses of futuristics it is important to recognize that all decision-making necessarily involves some kind of forecasting. It is not possible to make decisions, prepare plans, and take action without some idea about what may or may not happen in the future. Assumptions *will* be made about the future. They may be made carelessly or even unconsciously but they are inevitably made. Perhaps the most frequent assumption is that the world of the future will be so much like the world of the past that we can just assume, for the purpose of planning, that it will be identical with the world of the past. This assumption has beome increasingly invalid as the pace of social change has accelerated.

Forecasting crises and otherwise assisting people to make wiser decisions is only one of a number of important uses of futures studies. A list of these uses would include the following:

● Assisting the decision-making process by (a) providing useful frameworks for decision-making, (b) identifying dangers and opportunities, (c) suggesting a variety of possible approaches to solving a problem, (d) helping to assess alternative policies and actions, (e) enabling people to see the present, (f) increasing the degree of choice, (g) setting goals and devising means to reach them.

● Preparing people to live in a changing world by (a) providing "pre-experience" so that the future does not come as a shock, (b) offering a framework for understanding change as a normal process, (c) making the future an object of conscious study so that it becomes more interesting and exciting to contemplate.

● Offering a framework for reconciliation and cooperation. This applies not only for small organizations and communities but for nations and international communities.

● Contributing to science and thought.

● Aiding creativity.

● Helping to motivate people, both young and old, to learn.

● Providing a perspective for developing a well-integrated personal outlook or philosophy of life.

● Offering a means for recreation or "fun."

Assisting the Decision-Making Process

Assisting the decision-making process is perhaps the most important single role of futuristics, so important that many people can hardly imagine that the field has other important roles. The specific ways in which futuristics can be helpful include:

1. *Providing useful frameworks for decision-making and planning.* Plans, policies and decisions cannot be made without basic assumptions, and if these assumptions are erroneous, the planning can be disastrous. For example, French military planners in the period between the world wars decided that their principal problem in a war would be to halt a massive German infantry offensive and on that assumption they developed a powerful defensive system to halt the future attack. The Maginot Line was an impressive defensive system, but better designed for World War I than for World War II. New realities made the Maginot Line a sorry anachronism and France collapsed in 1940.

Based on the wrong assumptions, the most beautiful plans become tragedies—with undertones of comic irony. A magnificent educational institution is built—but stands empty for lack of students; millions of dollars are spent to develop an impressive automobile that people won't buy; a magnificent city center is created—but becomes a white elephant.

Futuristics can help to provide reasonable assumptions about what the future may be like. Often these assumptions must be expressed in terms of probability or possibility rather than certainty, but the planner can have at least some basis for making plans, and perhaps also can get some warning about assumptions that should be reviewed as the planning proceeds.

2. *Identifying future dangers and opportunities.* Decision-makers in business, government, and elsewhere need to know about both potential dangers and potential opportunities that lie on the horizon. In addition, futuristics can help assess the likelihood of a certain problem becoming critical, and if so, to monitor it so that action can be taken when needed to obviate serious difficulties. At the same time, futuristics can evaluate potential opportunities so that decision-makers can take action when appropriate.

3. *Suggesting a variety of possible approaches to solving a problem.* In addition to providing a framework for policy-making, futurists can suggest alternative approaches to issues. Such alternative policies develop almost naturally as various possible developments are identified.

4. *Helping to assess alternative policies and actions.* Besides suggesting alternative approaches, futuristics can help evaluate them by analyzing their possible impact on the future world.

5. *Enabling people to see the present.* People generally make decisions on the basis of what they think their present situation is. But their perception of the present is generally biased toward the past, that is, people assume that their situation is still essentially the same as they had perceived it in the past. Even when they have good reason to know that the situation has changed, it is often difficult to overcome this perceptual lag. For example, when we encounter a young person whom we have not seen for a number of years, we are often astounded at how much he has changed. We had retained an image of him based on what he was like in the past and nothing had really altered that image until he suddenly appeared before our eyes. If we had made a futuristic study of him, we might not have been so surprised, because we would have known that he would be much larger, more mature, etc. A similar perceptual lag is widespread in organizational policy making. Ian Wilson, a General Electric consultant, says that his group in the industrial relations department found that through the years the percentage of white-collar workers in the United States had gained on the number of blue-collar workers, and this trend was expected to continue. When Wilson and his colleagues reviewed the GE situation, they discovered that GE *already* had more white-collar than blue-collar workers, yet the company was set up administratively as if the blue-collar workers were in the majority. In effect, GE's research into the future enabled the company to see where it was in the present. Armed with this new perception, the company then took steps to bring its industrial relations department into line with the realities of the workforce.

6. *Increasing the degree of choice.* Without knowing that they have alternatives, people tend to accept current trends as manifest destiny. By identifying other possible developments, people gain freedom of choice and can avoid a slavish acceptance of current trends that may be leading in an unfortunate or even disastrous direction. Without forecasting the future, there is no freedom to choose a future: The future is simply thrust upon us. By studying future possibilities, we begin to realize new possibilities that are open to us. We are not locked into our present situation.

Preparing People to Live in a Changing World

One of the few certainties about the coming decades is that civilization will undergo continued rapid social change. People must be ready to adapt constantly. They will need to acquire new skills and attitudes and even new moral values in order to cope successfully in a changing society. Futuristics can help by informing people about what may happen in the future, giving them an outlook that accepts change as a normal process to be expected, and making the future an interesting and exciting field of study so that people can become more optimistic and self-confident.

By studying future possibilities, people can acquire the emotional outlook that they need—one of self-confidence in the face of rapid change. This self-confidence develops as people explore the future, because exploration of the future requires that people face forward rather than backward. As they begin to look ahead at what may happen and identify both the dangers and the opportunities, they cease backing into the future, which is what causes them to deal incompetently with new developments.

Today many people are suffering from future shock due to the rapid pace of change. They have withdrawn from a world that has become alien and incomprehensible, and are now largely incompetent to cope with today's world. If the pace of change accelerates (as seems likely), more and more people may become largely incompetent to cope with life. To live successfully, people must learn to accept the fact that society is changing and that they must learn constantly to adjust to the changes around them. Futuristics offers the means of doing so. Familiarizing people with the things that they may encounter in the future helps provide psychological preparation. A person who has heard of hovercraft is not likely to be completely baffled when he first encounters one, even though he may know virtually nothing about them. Similarly, a person who is aware that in the future he may be able to choose the sex of his children can begin thinking, very casually and in a relaxed manner, what he would do if ever he has to make the choice.

By studying the possible developments of the future, a person can prepare emotionally for the future, and get some idea of the context in which he will be making decisions. He can develop a general sense of what the future may be like—a sense of what may happen—and this sense of what is to come will provide a framework for confident and effective action. Futuristics provides a kind of "pre-experience" of the situations that we will confront in the future. Because we will encounter so much change, our past experience will lose much of its value as a frame of reference and we will need to rely increasingly on "pre-experience"—the imaging of possible changes and appropriate responses to those changes. This pre-experience can serve as a kind of substitute for experience. Futuristics can also give us a feeling of confidence and even of optimism about the future, because we know more about the future. We are in the situation of a person who is moving into territory for which he has several maps that are crude, but at least give him some idea of what to expect. Futuristics can help people accept change more easily because they have received some warning and can adjust to it; they can move into the future with less psychological disruption.

Futuristics can help give people the confidence needed to approach problems with excitement and interest rather than dread. Futurists tend to be optimistic about the future, because they have thought about the future, understand that it *can* be good, and are working to make it good.

The sorting out of feelings can lead to a goal-oriented, positive, optimistic approach to life, which makes effective action more likely.

Futuristics can give people a useful set of perceptions that can help them to cope with a rapidly changing world. These perceptions include:

1. The future is not fixed, but consists of a variety of alternatives among which we can choose those we want to realize.

2. Choice is necessary. Refusing to choose is itself a choice.

3. Small changes through time can become major changes.

4. The future world will probably be drastically different in many respects from the present world.

5. People are responsible for their future; the future doesn't just happen to them.

6. Methods successful in the past may not work in the future due to changed circumstances.

A Framework for Reconciliation and Cooperation

The peoples of the world do not share a common past, but they do share a common future. Through history, mankind has been divided into warring groups, each seeking to preserve its territory from incursions by other tribes and nations. Each of the world's peoples has sought to maintain itself in an environment filled with enemies. The past offers no common heritage which can be celebrated jointly by all people. Even the great religions have become rivals that divide rather than unite the world's people. But the future is different, because it has not yet been sullied by atrocities and jealousies, and offers a new realm in which the world's warring peoples can find reconciliation. Nations that today stand adamantly opposed to each other can find common ground in the future. A possibly significant sign of the future as the realm of reconciliation may be the 1975 linkup in space of the Soviet Union's Soyuz spacecraft with the U.S. Apollo vehicle. The event was commemorated by a set of nearly identical stamps issued simultaneously by both nations. In space—and in the world of the future—people are not yet locked into the rivalries and fears that so often imprison them; there is room and opportunity for everyone.

By focusing on the future, we can escape the rigidities of the present. The grievances of blacks and whites in America, of Catholics and Protestants in Northern Ireland, of Christians and Moslems in Lebanon can never be settled, but they can eventually be forgotten. The process of forgetting is accelerated when the focus is on the future rather than on the past, or what might be done tomorrow rather than what was done yesterday. The past is the domain of wrongs that can never be righted; the future is the realm of dreams that can be realized through common effort.

By thinking about what they would like to do in the future—and need each other to accomplish—small organizations and communities as well as large nations and international blocs can develop a framework for reconciliation and cooperation.

Contributions to Science and Thought.

Futuristic research promises to make a number of contributions to other disciplines. As young as the field is, it appears already to have made a major contribution to communications—computer conferencing. This novel use of computers did not develop from computer theory, but from the typical group process encountered in futuristic research. In the 1960s, Olaf Helmer and other researchers at the RAND Corporation were interested in policy formulation and Delphi techniques for aggregating expert information about the future. They began a series of experiments in which computers were used to aggregate group judgment. In the late 1960s, Murray Turoff, then at the Office of Emergency Preparedness in Washington, D.C., used the technique as a means of getting the opinions of experts and officials located at widely separate points and arriving at a group consensus on what needed to be done. In 1972 the Institute for the Future in Menlo Park, California, began implementing its network conferencing system (named *Forum*) under sponsorship of the National Science Foundation and the Pentagon's Advanced Research Projects Agency. The Institute used several versions of the system in experiments designed to analyze the behavior patterns of user groups. Among these activities, which extended from mid 1973 to the end of 1974, were:

- A conference, jointly arranged with Bell Canada, in which 35 researchers assessed telecommunications as a substitute for physical travel.
- A continuing research discussion between the Institute and the Communications Studies Group in London, England.
- A simulation of a meeting of an international working group on the future of digital data networks. Eighteen students played the roles of delegates to a Geneva meeting of the International Telecommunications Union and defended actual

positions of the countries involved. Negotiation and bargaining behavior were monitored.

- A planning conference on policy research in education, linking Institute researchers and the staff of Lilly Endowment, Inc.
- An international conference organized by the Brookhaven National Laboratory of the Atomic Energy Commission to study the effects of sulfur pollution on humans. Twenty participants contributed to this activity.
- A conference linking Dartmouth, Stanford, MIT, and other research centers to study experiential learning. This conference was sponsored by the National Institute of Social Sciences.

These experiments have now expanded with the introduction of an advanced version of this system on a commercial network. This version, known as *Planet*, is currently being used by the U.S. Geological Survey, the National Aeronautics and Space Administration, and several other major organizations. Although such usage is still experimental, the questions to be answered now concern the best range of tasks and the optimum organizational conditions for use, rather than the actual feasibility and usefulness of the concept. In the years ahead, computer conferencing is likely to expand far beyond the use that futurists originally planned for it. In fact, the futurists at the Institute for the Future have been actively seeking and studying possible uses.

Futuristics may also make a contribution to the field of history. In general, history is taught as if it were an inevitable unfolding of trends and events. But the future, as viewed by futurists, displays to us an infinite variety of alternative paths in a world that abounds in possibilities. Reconciling and unifying the two approaches may change people's concept of history.

An Aid to Creativity

Futuristics can stimulate and focus creative problem-solving. When people begin to contemplate the more distant future rather than their immediate problems, they can begin to think in a more relaxed and creative way. This freeing-up of thought permits new ideas to flow into consciousness, where they can later be evaluated for possible use. One can select the area in which one wishes to be creative and then begin thinking about possible future developments in that area. Almost automatically, new ideas begin to flow — ideas that are generally shut out when one focuses solely on the present.

An Educational Technique

The future offers an excellent tool for motivating students to learn. "Modern students appear to learn faster and with more enthusiasm if they participate very actively in producing knowledge rather than reading about the process," says H. Wentworth Eldredge, the Dartmouth professor of sociology who surveyed futuristic courses in colleges and universities. "They prefer to 'do futures' instead of studying what others have done." Eldredge also says that futures studies shakes up students' minds as they become "awed by the enormity and complexity of the future." He adds: "This is a useful form of 'gut-learning' for a generation whose arrogance is said to exceed its ignorance, but which must deal with the reality called 'future shock.'"

Futures studies also can counter the negativity of many students. Professor Julius Kane of the University of British Columbia says that "the key problem is to get the students to become aware of the fact that they have some control over future developments and to break them of their habit of merely criticizing the status quo. The key lessons learned from my teaching experience are that students are a good deal less innovative than the popular press would have us believe. Actually they are very uncertain and cautious of change."

The contrast between the traditional approach to a subject and a future-oriented approach may be suggested by comparing two ways to teach students about the problem of pollution. The traditional way might begin with a history of the deaths caused by pollution—such as the London smog of 1952-53 which killed thousands of people—and provide a general description of the damage done by pollution. The futurist approach might begin with a scenario describing what might happen to the world if pollution continues to increase. Biologist Paul Ehrlich, has, in fact, developed such a scenario for an "eco-catastrophe." Ehrlich tells how Soviet and U.S. rivalry for support in the underdeveloped countries led the Soviet Union to supply manufacturing facilities for a miracle pesticide called Thanodrin. At first the use of Thanodrin led to dramatic results, but nature soon developed superpests that could withstand Thanodrin. The Soviets counseled larger applications of Thanodrin to kill the superpests. As Thanodrin poured into the world's ecological system, it proved lethal to human beings. Angry mobs attacked the Thanodrin plants, tore them apart, and poured the Thanodrin into rivers and oceans. The massive infusions of the chemical upset the ecology of the oceans and within months all important animal life in the sea was extinct.

Such a scenario, describing what could happen in the future, can help a student begin to think about the future and become interested in the workings of the environment. Having an image of the possible importance of chemicals, he now has a reason for studying them. He also may gain a new sense of responsibility for the environment, because he begins to realize that his actions can injure—or preserve—it. Similarly, a student who begins thinking about the undersea dwellings of the future may acquire a new interest in the oceans, because he realizes he himself might some day be living in the seas. He may also perhaps become interested in engineering as he recognizes the challenges of building underwater structures.

Futuristic studies lead naturally to the identification of the world's unsolved problems, and it is the unsolved problems—not those that already are solved—that can stimulate a student's imagination. A student cannot help Robert Boyle to discover that reducing the volume of a gas by one half will double its pressure, nor can he help Crick and Watson to build the double helix model of DNA, but he still can help to solve some of today's mysteries. And it is the students who become excited about the future possibilities of science rather than its past triumphs who will become the scientists of tomorrow.

Futuristics can give students an awareness that they can build a world that will be better than anything people have yet dreamed of. Students know that they can do nothing about the past. All the horrors of history are fixed and unalterable. Only the future world remains open to change. As students begin to consider the various developments that could occur in the future—new forms of family relationships, new peace-keeping machinery, new ways of structuring business and governmental systems—they almost inevitably become involved in deciding which are the things they want to see realized, and perhaps even begin to take responsibility for making them happen.

Specific classroom assignments in futuristics might include:

1. Writing utopias (descriptions of each student's ideal world).
2. Planning a model community as a class project.
3. Writing scenarios for future developments in Antarctica, Florida, or some other area.
4. Assessing the impact of introducing a certain technology, for example, an extremely rapid transit system that would enable people to live in the Rocky Mountains and commute daily to Manhattan.
5. Trying to agree on the world's most urgent problems and then brainstorming various possible solutions.

Philosophy and Art

As we look at the various possibilities of the future and try to decide on those we want to realize, we inevitably must clarify what we want to have happen, that is, we must think more systematically about our goals and values. As we do this, we move necessarily toward a more unified perspective and a balanced "philosophy of life." Futuristics changes our ordinary functioning from being reactive to being proactive. Instead of simply responding to pressures from the environment as we encounter them, we begin to develop goals that we are willing to work to attain.

In addition, the study of future possibilities serves a cultural and recreational value. It can delight the spirit and elevate the emotions. Like a poem or a painting, a scenario indicating possible future developments can provide a vessel for our emotions and thoughts. Reading about future possibilities is an absorbing activity that can enlarge our minds so that we have new psychological resources with which to deal with problems.

13

A World of Utopias

We live in an age when the creation of a peaceful, prosperous, and happy world looms as a genuine possibility. But this vision of felicity fills many people with uneasiness. People who have learned to contemplate Armageddon with composure are horrified by utopia. They cannot imagine a society in which everyone is happy. Hence, they reassure themselves that utopia is an idle dream, that the human race will never burst the bonds that have enslaved it from the beginning to hunger, disease, and war.

If peace were to break out, fret the anti-utopians, life would become boring; if everybody had plenty to eat, no one would be willing to work—at least for reasonable wages; if everyone were happy, human existence would be meaningless. Thus, rather than face the dread specter of utopia, they soothe themselves with the myth that the human race is inevitably headed for collapse and barbarism, if not total destruction.

One reason that utopia unsettles people is the widespread belief that utopia requires conformity, if not uniformity. In a utopia, it is said, everyone is a robot. Individuality, freedom, and creativity are banned, and people lose their souls. What many people fail to realize is that they have come to confuse utopia with its opposite, dystopia. Dystopian novels like *1984* and *Brave New World* so dominate our thinking about the future that a dystopian novel now passes for a utopian novel, and utopia is thought to be a repressive police state or a robotized dream factory run by mad planners. The identification of utopia with dystopia shows how far we have come down the path toward the *1984* vision without benefit of a Ministry of Truth to teach us that WAR IS PEACE; FREEDOM IS SLAVERY; IGNORANCE IS STRENGTH.

Thus the first task in rehabilitating utopia is to recognize that a utopia is a person's concept of an *ideal* or desirable community or state, and not just any sort of future society, much less the sort of society he deplores. Aldous Huxley's *Brave New World* and George Orwell's *1984* were written as visions of bad or sinister societies that might exist in the future. They are *dys*topian novels that describe the horrors, not the beauties, of imagined future worlds. It seems ridiculous to belabor such an obvious point, but today's *newspeak* has stood utopia on its head.

A true utopian novel is psychologist B. F. Skinner's *Walden II*, in which the author presents a picture of a community that would offer a far better life than people now generally enjoy. Many readers of *Walden II* agree with Skinner's vision, and groups now are actually trying to create real communities based on the principles enunciated in the novel. (The best known such community, Twin Oaks, established near Louisa, Virginia, in 1967, is not only thriving but has even seeded other communities, one of which was given the name Acorn.) Some readers of *Walden II*, however, are shocked that the manager of Skinner's ideal community uses psychological principles to get people to behave properly and view this as sinister "behavior modification" constituting an intolerable injury to individual dignity and freedom.

This division of opinion about *Walden II* shows that one man's utopia can be another man's dystopia. Our demands on utopia have bounded up even more rapidly than the standard of living. Plato and Thomas More saw nothing wrong with having slavery in their utopias; today some people are shocked if rewards are used to guide people down the path of "righteousness." This insistence on absolute perfection poses a critical dilemma for today's utopian writer. If he fails to explain how his utopia operates, we will reject his work as meaningless and dishonest, but if he does explain how the benefits of his utopia are obtained, he can hardly fail to suggest means that some people will find disagreeable. A utopia in which peace is universal is presumably a utopia in which nations or localities have yielded some of their ability to make war and individuals have given up their freedom to use bombs and guns. Even these restrictions are offensive to people who insist on absolute freedom. All the residents of utopia may be happy people, but if that happiness results from chemicals or electrical stimulation of the brain, some readers will be horrified.

Thus we must recognize that it is impossible to describe an ideal world that would satisfy everyone's criteria of perfection. As soon as we go beyond generalities ("peaceful," "happy," "prosperous," etc.), we inevitably offend some people's sensibilities. However, we can develop concepts of highly desirable but not perfect societies, and these visions can help clarify our goals. It would be useful to develop thousands of concepts of desirable human societies and learn to compare them in terms of the benefits they provide and the costs that they demand. The construction of these imaginary communities could be one of the most worthwhile and exciting projects not only for young people but for adults. Developing a carefully thought-out plan for an ideal community requires that we learn more about what our values are and how societies work. Thus efforts expended to create realistic—though imaginary—utopias may prove one of the most effective ways to help us improve the real world.

Once we dismiss the sterile notion that a utopia must be perfect in all respects, we find ourselves free to think about a plurality of utopias. In fact, we can imagine myriads of utopias, each different but with its enthusiasts and critics. The ideal world might be composed of countless small utopias, ranging in size down to utopias consisting of a single individual living his own life according to his own highly individualistic principles.

A world divided into many communities—as interlinked or as independent as they freely chose to be—could not only provide scope for individual freedom, but would also offer a means for testing out all kinds of living arrangements, technologies, art forms, etc. It would be possible to create communities modeled after Athens in its golden age, imperial Rome, Venice in the days of Marco Polo, or Florence during the height of the Renaissance. These communities would be like today's Williamsburgs and Mystic Seaports, and would provide living museums for people who wanted a respite from change. Each person might expect to live in a number of communities during the course of his lifetime, moving on whenever he felt he could be happier or more productive somewhere else.

The development of a wide variety of communities, each with its own rules and life-style, provides a way for people to gain a better understanding of what their values really are. In the real world, people cannot have everything they want, because everything has a price: We pay for security with the money and time required to have locks, fences, watch dogs, police, etc., and we pay for liberty by allowing the publication of periodicals and books that anger or shock us, by supporting a judicial system that carefully protects the rights of defendants, etc. Since the flowers that beautify our parks, the museums that hold art treasures, and the medical services that care for our bodies must all be paid for, hard choices are required, yet often we cannot easily judge the benefits and costs.

A world that would encourage the formation of many little utopias could help both individuals and the larger societies to understand their own values. The clarification of human values is now an object of growing concern, because we have increasing ability to do the things we want. When people were very limited in what they could do, they did not need to worry so much about the problems of choice. Now that they can do so many things, they face difficult choices about what to do. If we can have any sort of world, what sort *do* we want?

Building a Greater Civilization

The problems and dangers of the present should not blind us to the real progress that has been made during the past few hundred years. Over the past few centuries, we have moved fairly steadily toward a world community that is reasonably well-fed, well-housed, and comfortable, at least by the standards of past ages. We have it within our power to create a better and happier human civilization than any that has ever before existed on this planet, but this greater world civilization is not foreordained: It may happen—or it may not. We may be able to avert disaster and continue creating a better world—but we may fail to do so. The issue is not settled.

What now prevents us from achieving the better world that seems to lie almost within our grasp? As we survey our situation, it might seem as if there is nothing to prevent us from attaining the goal. We have, for example, capabilities far greater than any available to any previous civilization. We possess fantastic economic wealth in the form of ships, airplanes, factories, railroads, power plants, highways, apartment houses, etc. Hence we can well afford enormous expenditures to overcome the obstacles to building a better world community. We also have huge numbers of highly educated people—vast phalanxes of engineers, scientists, scholars, and executives ready and able to take on important tasks. We have a worldwide communications system and a growing array of global institutions. A businessman in New York now can direct-dial the company's offices in Stockholm, Tokyo, and Hong Kong; ordinary people can see televised events on the other side of the world. Increasingly, the world is being unified, not only through the United Nations, but through such non-governmental groups as the International Telecommunications Satellite Consortium (INTELSAT).

We also have an important and often-unrecognized asset in the new intellectual technology. We have computers that can digest and store enormous amounts of information, retrieve it instantly upon demand, and manipulate it in complex ways that are beyond the capacity of human beings to accomplish within any reasonable time-frame. Our intellectual armory also includes videodiscs, microfiches, computer-output microfilms, and satellites that enable us to monitor conditions around the world. In addition, scientific knowledge of all kinds is accumulating faster than ever before in history, with the result that the sum of human knowledge is now doubling every decade, according to some estimates.

But with all these vast resources of economic wealth, educated people, sophisticated technology, and scientific knowledge, we do not seem able to address our problems very effectively. We seem to lack the collective wisdom to martial our resources for effective action. We seem unable to agree on the nature of our problems and how to solve them. And as many of our problems mount ominously, talk of doomsday is in the air.

In principle, the top leaders of the most powerful countries, acting, perhaps, through the United Nations, could provide the enlightened, forward-looking leadership that the world needs, but the leaders of democratic societies (and even, to a large extent, those of less than democratic societies) must follow the wishes of their people. The leaders must await the development of a public mood that will favor—or at least will tolerate—a given action; only then can they "lead." Furthermore, political leaders generally are so busy solving urgent day-to-day crises that they have little time to develop the long-range future-oriented programs that are required if the world is to solve its urgent problems.

If governments cannot provide the needed leadership, where else shall we look? To the multi-national corporations? To the academic community? To the churches? To scientific organizations? As we survey the array of institutions that we have in the world today, there does not seem to be any obvious place for the needed leadership to begin to develop, and we may have to face the fact that our present institutions are incapable of providing the needed leadership. Something new seems to be required.

The lack of leadership stems from a lack of a global consensus. The people of the world do not share the common values and goals that make it possible for leaders to lead effectively. People are so divided over what they want that no single leader or group of leaders is acceptable to more than a minority of the world's nations and interest groups. So long as there is no consensus, it is impossible for mankind as a whole to develop the unity required for collective action.

How can the required consensus develop? Here, perhaps, we can take a lesson from American history. In the colonial days, many people were angry at the British, but uncertain what to do. The 13 colonies distrusted each other and could not act together. In this situation, concerned people in each colony realized that they needed to know what was going on elsewhere if they were to reach agreement on what needed to be done and take joint action. So cities and towns set up what were called committees of correspondence to exchange information and ideas so that a consensus could develop throughout all the colonies on what needed to be done and how to do it. As a result of these committees of correspondence, the colonies were able to unite, expel the British, and gradually develop the United States of America.

The essential value of the committees of correspondence was that they provided *an effective system of communication among concerned people*. This system kept a large number of people informed about (1) what was happening, (2) what might be expected to happen, and (3) which methods were working. The system operated by quill pen, but it enabled the colonists to identify effective leaders, join forces behind them, and adopt rapidly the most workable solutions to the newly emerging problems.

Today mankind is in a situation that may be compared with that faced by the 18th-century colonists, and we may be able to benefit from their experience. Like them, we face common problems of enormous scope, and like them we are divided into separate constituencies and do not know how to unite for collective action. Perhaps we, too, can establish a communications system that will serve the modern world as effectively as the committees of correspondence served the colonists.

What we seem to require today is a global network of people seriously interested in the human future. It might be called the World Future Network. Once people within the network begin communicating regularly with each other, a consensus can develop concerning the actions that need to be taken in order for the world to avert catastrophe and move toward the better future that we know is possible. With consensus, good world leadership can be recognized and encouraged, and we can mobilize our vast resources toward solving our urgent global problems.

The Network could not, of course, solve all problems immediately, but it could lay the foundation of the global communication and consensus needed for mankind to begin to deal more intelligently with its future.

Collective Wisdom for Mankind

Specifically, the Network could do the following:

1. *Monitor social and technological change.* The speed-up of change makes it increasingly imperative to have better information concerning changes in social institutions, human values, individual personalities, the natural environment, and other aspects of human life. Better information would enable mankind to identify potentially dangerous trends and take timely corrective action to avert crises.

2. *Collect and evaluate forecasts and conjectures concerning major world and national developments.* Many forecasts are made, but are not generally assembled, compared, and evaluated, so that they can be maximally useful to decision-makers.

3. *Identify important problems and potential solutions.* The network should not be just an early warning system but should also alert us to emerging opportunities that we can take advantage of and to potential solutions that develop from scientific research and other activities.

4. *Harness expertise and imagination to solve problems.* The system should identify people with special talents and connect them with people needing their talents to solve problems. There are many highly creative people who could help find solutions if they were linked up effectively with problems that urgently require solutions.

5. *Encourage, collect, disseminate, and gather reactions to concepts and ideas (both written and graphic) of a future world that would be better than today's.* People have little difficulty imagining a world catastrophe, but their imaginations seem to fail when they try to imagine a better world.

6. *Encourage experimentation with new institutions and new social arrangements.* One way to determine whether a proposed solution will work is to try it out on a small scale. One can build a pilot model of a social invention just as one can build a pilot model of a machine. The network can identify areas where new social institutions might be set up on an experimental basis to determine how well they perform. At the same time, experiments in existing institutions might also be monitored and evaluated.

7. *Set priorities.* People in the network can be polled periodically to determine which problems are most urgent and which are most susceptible to solution. Effort can then be focused on those problems most likely to yield to determined action.

8. *Inform decision-makers.* Top decision-makers today are swamped with information, yet they often complain that they don't have the facts they need to make a decision. The network could help sift out the information that is really important to decision-makers and give it to them in a form that they would find useful.

The World Future Network might eventually consist of millions of people around the globe. They might be small in number relative to world population but they would be well represented in the leadership of government, business, and education. The Network might also include living-learning communities for people exceptionally interested in the future world. People in these communities could do research on world problems and teach others the new techniques and attitudes of holistic, futuristic thinking. The Network might also include libraries, computerized data banks, and other repositories of knowledge. The centers would be scattered around the world, but linked together by a variety of communications media.

Such a World Future Network could provide a nervous system for humanity, the beginning of a collective consciousness and intelligence for mankind. The Network would not, of course, dictate people's opinions and ideas anymore than a telephone system tells its users what to say when they are talking, but the Network would facilitate the communication, information-gathering, opinion-formation, and consensus that could eventually lead to joint action on collective problems.

The Manhattan Project and the Apollo program were outstanding examples of what man can accomplish with futuristics—that is, with careful and systematic exploration of the future. Similar projects could be mounted to deal with such problems as poverty, unemployment, and illiteracy. Futuristics today is developing rapidly in response to the urgent need for it. There is now a mounting impatience with government-by-crisis and businesses whose managements find themselves constantly in difficulties because they have not planned ahead. In the words of Harlan Cleveland, former U.S. Ambassador to NATO, "We know in our hearts that we are in the world for keeps, yet we are still tackling 20-year problems with five-year plans, staffed with two-year personnel, working on one-year appropriations. It's simply not good enough."

If we will really give serious attention to the future, rather than continue to lurch from crisis to crisis, we can hope for enormous benefits in the years ahead. Some of us may even live to experience life among the happy people in the multiple utopias which may someday dot the earth.

Appendix A

Future-Oriented Organizations
and Periodicals

Before 1960, there were few groups anywhere that could be called futurist in the current sense of the term. But during the mid 1960s, future-oriented associations, institutes, and periodicals suddenly blossomed, mainly in America, Europe, and Japan.

The appearance of future-oriented organizations opened a new era for the study of the future, because, as futurist Joseph F. Coates has said (with perhaps some exaggeration), "Nothing significant ever gets done until it's institutionalized." As they began working together, futurists found that they could accomplish far more than when they worked in isolation. As institutionalization progressed, futurists found it easier to meet one another, identify funding sources, locate friends in business and government, develop educational programs, and establish links with futurists in other scientific and scholarly fields. Futurists also could transcend national frontiers, because their publications now reached thousands of people around the world.

The development of future-oriented groups has moved forward steadily since the early 1960s. Not all the organizations have survived and prospered, but new groups have emerged to replace those that have fallen by the wayside. Though futuristics could hardly be described as a major industry, a few enterprises have developed from tiny cells into fairly sizable and stable organizations. The momentum developed by the mid 1970s suggests that future-oriented organizations may be expected to continue to gather strength, and have increasing influence on decision-making in government, business, and other areas in the decades ahead.

Classifying future-oriented organizations—or even deciding whether a given organization really is future-oriented—depends heavily on subjective judgment. A large research organization may have a number of staff members trying to make forecasts of possible future developments, yet these staffers may constitute only a tiny percentage of the organization's personnel. Can the organization as a whole be classified as futurist? Another problem is posed by the very small organization, which may consist of no more than a single individual or a husband-wife team; should it really be counted as "an organization"?

Some groups focus on a single aspect of the future (e.g., education, population, world order) while others are propagandist in character, seeking social change in line with their political or ideological goals, and have little interest in exploring the future in an open-minded way. Can such groups be properly termed *futurist*? Still another category of groups are those that try to create "alternative" life-styles or approaches to education, architecture, and other fields. These "alternative" groups include Ivan Illich's Centro Intercultural de Documentacion in Cuernavaca, Mexico, and Paolo Soleri's Arcosanti Foundation in Scottsdale, Arizona. Illich is perhaps best known for his radical alternatives in education, medicine, and other fields, while Soleri is famed for his "arcologies," single megastructures that would house and service hundreds of thousands of people apiece. In general, the people who identify themselves with the futurist movement are very interested in such alternative approaches, and often consider their spokesmen to be futurists. But are innovative people automatically futurists? If so, are people who are non-creative traditionalists to be read out of the futurist movement? Many people now identified with the futurist movement have great respect for tradition and are highly skeptical about many of today's innovations. However exciting and instructive, the innovation of today does not always foreshadow the shape of tomorrow.

Yet another question is raised by subgroups within larger organizations. Are the World Future Society's chapters to be counted as groups? How about a two-man department on the future in a large insurance company? Or three different future-oriented "centers" within a large research institute?

In the face of so many questions, it is impossible to say precisely how many future-oriented groups there are in the world. Even if the definition problem could be solved, there is the very serious additional problem of locating the groups that have sprung up. A new group often does not immediately make its presence known, nor does a defunct organization necessarily communicate the fact of its demise to all parties.

Despite the difficulties, it is still possible to offer what might be regarded as a reasonable guess concerning the number of futurist organizations in the world. Such an estimate may be based, first, on the 1975-76 survey by the World Future Society, which identified 230 organizations that the Society's staff felt merited inclusion in its directory (*The Future: A Guide to Information Sources*). In compiling this directory, the Society asked its members to submit the names of organizations that should be included and the staff personally contacted scholars in a number of nations for additional suggestions on organizations that should be included. The Society's staff sent questionnaires to groups that were nominated, and made repeated mailings whenever an organization did not respond promptly.

In processing the results of its survey, the Society's staff excluded from the directory about 100 organizations that returned questionnaires. In almost every instance, the exclusion was based on the determination that the organization did not seem sufficiently oriented toward the general study of the future to be viewed as a futurist organization. Since this was the primary reason for exclusions, many prestigious and well-staffed organizations were omitted from the directory while some less well known groups with very modest staffs were accepted.

To the figure of 230 groups, one may add the chapters of the World Future Society itself, since these chapters function independently (within certain guidelines) and each has its own officers, programs, and publications. Adding in an estimated 30 World Future Society chapters and local committees would bring the total number of futurist groups to 260. Allowing an additional five for subgroups of other organizations would bring the total to 265. Since it seems more likely that a greater number of qualified groups were missed by the survey than unqualified groups were counted, one may round off the total to 300, and regard this as a conservative estimate of the number of futurist groups in the world. If less strict standards were imposed, the figure could, of course, go into the thousands.

Research Centers

Among the groups that clearly belong on any list of future-oriented organizations are certain well-established research centers that specialize in making forecasts and analyses concerning technology and society in the decades ahead. These institutes are willing to provide forecasts for almost any area a client is interested in. The price will generally be $60,000 and up, although certain services may be available for less. The cost may seem high for what may amount to little more than some scholarly research, a typed report and a few consultations, but a study can pay for itself again and again when a firm or government agency is making decisions involving millions of dollars. An educational institution may realize enormous savings simply by not building facilities that it will not need five years hence. U.S. school systems have probably lost billions of dollars by constructing schools that were surplus shortly after they were occupied—or even, in some cases, before they were completed.

But why go to a research institute? Are there not other places to obtain forecasts? Numerous books, periodicals and other media such as tape recordings of seminars provide an inexpensive way to learn about current forecasts, and for the ordinary person they may suffice. One can also hire an individual futurist as a consultant. But for a major study of an important issue or subject area, many firms decide to contract with a research institute.

A research institute is organized specifically to conduct analyses and address problems that interest its clients. It thus differs greatly from a university department, which is a group of scholars organized to provide instruction in a certain field. Research institutes developed when companies and government agencies found they needed answers to certain questions, but discovered that no other institution was really set up to provide them. Research institutes have often sprung up in university communities, where they could draw on experts in many fields but could operate outside the constraints imposed by the university on its own departments.

Once established, a future-oriented research institute develops experience in the comprehensive, systematic approach needed to explore the future effectively. At the same time, an institute develops the management and support staff needed to make its information and advice maximally useful to clients. The background of the scholars and scientists in research institutes generally varies widely, but the natural and social sciences, engineering, and history are generally well-represented, and the institutes are also seasoned with lawyers, journalists, and many other professionals. One of the main strengths of a research institute is its ability to assemble a coherent team of experts to address systematically a given problem.

Among the best-known future-oriented research institutes that undertake many types of assignments for many types of clients are:

● *The Center for Futures Research, University of Southern California.* Located in USC's Graduate School of Business Administration, this Los Angeles-based group is headed by management scientist Burt Nanus and staffed by such noted futurists as James O'Toole and Selwyn Enzer. The Center develops methodologies for the study of social change and conducts multidisciplinary policy analyses and forecasts.

● *Forecasting International, Ltd.* This Arlington, Virginia, firm specializes in such areas as technology forecasting and

assessment. The firm is headed by Marvin J. Cetron, a former
U.S. Navy forecaster and author of such books as *Technological Forecasting: A Practical Approach.*

• *The Institute for the Future.* This non-profit group, located in Menlo Park, California, has traditionally devoted much of
its efforts toward developing better methods to study the future. The Institute has applied its methods to studies of the
corporate environment, telephones, wideband cable services
to the home, insurance, computer technology, energy, etc. In
1975, under President Roy C. Amara, the Institute initiated
a Corporate Associates Program designed specifically to assist private sector organizations in increasing their awareness of emerging trends and likely long-term consequences.

• *The Futures Group.* This profit-making (and profitable)
firm was created in 1971 by Theodore J. Gordon and two other
staff members of the Institute for the Future. Located in Glastonbury, Connecticut, the Futures Group has studied topics
ranging from the future of the Japanese economy to the potential of geothermal energy. In October 1972 the Dreyfus Corporation of New York acquired a 30% interest in the Futures
Group. Dreyfus's Board Chairman, Howard Stein, explained:
"This acquisition will enhance Dreyfus's abilities to anticipate
change and its consequences for the investors we serve."

• *The Hudson Institute.* Best known as the base of Herman
Kahn, the Hudson Institute was initially oriented mainly toward helping U.S. Defense Department strategists. In recent
years, it has actively sought (and found) clients in business,
civilian U.S. agencies, and other nations.

• *Social Policy Research Institute, Stanford Research Institute.* Inspired by Willis Harman, this group is oriented toward studies of the broad general trends of western society,
especially in such "soft" areas as human values.

Other future-oriented institutes are somewhat less general in
their approach, often specializing in a certain aspect of the future.
The following may serve as examples of the diversity in this group
of institutes:

• *Technological Forecasting Group, University of Dayton
(Ohio) Research Institute.* Staffed by leading forecasters
Ralph Lenz and Joseph Martino, this recently-formed group
provides consulting and research on future-oriented activities
for industrial clients and for government. The group is expected to concentrate on forecasting, assessing, and planning
of technology.

• *Program of Policy Studies in Science and Technology,
George Washington University,* Washington, D.C. This group

is directed by GWU Vice President Louis Mayo. The PPSST
has a special program on technology assessment directed by
Vary T. Coates.

● *Predicasts, Inc.* Located in Cleveland, Ohio, this business-
oriented, profit-making firm makes forecasts for various industries, with emphasis on plastics, electronics, and paper.

● *Science Policy Research Unit, University of Sussex.* This
British group has attracted wide attention for its evaluations
of the Club of Rome's limits-to-growth studies. Among its ma-
jor programs is a series of studies on forecasting techniques.
One current program focuses on "Future Patterns of Social
Organization."

● *Futuremics, Inc.* This consulting firm, located in Washington, D.C., offers educational services, publications, and workshops. Headed by psychologist Robert E. Maston, Futuremics
currently is focusing special attention on the future of education.

Not all research institutes concentrate on research commissioned
by outsiders. Some institutes, generally those funded mainly by
foundations and specializing in research in the public interest, have
"clients" that allow the scholars wide freedom to choose the problems they will study. Examples of this type of institute are:

● *Resources for the Future, Inc.* Funded mainly by the Ford
Foundation, this group was founded in Washington, D.C., in the
1950s to provide continuing research on natural resources.
Joseph L. Fisher, formerly president of RFF, was elected to the
U.S. Congress in 1974; the new president is Charles J. Hitch,
former Chancellor of the University of California.

● *Worldwatch Institute.* Headed by economist Lester Brown,
author of such books as *World Without Borders*, this Washington-based group began operating in 1974 with funding from
Rockefeller Brothers Fund and other foundations. The Institute
is producing a steady stream of papers and books on current
world trends that are shaping the future.

Associations

In addition to institutes, futurists have formed associations so
that they can communicate with each other through meetings, publications, etc. The associations generally have a headquarters or at
least a mailing address and one or more persons designated to serve
as officers or coordinators.

One of the first of these associations was Mankind 2000, which began in London in 1965, and has since co-sponsored a number of international meetings, starting with a conference in Oslo in 1967. Though never large in membership, Mankind 2000 has had considerable influence on the international development of futurism. Other membership groups include: The International Futuribles Association, based in Paris; the World Futures Studies Federation, whose secretariat is currently in Rome; the International Society for Technology Assessment, based in Washington, D.C.; the Swedish Society for Future Studies; the Norwegian Society for Futures Studies; the Committee for the Future, Washington, D.C.; and the Japan Futurological Society.

Two associations—the Club of Rome and the World Future Society—merit special attention, the first because of its international influence and the second because it provides a practical and easy way for people everywhere to participate in the futurist movement or at least to remain in touch with what is happening.

The Club of Rome. In 1967 Aurelio Peccei, a distinguished Italian industrialist and economist, had a meeting with Alexander King, scientific director of the Organization for Economic Cooperation and Development, the Paris-based group that provides a communications and research link for the United States, Japan, France, and other developed nations. Peccei and King agreed that the present world system is "a textbook case of mismanagement," demonstrated by skyrocketing population, increasing exhaustion of resources, pollution, poverty, etc.

Peccei and King also agreed that the present world institutions cannot handle the multitudes of complex interrelated global problems and something must be done. Accordingly, the two then invited 30 persons representing 10 countries to meet at the centuries-old Accademia dei Lincei in Rome. There in April 1968, the Club of Rome was formed: It was—and is—a highly exclusive association of scientists, industrialists, economists, educators, and statesmen, with a membership limited to 100. The structure of the Club is deliberately designed to be informal, loose, nonpolitical, and structureless. "We don't want to be an organization," explains Peccei. "There are already too many organizations in the world."

Despite its small membership and lack of structure, the Club quickly became known as an elite and somewhat mysterious group whose mission was to stimulate political action that would influence world affairs in a rational and humane direction. The real debut for the Club came with its well-publicized Project on the Predicament of Mankind. Led by Professor Dennis L. Meadows, an international group of scholars at the Massachusetts Institute of Technology used computers to simulate world trends and where they might lead. Supported by a $336,000 grant from the Volkswagen Foundation, the scholars used a computerized mathematical "model" of the world developed by Professor Jay W. Forrester and his System Dynamics Group at M.I.T. The model focuses on five major factors or components in the world situation: population, industrialization, food supply, depletion of nonrenewable resources, and pollution. Data regarding these factors were fed into the computer, which generated graphic projections of what might happen in the future, given different assumptions about each of the factors.

As a result of its studies, the scholars predicted global catastrophe within the next century if present rates of growth continue unchecked. The news that computers at M.I.T. had foretold world catastrophes made headlines around the world and aroused heated debate. The Club of Rome soon acquired a "doom and gloom" label, but a 1972 book based on the study, *The Limits to Growth* by Donella Meadows, Dennis L. Meadows, Jorgen Randers, and W.W. Behrens, III, had booming sales. The book has appeared in 34 languages and has sold three million copies.

Scholars have written whole books to refute the Club of Rome's findings. Critics argue that the assumptions of the report are unduly pessimistic, that the methods are biased, and that the model does not reflect actual global conditions. The Club's scholars, including Meadows and Forrester, have insisted from the beginning that their work was experimental and tentative in character, and that the "world model" was a highly simplified approximation of reality. In spite of this, the report became ammunition for people demanding various types of political and social action. The "limits to growth" topic soon emerged as a major controversy in futurist circles. The principal question seemed to be: Can the world's economy continue to grow at the present rate without disastrous consequences within a few more decades? The question remains unresolved. Certain futurists, like Herman Kahn in his 1976 book *The Next 200 Years*, are optimistic that technology will improve fast enough to allow the world to feed its growing population and to overcome the dangers posed by pollution. Other scholars, such as Rufus E. Miles in *Awakening from the American Dream*, believe that a terrible day of reckoning is coming. At the Club of Rome's 1976 meeting in Philadelphia, the consensus of the assembled scholars appeared less opposed to economic growth than the Club's first report suggested. What is needed, Club members seemed to agree, is not a complete halt to growth, but rather a more selective, managed type of growth. Growth must continue, especially in the underdeveloped countries if the worldwide quality of life is to improve, but the developed nations must strongly emphasize the conservation of resources.

The Club's second report, *Mankind at the Turning Point* by Mihajlo Mesarovic and Eduard Pestel, caused far less of a sensation than the first. Mesarovic and Pestel used a more sophisticated computer model of the world than the first study. The new model distinguished 10 regions (North America, Western Europe, Japan, etc.), unlike the first study which made no attempt to allow for regional differences. Mesarovic and Pestel described two great gaps—one between man and nature and a second between the rich countries in the northern part of the world and the poor countries of the south. To overcome these gaps, the researchers argue for a system of planned "organic" growth.

By the mid 1970s, scholars associated with the Club of Rome were working on a variety of projects. Professor Ervin Laszlo of the State University College of Arts and Sciences at Geneseo, New York, was working on *Goals for Global Society*, an investigation of "those ethical commitments, world views, and value judgments which could lead beyond perennial crises toward a healthier state of global society." Work on the project began in January 1975 with 12 researchers and 12 advisors. In 1976, more than a year after his project had begun, Laszlo stated that his research indicates that people can change their goals sufficiently to permit the establishment of a new world order that will be compatible with the preservation and prosperity of mankind. "Our researches show that the inner dimension of all major nations and cultures is capable of creative and humanistic transformation," Laszlo says, but he warns that the change might not happen fast enough—"before economic, political, and environmental pressures depress conditions and make voluntary adjustments difficult or impossible."

Another Club project, headed by Dutch economist Jan Tinbergen, has outlined new global arrangements that might ensure a life of dignity for everyone in the world. Tinbergen and his associates propose a number of concrete steps, including the establishment of an international monetary system, arms reduction, and first-class research institutes in the Third World. The results of the work by Tinbergen and his colleagues appear in *Reshaping the International Order* (E.P. Dutton, New York, 1976).

At the Philadelphia meeting, Laszlo seemed to sum up the general feeling of many Club members when he said, "The real issue is not whether to grow or not to grow. Rather it is how to grow, with which technologies, and in what sectors of the economy." Undifferentiated growth, he suggested, would deplete natural resources, overpollute the environment, and create unemployment and alienation among workers. At the same time, economic growth is needed to "assure basic minimum standards of need fulfillment to hundreds of millions in poor countries and in poor sectors of rich countries."

In general, the Club of Rome scholars agreed that the world

needs to change its social and political institutions if catastrophe is
to be avoided.

The World Future Society. By far the largest of the futurist associations, the World Future Society had about 24,000 members in 80
countries as of early 1977. Formed in Washington, D.C., in 1966 as a
nonprofit, nonpartisan scientific and educational association, the Society takes no stand on what the future can, will, or should be like. It
does, however, promote the study of the future, the development of
futuristic methodologies, and the education of the public concerning
possible future developments. It also serves as a clearinghouse for
ideas and information about the future. The Society is open to anyone interested in the future. Annual dues, which include a subscrip-
tion to its journal *The Futurist*, are kept modest ($15 per year). A
person can join the Society simply by sending his name, address,
and occupation along with his first year's dues to the Society's membership secretary. The Society publishes two journals—*The
Futurist: A Journal of Forecasts, Trends, and Ideas About the
Future*, and The *World Future Society Bulletin*. Both are bimonthly, but oriented toward slightly different audiences. *The Futurist*,
which goes to all Society members, seeks to reach a wide audience
of people interested in future developments. The *World Future Society Bulletin* is aimed at a more select group—people who have an
especially intense interest in the future or who are professionally
engaged in planning and forecasting. The aim of the *World Future
Society Bulletin* is reflected by recent articles like "Forecasting in
the Soviet Bloc," "State Goals Groups: Performance and Potential,"
and "Alternative Policies Tools."

In addition, the Society broadcasts a weekly radio program of interviews and future-related news over Station WAMU-FM, an educational station operated by American University in Washington,
D.C., and operates a book service which sells tape recordings and
simulation games as well as books. (The offerings are listed in a
catalog entitled *The Future: A Catalog of Resources.)*

The Society's first General Assembly, organized in 1971, drew
more than 1,000 registrants. The second Assembly, held four years
later, in 1975, drew about 2,800. Seven members of Congress—three
Senators and four Congressmen—addressed the Assembly, in addition to several hundred scholars, scientists, and others. In connection with the second Assembly, the Society published a book *The
Next 25 Years: Crisis and Opportunity*, a collection of papers by Assembly participants and others.

The Society began organizing chapters in 1968 and now has
groups or individual representatives in about 100 cities around the
world. Nobel Prize-winner Dennis Gabor was the first speaker before the Society's chapter in London; in 1976, Society members in

Bombay sponsored an all-day meeting on the future of India that attracted many of that nation's business and government leaders.

In 1975 the Society began organizing special-study sections for members interested in certain aspects of the future such as education, communications, business, etc. Section activity accelerated considerably during 1976 and about a dozen of the sections now produce their own newsletters—*Careers Tomorrow, Health Tomorrow, Life-Styles Tomorrow*, etc.

In the years ahead, the Society plans to improve and expand its services to members. The Society has in fact enlarged its publications and programs every year since it began. Membership dues are kept low so that no one interested in the future will be barred from membership for financial reasons. The Society offers a way for individuals everywhere to learn about the possibilities of the future and to contribute their own special skills and ideas to the creation of a better world.

Periodicals

Periodicals specializing in non-fiction articles about the future made their first widespread appearance in the 1960s. Though many books about the future had been published earlier, the only magazine of earlier date seems to have been the British journal *Tomorrow* whose life was terminated, after only a few issues, by World War II. *Tomorrow* is interesting not only because of its early appearance but because it provides a link between futurist publications and the science-fiction periodicals that preceded them. The writers and editors of *Tomorrow* operated under the heavy influence of science fiction. By contrast, the futurist periodicals of the 1960s appear to have been started by people with little connection to the science-fiction world.

In any event, periodicals appeared in both France and the United States almost simultaneously in 1966: In France, Helene de Jouvenel started the journal *Analyse & Prevision (Analysis & Forecasting)* to carry on the work of her husband and his Futuribles project, and in the United States, *The Futurist* made its initial appearance as a newsletter. After a trial issue in 1966, *The Futurist* began regular bimonthly publication the following year and expanded into a journal in 1968. In Britain, in 1968, Iliffe Science and Technology Publications began publishing *Futures*, a scholarly journal which soon entered into a collaborative relationship with the newly formed Institute for the Future in Middletown, Connecticut.

Other publications soon followed. In the United States they included technical or quasi-technical journals like *Technology Forecasting and Social Change* (founded in New York in 1969) and *Technology Assessment* (founded in Washington, D.C., in 1973), and also a variety of periodicals with different formats and styles. Examples:

FutuReports, a newsletter filled with one-paragraph descriptions of significant developments and findings.
Footnotes to the Future, a concise monthly review of recent publications, workshops, and seminars, published by Futuremics, Inc., of Washington, D.C.
Futures Conditional, a unique information service (a book, sheaf of reprints, or other material may substitute for an issue of the journal) inspired by British socio-economist Robert Theobald.
Lifestyles Tomorrow, Careers Tomorrow, etc. The World Future Society's special-studies sections produce newsletters, issued approximately bimonthly, in their areas of special interest. Other newsletters deal with education, government, technology, communication, food, life-styles, business, human values, resources, health, and international affairs.

Outside the United States, there are now a number of periodicals, including *Futuribles* (France), *Analysen und Prognosen* (Germany), *Futuriblerne* (Denmark), *Futures* (Great Britain), and *Futurology* (Switzerland).

The publications mentioned here constitute only a fraction of those now available. For a more complete listing of periodicals, see *The Future: A Guide to Information Sources* (World Future Society, 1977).

Futurism Around the World

France and the United States led the way in the development of future-oriented institutions during the 1960s, but other nations have followed close behind. Sweden may now lead the world in terms of incorporating the future into the processes of government. At the initiative of then Prime Minister Olof Palme, a working group headed by Minister of State Alva Myrdal was created in 1971 to review the role of future studies in Sweden. In 1973 the group presented its report, *To Choose a Future*, which was circulated for comments to some 145 governmental and non-governmental agencies and organizations. That same year, a Secretariat for Future Studies was created under the Office of the Prime Minister to explore the future on a continuing basis. Since then, the Secretariat has undertaken major studies on the labor market, resources and raw materials, and Sweden's role in the world. Two researchers for the Swedish secretariat, Goran Backstrand and Lars Ingelstam, stirred considerable controversy when they published a paper raising the question whether Sweden might want to limit its level of consumption in some key areas. Present rates of growth, said Backstrand and Ingelstam, seemed to lead to preposterous figures in a few decades. What will Sweden do with five times as much paper as it has now? Or with four times as many automobiles?

Elsewhere in Scandinavia, a Danish Committee on Futures Studies, funded by the Danish Social Science Research Council, has been preparing a report of "Denmark up to 1990," and an Institute for Future Studies in Copenhagen is forecasting economic and political developments.

German futurism has been strong under the inspiration of men like Ossip Flechtheim, a political scientist who has promoted the study of the future since 1943 when he was a refugee in the United States, and Heinz Hermann Koelle, former director of future plans for Wernher von Braun's rocket research, who has led the creation of a Berlin Center for Futures Research. The Center seems to straddle the border between a research institute and an association. The Center's members, mainly located in Berlin, serve on task forces that produce a variety of reports designed for government and business leaders. The Center does contract research, holds meetings, and publishes a journal, *Analysen und Prognosen*, which contains both scholarly articles and brief news items of interest to busy officials trying to look ahead.

Germany has a Society for the Advancement of Futures and Peace Research, founded in 1964 and based in Hannover, and a Society for the Future, founded in 1967 and now located in Berlin. Austria has an Austrian Society for Future Research. Berlin-born Robert Jungk, one of the world's best known futurists, maintains an apartment in Salzburg and spends much time there when not teaching in Berlin or on one of his frequent trips abroad. In a castle near Vienna is the International Institute for Applied Systems Analysis. This unique institute, which draws support from both the Soviet and Western blocs, does work so closely related to the study of the future that it may be viewed as a future-oriented institute. Early in 1977, famed futurist and mathematician Olaf Helmer, joined the Institute.

The Netherlands is perhaps best known in futurist circles for Fred Polak, a businessman who became a scholar while living in hiding during the Nazi occupation of his country. Polak's two-volume work, *The Image of the Future*, won the Council of Europe award following its publication in 1955. In *The Image of the Future*, Polak argues that man's creative ability for imagining the future shapes the dynamics of the historical process. In the western world, the image of the future has broken down, because man no longer believes either in heaven or in utopia; consequently, ways must be found to create new images of a desirable future. Later, Polak developed his ideas about the study of the future, for which he proposed the name *prognostics*, and published them in a book entitled *Prognostics: A*

Science in the Making Surveys Its Future. The Netherlands also has a foundation devoted to "the future shape of technology," which is funded partly by the Dutch Government, partly by Dutch business and industry, and partly by the Royal Institution of Engineers in the Netherlands.

In Italy in the late 1960s, a Rome-based economic research group, the Istituto per le Ricerche di Economia Applicata (IREA), began issuing the journal *Futuribili,* edited by Pietro Ferraro, an admirer of Bertrand de Jouvenel and his Futuribles group in France. Another research group in Rome, the Istituto Ricerche Applicata Documentazione e Studi (IRADES), began publishing news bulletins reporting on future studies, and in 1971 IRADES issued an 834-page English-language directory of future-oriented activities entitled *Social Forecasting: Documentation 1971.* The directory was revised several times, but after the 1975 edition, the IRADES project experienced difficulties, due apparently to a lack of adequate financing and to problems of political character, and it became uncertain whether further directories would appear. Both *Futuribili* and the IRADES directories apparently suffered from economic and political problems that beset Italy in the mid 1970s.

Great Britain, which historically has contributed so much to futurism, has not led so far in its institutionalization. However, Britain has had a Committee on the Next Thirty Years, organized by the Social Science Research Council, and chaired by Michael Young and Mark Abrams, and individual Britons have explored future possibilities with great enthusiasm. The World Future Society has had a strong London chapter under the leadership of David Berry, a lecturer in mass media and communications at London University. There is also a Futures Studies Centre at Leeds.

Elsewhere in Europe, the Swiss Association for Futures Research organizes seminars, courses and task forces, and publishes a monthly bulletin, and Spain has a Club de Amigos de la Futurologia.

Soviet futurism seems largely cut off from the West, despite occasional efforts by western futurists to develop closer relations with their Soviet counterparts and the friendliness of individual Soviet scholars. The Communist nations led the way in government planning, but so far do not appear to have pioneered in the study of the future, as it is known in the West. Communist officials seem to take the position that the most important part of the future is already known—capitalism will eventually collapse and communism will triumph—and therefore, the important thing is simply to reach that goal as quickly as possible. But scientists in the Communist countries speculate enthusiastically on the technological wonders of the future. They generally seem to feel that technology will continue to develop and that it will be good. Communist scholars so far do not appear very concerned about the potentially baneful effects of new technology on family life, population, human values, etc. In their view, it seems, these are problems only under capitalism.

In the Communist bloc countries, it is not possible for scholars to create an institute, association, or journal without government support. Hence, futurist organizations cannot emerge in the same way as in the West. But futurism is emerging nonetheless. One focus of Soviet futurism today is in the Academies of Science, where certain scholars are interpreting western futurism to their colleagues and compatriots. One such scholar is Igor V. Bestuzhev-Lada at the USSR Academy of Science's Institute of Social Research in Moscow. Located in the Institute's Section on Social Forecasting, Bestuzhev-Lada has written a number of books and papers explaining western futurism from a Marxist standpoint. Another Academy scholar is Andrei A. Kokoshin at the Institute of the United States and Canada, also in Moscow. Kokoshin attended the World Future Society's first General Assembly in Washington in 1971, and has since published a book on how U.S. scholars and officials forecast developments in international relations.

Poland's Academy of Sciences has two active futurist groups. The Academy's Presidium has a Research and Prognostics Committee chaired by Professor Witold Nowacki, which publishes about three issues each year of a journal entitled *Polska 2000* (Poland 2000). At the Academy's Institute of Philosophy and Sociology, located elsewhere in Warsaw, there is a Group on Social Prognoses headed by sociologist Andrzej Sicinski. A volume entitled *Problems of Forecasting Methodology*, edited by Sicinski, was published in 1976. Poland also has a Forecasting Research Center directed by Karol I. Pelc at the Research Institute of the Technical University of Wroclaw.

Romania has an International Center of Methodology for Future and Development Studies, directed by mathematician Mihai C. Botez, in Bucharest. Founded in 1970 under the title Laboratory for Prospective Research, this group has done a great deal of work in such areas as forecasting, global modeling, and system design. Hungary has a Group on Futurology located at the Karl Marx University of Economic Sciences. The group is working on very long-range research in the consistency of complex forecasts and in the connection between futures research and social planning.

In addition, the Soviet bloc has carried out what may have been the largest forecasting effort made anywhere. This effort, involving thousands of people, was conducted by the Council for Mutual Economic Assistance, (CMEA), generally known in the West as COMECON, which serves the East European countries, the Republic of Cuba, and the Mongolian People's Republic. The forecast focused special attention on the question of how soon the economic development of the non-European countries could be brought up to the European level. As explained by two CMEA researchers, Nikola Vylev and Fyodor Metelsky, the question is of more than theoretical interest because other countries may, in the future, wish to join CMEA. Vylev and Metelsky report that economic forecasting in CMEA is reaching a new stage with the countries engaged in joint forecasting of manpower, national income, and fixed assets. Eventually, according to Vylev and Metelsky, CMEA will conduct worldwide forecasts.

Japan has developed a number of future-oriented institutions in recent years. The Japan Techno-Economics Society, founded in Tokyo in 1966, has created an Institute of Future Technology, directed by Yujiro Hayashi, a professor at the Tokyo Institute of Technology. Hayashi formerly was a director of Japan's Economic Research Institute. Japan also has a future-oriented association, the Japan Society of Futurology, which hosted a major international meeting of futurists at Kyoto in 1970. Japanese futurists may stay reasonably current in western futurism, because of their ability to read English. But since most Japanese works are not translated into English, and few non-Japanese can read Japanese, Japanese futurism does not appear to have played a major role in international futurism.

India has a Center for the Study of Developing Societies, organized in 1963 in Delhi, India, and funded by the Indian Government. Directed by Rajni Kothari, author of *Footsteps into the Future*, the center is devoted to "analytic, normative, and policy-oriented work on the stresses and challenges facing societies."

South Korea has an Institute of Science and Technology, which is carrying out projects on such topics as "Korea in the Year 2000." The Korean Society for the Future, directed by Professor Hyung-Kook Kim of Seoul National University, currently is focusing major attention on the quality of life in Korea's rapidly changing society. The Society has held seminars on "Quality of Life in Industrializing Societies" and "Directions and Tasks of Social Development in the Future of Korea."

Canada now has a Canadian Association for Futures Studies, in addition to a number of World Future Society groups. The Association issues a quarterly bulletin *Futures Canada*.

The Republic of South Africa has a Unit for Futures Research at the University of Stellenbosch. The Unit expects to publish soon a report on long-term trends in South Africa and a Management Guide to Futures Studies.

The Futurist Impact on Society

The creation of future-oriented research institutes, associations, and publications means that futurists are increasingly in a position to have a major influence on government, business, education, and other areas of human life. It is now relatively easy for government officials and businessmen to commission studies of the future, and they are doing so in greater and greater numbers as they recognize the availability and importance of this new type of expertise. The development of future-oriented organizations has also established links between futurists located in very different fields. At the beginning of the 1960s, technological forecasters in the space industry knew almost nothing of sociological forecasters, and econometric forecasters knew nothing of theologians interested in the future of religion. By the 1970s, however, lines of communication across disciplinary boundaries had been established so that futurists could contact their colleagues in other fields. Most futurists were soberly aware that in the interconnected world of today, "everything depends on everything else."

Appendix B

A Field in Search of a Name

Futurists do not know what to call their subject. In fact, they are not even agreed on whether it is a science, an art, a philosophy, or something different from any of them. Names for the field that currently enjoy wide currency include *futures research*, *future studies*, *futuristics*, and *futurology*. And there is no shortage of alternatives such as *prognostics*, *futuribles*, *policy research*, *futures analysis*, etc.

If the study of the future is a science, then an *-ology* ending might be appropriate, but is the study of the future really a science? And should the field be limited to researchers, or should it include practitioners and creators as well? Until futurists are fully agreed on what the field really is, it will probably be somewhat difficult to be sure what to call it.

The notion that the world of the future might become a field of serious study traces at least as far back as 1902 when H.G. Wells envisioned teams of scholars at work on the future, and the field has antecedents of much earlier date: for instance, Francis Bacon, whose *New Atlantis*, written about 1620, imagined a research institute devoted to solving human problems. The first person to propose a name for the study of the future may have been sociologist S.C. Gilfillan, who in 1907 suggested that it might be called *mellontology*, a term derived from the Greek word for future events. "There is a call for mellontologists, students of future civilization in general, just as there are archaeologists who reason out all the interacting aspects of prehistoric culture," Gilfillan wrote.

Mellontology gained little acceptance in its day, and might have been forgotten except that its proposer was still alive and vigorous in the 1960s when interest in the future reached new heights, and able to remind scholars about his 1907 paper.

During the intervening years, in 1943, political scientist Ossip K.

Flechtheim proposed an alternative term, *futurology*. Flechtheim later commented:

> Time and again hitherto dispersed findings are brought together and integrated into a new discipline which treats the same materials in a new way. Thus sociology, the generalized study of society, or history are younger than some of the more special sciences upon which they draw. Since Futurology does not so much deal with a new and special segment of knowledge, but rather represents a new synthesis of varied materials, it is closely related to history and could indeed be pictured as a projection of history into a new time dimension. In the absence of written or unwritten records, however, Futurology must make use of a different method of approach. It cannot work with the chronological sequence of detailed facts; instead, it will avail itself of interpretation, generalization, and speculation to a considerably higher degree. In this respect, its kinship to cultural anthropology, theoretical sociology, and social philosophy becomes apparent.

A number of futurists have accepted *futurology* as a reasonable name for the futures field, but others are strongly opposed to it. The most common objection is that the term suggests that the future can be known scientifically.

French futurist Bertrand de Jouvenel writes, in *The Art of Conjecture:*

> The forecaster who takes care to give his best opinion does not want to make others believe that there is a "science of the future" able to set forth with assurance what will be. He is apprehensive of letting this misunderstanding arise. And it is to prevent this illusion that I reject the term *futurology*. This word would be very convenient for designating the whole of our forecasting activities except that it would suggest that the results of these activities are scientific—which they are not. . . .

Similarly, the Dutch scholar Fred Polak has written:

> The principal merit—and indeed no small one—of the term *Futurology* is that the component or dimension of "future" finds particularly clear linguistic expression in it. However, in my opinion this advantage should be carefully weighed against other, possibly greater, disadvantages.

Polak notes that anyone who is realistic must be aware that the future is regarded as unknown and therefore the supposed "science of the future" should be left to tea-leaf readers, crystal ball gazers, etc. Futurology "in the sense of some kind of knowledge of the future or precognition would likely be viewed as pretentious, reckless, misleading, and unfounded." A supposed science of the future, said Polak, runs the risk of exaggerating its own possibilities.

In a similar vein, the German-born writer Robert Jungk has said that *futurology* "is too close to astrology. It suggests the idea of a future made in advance which we could read like magicians. That's not at all what we do. I prefer 'future research,' that is, forecasts on the basis of tested hypotheses."

In English, *futurology* sounds like a pseudoscience and may be likened to such pretentious neologisms as *hamburgerology* and *garbology* (the science of garbage). Part of the problem is that the Greek ending *-ology* is married to the Latin stem *futur-*. The term proposed by Gilfillan, *mellontology*, would be more correct from a linguistic standpoint, but would be less easily remembered and recognized.

The Swedish Government's Secretariat for Future Studies explicitly rejected *futurology* in its 1974 report *Future Studies in Sweden*, and elected to use the term *future studies*. The Secretariat explained:

> The term *future studies* has been considered preferable to other terms in current use, e.g., *future research*. This is because future studies do not only involve research as such but also an inventory of the results of research already undertaken in various fields and the application of already known methods. And by using the term *future studies*, we emphasize the fact that the field is not a concern primarily of specialists and scientists.

The Swedish statement reflects widespread fear among many futurists that the field will be captured by experts, who are viewed as being narrow-minded and subservient to powerful interests.

The term *futures analysis*, popular in the U.S. Congress, is readily understandable. However, the term strongly suggests an activity limited to scientists, scholars, and other experts, and therefore is objectionable to people who want the field to involve many different types of people. Another objection is that the term seems to limit the field to analyzing future possibilities when it may be equally important to synthesize or create them.

Fred Polak has advocated the term *prognostics*, a term that is favored in Eastern Europe, perhaps partly because of the traditional Slavic orientation toward Greek rather than Roman culture. Based on the original Greek words, *prognostics* means fore-knowledge (pro-gnosis), which raises the issue whether it is possible to know the future world. So far, prognostics has found little acceptance in Western Europe or the United States, though Ferdinand Lundberg used it in his 1963 book *The Coming World Transformation*.

Poll on Name for the Field

The World Future Society polled its members in 1975 on their preferred term for the field. Only two terms received a net positive response: *future studies* and *futures research.* The other terms, in order of preference (that is, from least disliked to most disliked), were: *futures analysis, futuristics, forecasting, futurology, prognostics, futurics,* and *futuribles.*

The most popular term, *future studies,* is readily comprehensible and unpretentious. Artists paint "studies," children engage in them at school. But the term is often confusing because it could refer to studies to be made in the future rather than studies of the future. If the plural *futures* is used, that problem is overcome to some degree, but other problems arise: (1) the term loses its euphony, (2) there is a possible confusion with commodity futures, and (3) the pluralized futures is confusing to people new to the field.

The second most popular term, *futures research,* has many of the advantages of *future studies,* but seems to limit the field to scholarly or scientific research. The term seems very appropriate to the activities of certain research institutes, but less applicable to a course on the future given in a high school, or an artist's attempt to envision a city of the future. Furthermore, *futures research,* like *future studies,* lacks the distinctiveness and ease of manipulation that a single-word term would have.

Society members were asked to nominate alternative terms, and a few did so. Among the suggestions were: *futures field, probabilistics, forward studies, future planning, futurography, anthrospectunity, projective research, short-* and *long-range planning and projections, predictive studies, futury* (companion to history), *futory* (based on future and history), *alternative analysis, options analysis, decision option analysis, alternatives in futures.*

Nominations over the years from other sources have included *prospectivism, fustory* (like *futury* and *futory,* a contraction of future history), and *futurist* or *futuristic studies.*

The results of the poll seem to indicate:

1. There is no consensus on what the field should be called.

2. People want a new and distinctive word for the field— but shrink from any term that is proposed, perhaps partly because of various connotations attached to the term, but perhaps also because of its unfamiliarity.

3. A number of different words may be needed to indicate the various divisions or aspects of the futures field.

All things considered, the best of the proposed terms may be *futuristics,* for the following reasons:

1. It is a single word, and is easier to use and less confusing than double-word terms like *futures research, future studies,* and *futures analysis.*

2. *Futuristics* does not limit the field to strictly scientific or scholarly activities. One of the great virtues of the future is that everyone has a stake in it and can play a role in it. Hence, the term *futurology* is seriously misleading.

3. The Latin stem *futur-* is so firmly rooted in the field that its use appears to be almost compelling. Terms like *mellontology* pose a major learning problem, and it would be difficult to get them into general currency.

4. *Futuristics* avoids the plural futures issue, e.g., future(s) studies.

5. The ending *-ics* implies a field of study or an activity, which is what is meant.

6. The term *futurics* is less clear and euphonious than *futuristics* and also lacks the currency and acceptability now enjoyed by *futuristics*.

7. The term *futurism* implies a philosophy or style rather than a field of activity. However, futurism may still be used for the mood or movement that emphasizes the future.

Futuristics may be defined as follows:

> *futuristics:* A field of activity that seeks to identify, analyze, and evaluate possible future changes in human life and the world. The word implies a rational rather than mystical approach to the future, but also accepts artistic, imaginative, and experiential approaches as offering contributions that can be useful and valid.

Futuristics may be viewed as the discipline or field of activity that emerges from futurism. In other words, futurism is the philosophical attitude or approach of a futurist. Futuristics is the set of specific activities that emerge from that viewpoint.

A number of other terms also have possible uses:

> *prognostics:* The field of study that focuses on forecasting methods: their development, evaluation, and appropriate use.
> *futurible:* Any of various possible future developments.
> *futuristic research:* Scholarly or scientific research aiming at the description of possible future technological or social developments, assigning probabilities to such developments, and assessing their consequences.

Futuristics is a unique combination of science and art, management and morality, electronic intelligence and common sense that manages to avoid collapsing into total confusion because it maintains a unique perspective on reality—that of looking forward in time. This concentration on the future provides an organizing principle for the creation of a powerful framework for thought and action that can enable mankind to manage human civilization with increasing wisdom in the years ahead.

Bibliography

For a longer listing of future-oriented books, see The Future: A Guide to Information Sources *(World Future Society, Washington, D.C., 1977).*

Abt, Clark C. *Serious Games*. New York: Viking Press, 1970.

The president of Abt Associates, a consulting firm in Cambridge, Massachusetts, describes how games are being used as learning devices in schools, businesses, and even government agencies. Abt says that games permit players to test situations and "solutions" that are either irreversible or too risky or expensive to test in the real world. Games offer an opportunity for virtually risk-free, active exploration of intellectual and social problems.

Ayres, Robert U. *Technological Forecasting and Long-Range Planning*. New York: McGraw-Hill, 1969.

Robert Ayres, currently vice president of Delta Research Corp. in Arlington, Virginia, offers a clear and succinct introduction to forecasting methods. Ayres also describes the various failures of forecasting and the epistemology of forecasting.

Baier, Kurt, and Nicholas Rescher, eds. *Values and the Future*. New York: Free Press, 1969.

This is a collection of 17 essays by such futurists as Theodore Gordon, Olaf Helmer, Bertrand de Jouvenel, Kenneth Boulding, and others. The book is introduced by Alvin Toffler, who describes the "value impact forecaster" as "a profession of the future." Also included is "a questionnaire study of American values by 2000 A.D." by Nicholas Rescher. The volume concludes with two bibliographies dealing with technological progress, future-oriented studies, and the theory of value.

Bauer, Raymond, ed. *Social Indicators*. Cambridge, Massachusetts: M.I.T. Press, 1966.

Raymond Bauer, a psychologist and professor at the Harvard Business School, and Bertram Gross, an academician in the field of public administration, contribute major essays to this volume, which introduces the general topic of social indicators. This book was financed by a grant from the National Aeronautics and Space Administration to the American Academy of Arts and Sciences in Boston. NASA is only one of a number of U.S. agencies that have been interested in social indicators, that is, statistics on the many aspects of our society that are not covered by the traditional census statistics and economic indicators.

Beckwith, Burnham P. *The Next 500 Years: Scientific Predictions of Major Social Trends.* New York: Exposition Press, 1967.

This book contains more than 1,000 specific forecasts about what may happen in human society during the next five centuries. The book analyzes major social trends and covers such topics as population, education, knowledge, religion, the relationship of work and leisure, etc. In general, the forecast is optimistic and the forecasts appear highly integrated; that is, they tend to jibe fairly well with each other. The book is tightly written and stimulating but somewhat lacking in evidence to support its assertions.

Bell, Daniel. *The Coming of Post-Industrial Society: A Venture in Social Forecasting.* New York: Basic Books, 1973.

This book contains most of the concepts that sociologist Bell has developed in recent years. Scholarly and well-documented, it offers a thoughtful analysis of the great social trends that are shaping our future society. Bell argues that people can make meaningful forecasts about the future of modern society if they take the trouble to understand fully the present conditions of that society and the trends visibly at work in it.

Bell, Daniel. *The Cultural Contradictions of Capitalism.* New York: Basic Books, 1976.

Bell argues that capitalism may destroy itself if the polarities between its affective and rational elements are not reconciled. He says that capitalism as an economic system requires ever greater applications of rationality to solve problems of organization and efficiency and places an ever greater emphasis on such values as self-fulfillment and personal gratifications. As these two tendencies grow stronger, the rift between them widens. This book continues the analysis of Bell's earlier work *The Coming of Post-Industrial Society.* Bell describes the split character of the new capitalism of abundance: it demands a Protestant ethic in production, but encourages a fun ethic in consumption. Bell argues that modern society can best be analyzed by thinking of it as "an uneasy amalgam of three distinct realms: the social structure (principally the techno-economic order), the polity, and the culture." The three realms are ruled by contrary principles: efficiency, equality, and self-realization or self-gratification.

Bell, Daniel, ed. *Toward the Year 2000: Work in Progress.* Boston: Houghton Mifflin, 1968 (Beacon Press paperback, 1969).

This is the first report of the Commission on the Year 2000, formed in 1965 by the American Academy of Arts and Sciences and chaired by sociologist Daniel Bell. The volume summarizes the dialogue that occurred at the working sessions of the Commission in October 1965 and in February 1966. The book also includes a number of papers ranging from Leonard J. Duhl's ideas on planning to David Riesman's "Thinking on Meritocracy." This book is a highly compact compendium of stimulating ideas.

Bell, Wendell, and James A. Mau, eds. *The Sociology of the Future.* New York: Russell Sage Foundation, 1971.

Thirteen social scientists discuss the 1970s and the study of the future. The book offers a theory of social change based on the concept of the image of the future together with research strategies for studying the future. The book contains an annotated bibliography on social science studies of the future.

Berry, Adrian. *The Next Ten Thousand Years: A Vision of Man's Future in the Universe.* New York: E. P. Dutton, 1974.

The author, a fellow of Britain's Royal Astronomical Society, explores such possibilities as colonization of Venus, factories on the moon, intelligent life on other planets, and the extensive use of space ships. The book offers an optimistic and imaginative view of the possibilities of outer space. The emphasis is heavily on technology as the means for obtaining "ever more magnificent achievements."

Boulding, Kenneth E. *The Meaning of the Twentieth Century: The Great Transition.* New York: Harper and Row, 1964.

The author, a University of Colorado economist, argues that mankind is in a transition from civilized to "post-civilized" society and that he needs to avoid four "traps": (1) the war trap ("A major nuclear war would unquestionably set back the transition to a post-civilized world by many generations . . ."); (2) the population trap (Attempts to help people through medical services, says Boulding, could lead to disastrous overpopulation.); (3) the technological trap ("Technology at the present time, even the highest technology, is largely dependent for its sources of energy and materials on accumulations in the earth which date from its geological past. In a few centuries, or at most a few thousand years, these are likely to be exhausted."); and (4) the entropy trap (Borrowing a term from thermodynamics, Boulding suggests that the human potential may gradually diminish.) To avoid these traps, Boulding believes that man should use all his intellectual resources to create an image of the future, or set of long-range goals, which would stress the infinite possibilities open to him.

Bright, James R. *A Brief Introduction to Technology Forecasting Concepts and Exercises.* Austin, Texas: The Pemaquid Press, 1972.

James Bright is Professor of Technology Management at the University of Texas's Graduate School of Business Administration and President of the Industrial Management Center in Hilton Head, South Carolina. Since 1967 he has organized a series of seminars on technology forecasting and assessment. An integral part of Bright's seminars is the workshop in which students execute exercises based on case histories. Some of the most useful exercises are reproduced in this volume. Each group of exercises is preceded by a brief explanation of how forecasting techniques should be applied to the exercise, and in the process Bright offers some very clear explanations of the forecasting techniques now in use.

Bright, James R., and Milton E.F. Schoeman, eds. *A Guide to Practical Technological Forecasting.* Englewood Cliffs, New Jersey: Prentice-Hall, 1973.

A treasurehouse of papers by various authors on forecasting, technology transfer, innovation, decision-making, etc.

Bright, James R., ed. *Technological Forecasting for Industry and Government.* Englewood Cliffs, New Jersey: Prentice-Hall, 1968.

This volume resulted from Bright's May 1967 seminar at the Lake Placid Club in New York and provides a number of authoritative papers by professional forecasters.

Bronwell, Arthur B., ed. *Science and Technology in the World of the Future.* New York: John Wiley, 1970.

This volume brings together a number of authoritative and generally readable papers. Especially useful are the state-of-the-art summaries and the accompanying speculation for the various technological fields, such as transportation, biomedical engineering, science, cities, the oceans, etc.

Brown, Harrison. *The Challenge of Man's Future.* New York: Viking Press, 1954.

A California Institute of Technology geochemist discusses the major problems facing modern man such as rising population, the need to increase the food supply, dwindling supplies of fossil fuels, and the limited supplies of mineral resources. Brown sees three possible futures: (1) the reemergence of an agrarian world following a nuclear holocaust, which Brown regards as the most likely possibility, (2) a completely controlled, collectivized industrial society, and (3) a fully industrialized world in which everyone leads a good life.

Brown, Harrison, James Bonner, and John Wier. *The Next Hundred Years.* New York: Viking Press, 1957.

This volume results from a series of discussions between the authors, who are all professors at the California Institute of Technology, and the chief executives of thirty major corporations. The book focuses on trends in (1) availability of material resources and skilled manpower, (2) population growth and food production, and (3) the availability of creative people to solve technical dilemmas.

Brown, Harrison, *et al. The Next Ninety Years.* Pasadena, California: California Institute of Technology, 1967.

This volume results from a conference held in March 1967 in which the authors reviewed the forecasts that they had made 10 years earlier. Two basic surprises emerged: the fantastically rapid growth of population, which greatly exceeded the rates imagined earlier, and the revolution in the world energy picture brought about by the rapidly decreasing cost of nuclear power. The authors found two major disappointments: first, agricultural production had increased less rapidly than had been anticipated; second, while the technologically developed West was getting richer more rapidly than was thought possible, the poorer nations of the world were not sharing significantly in the bounty. (A conference on the next eighty years was held early in 1977 and may lead to a similar new volume.)

Brown, Lester R. *World Without Borders.* New York: Random House, 1972.

This book offers an overview of the current world situation regarding population, food production, pollution, etc. The author argues for an expanded world communications system, with English as the international lingua franca, and new supranational institutions such as a world environmental agency and international research institutes. The book is reasonably optimistic in its outlook, partly because Brown spells out a number of possible solutions to international dilemmas.

Bury, J. B. *The Idea of Progress.* New York: Macmillan, 1932.

In this classic work, a British historian describes the development of the notion of progress from its origins in Cartesianism to its efflorescence in the late 19th and early 20th centuries.

Butler, William F., Robert A. Kavesh, and Robert B. Platt, editors. *Methods and Techniques of Business Forecasting.* Englewood Cliffs, New Jersey: Prentice-Hall, 1974.

In this somewhat technical volume, about 30 economists offer descriptions of how they go about forecasting in a business setting.

Cetron, Marvin J. *Technological Forecasting: A Practical Approach.* New York: Gordon and Breach, 1969.

The author, president of Forecasting International of Arlington, Virginia, has set out to write a primer which would answer essential questions that a research manager would have about how technological forecasters go about their work, the basic methods they employ, and what one might expect them to deliver. The examples are derived primarily from the defense arena, since the author was employed by the U.S. Navy.

Cetron, Marvin J., and Christine A. Ralph. *Industrial Applications of Technological Forecasting: Its Utilization in R and D Management.* New York: John Wiley, 1971.

A useful anthology for anyone interested in the more technical aspects of forecasting and futuristics, especially those related to business and industry.

Chaplin, George, and Glenn D. Paige, eds. *Hawaii 2000: Continuing Experiment in Anticipatory Democracy.* Honolulu, Hawaii: University Press of Hawaii, 1973.

A collection of papers compiled in connection with one of the most vigorous programs aimed at preparing a state to manage its future.

Chase, Stuart. *The Most Probable World.* New York: Harper and Row, 1968.

Social critic and economist Chase, a professional writer for the past half a century, outlines the basic characteristics of tomorrow's world. He concentrates attention on ten areas: (1) technological advances; (2) population growth; (3) diminution of individual living space; (4) growing urbanization; (5) peaceful use of atomic energy; (6) the increasing mix of private and public enterprise; (7) the impact of automation on man; (8) the arms race; (9) mixed trends in nationalistic orientations; and (10) the development of a global community. In an optimistic epilogue Chase describes a world characterized by environmental beauty, a world language, reduced population growth, new towns, material abundance, and world order.

Ciba Foundation Symposium. *The Future as an Academic Discipline.* Amsterdam: Elsevier, 1975.

This volume summarizes a symposium in London on the study of the future in an educational setting. The participants include such distinguished figures as Harold Shane, Professor of Education, Indiana University; British biologist and Nobel prize winner C. H. Waddington, and many others.

Clarke, Arthur C. *Imperial Earth.* New York: Harcourt Brace Jovanovich, 1976.

This science-fiction novel, by one of the masters of the craft, tells about a space traveller who visits the United States during its Quincentennial celebration in 2276.

Clarke, Arthur C. *Profiles of the Future.* Rev. ed. New York: Harper and Row, 1973.

This is a new edition of one of the classics of futurist literature. The book was originally published in 1963 and some of the things that Clarke spoke of have already come true. The first two chapters explore the question of why prophets in the past often failed to foresee the future. Clark attributes this to (1) a failure of nerve and (2) a failure of imagination. In the one case, the would-be prophet has all the facts but cannot see that they point to an inescapable conclusion. In the other case, the prophet does not have the facts and can't imagine them. Later chapters explore such topics as transport, ground-effect machines, ocean mining, space, etc. This exceptionally well-written and scientifically balanced book presents the author's imaginative forecasts for the next 150 years. Clarke maintains that it is impossible to predict the actual future in any detail but one can delineate the general direction that development might take and indicate the realistic possibilities.

Cole, H. S. D., C. Freeman, M. Jahoda, and K. L. R. Pavitt, eds. *Models of Doom: A Critique of the Limits to Growth.* New York: Universe Books, 1973.

The Club of Rome's widely publicized work on *The Limits to Growth* suggested that computer simulations of global conditions indicate

that the world ecosystem is approaching collapse. In this book, 13
Sussex University scientists argue that the Club's world model did
not accurately reflect reality and the policy recommendations stemming from the Club's researchers are a counsel of despair, impossible
to implement.

Conger, D. Stuart. *Social Inventions*. Prince Albert, Canada: Saskatchewan
Newstart, 1970.

The author describes many social inventions through history and concludes with a forecast of some that may occur in the future such as
systems for voting at home with instantaneous nationwide tabulation
of the vote, government-guaranteed minimum annual income, renewable trial marriages, etc.

Cournand, Andre, and Maurice Levy, eds. *Shaping the Future: Gaston Berger and the Concept of Prospective*. New York: Gordon and Breach Science
Publishers, 1973.

This is an anthology of writings by Gaston Berger and others of the
French *Prospective* school that flourished in the 1950s, the era before
Bertrand de Jouvenel launched his Futuribles project.

Daly, Herman E., ed. *Toward a Steady-State Economy*. San Francisco: W.
H. Freeman, 1973.

This book seeks to present a single coherent point of view—that of a
steady-state economy, which is based on both physical and ethical
first principles. Daly, a Louisiana State University economist, says
that "we absolutely must revise our economic thinking, so that it will
be more in conformity with the finite energy and resource limits of
the earth, and with the finite limits of man's stomach." The volume
constitutes a vigorous attack on "growthmania." Included are such
articles as "The Economics of the Coming Spaceship Earth" by Kenneth E. Boulding, "Buddhist Economics" by E. F. Schumacher, and
Daly's own paper, "The Steady-State Economy: Toward a Political
Economy of Biophysical Equilibrium and Moral Growth."

De Jouvenel, Bertrand. *The Art of Conjecture*. New York: Basic Books,
1967; first published by Editions du Rocher, 1964.

Originally published in France in 1964, this book has become one of
the classics of futurist literature. De Jouvenel, widely known as an
economist and philosopher, regards looking into the future as an art
rather than a science. After laying the philosophical groundwork for
the new emerging field, he urges the creation of a "forecasting forum"
to develop the art for government, industry, and people at large.

Dickson, Paul. *Think Tanks*. New York: Atheneum, 1971.

This volume describes, in a rather breezy style, the activities of the
RAND Corporation, System Development Corporation, Hudson Institute, Institute for the Future, Urban Institute, etc. One chapter, entitled "Prospecting the Future," focuses special attention on futuristics.

Dickson, Paul. *The Future of the Workplace*. New York: Weybright and Talley, 1975.

A description of the innovations that may radically alter the way people work in the years ahead. (Note: Dickson was working in 1977 on a book about futurism.)

Dror, Yehezkel. *Crazy States: A Counterconventional Strategic Problem*. Lexington, Massachusetts: Heath, 1971.

An Israeli political scientist says that a number of nations may go "insane" in the future, and governments must prepare for that contingency.

Dror, Yehezkel. *Ventures in Policy Sciences: Concepts and Applications*. New York: American Elsevier, 1971.

Dror, a policy scientist and futurist, describes a concrete, operational approach to policy sciences through exploration of selected central concepts and their applications to actual economic, political, and social situations.

Encel, Solomon, Pauline K. Marstrand, and William Page. *The Art of Anticipation: Values and Methods in Forecasting*. New York: Pica Press, 1975.

Members of the Science Policy Research Unit at the University of Sussex, England, discuss the various methods of forecasting and their application.

Esfandiary, F. M. *Up-Wingers: A Futurist Manifesto*. New York: John Day, 1973.

An Iranian-born New Yorker offers an extremely optimistic view of the future.

Falk, Richard A. *This Endangered Planet: Prospects and Proposals for Human Survival*. New York: Random House, 1972.

A Princeton University professor discusses the growing need for world order and some of the inter-relationships involved in the global ecological crisis. He offers alternative images of the future—(1) a period of desperation leading to annihilation in the 21st century and (2) an optimistic scenario of world transformation which would usher in an era of world harmony in the 21st century.

Falk, Richard A. *A Study of Future Worlds*. New York: Free Press, 1975.

A professor of international law, Richard Falk details the structures and functions of new world organizations required to eliminate poverty, injustice, war, and environmental imbalance. Since today's major problems defy national solutions, the author proposes a reformed and integrated world policy. He suggests setting minimal goals compatible with present political realities adhering to a strict time frame, to the 1990s, and he develops a strategy for moving from the present to the future.

Feinberg, Gerald. *The Prometheus Project: Mankind's Search for Long-Range Goals.* New York: Doubleday, Anchor, 1969.

The author, a Columbia University physicist, argues that the emerging unity of mankind makes it desirable to create long-term goals for the whole world, thereby giving man a clear sense of purpose. The book classifies and analyzes goals, distinguishing between individual goals and collective goals as well as intermediate and final goals. He proposes a "Prometheus Project" as "a cooperative effort by humanity to choose its long-term goals."

Ferkiss, Victor. *The Future of Technological Civilization.* New York: George Braziller, 1971.

A political science professor calls for a new world view, "ecological immanentism," in order to bring about the peaceful revolution needed for human development on a finite planet. He argues that "the essence of humanity's current crisis is that we have allowed our collective destiny to be determined by the political philosophy usually called liberalism, which holds that the prime purpose of society is to encourage individual self-aggrandizement." In addition to liberalism, Ferkiss attacks other conventional ideologies such as Marxism, socialism, and anarchism. None of these ideologies, Ferkiss believes, can possibly cope with the crisis now gripping the world. But mankind can survive, he argues, through an "immanent revolution" that will involve a radical restructuring of society.

Ferkiss, Victor. *Technological Man: The Myth and the Reality.* New York: George Braziller, 1969.

Victor Ferkiss, a professor at Georgetown University in Washington, D.C., argues that world prospects for the long-run future are hopeful, if civilization safely survives the dangers of the near term. What is needed, he suggests, is "technological man"—a wise world citizen who can understand technology and the earth's environment as a complex system. At present, the world is dominated by what Ferkiss calls "bourgeois" man. Bourgeois man does not understand the modern world or see it in its totality and therefore uses technology piecemeal for selfish and limited purposes rather than for the general good of mankind. Ferkiss argues for a new philosophy based on three tenets: (1) "A new naturalism" (Man is viewed as an integral part of nature and must live in harmony with it.); (2) "A new holism" (Everything in the universe is interconnected.); and (3) "A new immanentism" (The whole is created from within.).

Flechtheim, Ossip K. *History and Futurology.* Meisenheim am Glan, Germany: Verlag Anton Hain, 1966.

This is a collection of essays by a professor of political science who has taught in the United States and Germany. Ossip Flechtheim published a prophetic article entitled "Teaching the Future" in a relatively obscure U.S. publication in 1943. In this article he called for the development of courses dealing with the future. Later he published other articles on what he called "futurology." This volume of essays, written primarily between 1941 and 1952, is about equally divided between history and futurology. During the late 1960s, the author founded the German journal *Futurum*, a scholarly journal devoted to studies of the future.

Forrester, Jay W. *World Dynamics*. Cambridge, Massachusetts: Wright-Allen Press, 1971.

Jay Forrester, Professor of Management at the Massachusetts Institute of Technology, has developed a technique known as "System Dynamics" to simulate the functioning of factories, cities, and the world as a whole. The computer simulation of the world described in this book suggests that man may now be living in a golden age that will soon disappear. The simulation of world trends indicates that catastrophe looms if man does not drastically slow down the growth of population and industrialization. Forrester's colleague, Dennis Meadows, used system dynamics in the now famous "Limits to Growth" study that became widely discussed in the early 1970s.

Fuller, R. Buckminster, and Robert Marks. *The Dymaxion World of Buckminster Fuller*. Carbondale, Illinois: Southern Illinois University Press, 1960; New York: Doubleday, Anchor, 1973.

An introduction—well-illustrated—to the thinking of one of the best-known American futurists.

Furnas, Clifford C. *The Next Hundred Years: The Unfinished Business of Science*. New York: Reynal and Hitchcock, 1936.

Chemist Furnas lived to review his own forecasts 30 years after he made them—and found them somewhat less than perfect. (See *"The Next Hundred Years* (Thirty Years Later!)" in *The Futurist*, June 1967.)

Gabel, Medard. *Energy, Earth and Everyone: A Global Energy Strategy for Spaceship Earth*. San Francisco: Straight Arrow Books, 1975.

An associate of comprehensive designer Buckminster Fuller, Medard Gabel describes today's wasteful shortlived energy systems and presents a global energy development strategy that insures a continuing supply of relatively clean energy by 1985 through the substitution of alcohol, methane, hydrogen, electricity, and solar heat for the combustion of coal, petroleum, natural gas, and nuclear energy. The book offers a sampling of the Fullerian approach to world problems. In this book, Fuller and the author make a special attempt at reaching the young people, whom they regard as the most hopeful segment of society.

Gabor, Dennis. *Inventing the Future*. New York: Knopf, 1964.

Dennis Gabor, a Nobel prize-winning physicist, has popularized the phrase "inventing the future." He argues that it is not possible to predict what will happen in the future but it is possible to create the future through imagination and effort. In this book, Gabor argues that civilization faces three dangers: nuclear war, overpopulation, and "the age of leisure." Gabor suggests that men may be able to cope with the first two dangers more easily than with the third, because of its novelty. In recent decades, man has moved rapidly toward the abolition of work but has done little to prepare himself for leisure. Gabor argues for more creative imagination both in short-range social engineering and in long-term visions of the future.

Hahn, Walter A., and Kenneth F. Gordon, eds. *Assessing the Future and Policy Planning.* New York: Gordon and Breach, 1973.

This volume consists of papers presented at a conference organized by the Washington, D.C., chapter of the Institute of Management Sciences, the World Future Society, and the National Bureau of Standards in Gaithersburg, Maryland, in March 1970. The contents include papers by Joseph P. Martino on "Methods of Technological Forecasting," Jack W. Carlson on "Impact of Future Forecasts on Federal Policy," and Charles W. Williams, Jr., on "The Role of National Goals Research."

Harman, Willis W. *An Incomplete Guide to the Future.* San Francisco: San Francisco Book Company, 1976.

Author Harman, director of Stanford Research Institute's Social Policy Research Center, here offers a synthesis of his thinking to date. Harman foresees a radical restructuring of human society in the years ahead.

Heilbroner, Robert L. *An Inquiry into the Human Prospect.* New York: W. W. Norton, 1974.

Economist Heilbroner suggests that mankind may not be able to take the measures necessary to surmount the present world crisis without repressive rule by governments capable of rallying obedience far more effectively than is possible in a democratic setting. Heilbroner discusses in some detail four "threats to mankind"—overpopulation, war, pollution, and knowledge. Knowledge, in the form of science and technology, is not ominous in and of itself, but has been and will continue to be used injudiciously. This is one of the most bleakly pessimistic books that has appeared in recent years.

Hellman, Hal. *Biology in the World of the Future.* New York: M. Evans and Company, 1971.

This is one of a series of volumes describing various aspects of the future. The books are well illustrated and suitable for high school-age people as well as adults. Other volumes in the series include *The City in the World of the Future* (1970), *Communications in the World of the Future* (1975), *Energy in the World of the Future* (1973), *Feeding the World of the Future* (1972), and *Transportation in the World of the Future* (1974).

Helmer, Olaf. *Social Technology.* New York: Basic Books, 1966.

Olaf Helmer, once Chief Mathematician at the RAND Corporation, was one of the principal founders of the Institute for the Future and the co-inventor of the now-famous Delphi technique of polling experts on their opinions about the future. This volume brings together several of his early papers on forecasting, including the now classic Delphi study that he and Theodore Gordon published in 1964.

Horn, Robert E., ed. *The Guide to Simulations/Games for Education and Training.* Crawford, New Jersey: Didactic Systems, 1977.

This comprehensive guide from Information Resources of Lexington, Massachusetts, contains descriptions and evaluations of approximately 1,200 games and simulations useful for schools, businesses, and community groups. A special section is devoted to games dealing with the future.

Hubbard, Barbara. *The Hunger of Eve.* Harrisburg, Pennsylvania: Stackpole, 1976.

Barbara Hubbard, widely known in futurist circles, tells the story of her life and development as an evolutionary thinker. This autobiography is enlivened by her encounters with well-known figures including Jonas Salk, Abraham Maslow, Herman Kahn, Buckminster Fuller, et al.

Ingelstam, Lars E., ed. *To Choose a Future.* Stockholm: Ministry of Foreign Affairs Secretariat for Future Studies, 1974.

The Swedish government has created a Secretariat for Future Studies under the Prime Minister's office. This volume suggests the reasoning behind that decision.

IRADES (Istituto Ricerche Applicate Documentazioni e Studi). *Social and Human Forecasting: Documentation 1975.* Rome: Edizioni Previsionali, 1975.

This is a directory of people and organizations active in the futures field. IRADES, an Italian organization, began publishing such directories in 1971 but in 1977 it was uncertain whether the project would continue. The directory covers most of the major nations of the world.

Judge, Anthony J., ed. *Yearbook of World Problems and Human Potential.* Brussels: Mankind 2000/Union of International Associations, 1976.

This massive tome (1,136 pages) is the result of a major attempt to compile a list of world problems and the means of solving them.

Jungk, Robert, and Johan Galtung, eds. *Mankind 2000.* London: Allen and Unwin, 1969.

This volume contains 35 papers which emerged from one of the first international conferences devoted to studies of the future.

Jungk, Robert. *The Everyman Project: A World Report on the Resources for a Humane Society.* New York: Liveright, 1977. (Originally published in German as *Der Jahrtausend Mensch* [Millennial Man] by C. Bertelsmann Verlag, Munich.)

One of Europe's best known futurists, Robert Jungk reports on the people who, he believes, are creating the society of the future. His topics include creativity, social experiments, simulations, anticipatory democracy, new schools, and changing values.

Jungk, Robert. *Tomorrow Is Already Here: Scenes from a Man-Made World.* English translation of *Die Zukunft hat schon begonnen* [Tomorrow Has Already Begun]. New York: Simon & Schuster, 1954.

A Berlin-born journalist reports on the technological wonders developing in the United States. The book created a major stir in Germany where many people were amazed and shocked by America's new technology.

Kahn, Herman, and Anthony J. Wiener. *The Year 2000: A Framework for Speculation on the Next Thirty-Three Years.* New York: Macmillan, 1967.

This volume summarizes the thinking of Herman Kahn and his Hudson Institute colleagues concerning the world of the future. At the time of its appearance, many futurists regarded the book as possibly the most impressive work available in terms of its disciplined and penetrating attempt to identify and describe the basic trends in western society. The book describes the "basic, long-term multifold trend" in western civilization, and projects economic and other trends to the end of the 20th century.

Kahn, Herman, and B. Bruce-Briggs. *Things to Come: Thinking about the Seventies and Eighties.* New York: Macmillan, 1972.

This volume appeared in 1972, five years after the earlier Hudson Institute volume, *The Year 2000,* and is shorter and somewhat less ponderous than its predecessor. The book presents a later stage in the evolving view of Kahn and his colleagues. The basic long-term multifold trend of western culture is described again with certain modifications based on suggestions developed in the wake of the earlier volume. Over all, the volume seems somewhat more optimistic in tone than *The Year 2000,* but not so optimistic as the later volume, *The Next 200 Years,* which appeared in 1976.

Kahn, Herman, William Brown, and Leon Martel. *The Next 200 Years: A Scenario for America and the World.* New York: William Morrow and Company, 1976.

Kahn and his Hudson Institute colleagues here present a highly optimistic view of America's future. They express confidence that Americans will become increasingly wealthy and that the problems associated with shrinking supplies of fossil fuels and increasing pollution can be overcome. This book might well be read in conjunction with the more pessimistic *Awakening from the American Dream* by Rufus E. Miles, Jr.

Kauffman, Draper L., Jr. *Teaching the Future: A Guide to Future-Oriented Education.* Palm Springs, California: ETC Publications, 1976.

An up-to-date, practical guide to classroom instruction in futuristics and the development of a future-oriented curriculum.

LaConte, Ronald T., and Ellen LaConte. *Teaching Tomorrow Today: A Guide to Futuristics.* New York: Bantam, 1975.

A useful guide to books and other materials that can be used in futuristics courses.

Linstone, Harold A., and Murray Turoff, eds. *The Delphi Method: Techniques and Applications*. Reading, Massachusetts: Addison-Wesley, 1975.

This volume constitutes a handbook on the Delphi Method, a polling technique designed to overcome some of the problems associated with earlier ways of compiling a consensus view of possible future developments. In their introduction, Linstone and Turoff discuss the characteristics and evolution of the Delphi technique. Later chapters contain essays on the philosophy of Delphi, an evaluation of the approach, and the use of cross-impact analysis. In one section, contributors discuss Delphi applications to such subjects as drug-abuse policy, the culprit environment, plastics and competing materials, and the future of the steel and ferroalloy industries.

Lippitt, Gordon L. *Visualizing Change: Model Building and the Change Process*. Fairfax, Virginia: Learning Resources Center, National Training Laboratory, 1973.

Gordon Lippitt, a professor at George Washington University, discusses ways in which a manager, consultant, or change agent can more effectively "picture" the change he is planning, so that those involved can understand the goals to be attained and forces that might resist the changes.

McCall, Robert, and Isaac Asimov. *Our World in Space*. Greenwich, Connecticut: New York Graphic Society, 1974.

This large format volume presents 72 color pages and 40 black and white illustrations by space artist Robert McCall, who offers an exhilarating vision of man's future in space. The text is provided by Isaac Asimov, who offers speculations on the colonization of the moon and Mars, voyages to the outer reaches of the solar system, and the exploration of distant star systems.

McHale, John. *The Future of the Future*. New York: George Braziller, 1969.

John McHale, artist, sociologist, and futurist, argues that mankind is headed toward a planetary society, and it is important that we begin to think and plan and act in terms of the shared planetary culture of the future. He argues that we must learn to anticipate and plan for the future because we will have the future that we learn to imagine and create.

McHale, John, and Magda Cordell McHale. *The Futures Directory*. Guildford, Surrey, England: IPC Press. Scheduled for publication in 1977.

A guide to future-oriented individuals and organizations.

McHale, John. *World Facts and Trends*. New York: Collier Books, 1972.

This volume brings together McHale's thought-provoking charts of world trends, such as the increase in the speed of travel, rising water consumption, advances in life expectancy, etc.

Marien, Michael. *Societal Directions and Alternatives: A Critical Guide to the Literature.* LaFayette, New York: Information for Policy Design, 1976.

A guide to the literature dealing with what various thinkers believe is happening in our society. This extensively annotated bibliography provides listings of books on a wide variety of topics, including: Optimists and Pessimists, Ecology and the Limits to Growth, World Order, Decentralization, Human Needs, Government Reform, Redistribution of Wealth and Power, etc. This is a fascinating volume to dip into.

Martin, Marie. *Films on the Future.* Washington, D.C.: World Future Society, 1976.

This guide identifies and describes films in such categories as Cities, Education, Energy, Human Values, Ocean Sciences, Sociology, Technology, Business, etc. The catalog provides information on how the films may be ordered from the suppliers.

Martino, Joseph P., ed. *An Introduction to Technological Forecasting.* New York: Gordon and Breach, 1972.

This is a collection of articles on technological forecasting by a variety of experts. Examples: "Industrial Implications of Technological Forecasting" by William L. Swager, "Prospects of Technological Progress" by Olaf Helmer, and "Thinking About Future Social Development" by Joseph M. Goldsen.

Martino, Joseph P. *Technological Forecasting for Decisionmaking.* New York: American Elsevier, 1972.

A comprehensive, authoritative treatise on the methodology of technological forecasting and its application to social, business, and government decision-making.

Maxmen, Jerrold S. *The Post-Physician Era: Medicine in the Twenty-First Century.* New York: John Wiley, 1976.

In 50 years, doctors will be obsolete, replaced by computers and a new breed of health care professional called "the medic," predicts Maxmen, who is himself a physician. He goes on to describe in detail his vision of the Post-Physician Era—the organizational issues that could arise, the interface of medicine and communication technology, the future of the health care professions, the biomedical revolution with its ethical implications, and the necessary changes in medical education. In the final chapter, he suggests that humanity must redefine its identity and learn to live harmoniously with the machine if we are to survive in a technological society.

Mead, Margaret. *Culture and Commitment: A Study of the Generation Gap.* New York: Doubleday, Natural History Press, 1970.

In this essay Mead presents her theory of prefigurative, cofigurative and postfigurative cultures. In the postfigurative cultures of the past, the central figures were the elders who had learned the most and were able to do the most with what they had learned. In the prefigurative society now emerging, the focus is on children who represent the world that is to come.

Meadows, Donella H., Dennis L. Meadows, Jorgen Randers, and William W. Behrens, III. *The Limits to Growth.* New York: Universe Books, 1972.

This is the report prepared by Dennis Meadows and his colleagues on The Club of Rome study of world trends. The researchers used the computerized system dynamics technique developed by Professor Jay Forrester. The report argues that if present patterns of rapid population and capital growth are allowed to continue, the world faces "a disastrous collapse."

Meadows, Dennis L., *et al. Dynamics of Growth in a Finite World.* Cambridge, Massachusetts: Wright-Allen, 1973.

This fairly technical volume is the third book to be written on the problem of growth by the system dynamics group at M.I.T. under the leadership of Jay W. Forrester. *Dynamics of Growth* reinforces the findings of its predecessors, *Limits to Growth* and *Toward Global Equilibrium: Collected Papers:* Uncontrolled growth will lead inexorably to world destruction. The models simulate man's total interaction with his environment and show possible global outcomes.

Mendlovitz, Saul H., ed. *On the Creation of a Just World Order: Preferred Worlds for the 1990s.* New York: Free Press, 1975.

In this volume, scholars from Japan, India, the United States, Africa, Western Europe, Latin America and China develop the theme "Preferred Worlds for the 1990s." Mendlovitz, who is the director of the World Order Models Project says in his introduction: "I believe that global community has emerged and global government is not far behind. Hopefully, this set of global essays will contribute to the creation of the social processes necessary for a just and peaceful world order."

Mesarovic, Mihajlo, and Eduard Pestel. *Mankind at the Turning Point: The Second Report to the Club of Rome.* New York: E. P. Dutton/Reader's Digest Press, 1974.

Whereas *The Limits to Growth,* The Club of Rome's first report, urged an immediate slowdown of economic growth, this second report concludes that a new differentiated kind of growth is required, balancing world population, food, energy, and world wealth distribution. The nature of many global crises, the authors state, lies in some form of uncontrolled growth. Based on the results of the World Modeling Project, Mesarovic and Pestel observe that the long-term interests of all the nations and peoples of the world would be best served by encouraging rational decision-making procedures based on worldwide and long-term perspectives.

Michael, Donald N. *On Learning to Plan—and Planning to Learn.* San Francisco: Jossey-Bass, 1973.

Though most people agree there is need for long-range social planning, almost no such planning is underway. The author, a social psychologist, explains the various resistances in individuals and groups that must be overcome in order to have long-range social planning.

Michael, Donald N. *The Unprepared Society: Planning for a Precarious Future*. New York: Basic Books, 1968.

Social psychologist Michael of the University of Michigan says the world is woefully unequipped to do the kind of radical long-range planning that is needed to cope with the stupendous changes ahead. Michael sees a profound societal crisis arising from "our growing intention to undertake long-range planning and our unpreparedness to do it well." Preparing students for tomorrow requires that the teacher teach *styles* of life as much or more than the "facts" of life, Michael believes.

Miles, Rufus E., Jr. *Awakening from the American Dream—The Social and Political Limits to Growth*. New York: Universe Books, 1976.

Formerly a top career official of the U.S. Department of Health, Education, and Welfare and later President of the Population Reference Bureau, Rufus Miles currently is senior fellow and lecturer at the Woodrow Wilson School of Public and International Affairs at Princeton University. In this book he analyzes 22 determinants that have brought American society to its present state. He believes that American society is highly vulnerable to further social deterioration, sabotage, and breakdown. This highly pessimistic work may be contrasted with Herman Kahn's highly optimistic volume, *The Next 200 Years*.

Miller, Walter. *A Canticle for Leibowitz*. New York: Lippincott, 1960.

After the destruction of civilization during a thermonuclear war, the survivors ruthlessly suppress technological knowledge, in the belief that technology was responsible for the catastrophe. Centuries later, a group of monks discovers some circuit diagrams by an electrical engineer who lived in southern California, and by patiently copying and studying the works of "St. Leibowitz" they eventually come to understand something of the ancient technological civilization. Thanks to their efforts, technology returns to the world and, as the novel ends, the world is again being engulfed in a thermonuclear war.

Moffitt, Donald, ed. *The Wall Street Journal Views America Tomorrow*. New York: AMACOM, 1977.

This book assembles a number of *Wall Street Journal* articles about the future up to the year 2000. Topics range from population and natural resources through speculation on new modes of transportation, food production and medical treatment, to such controversial issues as electronic warfare and the social impact of sexually-liberated lifestyles.

Murray, Bruce C. *Navigating the Future*. New York: Harper and Row, 1975.

Bruce Murray, Director of the Jet Propulsion Laboratory at the California Institute of Technology, challenges both the doomsday prophets and the fantasists by presenting his own "rationally optimistic" view of mankind's options for survival. Murray believes that man's best hope lies in a "World Confederation" of diverse peoples existing in largely autonomous states. The World Confederation would not be a Utopia, but simply "the least unsatisfactory means of governing a world racked by widespread social dissatisfaction and by ecological problems of unprecedented magnitude." He examines other scenarios, explaining why they are less probable or satisfactory.

National Goals Research Staff. *Toward Balanced Growth: Quantity with Quality*. Washington, D.C.: U.S. Government Printing Office, 1970.

While serving as a White House advisor under President Nixon, Daniel P. Moynihan led the creation of a National Goals Research Staff to explore the long-term future. Officially created by the President in 1969, the Staff produced this one report before being quietly disbanded. Though criticized in the press for not addressing the "important" issues, the report provided a balanced and insightful analysis of a number of significant problem areas, such as population growth and distribution, support for scientific research, education, etc.

O'Neill, Gerard K. *The High Frontier: Human Colonies in Space*. New York: Morrow, 1977.

By the 1990s, says Princeton physicist O'Neill, 10,000 people of various nationalities may be living and working in space in communities equidistant from the earth and the moon. O'Neill tells who will work in space and how they will get there and offers specific details on the possibilities for family life and earthlike living conditions.

Perloff, Harvey, ed. *The Future of the U.S. Government: Toward the Year 2000*. New York: George Braziller, 1971.

This is a report of a task force of the Commission on the Year 2000 of the American Academy of Arts and Sciences. The book includes 19 essays plus panel discussions. The book's editor is Harvey Perloff, Dean of the School of Architecture and Urban Planning at the University of California at Los Angeles. Perloff says that the activities of the task force centered on two themes: (1) the most significant problems and critical issues that the government of the United States will have to face and (2) the institutional changes and processes needed to enable the government to cope effectively with these changes.

Platt, John. *The Step to Man*. New York: John Wiley, 1966.

These essays, by a humanistic scientist long associated with the University of Michigan, take a searching look at the nature of man and his organizations and how they are changing. Platt suggests that the danger of the human race extinguishing itself cannot long continue. "No one lives very long walking on loose rocks at the edge of a precipice. Either, very soon, in ten or 20 years, or in 30 or 40, we fall over the nuclear precipice, or else, very soon, before that time runs out, we argue some sense into our collective heads and move back from danger." If humanity survives the next generation or so, Platt suggests it will move into a "steady-state" of history, when new ways of creative leisure and interaction will provide "the most interesting and satisfying ways of life."

Polak, Fred L. *The Image of the Future: Enlightening the Past, Orienting the Present, Forecasting the Future.* Two vols. New York: Oceana Publications, 1961. (A shortened version was published by Elsevier in Amsterdam in 1973.)

Dutch scholar Fred Polak examines here the various "images of the future" which man has constructed in the past. His retrospect encompasses Hellenic, Persian, Jewish, and Christian myths, as well as the imagistic historical periods of the Middle Ages, the Renaissance, the Enlightenment and the Age of Progress. He believes that modern man's "imaging" faculty is now seriously impaired. He attributes this primarily to the rise of de-Utopianism, that is, the trend towards believing that the future offers neither a heaven in the sky nor a utopia on earth. Polak believes that "the task before us is to reawaken the almost dormant awareness of the future and to find the best nourishment for a starving social imagination."

Polak, Fred L. *Prognostics: A Science in the Making Surveys and Creates the Future.* Amsterdam: Elsevier, 1971.

Dutch scholar Polak here offers a philosophical discussion of the future as a field of study. He argues that only by freeing ourselves of the dogmatism of the past can we comprehend the full spectrum of the future and realize its full potential.

Prehoda, Robert W. *Designing the Future: The Role of Technological Forecasting.* Philadelphia: Chilton Books, 1967.

Technological forecaster Robert Prehoda presents a rationale for man's potential ability to foresee accurately the future capabilities and results of applied science. The book defines technological forecasting as "the description or prediction of a foreseeable invention, specific scientific refinement, or likely scientific discovery that promises to serve some useful function." Prehoda describes several approaches to technological forecasting; his primary technique is through what he calls "the Hahn-Strassmann point." The name comes from the Hahn-Strassmann experiments in 1938, which showed the possibility of uranium fission. His method is to look for analogous situations, i.e., laboratory achievements which show the possibility of some major advance on a practical scale, then forecast the practical results which could be based on this laboratory achievement. About two-thirds of the book is devoted to examining various fields of science which, in Prehoda's opinion, have passed Hahn-Strassmann points, and which will therefore lead to major advances in the practical sphere.

President's Research Committee on Social Trends. *Recent Trends in the United States.* New York: McGraw-Hill, 1933.

This study presciently analyzed emerging U.S. problems. Social scientists still speak of this report with awe.

Roemer, Kenneth M. *The Obsolete Necessity: America in Utopian Writings 1888-1900*. Kent, Ohio: Kent State University Press, 1976.

The author analyzes the writings of a "utopian era" in the United States (1888-1900) when some 160 utopian, partially utopian, or anti-utopian works were published. Roemer reasons that the utopian writings can help understanding of early attempts to define the "American Dream" as well as present-day hopes and fears about the future.

Rosen, Stephen. *Future Facts*. New York: Simon and Schuster, 1976.

Billed as "a forecast of the world as we will know it before the end of the century," this book describes over 300 specific products, concrete ideas, and detailed processes that may be part of life in the 21st century, if not before. Among the "Future Facts" are Artificial Life, Nuclear-Powered Artificial Heart, "Electric Aspirin," Solar Power from Satellites, Quick-Ripening Produce, Deep-Sea Food Storage, Protein from Wastes, Flying Trains, Car Radar and Sonar, Chemical Transfer of Learning, Nonlethal Weapons, Ultrasonic Sewing, a Mobile Bridge, Portable Telephones, Life-Cycle Insurance, Remote Cassette Vendors, etc.

Schmalz, Anton B., ed. *Energy: Today's Choices, Tomorrow's Opportunities*. Washington, D.C.: The World Future Society, 1974.

This volume contains 47 articles by outstanding authorities and includes a foreword by Gerald Ford and an epilogue by John W. Gardner, chairman of Common Cause. Published in conjunction with the World Future Society's Energy Forum, April 1974, the book examines the energy question from eight perspectives: some new dimensions, resources, technology, economics, humanities, policy, implementation, and transitions.

Schumacher, E. F. *Small Is Beautiful: Economics as if People Mattered*. New York: Harper and Row, 1973.

A German-born British economist urges the decentralization of industry and an emphasis on providing jobs for people rather than increasing productivity. Schumacher advocates "intermediate technology"—technology that is neither primitive nor highly advanced—as a means for revitalizing the villages of the underdeveloped world.

Seaborg, Glenn T., and W. R. Corliss. *Man and Atom*. New York: E. P. Dutton, 1971.

Glenn Seaborg, the former chairman of the U.S. Atomic Energy Commission and winner of a Nobel prize for discovering plutonium and other elements, outlines his ideas for the peaceful use of atomic energy in creating a better world.

Shane, Harold G. *The Educational Significance of the Future*. Bloomington, Indiana: Phi Delta Kappa Educational Foundation, 1973.

The author, a professor of education at Indiana University, prepared this report for the U.S. Commissioner of Education on the basis of interviews with more than 80 futurists. The book offers a compact digest of what futurists are thinking about the future and specifically about education.

Somit, Albert, ed. *Political Science and the Study of the Future*. Hinsdale, Illinois: Dryden Press, 1974.

An unusually fine anthology of significant writing about the future. Theodore J. Gordon writes on "Current Methods of Futures Research"; Bertrand de Jouvenel discusses "Political Science and Prevision"; James Allen Dator talks about "Futuristics and the Exercise of Anticipatory Democracy in Hawaii."

Spekke, Andrew A., ed. *The Next 25 Years: Crisis and Opportunity*. Washington, D.C.: The World Future Society, 1975.

This volume is a selection of 47 thought-provoking papers submitted to the World Future Society's Second General Assembly, June 1975. The meeting was the largest gathering of futurists ever held (approximately 2,800 attendees). The papers were selected for their general interest and relevance to the theme of the meeting—a look at the prospects for mankind during the final quarter of the 20th century.

Taylor, Gordon Rattray. *How to Avoid the Future*. London: Secker and Warburg, 1975.

A British science writer offers an extremely pessimistic view of the human future.

Theobald, Robert. *An Alternative Future for America's Third Century*. Chicago: Swallow Press, 1976.

Ranging over many themes, socio-economist Theobald attempts to explore the problems mankind faces, the possibilities for deep change presented by these problems, and how people can hope to bring about the revolution in values, institutions, and systems needed to avoid extinction. He covers such themes as communications, the environment, education, the theory of guaranteed income, and income distribution.

Thomson, Sir George. *The Foreseeable Future*. Rev. ed. Cambridge, England: Cambridge University Press, 1960.

Nobel prize-winning British physicist Sir George Thomson published this book in 1955. The author focused on sources of energy, transportation, communication, meteorology, natural resources, food production, and intellectual development. Two decades after his book appeared, a reviewer in *The Futurist* reported that Thomson's twenty-year-old forecasts had generally turned out to be remarkably accurate. Thomson had correctly foreseen the energy crisis in the 1970s and the triumph of the computer.

Tinbergen, Jan, coordinator; Antony J. Dolman, editor; Jan van Ettinger, director. *RIO: Reshaping the International Order*. A Report to the Club of Rome. New York: Dutton, 1976.

Produced by a team of experts in the fields of food production, monetary systems, international trade, arms control, natural resources, and the human environment, this report addresses the question, "What new international order should be recommended to the world's statesmen and social groups so as to meet, to the extent practically and realistically possible, the urgent needs of today's population and the probable needs of future generations?" Among the massive reforms prescribed by the group are the creation of an international taxation system and a world treasury, a World Disarmament Agency, and a World Energy Research Authority.

Toffler, Alvin. *The Eco-Spasm Report.* New York: Bantam Books, 1975.

In this short work, Toffler argues that the world faces not just an economic upheaval but something far deeper. "What is happening, no more, no less," he says, "is the breakdown of industrial civilization on the planet and the first fragmentary appearance of a wholly new and dramatically different social order: a super-industrial civilization that will be technological but no longer industrial."

Toffler, Alvin. *Future Shock.* New York: Random House, 1970.

A best-seller that has sold some six million copies and been translated into 20 languages, *Future Shock* argues that increasing numbers of people are suffering from the impact of too rapid social change. Toffler believes that the problem may become increasingly severe in the years to come. A final chapter, "The Strategy of Social Futurism," proposes a number of ways in which society can learn to cope with future shock. The author outlines his ideas about how to make democracy more anticipatory in its character.

Toffler, Alvin, ed. *The Futurists.* New York: Random House, 1972.

In this well-edited anthology of writings by a number of well-known futurists, readers will find an introduction to many strains of current futurist thinking. Selections range from Arthur Clarke writing on "hazards of prophecy" to Kenneth Boulding describing "the economics of the coming spaceship earth."

Toffler, Alvin, ed. *Learning for Tomorrow: The Role of the Future in Education.* New York: Random House, 1974.

This anthology is essentially a call for "education in the future tense." The central thesis is that all education springs from images of the future, and all education creates images of the future. The volume includes a "Status Report, Sample Syllabi, and Directory of Future Studies" by Billy Rojas and H. Wentworth Eldredge.

Tugwell, Franklin, ed. *Search for Alternatives: Public Policy and the Study of the Future.* Cambridge, Massachusetts: Winthrop Publishers, 1973.

This excellent anthology of futurist writing includes many frequently quoted articles, such as "On the Epistemology of the Inexact Sciences" by Olaf Helmer and Nicholas Rescher, "What We Must Do" by John Platt, and "The Counter-Intuitive Behavior of Social Systems" by Jay W. Forrester.

Vacca, Roberto. *The Coming Dark Age*. New York: Doubleday, 1973.

The collapse of modern technology and modern life is forecast in this book by Italian computer scientist Roberto Vacca. He says that all the major systems on which modern life depends—transport, electricity, garbage removal, etc.—are hopelessly overloaded and about to crack. He says the breakdown will come sometime between 1985 and 1994 and will begin in the United States and Japan. A crisis in one system will aggravate the collapse of another and then another until the catastrophe becomes worldwide. The result of the collapse, Vacca suggests, will be a new dark age. Monastic communities for survival will be located in high places, because heights are easiest to defend. In the monasteries a few people may be able to preserve the remnants of civilization until a new renaissance dawns.

Wagar, W. Warren. *Building the City of Man: Outlines of a World Civilization*. New York: Grossman Publishers, 1971.

The author, a professor of history at the State University of New York at Binghamton, focuses on major trends in recent human history and then projects his own "blueprint for a global society" into the future. Wagar says that "the enemy of modern civilization is something quite commonplace and utterly impersonal. I shall not be clever. The enemy is change. The enemy is the geometrically accelerating pace of change in the growth of all the powers of mankind."

Watt, Kenneth E. F. *The Titanic Effect: Planning for the Unthinkable*. New York: E. P. Dutton, 1974.

Kenneth Watt, a professor of zoology at the University of California at Davis, argues that the world is in the grips of a critical disease, characterized by excessive, undirected, and destructive growth. The world's planners are failing to take adequate steps to deal with the disease because of a basic human tendency to ignore potential enormous disasters as "unthinkable," since they have never happened before. Consequently, appropriate counter-measures are not taken. Watt urges adopting the point of view of ecology and systems analysis to make more accurate future projections, plan accordingly, and use vital resources effectively.

Winner, Langdon. *Autonomous Technology: Technics-out-of-Control as a Theme in Political Thought*. Cambridge, Massachusetts: MIT Press, 1977.

This scholarly volume by a professor at the Massachusetts Institute of Technology analyzes the wide-ranging influences of technology on modern life. The book is packed with ideas and insights and will repay close study by people interested in the far-reaching effects of technology.

World Future Society. *The Future: A Guide to Information Sources*. Washington, D.C.: World Future Society, 1977.

This 603-page directory, whose preparation was supported in part by the National Science Foundation and the Library of Congress's Congressional Research Service, provides information on some 450 individuals, 230 organizations, 116 research projects, 400 books and reports, 107 periodicals, 354 films (including 11 film series), one series of 28 video cassettes, 64 audiotapes and tape series, 31 games and simulations, six mixed-media presentations, and more than 200 courses and programs offered by educational institutions.

Notes

A description of many of the books mentioned in the Notes may be found in the Bibliography.

Chapter 1: An Age of Convulsive Change

Page

1 Figures on the number of new nations, world population, and the gross world product were supplied by the National Geographic Society, Washington, D.C.

1 John Platt's quote on the enormity of the current transformation is from a document entitled "Beliefs That Can Link Men Together" presented at the Rome Special World Conference on Futures Research, 1973. The document appears in *Human Needs, New Societies, Supportive Technologies* (Rome: IRADES, 1974), Vol. IV, p. 100.

2 Charles Williams is quoted from his article entitled "Inventing a Future Civilization" in *The Futurist*, Vol. 6, No. 4 (August 1972), p. 138.

2 For McHale's comment, see page 17, *The Future of the Future* (described in the Bibliography).

2 John Platt's quote about a "crisis of crises" is from his essay "What We Must Do" included in his book *Perception and Change: Projections for Survival* (Ann Arbor, Michigan: The University of Michigan Press, 1970), p. 163.

3 Samuel Lilley is quoted from his essay "Can Prediction Become a Science?" *Discovery*, November 1946, pp. 336-340.

3 Max Ways's estimation of the pace of change is from his book *Beyond Survival* (New York: Harper & Brothers, 1959), p. 25.

3 Alvin Pitcher is quoted in Max Ways's article "The Era of Radical Change," *Fortune*, May 1964, which also includes Ways's proposed categories of change.

4 Charles de Gaulle and Marshall M. Fishwick are quoted in Max Ways's article "The Era of Radical Change," *Fortune*, May 1964.

5 For more about the pace of change, see Platt's discussion of the ideas of Jonas Salk in "World Transformation: Changes in Belief Systems," *The Futurist*, Vol. 8, No. 3 (June 1974), pp. 124-125.

5 Kenneth Boulding's quote is from a lecture, "The Challenge of Change," in the "Courses by Newspaper" learning kit *America and the Future of Man* (San Diego: University of California, University Extension, 1974), p. 28.

5 Willis Harman's statement is from the preface to his book, *An Incomplete Guide to the Future* (San Francisco: San Francisco Book Company, Inc., 1976), p. xi.

Page

5 William F. Ogburn's quote is from his book *On Culture and Social Change* (Chicago: Phoenix Books, 1964), p. 131.

6 For Jacques Ellul's views, see his book *The Technological Society* (New York: Knopf, 1964).

6 Warren Wagar *Building the City of Man* (See Bibliography.), p. 25.

7 The automobile statistics were supplied by the National Safety Council, Washington, D.C.

8 The Hidden Effects of Technology is adapted from "The Effects of Technology" in *The Futurist*, Vol. 5, No. 6 (December 1971), pp. 228-229.

10 The quotation from a drug executive appeared in *Newsweek*, June 16, 1958.

10 "If it works . . ." stated by Kenneth Julin, president of Leach Corp., Los Angeles and appeared in an article "The Makers of Magic," *Newsweek*, May 25, 1959.

10 Paul Armer is quoted from his testimony before the U.S. Congress, January 28, 1970. See "The Paul Principle," *The Futurist*, Vol. 4, No. 3 (June 1970), p. 77.

10 Gordon Rattray Taylor is quoted from his book *Rethink* (New York: E. P. Dutton, 1973), pp. 324-325.

12 Willis W. Harman's table on the "problems of success" is from "The Coming Transformation in Our View of Knowledge," *The Futurist*, Vol. 8, No. 3 (June 1974), p. 127.

13 Herman Kahn and B. Bruce-Briggs's list of the "mixed blessings of progress" is from their book *Things to Come* (See Bibliography.), p. 210.

14 Lyman Bryson is quoted from his book *The Next America* (New York: Harper & Bros., 1952), p. 67.

15 Abraham Maslow's "Hierarchy of Needs" is taken from an article entitled "How Our Values Are Changing" by Ian H. Wilson in *The Futurist*, Vol. 4, No. 1 (February 1970), p. 6.

18 E. J. Mishan is quoted from *Encounter*, March 1971.

18 Reference to the disturbances caused by the wage gap between the two classes of workers in Sweden is found in Daniel Bell's *The Cultural Contradictions of Capitalism* (See Bibliography.), p. 246.

20 Statistics on youth suicides are from "Youth and Suicide: Debunking the Myths," by Donna Landry, *Washington Post*, December, 30, 1976.

Chapter 2: The Terrors of Tomorrow: Realities and Bugaboos

21 Jay W. Forrester is quoted from his book *World Dynamics* (See Bibliography.), p. 11.

21 Roberto Vacca is quoted from his book *The Coming Dark Age* (See Bibliography.), pp. 30-31.

21 The Gordon Rattray Taylor quote is from the introduction to his book *How to Avoid the Future* (See Bibliography.), p. x.

22 The U Thant quote is from *Changing Images of Man*, Policy Research Report 4 (Center for the Study of Social Policy, Stanford Research Institute, Menlo Park, California, May 1974), p. iii.

22 The John Platt quote is from his book *Perception and Change: Projections for Survival* (Ann Arbor, Michigan: The University of Mich-

Page

igan Press, 1970), p. 163; see also Platt's article, "What We Must Do," *Science*, Vol. 166, November 28, 1969.

24 The Wagar quote is from his book *Building the City of Man* (See Bibliography.), p. 16.

25 Colin Turnbull describes the Ik People in his book *The Mountain People* (New York: Simon and Schuster, 1973).

25 Gota Ehrensvaerd is quoted in Harold Shane's *The Educational Significance of the Future* (See Bibliography.), p. 86.

26 Stephen H. Schneider was quoted in the *Washington Star*, February 26, 1976.

26 The forecasts of Mexico's projected population were drawn from Bruce C. Murray's *Navigating the Future* (See Bibliography.), p. 46.

26 Bruce Murray's comment is in *Navigating the Future*, p. 140.

26 The quote from the editors of *The Ecologist* appears in Edward Goldsmith, et al., *Blueprint for Survival* (New York: The New American Library, Signet Book, 1974), p. 14.

27 The Heilbroner quote is from his book *An Inquiry into the Human Prospect* (See Bibliography.), p. 110.

27 Herbert W. Robinson's calculations and views on required world output in the year 2000 can be found in his article, "Can the World Stand Higher Productivity and Incomes?," *The Futurist*, Vol. 5, No. 5 (October 1971), pp. 195-196.

29 The Warren Wagar quotation is from his book *Building the City of Man* (See Bibliography.), p. 155.

29 The Yehezkel Dror citation is from his book *Crazy States: A Counterconventional Strategic Problem* (See Bibliography.). See also Yehezkel Dror, "Crazy States," *The Futurist*, Vol. 7, No. 5 (October 1973), p. 216.

30 The Toffler quote is from his book *The Eco-Spasm Report* (See Bibliography.), p. 3.

30 The Brian Aldiss quote is from his article, "Learning to Live with a Doom-laden Future," in G. R. Urban, ed., *Can We Survive Our Future?* (New York: St. Martin's Press, 1971), p. 390.

31 Alan Seymour's novel *The Coming Self-Destruction of the United States of America* was published by Grove Press, New York, 1969.

32 See Wagar, *Building the City of Man*, p. 22 & p. 70.

32 Vacca's views on the initial manifestations of the future Dark Age appear in *The Coming Dark Age* (See Bibliography.). Other quotes are from pages 181, 215, and 221 of *The Coming Dark Age*.

34 See the Bibliography for a description of *A Canticle for Leibowitz* by Walter Miller.

35 Harold G. Shane made this comment in *The Educational Significance of the Future* (See Bibliography.), p. 18.

35 The George Boehm quote is from his article in *Think* magazine, July-August 1970. *Think* (now defunct) was published by the IBM Corporation in Armonk, New York.

38 Glenn T. Seaborg is quoted from his article "The Birthpangs of a New World," *The Futurist*, Vol. 4, No. 5 (December 1970), p. 205.

Chapter 3: The Shape of Things to Come

41 The "Long-Term Multifold Trend of Western Culture" is described in

Herman Kahn and Anthony J. Wiener's book *The Year 2000: A Framework for Speculation on the Next Thirty-Three Years,* and other books by Kahn and his Hudson Institute colleagues (See Bibliography.).

41 The Burnham P. Beckwith list of trends is from his book *The Next 500 Years: Scientific Predictions of Major Social Trends* (See Bibliography.).

43 For more on the debate between the "technological optimists" and the "technological pessimists," compare the optimistic view of *The Next 200 Years* by Herman Kahn with the pessimistic *Awakening from the American Dream* by Rufus Miles. (See Bibliography.)

44 For more on standardization of measurements, contact the International Organization for Standardization, 1, rue de Varembe, Geneva, Switzerland. IOS is actively working to standardize all kinds of things—from film cartridges to motor vehicle helmets.

45 Barbara Ward and Rene Dubos are quoted from their book *Only One Earth* (New York: W. W. Norton, 1972), p. 219.

45 The Willis Harman quote ("We often assume. . . .") is from his book *An Incomplete Guide to the Future* (See Bibliography.), pp. 1-2.

46 E. F. Schumacher is quoted from his book *Small is Beautiful* (See Bibliography.), p. 27.

46 The Harman quote ("Something like these first two steps. . . .") is from his book *An Incomplete Guide to the Future* (See Bibliography.), p. 7.

48 Tom Lehrer's song "So Long, Mom: A Song for World War III," was recorded in July 1965 at the Hungry I in San Francisco (Reprise Label, *That Was the Year That Was,* Warner Brothers Record).

Chapter 4: The Discovery of the Future

52 The Thucydides quote is from the *Encyclopaedia Britannica,* 14th Edition, Vol. 22, p. 165, subject heading *Thucydides.*

53 The quote from Plato and I. F. Clarke's comment are from "The Utility of Utopia," *Futures,* Vol. 3, No. 4 (December 1971), p. 396.

53 For more on Harvey Cox's three ways of looking at the future, see "Christianity's Conflicting Views of the Future," *The Futurist,* Vol. 3, No. 4 (August 1969), pp. 95-96.

54 See the discussion of More's *Utopia* in I. F. Clarke's article "More's Utopia: The Myth and the Method," *Futures,* Vol. 4, No. 2 (June 1972), pp. 173-178.

55 For the quote from Sir Francis Bacon and comments on Bacon's thinking, see I. F. Clarke's article "Bacon's New Atlantis: Blueprint for Progress," *Futures,* Vol. 4, No. 3 (September 1972), pp. 273-279.

55 See Sir Francis Bacon, *Novum Organum* (1620), p. 129. This quote appears in J. B. Bury's *The Idea of Progress* (New York: Macmillan, 1932), which also offers a discussion of Bacon's views.

56 The Wagar quote is from the jacket to his book *Good Tidings: The Belief in Progress from Darwin to Marcuse* (Bloomington, Indiana: Indiana University Press, 1972).

56 Charles Beard is quoted from his Introduction to J. B. Bury's *The Idea of Progress* (New York: Macmillan, 1932), p. xi.

56 For more on the battle between the Ancients and the Moderns, see J. B. Bury's *The Idea of Progress* (New York: Macmillan, 1932).

Page

57 Socrates is quoted by J. B. Bury in *The Idea of Progress* (New York: Macmillan, 1932), p. 100.

57 Bury's comments about Fontenelle are from *The Idea of Progress* (New York: Macmillan, 1932), pp. 108-109, 110.

57 Fontenelle is quoted from *Preface des elemens de la geometrie de l'infini* (OEuvres, 1790), p. 40. This quote appears in J. B. Bury's *The Idea of Progress* (New York: Macmillan, 1932), p. 110.

58 Turgot is quoted by I. F. Clarke in his article "1750-1850: The Discovery of the Future," *Futures*, Vol. 5, No. 5 (October 1973), pp. 494-495.

58 Leibnitz is quoted by J. B. Bury in *The Idea of Progress*, (New York: Macmillan, 1932), p. 194.

58 Bury's synopsis of *The Year 2440* is in *The Idea of Progress*, pp. 194-197.

59 Benjamin Franklin is quoted by Roger Adams in an article "Man's Synthetic Future" in the *Annual Report of the Smithsonian Institution*, 1952, p. 230.

60 Marquis de Condorcet *Sketch for a Historical Picture of the Progress of the Human Mind*, translated by June Barraclough (New York: The Noonday Press, 1955). The *Sketch* was first published in 1795.

60 For more on Condorcet, see J. B. Bury's *The Idea of Progress* (New York: Macmillan, 1932), pp. 202-216.

61 S. Colum Gilfillan is quoted from "A Sociologist Looks at Technical Prediction" in James R. Bright, ed., *Technological Forecasting for Industry and Government* (Englewood Cliffs, New Jersey: Prentice-Hall, 1965), p. 15.

61 References to 18th-century living conditions are from I. F. Clarke's article "1750-1850: The Shape of the Future," *Futures*, Vol. 5, No. 6 (December 1973), pp. 580-583.

61 Material on the progress of the railroad in the early 19th century is from Bury's *The Idea of Progress*, pp. 326, 327, 329.

61 Tennyson's poem "Locksley Hall" was first published in 1842 in a two-volume edition entitled *Poems*.

62 The Prince Consort is quoted in Bury's *The Idea of Progress*, p. 330.

62 The *Times* is quoted by Bury (op. cit.), p. 331.

62 The reference to Andersen's *Foedrelandet* is from I. F. Clarke's "The Calculus of Probabilities, 1870-1914," *Futures*, Vol. 7, No. 3 (June 1975), p. 239.

63 For Verne's role, see William T. Gay's article "Jules Verne: The Prophet of the Space Age," *The Futurist*, Vol. 5, No. 2 (April 1971), pp. 76-78.

64 The references to *The Coming Race* and Edward Bellamy are from I. F. Clarke's "The Pattern of Prediction, 1871-1914," *Futures*, Vol. 2, No. 1 (March 1970), p. 66.

64 Franklin is quoted from his article "Fictions of the Future," *The Futurist*, Vol. 4, No. 1 (February 1970), p. 26.

65 Reference to a *Report on Coal* is found in I. F. Clarke's article "The Calculus of Probabilities, 1870-1914," *Futures*, Vol. 7, No. 3 (June 1975), p. 240.

65 References to Max Plessner's book *A Look at the Great Discoveries of the 20th Century: The Future of Electrical Television* (1892) are from S. C. Gilfillan's article "A Sociologist Looks at Technical Prediction" in *Technological Forecasting for Industry and Government* (James Bright, editor), p. 17.

Page
65 The forecasts by Richet are from I. F. Clarke's article "The Calculus of
    Probabilities, 1870-1914," *Futures*, Vol. 7, No. 3 (June 1975), pp.
    243-244.
65 Darwin is quoted by Bury in *The Idea of Progress*, p. 336.
66 Bury's comments on posterity and the "illusion of finality" are in *The
    Idea of Progress*, pp. 347-351.
66 Dewey's quote appears in Robert M. Hutchins's essay "Permanence
    and Change" in *The Establishment and All That* (Santa Barbara,
    California: The Center for the Study of Democratic Institutions), p.
    120.

Chapter 5: How the Future Became Foreboding

68 The early 19th-century forecasts are found in S. C. Gilfillan's "A Soci-
    ologist Looks at Technical Prediction" in James Bright's *Technologi-
    cal Forecasting for Industry and Government*, pp. 18-19.
68 H. G. Wells *Anticipations of the Reaction of Mechanical and Scientific
    Progress upon Human Life and Thought* (1901).
69 "It is into the future we go . . ." Wells's quote is from "The Discovery of
    the Future," *Nature*, Vol. 65, No. 1684 (February 6, 1902), p. 327.
69 Wells's quote about uncertainty of the future is from "The Discovery of
    the Future," p. 328.
69 Wells's remarks on how science might help man discover his future are
    from "The Discovery of the Future," p. 329.
69 Wells's quotes about an inductive future are from "The Discovery of
    the Future," p. 329.
70 Wells's concluding statements about the promise of the future are
    found in "The Discovery of the Future," p. 331.
71 Wells's quote is from *The Outline of History* (Garden City, New York:
    Doubleday, first published 1920).
72 H. Bruce Franklin describes the novel *We* in his article "Fictions of the
    Future," *The Futurist*, Vol. 4, No. 1 (February 1970), p. 27.
72 Aldous Huxley *Brave New World* (New York: Harper & Row, 1932).
72 George Orwell *1984* (New York: Harcourt, Brace, 1949).
72 Kurt Vonnegut *Player Piano* (New York: Avon, 1970).
72 Anthony Burgess *A Clockwork Orange* (New York: Random House,
    Modern Library, 1962).
72 Oswald Spengler *The Decline of the West* (New York, 2 volumes,
    1926-8).
72 Charles Steinmetz's forecasts were first published in an article "You
    Will Think This a Dream: A 1915 Vision of Tomorrow" in the *Ladies
    Home Journal*, September 1915, p. 12 and reproduced in *The Futur-
    ist*, Vol. 8, No. 5 (October 1974), pp. 223-226.
72 The forecasts published in "The Future as Suggested by the Develop-
    ments of the Past 72 Years," *Scientific American*, October 2, 1920,
    pp. 320-321 were unsigned, but were made by A.C. Lescarboura and
    his collaborators, according to S. C. Gilfillan's "Prediction of Inven-
    tions," in the U.S. National Resources Committee report *Technologi-
    cal Trends and National Policy* (1937), p. 15.
73 The Edison and Tesla predictions were published in *Popular Science
    Monthly*, May 1922, pp. 21, 22, 26-28 and noted by S. C. Gilfillan in "A

Page

Sociologist Looks at Technical Prediction" in James Bright, ed. *Technological Forecasting for Industry and Government.*

73 For more on the role of Gilfillan, see Wayne Boucher's comments in Boucher *The Study of the Future,* (Washington, D.C.: Government Printing Office, in press).

73 Bertrand Russell's quote, taken from his book *Icarus or The Future of Science,* is found in I. F. Clarke's "The Pattern of Prediction," *Futures,* Vol. 2, No. 4 (December 1970), p. 376.

73 See Furnas' article "The Next Hundred Years (Thirty Years Later!)" *The Futurist,* Vol. 1, No. 3 (June 1967), pp. 46-47.

74 See Frederick Lewis Allen, *The Big Change* (New York: Harper, 1952), p. 84.

74 Hoover's role is described in an unpublished manuscript by Kathryn Humes, Washington, D.C.

74 Gilfillan's comments about William F. Ogburn are found in "A Sociologist Looks at Technical Prediction" in *Technological Forecasting for Industry and Government* edited by James Bright, p. 28.

75 *Technological Trends and the National Policy: Including the Social Implications of New Inventions.* Report of the Subcommittee on Technology to the National Resources Committee (Washington, D.C.: Government Printing Office, June 1937).

75 The long quote comes from *Technological Trends and National Policy: Including the Social Implications of New Inventions,* Report of the Subcommittee on Technology to the National Resources Committee (Washington, D.C.: Government Printing Office, June 1937), pp. 142-144. Reprinted in *The Futurist,* Vol. 4, No. 5 (October 1970), p. 162.

76 Orville Freeman's comments are from *War on Hunger,* A Report from the Agency for International Development, Vol. 4, No. 5 (May 1970), p. 7. Freeman's comments were quoted in *The Futurist,* Vol. 4, No. 5 (October 1970), p. 162.

76 Professor Low's idea for a "Minister of the Future" appears in his article "Why Not a Minister for the Future?" *Tomorrow,* Vol. 2, No. 1 (Spring 1938), p. 2.

77 The reference to Szilard is from Daniel Bell's *The Coming of Post-Industrial Society,* p. 388.

Chapter 6: A New Attitude Toward the Future

78 Wells's comment that great leaders do not make the future comes from his discourse at the Royal Institution titled "The Discovery of the Future," *Nature,* Vol. 65, No. 1684 (February 6, 1902), p. 330.

79 Sartre's comments on the wartime mood of the French are from his article in *Les Lettres Francaises,* September 9, 1944.

79 Sartre's statement about individual freedom is from a lecture titled *L'existentialisme est un humanisme* (translated into English as *Existentialism and Humanism),* 1946.

80 For more on Berger and his Prospective movement, see *Shaping the Future,* edited by Andre Cournand and Maurice Levy (New York: Gordon and Breach, Science Publishers, Inc., 1973).

81 Berger's views of Prospective are from *Prospective,* No. 1, May 1958, pp. 1-10, reprinted in Section VI of *Shaping the Future,* pp. 245-249.

Page

81 Berger's later corrections of misinterpretations of Prospective were published in *Prospective*, No. 6, November 1960, pp. 1-14, also reprinted in *Shaping the Future*, pp. 101-106.

83 Hetman's comment was made in a letter to the author.

84 For more on von Karman's influence on technological forecasting, see Joseph Martino's article "Technological Forecasting in the U.S. Air Force," *The Futurist*, Vol. 5, No. 6 (December 1971), p. 251.

84 For more on the creation of RAND, see Paul Dickson's *Think Tanks* (New York: Atheneum, 1971), pp. 22-25.

85 Helmer and Rescher's paper "On the Epistemology of the Inexact Sciences" is included in Franklin Tugwell's *Search for Alternatives: Public Policy and the Study of the Future* (Cambridge, Massachusetts: Winthrop, 1973), pp. 50-74.

85 See T. J. Gordon and Olaf Helmer, *Report on a Long-range Forecasting Study*, The RAND Corporation, Paper P2982, September 1964.

85 Murray Turoff pioneered in creating the Delphi Conference while he was at the U.S. Office of Emergency Preparedness. See Turoff's article "The Delphi Conference," *The Futurist*, Vol. 5, No. 2 (April 1971), pp. 55-57.

86 The game *Future* is described in *The Futurist*, Vol. 1, No. 1 (February 1967), p. 7.

86 The purposes for creating the Institute for the Future are listed in the *Prospectus*, May 25, 1966, p. 1.

86 "Today, because resources available to governments . . ." *Prospectus*, May 25, 1966, p. 2.

86 "Change in attitude toward the future . . ." *Prospectus*, May 25, 1966, p. 19.

87 The Institute for the Future is now located at 2725 Sand Hill Road, Menlo Park, California 94025.

87 The address of the Futures Group is 124 Hebron Avenue, Glastonbury, Connecticut 06033.

88 Hudson Institute's address is Quaker Ridge Road, Croton-on-Hudson, New York 10520.

88 Herman Kahn *On Escalation: Metaphors and Scenarios* (New York: Frederick A. Praeger, 1965).

88 Herman Kahn *Thinking about the Unthinkable* (New York: Horizon Press, 1962).

88 Herman Kahn and Anthony J. Wiener *The Year 2000: A Framework for Speculation on the Next Thirty-Three Years* (New York: Macmillan, 1967).

88 Donald Michael *The Next Generation: The Prospects Ahead for the Youth of Today and Tomorrow* (New York: Random House, Vintage Books, 1963).

88 Kenneth Boulding *The Meaning of the Twentieth Century: The Great Transition* (New York: Harper and Row, 1964).

89 Resources for the Future, Inc., 1755 Massachusetts Avenue, Washington, D.C. 20036.

90 For more on the "endless frontier," see Vannevar Bush's book *Science: The Endless Frontier* (Washington D.C.: U.S. Office of Scientific Research & Development, 1946).

90 For a discussion of the science policy issues of the 1960s, see chapter on "Basic Natural Science" in *Toward Balanced Growth: Quantity with*

Quality, Report of the National Goals Research Staff (Washington, D.C.: Government Printing Office, 1970), pp. 103-117.

Chapter 7: Basic Principles of Futurism

98 For more information about Joseph's five basic periods of the future, see his article "What Is Future Time?" *The Futurist*, Vol. 8, No. 4 (August 1974), p. 178.

Chapter 8: Methods for Studying the Future

Readers wishing to know more about the methods used by futurists may turn to: "Surveys of Forecasting Methods" by Joseph P. Martino, a two-part series which appeared in the November-December 1976 and January-February 1977 issues of the *World Future Society Bulletin*, as well as the following books which may be found in the bibliography:

An Introduction to Technological Forecasting by Joseph Martino
A Guide to Practical Technological Forecasting. Edited by James Bright
Industrial Applications of Technological Forecasting. Edited by Marvin Cetron and Christine Ralph
Technological Forecasting and Long-Range Planning by Robert U. Ayres
Technological Forecasting: A Practical Approach by Marvin J. Cetron

106 *Think Tank* was invented by Savo Bojecic, Think Tank Corporation, 2245-7 Midland Avenue, Scarborough, Ontario, MIP 3E7, Canada.

107 The blunders of forecasting are cited from *Erroneous Predictions and Negative Comments Concerning Exploration, Territorial Expansion, Scientific and Technological Development*, prepared by Nancy T. Gamarra for the Senate Committee on Aeronautical and Space Sciences and reprinted in "Blunders of Negative Forecasting" by Maj. Joseph Martino and "Faulty Forecasting through History," both in *The Futurist*, Vol. 2, No. 6 (December 1968), pp. 120-121.

110 For more about the influence of new breakthroughs in aircraft technology on growth trends see Joseph Martino's article "Survey of Forecasting Methods," *World Future Society Bulletin*, Vol. 10, No. 6 (November-December 1976), pp. 5-6.

112 Fletcher Knebel and Charles W. Bailey *Seven Days in May* (New York: Harper, 1962).

112 For more on Arthur Waskow's German scenario, see "The Berlin Crisis of 1999," *The Futurist*, Vol. 1, No. 2 (April 1967), pp. 24-25.

116 Theodore J. Gordon and his colleagues at the Futures Group in Glastonbury, Connecticut, have developed highly sophisticated cross-impact matrices.

118 For more about Delphi, see Murray Turoff and Harold Linstone, eds., *The Delphi Method: Techniques and Applications* (Reading, Massachusetts: Addison-Wesley, 1975).

121 A description of the "robot patient" appears in "Robots May Train Tomorrow's Doctors," *The Futurist*, Vol. 1, No. 5 (October 1967), p. 73.

122 Military games developed by RAND are discussed in Paul Dickson's book *Think Tanks* (New York: Atheneum, 1971), pp. 62-63.

123 Information about Data Resources, Inc., is from an article by John Holusha titled "How Accurate Are the Economic Forecasters?" in the *Washington Star*, January 23, 1977.

123 For more about Forrester's models, see his books in the Bibliography.

123 See "Counter-intuitive Behavior of Social Systems" in *Collected Papers of Jay W. Forrester* (Cambridge, Massachusetts: Wright-Allen, 1975), pp. 211-244.

125 Snyder's comments are from his article "Informing the Decision-Makers," *World Future Society Bulletin*, Vol. 10, No. 6 (November-December 1976), p. 17.

126 For descriptions of operations research, cost-benefit analysis, and technology assessment, see Appendix A to *Information and Policy: Inquiries into the Future Information Needs of Congress* (Columbus, Ohio: The Academy for Contemporary Problems, 1975).

Chapter 9: Futurists and Their Ideas

128 Mead's quote about the generation gap is from her book *Culture and Commitment* (Garden City, New York: Doubleday, Natural History Press, 1970), p. 68.

128 Mead's comments about the emergence of a world community are from *Culture and Commitment*, p. 69.

128 Mead's quote about "immigrants into the new era" is from *Culture and Commitment*, p. 72.

129 Mead's quotation about no guides to the future is from *Culture and Commitment*, p. 78.

130 Mead's quote about the unborn child as the symbol of the future is from *Culture and Commitment*, p. 88.

130 Mead's quote about the creation of new models is from *Culture and Commitment*, pp. 92-93.

130 Mead's quote about direct participation of the young is from *Culture and Commitment*, p. 94.

130 Mead's suggestion that every university have a Chair of the Future is mentioned in *The Futurist*, Vol. 8, No. 3 (June 1974), p. 123.

131 Margaret Mead *Coming of Age in Samoa* (New York: Morrow, 1928).

131 Margaret Mead *Growing Up in New Guinea* (New York: Morrow, 1930).

131 Margaret Mead *Sex and Temperament in Three Primitive Societies* (New York: Morrow, 1935).

131 Margaret Mead *Male and Female* (New York: Morrow, 1949).

131 Margaret Mead *New Lives for Old: Cultural Transformation—Manus, 1928-1953* (New York: Morrow, 1956).

131 Mead's quote about the transformation period is from her article "Ways to Deal with the Current Social Transformation," *The Futurist*, Vol. 8, No. 3 (June 1974), p. 122.

132 Mead's comment about global interdependence is from her article "Ways to Deal with the Current Social Transformation," *The Futurist*, Vol. 8, No. 3 (June 1974), p. 123.

133 De Jouvenel's observations on the Treaty of Versailles and the League of Nations are from his article "The Planning of the Future" in *The Great Ideas Today, 1974* (Encyclopaedia Britannica, Inc., 1974).

134 De Jouvenel's comments about long-range consequences of political action are from a letter to the author dated October 3, 1975.

135 Bertrand de Jouvenel *The Art of Conjecture*. Translated by Nikita

Page

Lary (New York: Basic Books, 1967; First published in Monaco by Editions du Rocher, 1964).

135 Quotes regarding the past are from *The Art of Conjecture*, pp. 3, 4, 5, 6.

137 The quotation on the "order of urgency" is from *The Art of Conjecture*, p. 276.

137 The quotation about the "Surmising Forum" is from *The Art of Conjecture*, p. 277.

139 See separate biographies of Daniel Bell and Herman Kahn included in this chapter and the description of Olaf Helmer's role in the development of RAND in the chapter entitled "A New Attitude Toward the Future."

139 De Jouvenel's comments about Helene's role in the journal and the Association are from a letter to the author, October 3, 1975.

139 *Futuribles: Analyse, Prevision, Prospective*, 10, rue Cernuschi, 75017 Paris, France.

140 De Jouvenel's comments about a father's role are from a letter to the author, October 3, 1975.

140 De Jouvenel's discussion of La Fontaine's fable is from his article "La civilisation de l'ephemere" in *Futuribles*, No. 1-2 (Winter-Spring 1975), pp. 5-18.

141 Seaborg's comments on nuclear energy as a key to resolving civilization's crises are from his and William Corliss's book *Man and Atom* (New York: Dutton, 1971), p. 13.

141 Quotes about living wisely with the atom are from Seaborg's testimony before the Joint Committee on Atomic Energy, October 29, 1969 and reprinted in *Peaceful Uses of Nuclear Energy* (Oak Ridge, Tennessee: U.S. Atomic Energy Commission/Division of Technical Information, 1970), p. 5.

142 Seaborg's warning about power failures is from his testimony before the Joint Committee on Atomic Energy, October 29, 1969 and reprinted in *Peaceful Uses of Nuclear Energy* (Oak Ridge, Tennessee: U.S. Atomic Energy Commission/Division of Technical Information, 1970), p. 7.

143 Seaborg's reminiscences about the discovery of plutonium are from his speech at the dedication of Room 307 in Gilman Hall as a National Historic Landmark (University of California, Berkeley, California, February 21, 1966) and reprinted in his book *Nuclear Milestones* (San Francisco, Calif.: W. H. Freeman & Company, 1972), pp. 3-13.

145 The quotation about the use of science in solving some basic human problems is from Seaborg's remarks at Fairleigh Dickinson University, Teaneck, New Jersey, March 7, 1968. His comments, entitled "Man and the Atom—by the Year 2000," were reprinted in *Peaceful Uses of Nuclear Energy* (Oak Ridge, Tennessee: U.S. Atomic Energy Commission/Division of Technical Information, 1970), pp. 146-147.

146 For more on Seaborg's ideas about nuclear powered agro-industrial plants see "Some Long-Range Implications of Nuclear Energy" by Glenn T. Seaborg, *The Futurist*, Vol. 2, No. 1 (February 1968), pp. 12-13.

147 The quotation about "mankind as a global civilization" is from Seaborg's remarks at Fairleigh Dickinson University, Teaneck, N.J.,

March 7, 1968, reprinted in *Peaceful Uses of Nuclear Energy* (Oak Ridge, Tennessee: U.S. Atomic Energy Commission/Division of Technical Information, 1970), p. 143.

147 Seaborg's quote about directing the future is from his address before the World Future Society on December 13, 1967, published as "Some Long-Range Implications of Nuclear Energy" in *The Futurist*, Vol. 2, No. 1 (February 1968), p. 12.

147 Seaborg is quoted from his remarks at Fairleigh Dickinson University, Teaneck, N.J., March 7, 1968 and reprinted as "Man and the Atom—by the Year 2000," *Peaceful Uses of Nuclear Energy* (Oak Ridge, Tennessee: U.S. Atomic Energy Commission/Division of Technical Information, 1970), p. 156.

148 The quotation from atomic bomb victim is from an interview with Robert Jungk in the French magazine *L'Express* (Paris), No. 966 (January 18, 1970), p. 93.

148 Jungk's ideas on prevention of crises are from the previously cited interview published in *L'Express*.

148 Mankind 2000, 1 rue aux Laines, 1000 Brussels, Belgium.

150 Robert Jungk *Tomorrow Is Already Here* (New York: Simon & Schuster, 1954).

150 Robert Jungk *Brighter than a Thousand Suns* (New York: Harcourt Brace, 1958, originally published in Germany in 1956).

150 The Institute for the Future (Institut fur Zukunftsfragen) faded from the scene about 1970 when Jungk became a professor in Berlin.

150 Robert Jungk *Outline of a European Look-out Institution* (First draft), (April 1967), commissioned by the Council of Europe, Strasbourg, p. 1 and 2.

151 Jungk's comment about his conflicts of interests is from a letter to John Dixon, November 9, 1967.

151 Robert Jungk *The Big Machine* (New York: Charles Scribner's Sons, 1968).

151 Robert Jungk *Der Jahrtausend Mensch* (Munich: C. Bertelsmann, Verlag, 1973). A revised version of the book has been published in English with the title *The Everyman Project: A World Report on the Resources for a Humane Society* (New York: Liveright, 1976).

151 Jungk's comments about democratizing the field of research into the future are from a discussion at the Center for the Study of Democratic Institutions, Santa Barbara, California and published as "The Need for Social Invention," *The Center Diary*, May-June 1967, p. 48.

152 Jungk's comments about a "participation crisis" and the need for "future creating workshops" are from his interview in *L'Express* (Paris), No. 966 (January 18, 1970), p. 94.

153 Jungk's optimistic statement on the problems of the world is from a discussion at The Center for the Study of Democratic Institutions, Santa Barbara, California and published as "The Need for Social Invention" in *The Center Diary*, May-June 1967, p. 50.

153 "Extraterrestrial Relays," *Wireless World*, October 1945.

153 Clarke's comments about his idea for communications satellites are from an interview in *Newsweek*, October 31, 1961.

153 Clarke's description of his early "scientific gadgets" and his discovery of science-fiction magazines appears in an autobiographical sketch at the conclusion of the 1974 edition of his book *Childhood's End* (New York: Ballantine Books, 1953), p. 219.

Page

154 Arthur C. Clarke *Interplanetary Flight* (Philadelphia: Temple Press, 1950).

154 Arthur C. Clarke *The Exploration of Space* (New York: Harper, 1951).

154 Arthur C. Clarke *Childhood's End* (New York: Ballantine Books, 1953).

154 Basil Davenport reviewed *Childhood's End* in *The New York Times*, August 23, 1953.

155 Arthur C. Clarke *Profiles of the Future*, rev. ed., (New York: Harper & Row, 1973).

155 Clarke's comments about his book *Profiles of the Future* are from the Introduction to the book, pp. xiii and xvii.

155 Clarke's quote about failures of prophets is from *Profiles of the Future*, pp. 1 and 2.

156 Arthur C. Clarke *The Lost Worlds of 2001* (New York: New American Library, 1972).

156 Arthur C. Clarke *The Wind from the Sun* (New York: Harcourt Brace Jovanovich, 1972).

156 Arthur C. Clarke *Rendezvous with Rama* (New York: Harcourt Brace Jovanovich, 1973).

156 Arthur C. Clarke *Imperial Earth* (New York: Harcourt Brace Jovanovich, 1975).

157 Clarke's remarks at the signing ceremony of the INTELSAT agreements, August 20, 1971. Text of his remarks was reprinted as "Satellites and the 'United States of Earth,'" *The Futurist*, Vol. 6, No. 2 (April 1972), p. 61.

157 Most of the material about Harman's life comes from lengthy answers to questions posed by the World Future Society.

160 Charles Williams later founded Charles W. Williams, Inc., a consulting firm in Alexandria, Virginia.

162 Statistics on the American workforce are from a review by Dennis Little of Daniel Bell's book *The Coming of Post-Industrial Society* (New York: Basic Books, 1973) in *The Futurist*, Vol. 7, No. 5 (December 1973), p. 259.

163 Daniel Bell *The End of Ideology* (Glencoe, Illinois: Free Press, 1960).

163 Andrew Hacker's review of Bell's *The End of Ideology* appeared in *The New York Times*, May 1, 1966.

164 Daniel Bell "Twelve Modes of Prediction," *Daedalus*, Summer 1964, p. 869.

164 Daniel Bell *Toward the Year 2000* (Boston: Houghton, Mifflin, 1968; paperback edition published by Beacon Press, 1969).

165 Bell's preface to Harvey S. Perloff's *The Future of the U.S. Government* (New York: George Braziller, 1971; paperback edition published by Prentice-Hall, 1972), pp. ix-xix.

166 Bell's comments about the student disruptions at Columbia affecting his workshop are from a letter to the author, February 14, 1969.

166 Bell's description of his activities is from the Preface to his book *The Coming of Post-Industrial Society* (New York: Basic Books, 1973), p. xii.

166 Daniel Bell *The Cultural Contradictions of Capitalism* (New York: Basic Books, 1976).

167 The quotation about dangers of merging Utopia with reality is from Bell's book *The Coming of Post-Industrial Society* (New York: Basic Books, 1973), pp. 488-489.

167 The quotation about predicting the future is from Asimov's book *Is Anyone There?* (Garden City, New York: Doubleday, 1967), p. 217.

167 Asimov's remarks about the change of public opinion toward science fiction are from his book *Is Anyone There?* (Garden City, New York: Doubleday, 1967), pp. 287 and 290.

168 Asimov's comments about other writers' dislike for writing are from a conversation with the author.

168 The comments about Campbell's influence on Asimov's early writings are from a story in *Luna Monthly*, August 1971.

169 Campbell's comments about Asimov's ability to tell a story are from *Current Biography 1968* (New York: H. W. Wilson), p. 30.

169 The figure for Asimov's total book production is from the monthly newsletter of the Literary Guild, May 1977. However, the figure must constantly be revised upward.

170 Asimov's remark about his compulsion to write is from an interview by Harvey Aronson in *Newsday*, March 18, 1967.

171 The quotation about science fiction is from Asimov's book *Is Anyone There?* (Garden City, New York: Doubleday, 1967), p. 290.

171 The quotation about "world community" is from McHale's book *The Future of the Future* (New York: George Braziller, 1969), p. 13.

172 For more about the World Resources Inventory project and *World Design Science Decade* 1965-1975, see Robert Horn's review in *The Futurist*, Vol. 1, No. 4 (August 1967), pp. 56-57.

172 John McHale *The Ecological Context* (New York: George Braziller, 1970).

173 In late 1976 McHale transferred his base to Texas. He is now Director, Center for Integrative Studies, College of Social Studies, University of Houston, Houston, Texas.

173 John McHale *World Facts and Trends* (New York: MacMillan, 1972).

174 This three-line epigram was written by McHale in 1965 and published in *The Futurist*, Vol. 1, No. 1 (February 1967), p. 11.

174 McHale is cited from *The Future of the Future*, p. 3.

174 The quotation about the Western view of the future is from McHale's book *The Future of the Future*, p. 4.

175 McHale's comment about long-range social programs is from his book *The Future of the Future*, p. 9.

175 Comments about failure of city planners to plan for accommodation of human idiosyncratic requirements are from *The Future of the Future*, p. 293.

176 The review by James R. Newman was published in *Scientific American*, March 1961.

176 Herman Kahn *On Thermonuclear War* (Princeton, N.J.: Princeton University Press, 1960).

176 From an interview entitled "How Peace Will Change Life in America" in *U.S. News and World Report* March 12, 1973, p. 42.

176 Kahn's comments about his optimism are from an interview with *The Washington Star*, August 3, 1975.

177 Kahn's statement on widespread starvation is from his interview with *The Washington Star*, August 3, 1975.

179 Herman Kahn and Anthony J. Wiener *The Year 2000: A Framework for Speculation on the Next Thirty-Three Years* (New York: MacMillan, 1967).

Page

179 Herman Kahn and B. Bruce-Briggs *Things to Come: Thinking about the 70s and 80s* (New York: Macmillan, 1972).

179 Herman Kahn, William Brown and Leon Martel *The Next 200 Years: A Scenario for America and the World* (New York: William Morrow & Co., 1976).

179 Comments about the educational system were made by Kahn in an interview with *The Washington Star*, August 3, 1975.

179 Remarks about the environment and population are from an address at a meeting in New York of Prospects for Mankind.

180 Paul Dickson's comments about the Hudson Institute are contained in his book *Think Tanks* (New York: Atheneum, 1971), p. 102.

181 Alvin Toffler *The Culture Consumers* (New York: St. Martin's Press, 1964).

181 Toffler first explained his "future shock" concept in an article entitled "The Future as a Way of Life," *Horizon*, Vol. 7, No. 3 (Summer 1965), pp. 108-116.

182 Ignorance of how to cope with "future shock" is discussed in *Future Shock*, pp. 2-3 (originally published by Random House, New York, 1970).

182 Alvin Toffler, ed., *The Schoolhouse in the City* (New York: Praeger, 1968).

182 Alvin Toffler, ed., *Learning for Tomorrow* (New York: Random House, 1974).

182 The comment on a democracy's need to anticipate change appeared in a paper circulated by the Committee on Anticipatory Democracy.

183 Toffler is quoted from his speech "Congress and the Future" at the conference organized by Committee on Anticipatory Democracy for members and staff of Congress, September 11, 1975.

183 Alvin Toffler *The Eco-Spasm Report* (New York: Bantam, 1975).

183 The "crisis of industrialism" quotation is from Toffler's *The Eco-Spasm Report* (New York: Bantam, 1975), p. 3.

184 Toffler's optimistic outlook for the years ahead appears in his book *The Eco-Spasm Report* (New York: Bantam, 1975), p. 108.

Chapter 10: Futuristics in Practice (With Case Histories)

189 The account of the British Parliament's reaction to Edison's electric lamp is from Arthur Clarke's *Profiles of the Future*, rev. ed., (New York: Harper & Row, 1973), p. 2.

189 The original Xerox machine, now displayed by the Smithsonian Institution's Museum of History and Technology in Washington, D.C., is not a large and fancy apparatus, and one can understand perhaps why its merits were not immediately appreciated.

191 For more information on the TRW "probe," see North and Pyke's article "Probes of Technological Future" in the *Harvard Business Review*, May 1969, pp. 68-82.

192 For more on G.E.'s report *Our Future Business Environment* see "Industry Study Foresees Educational Institutions Dominant in United States," *The Futurist*, Vol. 3, No. 1 (February 1969), pp. 17-19.

193 The Northern States Power experience was described by Donald O. Imsland in "The Futurizing of a Power Company," *The Futurist*, Vol. 3, No. 4 (August 1973), pp. 175-176.

194 The material on Shell Oil and the Institute of Life Insurance's Trend

Analysis Program was provided by James Webber and Rebecca Ojala of the Cambridge Research Institute.

198 For more information about the Bolling Committee and the futurists'
testimony, see "Futurists Testify Before U.S. Congress," *The Futurist*, Vol. 7, No. 5 (October 1973), pp. 228-230 and "Congress and the
Future," *The Futurist*, Vol. 9, No. 3 (June 1975), pp. 132-142.

200 David Baker of the Population Institute in Washington, D.C., has
worked extensively with state goals groups. For more on this topic,
see his articles "The States Experiment with 'Anticipatory Democracy,'" *The Futurist*, Vol. 10, No. 5 (October 1976), pp. 262-271 and
"State Goals Groups: Performance and Potential," *World Future Society Bulletin*, Vol. 10, No. 2 (March-April 1976), pp. 5-14.

204 Much of the information about other organizations' long-range projections was provided by James Webber and Rebecca Ojala of the Cambridge Research Institute.

Chapter 11: The Coming Revolution in Education

210 The future-oriented curriculum is drawn from Draper Kauffman's
Teaching the Future (Palm Springs, California: ETC Publications,
1976), p. 30.

211 For more about the paracurriculum concept, see Harold Shane's *The
Educational Significance of the Future* (Bloomington, Indiana: Phi
Delta Kappa, 1973), pp. 71-76.

212 Ossip K. Flechtheim, "Teaching the Future," *History and Futurology*
(Meisenheim am Glan, Germany: Verlag Anton Hain, 1966), pp.
63-68.

212 For reports of Eldredge's surveys, see "Education in Futurism in
North America," *The Futurist*, Vol. 4, No. 5 (December 1970), pp.
193-196; "Teaching the Future at North American Universities,"
The Futurist, Vol. 6, No. 6 (December 1972), pp. 250-252; and "Uni-
versity Education in Future Studies," *The Futurist*, Vol. 9, No. 2
(April 1975), pp. 98-102.

212 References to James Duran and Ronald Abler's courses are from Billy
Rojas' article "Futuristics, Games and Educational Change" in
Learning for Tomorrow edited by Alvin Toffler (New York: Vintage
Books Edition, 1974), p. 221.

213 Jib Fowles, Committee on Studies of the Future, University of Houston at Clear Lake City, 2700 Bay Area Blvd., Houston, Texas 77058.

213 Peter Wagschal, Future Studies Program, University of Massachusetts, Amherst, Massachusetts 01002.

213 For more on courses in futuristics, see James Stirewalt's two-part
series "The Future as an Academic Subject," *World Future Society
Bulletin*, Vol. 11, Nos. 1 and 2 (January-February and March-April,
1977), pp. 16-20.

214 Singer is quoted from his article "The Future-Focused Role-Image" in
Learning for Tomorrow edited by Alvin Toffler (New York: Vintage
Books Edition, 1974), pp. 20-21, 24.

215 Howard Didsbury's statements were made to the author.

216 The quotation from Steve Mathews is taken from a report on the future
studies program at Burnsville Senior High, Burnsville, Minnesota.
The report is titled "Futuristics Cures 'Doomsday Syndrome,'" *The
Futurist*, Vol. 8, No. 4 (August 1974), pp. 183-184.

216 For a report on Wilkerson and Epping's course see *Education Tomorrow* (newsletter published by the World Future Society), Vol. 1, No. 3 (August 1976), p. 8.

Chapter 12: The Uses of the Future

221 Ian Wilson's comments are from a discussion with the author.
224 Information about the activities of the Institute for the Future was supplied by Roy Amara, President of the Institute.
226 H. Wentworth Eldredge's findings were reported in his article "Education and Futurism" in *The Futurist*, Vol. 4, No. 5 (December 1970), p. 106.
226 Professor Kane's remarks are found in "Teaching the Future at North American Universities" by H. Wentworth Eldredge, *The Futurist*, Vol. 6, No. 6 (December 1972), p. 252.
226 Paul Ehrlich's scenario about a Thanodrin catastrophe was first published in *Ramparts* (September 1969) and reprinted in Franklin Tugwell's *Search for Alternatives: Public Policy and the Study of the Future* (Cambridge, Massachusetts: Winthrop Publishers, 1973), pp. 193-194.

Chapter 13: A World of Utopias

230 Twin Oaks, Route 4, Box 169, Louisa, Virginia 23093.
236 Cleveland is quoted from *The Futurist*, Vol. 10, No. 3, (June 1976), p. 165.

Appendix A: Future-Oriented Organizations and Periodicals

237 For more information on the organizations and periodicals listed in Appendix A, readers should turn to *The Future: A Guide to Information Sources* (Washington, D.C.: World Future Society, 1977). This 603-page guide provides addresses, telephone numbers, and a wide variety of other information about organizations, individuals, periodicals, educational programs, films, audiotapes, research projects, etc.

Appendix B: A Field in Search of a Name

254 For more details on the search for a name, see "The Study of the Future: What It Is and Why It Has No Accepted Name" in *An Introduction to the Study of the Future:* Part 1 of *Resources Directory for America's Third Century* (Washington, D.C.: World Future Society, 1977), pp. 141-157.
254 For more on Wells's proposal to study the future, see Chapter 6 ("Distrust of the Future"). See also Notes for Chapter 6.
254 Gilfillan issued a call for mellontologists in his unpublished M.A. thesis, "Successful Social Prophecy in the Past," May 3, 1920.
255 Flechtheim's comments about Futurology are from his book *History*

Page

   and Futurology (Meisenheim am Glan, Germany: Verlag Anton
   Hain, 1966), p. 73.
255 De Jouvenel's rejection of the term "futurology" appears in his book
   The Art of Conjecture, p. 17.
255 Polak's comments about the term "futurology" appear in his book
   Prognostics (Amsterdam: Elsevier, 1971), pp. 15-16.
256 Jungk's comments about the term "futurology" occur in an interview
   with *L'Express* (Paris), No. 966 (January 18, 1970), pp. 92-93.
256 The Swedish statement is from the Secretariat for Future Studies report *Future Studies in Sweden* (Stockholm, 1974), p. 1.
256 Ferdinand Lundberg *The Coming World Transformation* (Garden
   City, N.Y.: Doubleday, 1963).
257 The World Future Society issued its survey form in *The Futurist*, Vol.
   9, No. 4 (August 1975), pp. 191-194.

Index

About the Author

Edward Cornish is president of the World Future Society and editor of its journals *The Futurist* and the *World Future Society Bulletin*. He was a member of the group that founded the Society in 1966 and has worked full-time for the Society since 1969. Before joining the Society's staff, he served as a United Press International correspondent in Richmond, Virginia; Raleigh, North Carolina; London; Geneva; Paris; and Rome. He also worked as a science writer for the National Geographic Society's News Service. His articles have appeared in newspapers and magazines in many nations.

WORLD FUTURE SOCIETY
An Association for the Study of Alternative Futures

The Society is an association of people interested in future social and technological developments. It is chartered as a non-profit scientific and educational organization in Washington, D.C., and is recognized as tax-exempt by the U.S. Internal Revenue Service. The World Future Society is independent, non-political and non-ideological.

The purpose of the World Future Society is to serve as an unbiased forum and clearinghouse for scientific and scholarly forecasts, investigations and intellectual explorations of the future. The Society's objectives, as stated in its charter, are as follows:

1. To contribute to a reasoned awareness of the future and the importance of its study, without advocating particular ideologies or engaging in political activities.
2. To advance responsible and serious investigation of the future.
3. To promote the development and improvement of methodologies for the study of the future.
4. To increase public understanding of future-oriented activities and studies.
5. To facilitate communication and cooperation among organizations and individuals interested in studying or planning for the future.

Membership is open to anyone seriously interested in the future. Since its founding in 1966, the Society has grown to more than 45,000 members in over 80 countries. Most members are U.S. residents, with growing numbers in Canada, Europe, Japan, and other countries. Members include many of the world's most distinguished scientists, scholars, business leaders and government officials.

SOCIETY PROGRAMS

THE FUTURIST: A Journal of Forecasts, Trends, and Ideas About the Future.
This unique bimonthly journal reports the forecasts made by scientists and others concerning the coming years. It explores the possible consequences of these developments on the individual, institutions and society,

and discusses actions people may take to improve the future.

Publications
The Society publishes books, reports, films and other specialized documents on future-related subjects. Among these are the book, *The Next 25 Years: Crisis and Opportunity,* and a report on "The Educational Significance of the Future."

Book Service
World Future Society members can purchase books, audio tapes, games and other educational materials dealing with the future, at substantial savings. The Society's unique "Bookstore of the Future" carries about 200 titles.

Tape Recordings
The Society has a rapidly growing inventory of more than 100 audio

tapes available at low cost to members. This cassette series includes coverage of most major areas and issues of the future, such as science and technology, government, education, environment and human values.

Chapter and Local Activities
Society chapters and local activities in many cities offer speakers, educational courses, seminars, discussion groups and other opportunities for members to get to know each other. They provide personal contacts with people interested in alternative futures.

Meetings
Meetings offer special opportunities for participation and interaction. The *General Assemblies* are large, multi-disciplinary convocations where Society members can hear and meet frontier thinkers and doers. The Second General Assembly, held in June, 1975, drew 2,500 participants. Specialized conferences are also held, such as a forum on energy in April, 1974, and a workshop on "Futurizing Education" in October, 1974.

Employment Services
The Society helps provide contact between potential employers and individuals seeking positions in future-oriented business, university or governmental activities.

Insurance
Society members are eligible to participate in a low-cost group insurance program.